Network Programming in .NET

Network Programming in .NET
With C# and Visual Basic .NET

Fiach Reid

ELSEVIER
DIGITAL
PRESS

AMSTERDAM • BOSTON • HEIDELBERG • LONDON
NEW YORK • OXFORD • PARIS • SAN DIEGO•
SAN FRANCISCO • SINGAPORE • SYDNEY • TOKYO

Elsevier Digital Press
200 Wheeler Road, Burlington, MA 01803, USA
Linacre House, Jordan Hill, Oxford OX2 8DP, UK

∞ Recognizing the importance of preserving what has been written, Elsevier prints its
books on acid-free paper whenever possible.

Library of Congress Cataloging-in-Publication Data
Application submitted.

ISBN: 1-55558-315-6

British Library Cataloguing-in-Publication Data
A catalogue record for this book is available from the British Library.

For information on all Digital Press publications
visit our Web site at www.digitalpress.com and www.bh.com/digitalpress

04 05 06 07 08 09 10 9 8 7 6 5 4 3 2 1

Printed in the United States of America

To my parents, thank you for everything.

Contents

Preface

This book will help you develop network applications with .NET, using either the C# or VB.NET programming language.

It covers everything you need to know about network programming in .NET, from basic get-started information, to a huge selection of advanced networking technologies that may have seemed like science fiction—until now. Whether you're looking for a solution to a specific networking issue or for a general all-round knowledge of network application development, you'll find it in this book!

Who should read this book?

This book is aimed at professional developers with some previous programming experience. Basic knowledge of either C# or VB.NET is an advantage, but not essential. This is not a beginners guide to .NET, and as such it is assumed that you already know basic programming constructs such as `if` statements and loops.

No previous experience with network programming is assumed, so even complete newcomers will find this book comprehensive enough cover all the basics. Seasoned programmers may skip the first chapter, and readers will quickly find the pace fast enough to keep even the most expert developers glued to the pages.

Although the book is geared for developers, as a solution architect, IT manager, or even computer science undergraduate, you will also find this book of enormous benefit. Every new concept is introduced with its associated technology theory and commercial implications for IT businesses. This book keeps a keen eye on best practice techniques, as well as provides ground-up implementations. Using this approach, project managers can help guide developers towards an implementation that could provide future flexibility or lead to faster end-product deployment.

What hardware and software do you need?

In order to use the code examples provided in this book, you should install the latest version of the .NET framework from Microsoft's Web site. It is also highly recommended that you install Visual Studio .NET, rather than use the command-line based compilers supplied with the .NET SDK.

The minimum hardware requirements for Visual Studio .NET are

- Intel Pentium processor; 450 MHz or equivalent
- Microsoft Windows 2000, NT 4.0, or XP
- 128 Mb RAM
- 3 Gb of available disk space

The telephony examples in chapter 14 require the use of a voice modem and access to a live analog phone line.

How this book is organized

The book is divided into three main parts. The following sections will describe what is covered in each part of the book.

Part I: Basic network applications

Chapters 1 to 6 cover the established Internet technologies. These include the main activities that we all carry out in our daily lives, everything from browsing the Web, sending e-mail, and maybe uploading files with FTP. Knowing how to implement these basic networking operations from .NET is a must for any serious developer. Ever wanted to link to your company Web site from your application or to send an e-mail whenever the program crashes? These chapters show you how.

Part II: Network application design

Chapters 7 to 11 discuss network application design. These chapters are aimed at enterprise-scale development of heavy-duty distributed applications. Provided are five chapters on hardware, encryption, authentication, scalability, and performance. Encryption and authentication provide you with the confidence to know that nobody can defraud your system or compromise the confidentiality of the information held within it. Scalability ensures that you can keep your service working at full tilt even under extreme loads. With an excellent chapter on performance enhancing techniques, after reading this section you can be sure that no customer turns away because they were "bored waiting." All together this handful of pages equates to a huge step forward in application quality.

Part III: Specialized networking topics

Chapters 12 to 17 are geared toward the more specialized networking topics and the more advanced developer with a keen interest in niche or cutting-edge technologies. Each chapter in this section is the result of months of research, brought to you in simple step-by-step examples. This section includes possibly the first published implementation of frame-level packet capture in .NET, as well as a cool telephony application built from scratch in .NET.

These chapters also cover MSMQ, IPv6, WMI, DNS, Ping, WHOIS, Telnet, ARP, RIP, OSPF, BGP/EGP, SNMP, PPP, Web services, remoting, and more!

Conventions used in this book

Typographical conventions

This book uses `fixed-spaced` font to differentiate between English text and keywords that are used verbatim in computer code. Words highlighted in *italic* are used to emphasize a new programming term.

Note: A note such as this is used to emphasize an important point or a worthwhile observation.

Code

Code examples in this book are labeled as either C# or VB.NET and are printed with fixed-spaced fonts, such as the following example:

```
C#
public int addition(int a, int b)
{
  return a+b;
}
```

In some cases, other scripts, such as SQL, ASP.NET, or MS-DOS are used and labeled accordingly.

Further information

You can find help for specific problems and questions by investigating several Web sites. A good place to start for issues relating to .NET is always Microsoft's official Web site at *msdn.Microsoft.com/net*.

For definitive information on specific network protocols, you should consult the IETF (Internet Engineering Task Force) Web site at *http://www.ietf.org/rfc.html*.

You may also contact the author with any questions or comments regarding this book. While every care has been taken to ensure that all the information within is correct and accurate, you are free to report anything you feel is missing or erroneous, so that these can be corrected in future revisions.

Fiach Reid
fiach@eircom.net
Co. Donegal, Ireland
February 2004

Acknowledgments

This book was made possible by a wonderful network of people at Digital Press. Of these people I would like to personally thank Pam Chester and Theron Shreve, without whom this book would have never been published. I would also like to thank Alan Rose and all at Multiscience Press for their efforts in getting this book into print.

I am extremely grateful to the assistance of my technical reviewer, David Stephenson at HP. His technical expertise improved the code examples in this book one hundred fold. A big thank you goes out to all those at Microsoft who offered their assistance in the writing of this book, especially Christopher Brown and Lance Olson.

I would like to also like to say thanks to everybody at eyespyfx.com for their help and support and also to the guys at cheapflights.ie for their expertise and sense of humor. Above all else, I would like to thank my parents for being so supportive of me for the past twenty-three years.

Understanding the Internet and Network Programming

1.1   Introduction

This book will help you develop network applications with .NET, using either the C# (pronounced C-sharp) or VB.NET programming language. It is broken up into three distinct sections: networking basics, distributed application design, and specialized networking topics.

The first six chapters of the book cover the established Internet technologies, such as email and the World Wide Web. Leveraging established technologies such as these gives the general public greater access to your software service because most users will already have a Web browser or email client on their computers.

The next five chapters discuss network application design. This includes application security, performance, and scalability. Contained within these chapters is practical, hands-on advice to help improve the overall quality of your software. With tougher security, your applications will be less susceptible to theft of intellectual property and privileged information. The performance and scalability improvements described in this section will ensure that your application remains responsive even under the most extreme loads.

The specialized networking topics section provides a wealth of information about both niche and cutting-edge Internet technologies. These include chapters on telephony, packet capture, message queues, IPv6, and Microsoft's latest offerings in the field of distributed application development: Web services and remoting.

1.2   **Why network programming in .NET?**

One of the first technical decisions to be made whenever a new project is undertaken is what language to use. .NET is a capable platform on which to develop almost any solution, and it offers substantial support for network programming. In fact, .NET has more intrinsic support for networking than any other platform developed by Microsoft.

This book assumes that you have already decided to develop with .NET, and languages outside the .NET platform will not be discussed in any great detail, except for comparative purposes. This is not to say that .NET is the be-all and end-all of network-programming applications. If your application runs over a UNIX-only infrastructure communicating via Java remote method invocation (RMI), then .NET is not the way to go. In most circumstances, however, you will find that .NET is more than capable of handling whatever you throw at it.

1.3   **What can a network program do?**

A network program is any application that uses a computer network to transfer information to and from other applications. Examples range from the ubiquitous Web browser such as Internet Explorer, or the program you use to receive your email, to the software that controls spacecraft at NASA.

All of these pieces of software share the ability to communicate with other computers, and in so doing, become more useful to the end-user. In the case of a browser, every Web site you visit is actually files stored on a computer somewhere else on the Internet. With your email program, you are communicating with a computer at your Internet service provider (ISP) or company email exchange, which is holding your email for you.

This book is largely concerned with creating network programs, not Web sites. Although the capabilities of Web sites and network programs are quickly converging, it is important to understand the arguments for and against each system. A service accessed via a Web site is instantly accessible to users across many different platforms, and the whole networking architecture is ready-built for you; however, there is a point at which features are simply unfeasible to implement using Web sites and at which you have to turn to network applications.

Users generally trust network applications; therefore, these programs have much greater control over the computers on which they are running than a Web site has over the computers viewing it. This makes it possible for a network application to manage files on the local computer, whereas a Web site, for all practical purposes, cannot do this. More importantly, from a networking perspective, an application has much greater control over how it can communicate with other computers on the Internet.

To give a simple example, a Web site cannot make the computer that is viewing it open a persistent network connection to another computer (except the computer from which the Web site was served). This applies even when the Web site contains embedded content such as a Java applet or Flash movie. There is one exception to this rule, when executable content (such as an ActiveX control) is included in a page. In this case, the page is capable of everything a network program could do, but most browsers and antivirus software will warn against or deny such executable content. Therefore, this scenario is commonly accepted as being unfeasible because of public distrust.

1.4   IP addresses

Every computer that connects directly to the Internet must have a globally unique IP address. An IP address is a four-byte number, which is generally written as four decimal, period-separated numbers, such as 192.168.0.1. Computers that connect indirectly to the Internet, such as via their company network, also have IP addresses, but these do not need to be globally unique, only unique within the same network.

To find out what the IP address of your computer is, open a DOS console window and type `IpConfig` (Windows NT, 2000, and XP) or `winIpcfg` (Windows 95, 98, and ME).

In Figure 1.1, the PC has two IP addresses: 192.618.0.1 and 81.98.59.133. This is unusual because this particular PC contains two network cards and is connected to two different networks. Only one of those IP addresses is publicly accessible.

If you receive the IP address 127.0.0.1, your computer is not connected to any network. This IP address always refers to the local machine and is used in later examples.

In the same way that you can tell whether a phone number is local or international by looking at the prefix, you can tell whether the computer with that IP address is on the same local area network or somewhere else on the Internet by looking closely at an IP address. In the case of IP addresses, they are always the same length, but certain prefixes (192.168 being the

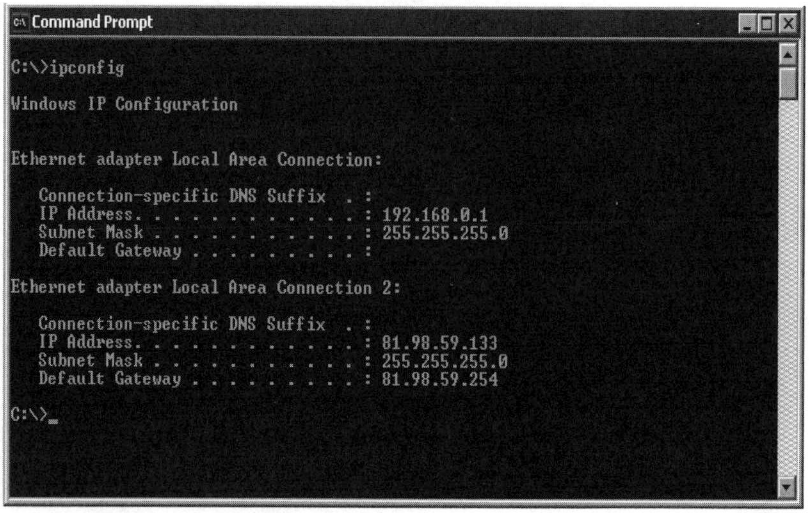

Figure 1.1
IPConfig.

most common) indicate that the computer is in a local area network, or intranet, and not accessible to the outside world.

If you share your Internet connection with other computers on your network, you may have a private IP address. These can be recognized as being within the IP address ranges listed in Table 1.1.

Table 1.1   *Private IP families.*

IP Address Range	Number of Distinct Addresses
10.0.0.0 to 10.255.255.255	Up to 16 million computers (Class A)
172.16.0.0 to 172.31.255.255	900,000 computers (Class B)
192.168.0.0 to 192.168.255.255	65,000 computers (Class C)

The same private IP address may exist on two computers in different local area networks (LANs). This does not cause a problem because neither computer can directly contact the other. Whereas a privately addressed computer can initiate a request for information from a foreign computer, no foreign computer can initiate a request for information from a privately addressed computer.

The exception to this rule would be where network address translation (NAT) or port forwarding is set up on the router that lies upstream of the privately addressed computer. This is where requests from foreign machines destined for the IP address of the router are forwarded to a designated computer behind the router. Responses from this computer are forwarded from the router back to the foreign machine that initiated the request. The benefits of such an architecture are security and the possibility for load balancing, which is described in more detail in later chapters.

All computers with private IP addresses must be connected to at least one computer or network router with a public IP address to access the Internet.

In order to ensure that no two computers on the Internet have the same IP address, there is a central regulatory body known as the Internet Assigned Numbers Authority (IANA), and more recently the Internet Corporation for Assigned Names and Numbers (ICANN). This body acts through ISPs to assign public IP addresses to organizations and individuals. Although it is possible to be allocated one IP address at a time, it is more common to be allocated IP addresses in contiguous blocks.

Contiguous blocks come in three classes: A, B, and C. Class A addresses are blocks of IP addresses with the same first byte only. Class A is more than 16 million IP addresses in size. Class B addresses are blocks of IP addresses with the same first and second byte. Class B holds 65,024 public IP addresses. The full 2^{16} byte range is not available because the last byte of an IP address cannot be 0 or 255 because these are reserved for future use. Class C addresses are blocks of IP addresses with the same first, second, and third byte. Class C holds 254 public addresses, and class C addresses are routinely allocated to companies.

A computer may not always have the same IP address. It may obtain its IP address from your ISP's dynamic host control protocol (DHCP) server. This means that your IP address may change every time you go online. Such an IP address is called a dynamic IP address. If you are on an intranet, you can check to see if your IP address is liable to change by checking the "obtain IP address automatically" radio button in TCP/IP properties, under Network in the control panel.

The purpose of DHCP is that if there is a limited number of IP addresses available to the ISP, it will allocate its subscribers with IP addresses from a pool on a first-come, first-served basis. IP addresses are 32-bit numbers, with a maximum value of about 4 billion, and the number of computers in the world is fast approaching that figure. IPv6 is a solution to that problem and is discussed in later chapters.

There is one identifier built into every network card that is genuinely unique and cannot be changed. This is called the hardware, or media access control (MAC) address. A sample MAC address is 00-02-E3-15-59-6C.

This is used on intranets to identify computers when they log on to the network. A system called address resolution protocol (ARP) is used to associate MAC addresses with IP addresses.

1.5   The network stack

The digital signals that travel between computers on the Internet are extremely complex. Without the concept of encapsulation, programmers would quickly become bogged down with insignificant details.

This technique is used in everyday life, where you may ask a taxi driver to take you to the city center. It is the taxi driver's responsibility to find the quickest route and to operate the car. At a lower level again, it is the car manufacturer's responsibility to ensure that gasoline will be present in the engine pistons while the accelerator is depressed.

Encapsulation is where the more complex details of a task are hidden, and the programmer only needs to concentrate on what is happening at a higher level. The open systems interconnection (OSI) network stack model has seven layers of encapsulation, as shown in Table 1.2.

In modern programming, however, the network stack looks more like Table 1.3.

The most important layer for any programmer is the uppermost layer because this will afford the greatest ease of use and will suit most applications. When you head down the stack, implementation becomes more difficult, albeit more flexible.

Table 1.2   *The traditional network stack.*

Level Name	Layer Name	Example Protocol
Level 7	Application layer	FTP
Level 6	Presentation layer	XNS
Level 5	Session layer	RPC
Level 4	Transport layer	TCP
Level 3	Network layer	IP
Level 2	Data-Link layer	Ethernet Frames
Level 1	Physical layer	Voltages

Table 1.3 *The modern network stack.*

Level Name	Layer Name	Example Protocol
Level 4	Structured Information layer	SOAP
Level 3	Messaging layer	HTTP
Level 2	Stream layer	TCP
Level 1	Packet layer	IP

This book covers the application layer primarily, but coverage is given to all of the various layers, excluding the physical layer, which would apply only to electronics engineers.

In network programming, you generally do not need to concern yourself with how information travels between two computers, just with what you want to send. The finer details are handled at lower levels and are controlled by the computer's operating system.

1.6   Ports

If you want to browse the Web and receive emails at the same time, your computer needs to decide which bits of network traffic are emails and which are Web pages. To tell the difference, every piece of data on the network is tagged with a port number: 80 for Web pages, 110 for incoming email. This information is contained within either the transmission control protocol (TCP) or user datagram protocol (UDP) header that immediately follows the IP header. Table 1.4 lists common protocols and their associated port numbers.

1.7   Internet standards

When developing a networked application, it is important not to reinvent the wheel or otherwise create an application that is unnecessarily incompatible with other applications of the same genre. This book often refers to standards documents, so it is worthwhile knowing where to find them.

A shining example is dynamic HTML, which was implemented differently on Internet Explorer and Netscape Navigator. This meant that most Web sites that used dynamic HTML would fail to work properly on all browsers. Thus, Web developers avoided it and moved toward cross-

Table 1.4   *Well-known port numbers.*

Port	Protocol
20	FTP (data)
21	FTP (control)
25	SMTP (email, outgoing)
53	DNS (domain names)
80	HTTP (Web)
110	POP3 (email, incoming)
119	NNTP (news)
143	IMAP (email, incoming)

Source: *www.iana.org/assignments/port-numbers.txt.*

browser technologies, such as Macromedia Flash and Java Applets. The reason for this downfall is lack of standardization.

Two organizations are largely responsible for regulating Internet standards: the Internet Engineering Task Force (IETF) and the World Wide Web Consortium (W3C). The IETF is a not-for-profit organization, which regulates the most fundamental protocols on the Internet. Anyone can submit a protocol to them, and it will be publicly available as a request for

Table 1.5   *Important RFCs.*

RFC Document	Protocol Described
RFC 821	SMTP (email, outgoing)
RFC 954	WHOIS
RFC 959	FTP (uploading and downloading)
RFC 1939	POP3 (email, incoming)
RFC 2616	HTTP (Web browsing)
RFC 793	TCP (runs under all above protocols)
RFC 792	ICMP (ping)
RFC 791	IP (runs under TCP and ICMP)

comments (RFC) on their Web site at *www.ietf.org/rfc.html*. Table 1.5 lists some important RFC documents.

The W3C (*www.w3c.org*) is designed to facilitate standard interoperability among vendors. Only large corporations can become members of the W3C. The W3C is responsible for hypertext markup language (HTML), cascading style sheets (CSS), and extensible markup language (XML).

1.8   What is .NET?

.NET is not a programming language. It is a development framework that incorporates four official programming languages: C#, VB.NET, Managed C++, and J# .NET. Where there are overlaps in object types in the four languages, the framework defines the framework class library (FCL).

All four languages in the framework share the FCL and the common language runtime (CLR), which is an object-oriented platform that provides a runtime environment for .NET applications. The CLR is analogous to the virtual machine (VM) in Java, except it is designed for Windows, not cross-platform, use; however, a stripped-down version of the .NET framework, known as the .NET compact framework, is capable of running on Windows CE devices, such as palmtops and certain cell phones. Furthermore, there are initiatives to port the CLR to Linux, such as the MONO project (*www.go-mono.com*).

In this book, the two most popular .NET programming languages, C# and VB.NET, are used. Both languages differ syntactically, but are equally capable and offer identical performance characteristics. Languages in the .NET framework are highly interoperable, so there is no need to be confined to a single language. A class compiled from VB.NET can be called from a C# application and vice versa. Similarly, a class written in VB.NET can derive from a compiled class written in C#. Exceptions and polymorphism are also supported across languages. This is made possible by a specification called the Common Type System (CTS).

When an application written in a .NET language is compiled, it becomes the Microsoft intermediate language (MSIL) byte code, which is then executed by the CLR. MSIL code generated from compiling C# is generally identical to MSIL code generated from compiling VB.NET code. Exceptions to this lie with a few language-specific features, such as how C# can use classic C-style pointers within unsafe code and how VB.NET can use VB6-style Windows API definitions.

One of the failings of interpreted, or semicompiled, languages is a performance loss. .NET avoids this problem by using a just-in-time (JIT) compiler, which is generally transparent to the user. JIT acts ondemand, whenever MSIL code is first executed. JIT compiles MSIL code to machine code, which is optimized for the processor of the computer that is executing the code. In this way, JIT can leverage new features as they become available in new Intel processors without rendering older computers obsolete.

.NET languages are object-oriented rather than procedurally based. This provides a natural mechanism to encapsulate interrelated data and methods to modify this data within the same logical construct. An object is a programmatic construct that has properties or can perform actions. A core concept of object orientation is the ability of one class to inherit the properties and methods of another. The most common example used in this book is inheritance from `System.Windows.Forms.Form`. This provides the standard Windows user interface (i.e., a grey window with a title bar and the Minimize/Restore/Close button set at the top right).

You can make your own classes, which could form a base class from which other classes inherit. A typical example would be a class representing a car that could inherit from the vehicle class. .NET does not support multiple inheritance, so the car class cannot inherit from a vehicle class and a Windows form. Interestingly, every class within .NET derives from a root called `System.Object`.

An interface is a contract that stipulates what methods and properties a class must expose. To return to the previous example, the vehicle interface could be that it must be able to move, hold people, and be bought and sold. The benefit of interfaces is that software designed to auction vehicle objects would work with cars, motorcycles, and boats. An object can inherit from multiple interfaces. Thus, a boat could inherit from the vehicle interface and expose extra methods that satisfy with the marine interface (e.g., buoyancy ratings, nationality).

The code examples in this book are designed to be stand-alone Windows applications, rather than portable, self-contained classes. This approach is used to ensure that examples are kept as concise as possible. In real-world applications, networking code is generally kept separate from other facets of the application (e.g., user interface (UI), database access). Therefore, it is commonplace to keep classes associated with networking in a separate assembly.

An assembly is generally a .DLL file that contains precompiled (MSIL) code for a collection of .NET classes. Unlike standard Win32 DLLs in which developers had to rely on documentation, such as header files, to use any given DLL, .NET assemblies contain metadata, which provides enough information for any .NET application to use the methods contained within the assembly correctly. Metadata is also used to describe other features of the assembly, such as its version number, culture, the originator of the code, and any custom attributes that were added to the classes.

.NET provides a unique solution to the issue of sharing assemblies between multiple applications (aptly named DLL Hell). Generally, where an assembly is designed for use with only one application, it is contained within the same folder (or `bin` subfolder) as the application. This is known as a *private assembly*. A *public assembly* is copied into a location where all .NET applications on the local system have access too. Furthermore, this public assembly is designed to be versioned, unique, and tamperproof, thanks to a clever security model. This location into which public assemblies are copied is called the global assembly cache (GAC).

If you are developing a component that will be shared among many applications, you can transfer it to the GAC with these simple steps. First, create a key-pair file by typing `sn -k c:\keys.snk` at the command prompt. You then associate the key file with your assembly by adding the code `[assembly:AssemblyKeyFile("c:\keys.snk")]` to the head of your class. Finally, it can be copied into the GAC, either by copying and pasting into windows\ assembly with Windows Explorer or by typing `gacutil /I:MyAssembly.dll`.

1.9   Getting started

The examples in this book require you to have access to Microsoft Visual Studio .NET. To program in Microsoft .NET, you need to have the Microsoft .NET SDK or Microsoft Visual Studio .NET. The former is freely available at the Microsoft Web site (*http://msdn.microsoft.com/netframework/ technologyinfo/howtoget/*). The SDK can be used to create .NET applications, but it is awkward to create graphical user interfaces (GUIs) and use command-line-based compilers.

Visual Studio .NET is not free, but no serious .NET developer should attempt to write .NET applications without it. A free alternative to Visual Studio .NET is SharpDevelop (http://www.icsharpcode.net/OpenSource/ SD/Default.aspx). This first example will include instructions for developers opting to use the .NET SDK, as well as Visual Studio .NET users, but no further examples will use the .NET SDK.

Figure 1.2
*Visual Studio
.NET, New Project
dialog.*

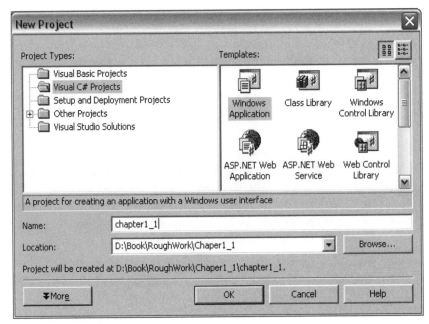

All examples are given in the two most popular .NET languages: C# and Visual Basic .NET. Both languages have exactly the same capabilities, and there is absolutely no difference in performance between the two languages. If you are familiar with C or C++, you should choose to develop in C#. If you are familiar with Visual Basic, you should choose to develop in Visual Basic .NET. When developing an application, you should not swap between languages.

The first example demonstrates how to display a Web page within a .NET application.

1.10 Using Visual Studio .NET

Open Visual Studio .NET, and click New Project. Then type in a name and location for your project (Figure 1.2).

Select the Visual Basic Windows application or Visual C# Windows application, depending on which language you wish to develop in.

When the form appears, right-click on the toolbox and select Customize Toolbox (Visual Studio .NET 2002) or Add/Remove Items (Visual Studio .NET 2003). Then select Microsoft Web Browser from the dialog box (as shown in Figure 1.3), and press OK.

Figure 1.3
*Visual Studio
.NET, Customize
Toolbox dialog.*

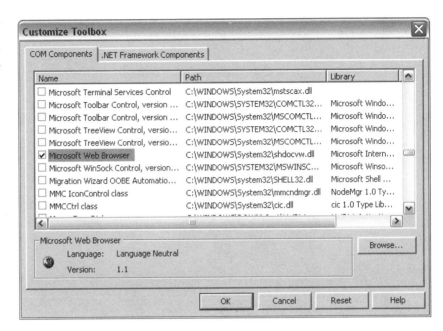

Drag the Explorer icon onto the form, and then drag a button and text-box onto the form. The finished form should look like Figure 1.4.

The next step is to set the properties of all the user interface elements. Right-click on the button and select the Properties option. You will see the Properties snap-in window appearing. Scroll up to the top of this window, and click on the property labeled (Name). Enter in the new name, btn-Browse, as shown in Figure 1.5.

Similarly, name the textbox tbURL and the Microsoft Web Browser control webBrowser.

If you double-click on the button, you will see a page of code already written for you. Find the reference to btnBrowse_Click and insert the following code:

VB.NET

```
Private Sub btnBrowse_Click(ByVal sender As _
System.Object, ByVal e As System.EventArgs) Handles _
 btnBrowse.Click
   webBrowser.Navigate(tbURL.Text)
End Sub
```

Figure 1.4
*Visual Studio
.NET, form design
view.*

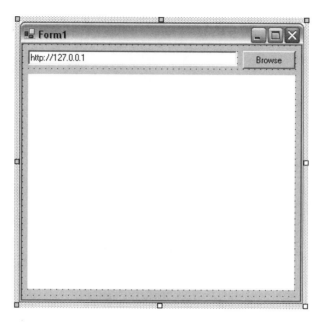

Figure 1.4
*Visual Studio
.NET, form design
view.*

C#

```
private void btnBrowse_Click(object sender, System.EventArgs
e)
{
  object notUsed = null;
  webBrowser.Navigate(tbURL.Text,ref notUsed,ref notUsed, ref
notUsed, ref notUsed);
}
```

The code consists simply of a single method call, navigate. This invokes the standard process that Internet Explorer goes through as it navigates the Web. The reason for the extra parameters to the method in the C# version is that C# does not support optional parameters. The navigate method has four optional parameters: Flags, targetFrameName, postData, and Headers. None of these is needed for this simple example.

In the application, click Debug→Start, type in the name of a Web page in the space provided, and press the Browse button. You will see that Web page appearing in the Web Browser control on the page, such as that shown in Figure 1.6.

You will quickly notice that the Web browser window behaves identically to Internet Explorer. This is because the component that was added to the toolbox is the main processing engine behind Internet Explorer. This

Figure 1.5
*Visual Studio
.NET, Properties
tool window.*

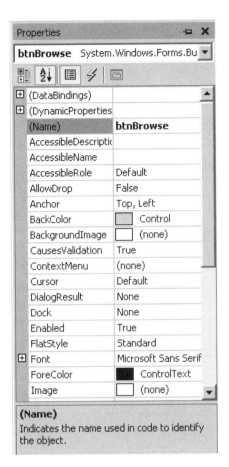

component was developed before .NET arrived on the scene, so it uses an older component model than the native .NET-managed controls.

Applications written in .NET are referred to as *managed*, or *type-safe*, *code*. This means that the code is compiled to an intermediate language (IL) that is strictly controlled, such that it cannot contain any code that could potentially cause a computer to crash. Applications written in native code have the ability to modify arbitrary addresses of computer memory, some of which could cause crashes, or general protection faults.

Components designed before the advent of .NET are written in native code and are therefore unmanaged and deemed unsafe. There is no technical difficulty in combining unsafe code with a .NET application, as shown previously; however, if an underlying component has the potential to bring down a computer, the whole application is also deemed unsafe. Unsafe

Figure 1.6
*Visual Studio
.NET, form at
runtime.*

applications may be subject to restrictions; for instance, when they are executed from a network share, they could be prevented from operating. On
the whole, though, if a component can do the job, use it.

The Internet Explorer component is a Common Object Model (COM)
control. This type of model was used most extensively in Visual Studio 6.0.
When a COM object is imported into a .NET application, a Runtime call-
able wrapper (RCW) class is created. This class then exposes all the properties and methods of the COM object to .NET code. In some cases, this
importing process produces an interface that is virtually identical to the
original COM object; however, as aptly demonstrated in the previous
example, there may be some differences in the syntax of function calls.

In the original COM object, the `Navigate` method's last four parameters
were optional, but in the case of C#, the optional parameters had to be
passed `ref notUsed`.

1.11   Using the .NET SDK

Using the .NET SDK to develop .NET applications makes a lot more work
for a developer. This section shows you how to write and compile a .NET
application from the command line.

The command line may be adequate for development of console applications, ASP.NET, and components, but it is not feasible to develop large

Windows forms applications from the command line. The previous example, although easy to implement in Visual Studio .NET, would require a large and complex program. Nevertheless, it should be informative to Visual Studio .NET developers to be aware of the code that is autogenerated by Visual Studio .NET.

In the true programming tradition, we shall start with a program that simply displays "Hello World." To make this different, the program will be written as a Windows form. After all, DOS console applications are very much past their sell-by date, and there seems little point in using them at all.

The code for this application may seem daunting at first, but this should illustrate how much extra work is required to implement applications without Visual Studio .NET.

First, decide which language you want to develop in, either C# or Visual Basic .NET. Open a text editor, such as Notepad, and type in the following code:

C#

```
using System;
using System.Windows.Forms;
namespace helloWorld
{
  public class Form1 : System.Windows.Forms.Form
  {
    public Form1()
    {
      this.Text = "Hello World";
    }
    [STAThread]
    static void Main()
    {
      Application.Run(new Form1());
    }
  }
}
```

VB.NET

```
Imports System
Imports System.Windows.Forms
Public Class Form1
  Inherits System.Windows.Forms.Form
```

```
Public Sub New ( )
  InitializeComponent( )
End Sub

Private Sub InitializeComponent( )
  Me.Text = "Hello World"
End sub
End Class

Module Module1
  Sub Main ( )
   Application.Run ( new Form1 ( ) )
  End sub
End Module
```

All this code does is open a window with the caption "Hello World," which is somewhat underwhelming for the amount of code entered. Looking closely at the code, you can see the process of events that make up a Windows application in .NET.

An application in .NET is made up of namespaces, some of which are system defined and others are coded in. This application contains three namespaces: System, System.Windows.Forms, and helloWorld. The latter is the only namespace of the three that is actually supplied by the programmer. The helloWorld namespace contains a class, named Form1. This class inherits from System.Windows.Forms.Form. This means that the class will have a visible presence on screen.

Whenever a class is created, a function known as the *constructor* is called. This function can be recognized in C# when the name of the function is the same as that of the class. In VB.NET, the constructor is a subroutine named New. In the case of the previous example and in most Windows applications, this constructor is used to place user interface elements (sometimes referred to as *widgets*) on the form. In the previous example, the constructor calls InitializeComponent, which then sets the window name of the current form (this) to "Hello World."

Every application must have a starting point. It is tradition in virtually every programming language that the stating point should be called Main. In C#, the [STAThread] attribute indicates the function which acts as the entry point for this single threaded apartment (STA) application. Every application must have one, and only one, entry point.

```
[STAThread] static void Main()
```

In VB.NET, the main function is coded in a different way but operates identically. The main function must appear in a separate module and be coded as follows. A module is a programmatic element that contains code that is global to the entire application.

```
Module Module1: Sub Main ( )
```

Once a Windows application starts, at least one form (a class inheriting from `System.Windows.Forms.Form`) must be created in order for there to be a visual interface. To create a new form, we call `Application.Run`, passing an instance of the form.

1.11.1 Compiling with Visual Basic.NET

Save the file to `d:\temp\helloworld.vb`. Open the command prompt by pressing Start→Run and then typing `cmd` for Windows NT, 2000, or XP or `command` for Windows 95, 98, or ME.

Note: Path names mentioned differ among computers, depending on installation options.

Type the following:

DOS

```
D:\temp> path %path%;C:\WINDOWS\Microsoft.NET\Framework\v1.0.3705
D:\temp> Vbc /t:winexe /r:system.dll /r:system.windows.forms.dll
helloworld.vb
D:\temp> helloworld
```

Figure 1.7
"Hello World"
application.

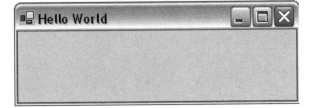

1.11.2   Compiling with C#

Save the file to d:\temp\helloworld.cs. Open the command prompt by pressing Start > Run and then typing cmd for Windows NT, 2000, or XP or command for Windows 95, 98, or ME.

Note: Path names mentioned differ among computers, depending on installation options.

DOS

```
D:\temp> path %path%;C:\WINDOWS\Microsoft.NET\Framework\v1.0.3705
D:\temp> csc /t:exe helloworld.cs
D:\temp> helloworld
```

1.11.3   Testing the application

To run the application, you need to compile it first. Depending on what language you used to program the application, skip to the relevant section. Once it has compiled, you can run the application by clicking on the executable (.exe) file generated from the compilation. You should see a form resembling Figure 1.7.

1.12   Conclusion

This chapter should whet your appetite for .NET network programming and give you a better understanding of what you have to bear in mind when working with networks.

The following chapter deals with input and output (I/O) in .NET, which forms the foundation for all native .NET networking functions.

2

I/O in the .NET Framework

2.1   Introduction

This chapter lays the foundation for virtually every networking example contained in this book. Without a working knowledge of how .NET handles I/O, it may prove difficult to adapt the code examples in this book to your own needs.

I/O applies to network data transfers, as well as saving and loading to your computer's hard disk Later chapters will describe how to perform network transfers; however, this chapter will be concerned with the underlying I/O operations that are common to both types of transfers. The first half of this chapter will demonstrate how to read and write to disk, using .NET streams.

The second half of this chapter develops the stream concept by demonstrating how to convert complex objects, such as database queries, into a format that can be written to a .NET stream.

2.2   Streams

In order to provide similar programmatic interfaces to the broad range of I/O devices with which a programmer has to contend, a stream-based architecture was developed in .NET. I/O devices can be anything from printers to hard disks to network interfaces.

Not all devices support the same functions. For example, it is possible to read only the second half of a 1-Mb file, but not possible to download only the second half of a Web page. Therefore, not all streams support the same methods.

Properties such as canRead(), canSeek(), and canWrite() indicate the capabilities of the stream when applied to a particular device.

The most important stream in the context of this book is the network-Stream, but another important stream is fileStream, which is used extensively throughout this book to demonstrate file transfers over networks.

Streams can be used in two ways: asynchronously or synchronously. When using a stream synchronously, upon calling a method, the thread will halt until the operation is complete or fails. When using a stream asynchronously, the thread will return from the method call immediately, and whenever the operation is complete, a method will be called to signify the completion of the operation, or some other event, such as I/O failure.

It is not user friendly to have a program "hang" when it is waiting for an operation to complete. Therefore, synchronous method calls must be used in a separate thread.

Through the use of threads and synchronous method calls, computers achieve the illusion of being able to do several things at once. In reality, most computers have only one central processing unit (CPU), and the illusion is achieved by quickly switching between tasks every few milliseconds.

The following application illustrates the two techniques. The code in this book will tend toward using synchronous streams, but it is important to be able to recognize and understand asynchronous streams.

2.2.1   Streams for files

Start a new Visual Studio .NET Windows application project.

Drag an File Open Dialog control onto the form. Name this control openFileDialog. Then add a textbox, to be named tbResults, which should be set with multiline=true. Add two buttons to the form, and name them btnReadAsync and btnReadSync.

First, we shall implement asynchronous file reading. Press Read Async and enter the following code:

C#

```
FileStream fs;
byte[] fileContents;
AsyncCallback callback;


private void btnReadAsync_Click(object sender,
System.EventArgs e)
{
  openFileDialog.ShowDialog();
```

```
    callback = new AsyncCallback(fs_StateChanged);
    fs = new FileStream(openFileDialog.FileName, FileMode.Open,

    FileAccess.Read, FileShare.Read, 4096, true);
    fileContents = new Byte[fs.Length];
    fs.BeginRead(fileContents, 0, (int)fs.Length, callback,
null);
}
```

VB.NET

```
Dim fs As FileStream
Dim fileContents As Byte()
Dim callback As AsyncCallback
Private Sub btnReadAsync_Click(ByVal sender As _
    System.Object, ByVal e As System.EventArgs) _
    Handles btnReadAsync.Click
 OpenFileDialog.ShowDialog()
 callback = New AsyncCallback(AddressOf fs_StateChanged)
 fs = New FileStream(OpenFileDialog.FileName,
    FileMode.Open, FileAccess.Read, FileShare.Read, _
    4096, True)
 ReDim fileContents(fs.Length)
 fs.BeginRead(fileContents, 0, fs.Length, callback, Nothing)
End Sub
```

This code requires a little explanation. First, the magic number, 4096, is simply a performance characteristic because it is quicker to transfer data from disks in 4-Kb chunks than 1 byte at a time.

The final parameter in the `FileStream` constructor indicates whether the operation is to be completed asynchronously or synchronously.

The most important thing to note is that there is no reference to `tbResults`; this implies that some other function must handle the data once the read is complete. The `AsyncCallback` constructor refers to another function, which is also referenced in the `BeginRead` method, so this must be it.

As you can see from the code, the `fs_StateChanged` function has not yet been implemented. This function is called whenever the file is finished reading.

Note: Synchronous use of `FileStream` is more efficient when the file size is less than 64 Kb and the file is located on the local machine.

C#

```
private void fs_StateChanged(IAsyncResult asyncResult)
{
  if (asyncResult.IsCompleted)
  {
    tbResults.Text = Encoding.UTF8.GetString(fileContents);
    fs.Close();
  }
}
```

VB.NET

```
Private Sub fs_StateChanged(ByVal asyncResult As _
      IAsyncResult)
  If asyncResult.IsCompleted Then
      tbResults.Text = Encoding.UTF8.GetString(fileContents)
      fs.Close()
  End If
End Sub
```

Now, let's look at how the same operation is carried out using synchronous streams and threading.

Click on the Read Sync button, and enter the following code:

C#

```
private void btnReadSync_Click(object sender,
System.EventArgs e)
{
  Thread thdSyncRead = new Thread(new ThreadStart(syncRead));
  thdSyncRead.Start();
}
```

VB.NET

```
Private Sub btnReadSync_Click(ByVal sender As _
System.Object, ByVal e As System.EventArgs) Handles _
      btnReadSync.Click
```

```
            Dim thdSyncRead = New Thread(New ThreadStart _
            (AddressOf syncRead)) thdSyncRead.Start();
    End Sub
```

This code doesn't perform any file handling; instead, it creates a new thread, whose entry point is the syncRead function. When this thread runs, it does so in parallel with any other code that is running at the same time, which includes the background operating system (OS) "housekeeping" (Windows message handling) functions.

If the code above were replaced by a simple call to syncRead( ), the program would still operate; however, if the file happened to be several gigabytes in size, the user would quickly perceive the application to be "hung." A hung application is notably nonresponsive and may turn white when dragged behind another application. What is actually happening is that the main thread of application is taking 100% processor time and does not give the OS time to handle simple tasks such as redrawing the user interface.

In certain time-critical applications, it may be necessary to take 100% processor time, but any application with a user interface should remain responsive at all times.

The next task is to implement the syncRead function:

C#

```csharp
public void syncRead()
{
  openFileDialog.ShowDialog();
  FileStream fs;
  try
  {
    fs = new FileStream(ofd.FileName, FileMode.OpenOrCreate);
  }
  catch(Exception ex)
  {
    MessageBox.Show(ex.Message);
    return;
  }
  fs.Seek(0, SeekOrigin.Begin);
  byte[] fileContents = new byte[fs.Length];
  fs.Read(fileContents, 0, (int)fs.Length);
  tbResults.Text = Encoding.UTF8.GetString(fileContents);
```

```
        fs.Close();
    }
```

VB.NET

```
    Public Sub syncRead()
        OpenFileDialog.ShowDialog()
        Dim fs As FileStream
        Try
            fs = New FileStream(ofd.FileName, _
            FileMode.OpenOrCreate)
        Catch ex As Exception
            MessageBox.Show(ex.Message)
            Return
        End Try
      fs.Seek(0, SeekOrigin.Begin)
        ReDim fileContents(fs.Length)
        fs.Read(fileContents, 0, fs.Length)
      tbResults.Text = Encoding.UTF8.GetString(fileContents)
        fs.Close()
    End Sub
```

In the above code, you will notice that the FileStream constructor is enclosed in a try/catch block. This allows the program to recover gracefully from problems such as a missing file or an unreadable disk. In real-world applications, any operation that relies on the existence of files or network resources should be contained within a try/catch block. This allows programs to continue execution, even if something unexpected happens. In most examples throughout this book, try/catch blocks are not used in order to keep the examples concise and readable.

Three namespaces must be included in the code as follows:

C#

```
using System.IO;
using System.Text;
using System.Threading;
```

VB.NET

```
Imports System.IO
Imports System.Threading
Imports System.Text
```

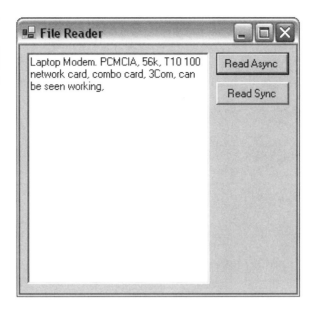

Figure 2.1
Reading files using synchronous and asynchronous methods.

Note: The most concise way to read text files (under 1 Gb) is:
```
(new StreamReader(filename)).ReadToEnd();
```

To test the application, press Debug→Start. Press either button, and then open a file, and you will see its contents in the textbox opposite, as shown in Figure 2.1. Many files, such as those designed to hold audio or video data, will display as pages of seemingly random characters because the data is not designed to be displayed as text and requires another program to interpret into something we can see or hear.

An interesting observation you can make with this application is that if you compare the textual representation of a database file (.mdb) with an Mp3 (.mp3), you will notice that the database file contains many identical pages of text, whereas the Mp3 file contains a real mixture of characters. The similarity of data within a file is known as its *entropy*. By reducing the entropy of data in a file, the file size can be reduced. This is why a database shrinks in size when compressed, but an Mp3 doesn't. Chapter 11 deals with this topic in more detail.

The significant methods and properties for `FileStream` are shown in Table 2.1.

Table 2.1   *Significant members of* FileStream.

Method or Property	Purpose
Constructor	Initializes a new instance of the FileStream. It may be invoked thus: FileStream(string, FileMode).
Length	Gets the length of the file. Returns long.
Position	Gets or sets the current position of the file pointer. Returns long.
BeginRead()	Begins an asynchronous read. It may be invoked thus: BeginRead(byte[] array,int offset,int numBytes, AsyncCallback userCallback, object stateObject).
BeginWrite()	Begins an asynchronous write. It may be invoked thus: BeginWrite(byte[] array,int offset,int numBytes, AsyncCallback userCallback, object stateObject).
Write	Writes a block of bytes to this stream using data from a buffer. It may be invoked thus: Write(byte[] array,int offset,int count).
Read	Reads a block of bytes from the stream and writes the data in a given buffer. It may be invoked thus: Read(in byte[] array,int offset, int count).
Lock	Prevents access by other processes to all or part of a file. It may be invoked thus: Lock (long position, long length).

2.2.2   Encoding data

In the previous example, in both synchronous and asynchronous modes, a call was made to Encoding.UTF8.GetString() in order to convert the byte array to a string. The reason for such a verbose statement is the variety of ways in which a byte array can represent a string. Other valid formats are Unicode (Encoding.Unicode), ASCII, and UTF7.

Unicode Transformation Format 8 (UTF8) represents each byte as a different character; Unicode represents every two bytes as a character. This system is used for Eastern languages such as Japanese, but also covers English. Applications designed for worldwide markets should have all human-readable strings encoded in Unicode to facilitate localization at a later date.

2.2.3 **Binary and text streams**

When data contained in streams is of a well-known format, such as XML, plain text, or primitive types, there are methods available to greatly simplify the parsing of such data.

Plain text is most commonly used in streams that are designed to be human readable and editable. Plain-text streams exist in many network protocols that were originally designed for text-only UNIX computers. A common guise for plain-text files is the end-user modifiable application configuration files such as the ubiquitous .INI or .CSV; however, these are being somewhat replaced by XML in .NET.

A common feature of plain text is that each unit of information is terminated with an {enter}. This is actually a sequence of two UTF8 codes, 10 and 13 (represented in C# by \n and by VBCrLf in VB.NET). This can be tricky to parse out of a string, so methods such as ReadLine have been implemented in the textReader class.

To read a file one line at a time to the end, you could use code similar to the following application. Start a new project in Visual Studio .NET, and draw a button on the form. Name this button btnRead. Click on this button, and enter the following code:

C#

```
private void btnRead_Click(object sender, System.EventArgs e)
{
OpenFileDialog ofd = new OpenFileDialog();
ofd.ShowDialog();
FileStream fs = new FileStream(ofd.FileName,
FileMode.OpenOrCreate);
StreamReader sr = new StreamReader(fs);
int lineCount=0;
while (sr.ReadLine()!=null)
{
  lineCount++;
}
fs.Close();
MessageBox.Show("There are " + lineCount + " lines in " +
ofd.FileName);
}
```

VB.NET

```
Private Sub btnRead_Click(ByVal sender As System.Object, _
ByVal e As System.EventArgs) Handles btnRead.Click

  Dim ofd As OpenFileDialog =  New OpenFileDialog()
  ofd.ShowDialog()
  Dim fs As FileStream =  New _
      FileStream(ofd.FileName,FileMode.OpenOrCreate)
  Dim sr As StreamReader =  New StreamReader(fs)
  Dim lineCount As Integer = 0
  While Not sr.ReadLine() Is Nothing
    lineCount = lineCount + 1
  End While
  fs.Close()
  MessageBox.Show("There are " & lineCount & _
      " lines in " &  ofd.FileName)
End sub
```

The following namespace must be included in the code in order for it to compile correctly:

C#

```
using System.IO;
```

VB.NET

```
Imports System.IO
```

To test the application, run it from Visual Studio .NET. Press the Read button, and then select a text file from the hard disk. Press OK, and a message box similar to Figure 2.2 will appear shortly.

When porting a .NET application from a console application to a Windows application, you will notice that the familiar format of the `Console.WriteLine` method is not reflected in standard string handling. It is, however, available in `StringBuilder.AppendFormat` and `StreamWriter.WriteLine`.

Not everything stored on disk or sent across a network has to be human readable. In many cases, significantly more efficient code can be written, which leverages the compact binary representations of variables. For instance, the number 65000 in a 16-bit unsigned Integer binary (`Uint16`) is 11111101 11101000 (2 bytes); in text it is "6," "5," "0," "0," "0" (5 bytes).

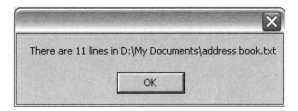

Figure 2.2
Using streams to help read files.

Table 2.2   *The significant methods and properties for* `StreamReader`.

Method or Property	Purpose
`Constructor`	Initializes a new instance of the object. May be invoked thus: `StreamReader(Stream)`.
`Peek`	Returns the next available character, but does not consume it. Returns −1 at the end of a stream. Takes no parameters.
`Read`	Reads the next character or next set of characters from the input stream. It may be invoked thus: `Read(char[], int, int)`.
`ReadBlock`	Reads characters from the current stream and writes the data to buffer, beginning at index. It may be invoked thus: `ReadBlock(in char[] buffer, int index, int count)`.
`ReadLine`	Reads a line of characters from the current stream and returns the data as a string. Takes no parameters; returns `string`.
`ReadToEnd`	Reads the stream from the current position to the end of the stream. Takes no parameters; returns `string`.

To save an array of variables to disk, you could use the following application. Start a new project in Visual Studio .NET and draw a button on the form. Name this button `btnWrite`. Click on this button and enter the following code:

C#

```
private void btnWrite_Click(object sender, System.EventArgs
e)
{
 SaveFileDialog sfd = new SaveFileDialog();
 sfd.ShowDialog();
 FileStream fs = new FileStream(sfd.FileName,
 FileMode.CreateNew);
```

```
BinaryWriter bw = new BinaryWriter(fs);
int[] myArray= new int[1000];
for(int i=0;i<1000;i++)
{
  myArray[i]=i;
  bw.Write(myArray[i]);
}
bw.Close();
}
```

VB.NET

```
Private Sub btnWrite_Click(ByVal sender As System.Object, _
ByVal e As System.EventArgs) Handles btnRead.Click
 Dim sfd As SaveFileDialog =  New SaveFileDialog()
 sfd.ShowDialog()
 Dim fs As FileStream =  New _
 FileStream(sfd.FileName,FileMode.CreateNew)
 Dim bw As BinaryWriter =  New BinaryWriter(fs)
 Dim myArray() As Integer =  New Integer(1000) {}
 Dim i As Integer
 For  i = 1 to 1000
   myArray(i)=i
  bw.Write(myArray(i))
 Next
 bw.Close()
End Sub
```

The following namespace must be included in the code in order for it to compile correctly:

C#

```
using System.IO;
```

VB.NET

```
Imports System.IO
```

To test the application, run it from Visual Studio .NET. Press the Write button and then select a location on the hard disk. Press OK, and a file will be written to that location shortly.

> **Note:** `int` in C# is a signed 4-byte number; thus the resultant file is exactly 4,000 bytes long.

The significant methods and properties for `BinaryWriter` are shown in Table 2.3.

Table 2.3 *Significant members of the `BinaryWriter` class.*

Method or Property	Purpose
`Constructor`	Initializes a new instance of the object. May be invoked thus: `BinaryWriter(Stream)`.
`Close`	Closes the current `BinaryWriter` and the underlying stream. It takes no parameters.
`Seek`	Sets the position within the current stream. It may be invoked thus: `Seek(int offset, SeekOrigin origin)`.
`Write`	Writes a value to the current stream. It may be invoked thus: `Write(byte[])`.
`Write7BitEncodedInt`	Writes a 32-bit integer in a compressed format. It may be invoked thus: `Write7BitEncodedInt(int value)`.

2.2.4 Serialization

Serialization is the process by which a .NET object can be converted into a stream, which can easily be transferred across a network or written to disk. This stream can be converted into a copy of the original object through a process called *deserialization*.

The following examples are modeled on a purchase order system. A purchase order is a request to supply goods on a credit basis. The process must be highly bug resilient because an error in purchasing information could cost millions of dollars in unfulfilled sales and audits. This means that each stage of the process must be recorded, from issuance to payment. The process must follow a set pattern, and dates must be recorded. These rules must be enforced by the object itself, so that any bugs can be traced quickly back to the offending class.

To demonstrate serialization, you could use code similar to the following application. Start a new project in Visual Studio .NET and draw two buttons on the form. Name the buttons `button1` and `button2`, respectively. Click on the form, and enter the following code:

C#

```csharp
public enum purchaseOrderStates
{
  ISSUED,
  DELIVERED,
  INVOICED,
  PAID
}
[Serializable()]
public class company
{
  public string name;
  public string address;
  public string phone;
}
[Serializable()]
public class lineItem
{
  public string description;
  public int quantity;
  public double cost;
}
[Serializable()]
public class purchaseOrder
{
  private purchaseOrderStates _purchaseOrderStatus;
  private DateTime _issuanceDate;
  private DateTime _deliveryDate;
  private DateTime _invoiceDate;
  private DateTime _paymentDate;

  public company buyer;
  public company vendor;
  public string reference;
    public lineItem[] items;

  public purchaseOrder()
  {
```

```
        _purchaseOrderStatus=purchaseOrderStates.ISSUED;
        _issuanceDate=DateTime.Now;
    }
    public void recordDelivery()
    {
      if ( _purchaseOrderStatus==purchaseOrderStates.ISSUED)
      {
        _purchaseOrderStatus=purchaseOrderStates.DELIVERED;
        _deliveryDate=DateTime.Now;
      }
    }
    public void recordInvoice()
    {
      if
( _purchaseOrderStatus==purchaseOrderStates.DELIVERED)
      {
        _purchaseOrderStatus=purchaseOrderStates.INVOICED;

        _invoiceDate=DateTime.Now;
      }
    }
    public void recordPayment()
    {
      if ( _purchaseOrderStatus==purchaseOrderStates.INVOICED)
      {
        _purchaseOrderStatus=purchaseOrderStates.PAID;
        _paymentDate=DateTime.Now;
      }
    }
}
```

VB.NET

```
Public Enum purchaseOrderStates
    ISSUED
    DELIVERED
    INVOICED
    PAID
End Enum
  <Serializable()> _
  Public Class company
    Public name As String
    Public address As String
```

```
      Public phone As String
  End Class
  <Serializable()> _
  Public Class lineItem
    Public description As String
    Public quantity As Integer
    Public cost As Double
  End Class
  <Serializable()> _
  Public Class purchaseOrder
    Private _purchaseOrderStatus As purchaseOrderStates
    Private _issuanceDate As DateTime
    Private _deliveryDate As DateTime
    Private _invoiceDate As DateTime
    Private _paymentDate As DateTime

    Public buyer As company
    Public vendor As company
    Public reference As String
      Public items() As lineItem

    Public sub New()
      _purchaseOrderStatus=purchaseOrderStates.ISSUED
      _issuanceDate=DateTime.Now
    End sub

    Public sub recordDelivery()
      if _purchaseOrderStatus=purchaseOrderStates.ISSUED
        _purchaseOrderStatus=purchaseOrderStates.DELIVERED
        _deliveryDate=DateTime.Now
      end if
    end sub
    Public sub recordInvoice()
      if _purchaseOrderStatus=purchaseOrderStates.DELIVERED
        _purchaseOrderStatus=purchaseOrderStates.INVOICED
        _invoiceDate=DateTime.Now
      end if
    end sub

    Public sub recordPayment()
      if _purchaseOrderStatus=purchaseOrderStates.INVOICED
```

```
        _purchaseOrderStatus=purchaseOrderStates.PAID
        _invoiceDate=DateTime.Now
     end if
  end sub
End Class
```

Note: The use of the [Serializable()] tag facilitates deep seilalization. It is possible to perform deep serialization without this tag by using surrogates. A surrogate is where the a class implements ISerializationSurrogate, and is passed to the AddSurrogate method of a SurrogateSelector object. The SurrogateSelector property of the formatter is then set equal to this object prior to serialization.

The _purchaseOrderStatus variable is private and can only be modified by recordDelivery(), recordInvoice(), and recordPayment(). This ensures that a bug elsewhere in the code will not cause undelivered goods to be paid for (i.e., _purchaseOrderStatus cannot change directly from ISSUED to PAID). Similarly, the date recording is encapsulated within the object and cannot be externally manipulated.

To place a purchase order on a stream (either to disk or to the network), you could write each value one after the other as text, separated by commas, and have the receiver parse out the values and re-create the object; however, there is an easier way: serialization.

To write the object to a stream and save the object to disk, you could use the following code:

C#

```
private void button1_Click(object sender, System.EventArgs e)
{
   company Vendor = new company();
   company Buyer = new company();
   lineItem Goods = new lineItem();
   purchaseOrder po = new purchaseOrder();

   Vendor.name = "Acme Inc.";
   Buyer.name = "Wiley E. Coyote";
   Goods.description = "anti-RoadRunner cannon";
   Goods.quantity = 1;
   Goods.cost = 599.99;
```

```
        po.items = new lineItem[1];
        po.items[0] = Goods;
        po.buyer = Buyer;
        po.vendor = Vendor;
        SoapFormatter sf = new SoapFormatter();
        FileStream fs = File.Create("C:\\po.xml");
        sf.Serialize(fs,po);
        fs.Close();
    }
```

VB.NET

```
    Private  Sub Button1_Click(ByVal sender As Object, ByVal e As _
    System.EventArgs) Handles Button1.Click
        Dim Vendor As company =  New company()
        Dim Buyer As company =  New company()
        Dim Goods As lineItem =  New lineItem()
        Dim po As purchaseOrder =  New purchaseOrder()

        Vendor.name = "Acme Inc."
        Buyer.name = "Wiley E. Coyote"
        Goods.description = "anti-RoadRunner cannon"
        Goods.quantity = 1
        Goods.cost = 599.99

        po.items = New lineItem(1) {}
        po.items(0) = Goods
        po.buyer = Buyer
        po.vendor = Vendor

        Dim sf As SoapFormatter =  New SoapFormatter()
        Dim fs As FileStream =  File.Create("C:\po.xml")
        sf.Serialize(fs,po)
        fs.Close()
    End Sub
```

To read the object back into memory, we can deserialize it thus:

C#

```
    private void button2_Click(object sender, System.EventArgs e)
    {
        SoapFormatter sf = new SoapFormatter();
```

```
FileStream fs = File.OpenRead("C:\\po.xml");
purchaseOrder po = (purchaseOrder)sf.Deserialize(fs);
fs.Close();
MessageBox.Show("Customer is " + po.buyer.name);
}
```

VB.NET

```
Private  Sub button2_Click(ByVal sender As Object, ByVal e As_
System.EventArgs) Handles Button2.Click
   Dim sf As SoapFormatter =  New SoapFormatter()
   Dim fs As FileStream =  File.OpenRead("C:\po.xml")
   Dim po As purchaseOrder = CType(sf.Deserialize(fs),_
   purchaseOrder)
   fs.Close()
   MessageBox.Show("Customer is " + po.buyer.name)
End Sub
```

Before this code will work, you will need an assembly reference for
SoapFormatter. This is done by clicking Project→Add Reference and selecting System.Runtime.Serialization.Formatters.Soap, then adding this
line to the top of the code:

C#

```
using System.IO;
using System.Runtime.Serialization.Formatters.Soap;
```

VB.NET

```
imports System.IO
imports System.Runtime.Serialization.Formatters.Soap
```

To test this application, run it from Visual Studio .NET. Press the Serialize button and then the Deserialize button. You will see the message "Customer is Wiley E. Coyote," as depicted in Figure 2.3.

If you open the file C:\PO.XML, you will see a human-readable representation of the object, as shown in Figure 2.4. This format is known as simple
object access protocol (SOAP) and is very portable between platforms (e.g.,
WebSphere for UNIX can read it).

Figure 2.3
*Serializing .NET
classes.*

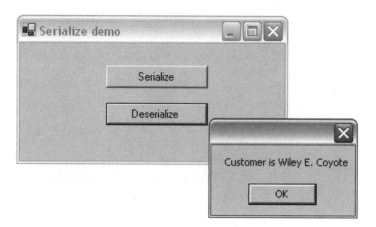

Note: The constructor is not called during deserialization. In the above example, you will see that the issue date does not change when the object is re-created from disk.

The significant methods and properties for `SoapFormatter` are shown in Table 2.4.

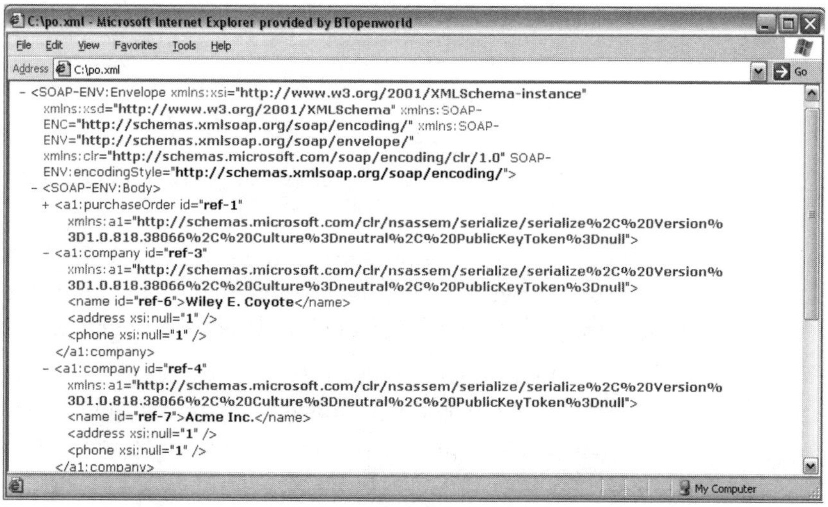

Figure 2.4
*XML view of a
serialized object.*

Table 2.4 *Significant members of* `SoapFormatter`.

Method or Property	Purpose
Constructor	Initializes a new instance of the `SoapFormatter` class. It may be invoked without any parameters.
Deserialize	Deserializes a stream into an object graph. It may be invoked thus: `Deserialize(Stream)`.
Serialize	Serializes an object or graph of connected objects. It may be invoked thus: `Serialize(Stream, object)`.
AssemblyFormat	Gets or sets the format in which assembly names are serialized. Returns `FormatterAssemblyStyle`.
TypeFormat	Gets or sets the format in which type descriptions are laid out in the serialized stream. Returns `FormatterTypeStyle`.
TopObject	Gets or sets the `ISoapMessage` into which the SOAP top object is deserialized. Returns `ISoapMessage`.

Serializing to binary

SOAP formatting may be very impressive, but it is far from compact and may be quite bandwidth consuming if sent over a slow network. We can therefore use the native binary format to store the array by substituting `SoapFormatter` with `BinaryFormatter` in the above example thus:

C#

```
BinaryFormatter bf = new BinaryFormatter();
FileStream fs = File.Create("C:\\po.bin");
bf.Serialize(fs,po);
fs.Close();
```

VB.NET

```
Dim bf As BinaryFormatter =  New BinaryFormatter()
Dim fs As FileStream =  File.Create("C:\po.bin")
bf.Serialize(fs,po)
fs.Close()
```

And deserialize with this code:

C#

```
BinaryFormatter bf = new BinaryFormatter();
FileStream fs = File.OpenRead("C:\\po.bin");
```

```
purchaseOrder po = (purchaseOrder)bf.Deserialize(fs);
fs.Close();
```

VB.NET

```
Dim bf As BinaryFormatter =  New BinaryFormatter()
Dim fs As FileStream =  File.OpenRead("C:\po.bin")
Dim po As purchaseOrder = CType(bf.Deserialize(fs), _
    purchaseOrder)
fs.Close()
```

When substituting the `SoapFormatter` with the `BinaryFormatter`, a reference to `System.Runtime.Serialization.Formatters.Soap` is no longer required. Instead, the `Formatters.Binary` namespace is required; it can be added by inserting this line to the top of the code:

C#

```
using System.Runtime.Serialization.Formatters.Binary;
```

VB.NET

```
imports System.Runtime.Serialization.Formatters.Binary
```

This produces a file that is considerably smaller than the previous SOAP version. The resulting file is not human readable, and it is unfeasible to port to other platforms.

Note: Binary representations, although difficult to read, are not a secure way of protecting sensitive data.

The `BinaryFormatter` object is programatically identical to the `Soap-Formatter` object, except that it does not support the `topObject` method.

Shallow serialization

Whenever an object is serialized without its private and protected members, this is known as *shallow serialization*. This may cause problems as a result of inaccurate copies of objects; for instance, in the purchase order application, users would find their orders reverting from PAID to ISSUED. Furthermore, shallow serialization cannot resolve circular references within objects. For instance, if a `BookCatalog` class has a member of type `Book`, and the `Book` class has a member of type `BookCatalog`, then neither object can be serialized shallowly.

One benefit of shallow serialization is that it uses XML schema definition (XSD) to define types. The XSD standard ensures faithful representations on other platforms. The SOAP formatter, as used in deep serialization, uses the CLR-type system and is not standardized across non-.NET platforms.

Code for shallow serialization can be seen by the use of code similar to the following:

C#

```
XmlSerializer xs = new XmlSerializer(po.GetType());
FileStream fs = File.Create("C:\\po.xml");
xs.Serialize(fs,po);
fs.Close();
```

VB.NET

```
Dim xs As XmlSerializer =  New XmlSerializer(po.GetType())
Dim fs As FileStream =  File.Create("C:\po.xml")
xs.Serialize(fs,po)
fs.Close()
```

Shallow deserialization is performed with the following code:

C#

```
purchaseOrder po = new purchaseOrder();
XmlSerializer xs = new XmlSerializer(po.GetType());
FileStream fs = File.OpenRead("C:\\po.xml");
po = (purchaseOrder)xs.Deserialize(fs);
fs.Close();
MessageBox.Show("Customer is " + po.buyer.name);
```

VB.NET

```
Dim po As purchaseOrder =  New purchaseOrder()
Dim xs As XmlSerializer =  New XmlSerializer(po.GetType())
Dim fs As FileStream =  File.OpenRead("C:\po.xml")
po = CType(xs.Deserialize(fs), purchaseOrder)
fs.Close()
MessageBox.Show("Customer is " + po.buyer.name)
```

The following namespace is required for the `XmlSerializer` object:

C#

```
using System.Xml.Serialization;
```

VB.NET

```
imports System.Xml.Serialization
```

The significant methods and properties for `XMLSerializer` are shown in Table 2.5.

Table 2.5 *Significant members of the XMLSerializer class.*

Method or Property	Purpose
Constructor	Initializes a new instance of the object. It may be invoked thus: `XmlSerializer(Type)`.
Deserialize	Deserializes an XML document. May be invoked thus: `Deserialize(Stream)`.
FromTypes	Returns an array of `XmlSerializer` objects created from an array of types. May be invoked thus: `FromTypes(Type[] types)`.
Serialize	Serializes an object into an XML document. May be invoked thus: `Serialize(Stream stream, object o)`.
CanDeserialize	Gets a value indicating whether this `XmlSerializer` can deserialize a specified XML document. Can be invoked thus: `CanDeserialize(XmlReader xmlReader)`.

2.2.5 Writing a database to a stream

Most business applications use databases to store their data. In order to transport data from the database across a network, it must be written to a stream. The easiest way of doing this is to serialize the dataset.

Note: SQL Server and Oracle provide direct network access to their databases and should be used in preference to serialization.

Database programming overview

Whole books have been written on database programming, and it would be impossible to do the topic justice in this chapter; however, a brief overview is provided here to help explain the basics of database access in .NET and the concept of dataset serialization.

Database programming is centered on two key strings: the connection string and structured query language (SQL) statements. The connection string indicates the location and type of the database. The SQL statement describes the operation to be performed on the data.

Table 2.6 *Connection strings for common databases.*

Database type	Connection string
Microsoft Access	`Provider=Microsoft.Jet.OLEDB.4.0;` `Data Source=<location of .mdb file>`

SQL Server	`Provider=sqloledb;`
	`Network Library=DBMSSOCN;`
	`DataSource=<IP address>,1433; Initial`
	`Catalog=<database name>; User ID=<user>;`
	`Password=<password>;`

To open a connection to a database in .NET, you need to import the `System.Data.OleDb` namespace:

C#

```
using System.Data.OleDb;
```

VB.NET

```
imports System.Data.OleDb
```

This task is followed by the creation of an `OleDbConnection` object, where the constructor is passed the connection string (Table 2.6). Here the database is a Microsoft Access file located at `c:\purchaseOrder.mdb`

C#

```
string szDSN = "Provider=Microsoft.Jet.OLEDB.4.0;" +
        "Data Source=C:\\purchaseOrder.mdb";
OleDbConnection DSN = new OleDbConnection(szDSN);
```

VB.NET

```
String szDSN = "Provider=Microsoft.Jet.OLEDB.4.0;" + _
              "Data Source=C:\purchaseOrder.mdb"
Dim DSN As OleDbConnection =  New OleDbConnection(szDSN)
```

Once we have a connection to the database, SQL statements can be executed against it to read and manipulate data. The constructor of the OleDb-Command object is passed the SQL string.

Depending on the intended use of the data, there are three ways to make the OleDbCommand act upon the SQL: (1) data binding and serialization pass the object to the constructor of an OleDbDataAdapter; (2) manipulation statements use the executeNonQuery method; and (3) everything else uses the executeReader method.

Four main operations can be performed on a database: reading data (Select), adding new rows to a table (Insert), removing rows from a table (Delete), and changing the contents of an existing row (Update).

A select statement takes the form

```
Select * from table
```

Where table is the name of a table in the database. The preceding statement would return all of the rows from the selected table. It is possible to limit the amount of data returned by using where clauses:

```
Select * from table where column='some data'
```

Note: It is possible to increase the amount of data returned by using join to combine two or more tables on a common field.

Update statements may take the following form:

```
Update table set column='new data' where column='old data'
```

Delete statements may take the following form:

```
Delete from table where column='old data'
```

Insert statements may take the following form:

```
Insert into table (column) values ('new data')
```

To perform an Update, Delete, or Insert function, we use the executeNonQuery method:

C#

```
Public void nonQuery(string szSQL,string szDSN)
{
  OleDbConnection DSN = new OleDbConnection(szDSN);
  DSN.Open();
  OleDbCommand SQL = new OleDbCommand(SQL,DSN);
   SQL.ExecuteNonQuery();
   DSN.Close();
}
```

VB.NET

```
Public  Sub nonQuery(ByVal szSQL As String, ByVal szDSN _
    As String)
  Dim DSN As OleDbConnection =  New OleDbConnection(szDSN)
  DSN.Open()
  Dim SQL As OleDbCommand =  New OleDbCommand(SQL,DSN)
  SQL.ExecuteNonQuery()
  DSN.Close()
End Sub
```

To perform a Select query, without requiring any serialization or data binding, the executeReader method is used:

C#

```
Public void Query(string szSQL,string szDSN)
{
  OleDbConnection DSN = new OleDbConnection(szDSN);
  DSN.Open();
  OleDbCommand SQL = new OleDbCommand(szSQL,DSN);
  OleDbDataReader dataReader = SQL.ExecuteReader();
  While(dataReader.Read())
  {
    // process data
  }
  DSN.Close();
}
```

VB.NET

```vbnet
Public sub Query(String szSQL,string szDSN)
   Dim DSN As OleDbConnection =  New OleDbConnection(szDSN)
   DSN.Open()
   Dim SQL As OleDbCommand =  New OleDbCommand(szSQL,DSN)
   Dim dataReader As OleDbDataReader =  SQL.ExecuteReader()
   Do while dataReader.Read()
      ' process data.
   loop
   DSN.Close()
end sub
```

To perform a select query, requiring further serialization or data binding, the OleDbDataAdapter object is used to fill a dataset object with the
SQL query results:

C#

```csharp
Public DataSet Query(string szSQL,string szDSN)
{
   DataSet ds = new DataSet();
   OleDbConnection DSN = new OleDbConnection(szDSN);
   DSN.Open();
   OleDbCommand SQL = new OleDbCommand(szSQL,DSN);
   OleDbDataAdapter Adapter = new OleDbDataAdapter(SQL);
   Adapter.Fill(ds,"sql");
   DSN.Close();
   return(ds);
}
```

VB.NET

```vbnet
Public  Function Query(ByVal szSQL As String, ByVal szDSN _
     As String) As DataSet
   Dim ds As DataSet =  New DataSet()
   Dim DSN As OleDbConnection =  New OleDbConnection(szDSN)
   DSN.Open()
   Dim SQL As OleDbCommand =  New OleDbCommand(szSQL,DSN)
   Dim Adapter As OleDbDataAdapter =  New OleDbDataAdapter(SQL)
   Adapter.Fill(ds,"sql")
   DSN.Close()
   Return(ds)
End Sub
```

Creating a database

In order to try out the following demo, you will need either Microsoft SQL Server 2000 Desktop Engine (available free at *www.microsoft.com/sql/msde/downloads/download.asp*) or Microsoft Access to create the database.

If you are using SQL Server, you can set up the necessary tables and data using the SQL statements below. Open Query Analyzer, log onto the database, and execute the following SQL code:

SQL

```
create table purchaseOrder
(
 id int identity(1,1) not null,
 purchaseOrderStatus int,
 issuanceDate datetime,
 deliveryDate datetime,
 invoiceDate datetime,
 paymentDate datetime,
 buyer int,
 vendor int,
 reference varchar(50)
)

create table company
(
 id int identity(1,1) not null,
 name varchar(50),
 address varchar(50)
)

create table lineitem
(
 id int identity(1,1) not null,
 description varchar(50),
 quantity int,
 cost money,
 purchaseOrderID int
)

insert into company (name,address) values (
'Wiley E coyote','sandy desert')
```

```
insert into company (name,address) values ('Acme corp.',
'big city')
insert into purchaseorder ( issuanceDate, buyer,vendor)
values (getDate(),1,2)
insert into lineitem
(description,quantity,cost,purchaseorderid) values
('Road runner trap',1,100,1)
```

If you are using Access, open Microsoft Access, select Blank Access database, and press OK (Figure 2.5).

Save the file to c:\purchaseOrder.mdb, and press New to create a new table. You should select Design View. Then press OK.

Enter in the table fields as illustrated below. Set Allow Zero Length to Yes for the reference field.

Close the window and save the table as purchaseOrder. Create two other tables named company and lineItem.

The company table should have the following fields: id, name, address, and phone. The lineItem table should have the following fields: id, description, quantity, cost, and purchaseOrderID.

Figure 2.5
Microsoft Access,
new database
dialog.

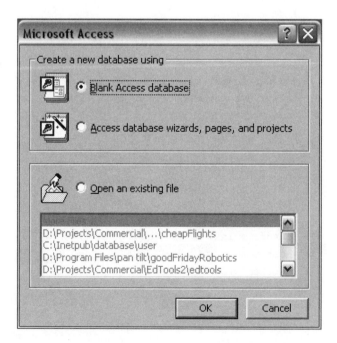

Enter details for two companies into the company table by selecting the table name and pressing "open." A corresponding row in the `purchaseOrder` table should also be entered, ensuring that the `buyer` and `vendor` fields match the `ID` fields in the company table. Enter one item into the `lineItem` table, where `purchaseOrderID` is equal to the `ID` of the newly entered row in the `purchaseOrder` table.

Dataset serialization

The following application runs SQL queries against the database just created in the previous section. The results of the queries are displayed as XML in a browser window. The ability to convert datasets into XML is useful because it is transferable across networks and can be read from other platforms without too much extra work.

Start a new Visual Studio .NET project, and select a Windows application as before.

Right-click on the toolbox, and select Customize toolbox (Visual Studio .NET 2002) or Add/Remove Items (Visual Studio .NET 2003). Then select Microsoft Web Browser, and press OK. Drag this onto the form, and name it `WebBrowser`. Also drag a button and textbox named `btnQuery` and `tbSQL`, respectively.

You will need to add references to the required namespaces first:

C#

```
using System.Data.OleDb;
using System.IO;
using System.Xml.Serialization;
```

VB.NET

```
imports System.Data.OleDb
imports System.IO
imports System.Xml.Serialization
```

To remove the unsightly error message on the Web browser, we can set the initial page to be `about:blank` thus:

C#

```
private void Form1_Load(object sender, System.EventArgs e)
{
  object notUsed = null;
```

```
    WebBrowser.Navigate("about:blank",ref notUsed,ref notUsed,
ref notUsed, ref notUsed);
    }
```

VB.NET

```
Private  Sub Form1_Load(ByVal sender As Object, ByVal e _
As System.EventArgs)
  WebBrowser.Navigate("about:blank")
End Sub
```

Now, click on the Query button, and enter the following code:

C#

```
private void button1_Click(object sender, System.EventArgs e)
{
    string szDSN = "Provider=Microsoft.Jet.OLEDB.4.0;" +
                   "Data Source=C:\\purchaseOrder.mdb";

    OleDbConnection DSN =  new OleDbConnection(szDSN);
    XmlSerializer xs = new XmlSerializer(typeof(DataSet));
    DataSet ds = new DataSet();
    DSN.Open();
    OleDbCommand odbc = new OleDbCommand(tbSQL.Text,DSN);
    OleDbDataAdapter odda = new OleDbDataAdapter(odbc);
    odda.Fill(ds,"sql");
    TextWriter tw = new StreamWriter("c:\\sql.xml");
    xs.Serialize(tw, ds);
    tw.Close();
    DSN.Close();
    object notUsed = null;
    WebBrowser.Navigate("c:\\sql.xml",ref notUsed,ref notUsed,
ref notUsed, ref notUsed);
    }
```

VB.NET

```
Private  Sub button1_Click(ByVal sender As Object, ByVal _
e As System.EventArgs) Handles btnQuery.Click
  Dim szDSN as String = _
   "Provider=Microsoft.Jet.OLEDB.4.0;" + _
              "Data Source=C:\purchaseOrder.mdb"
  Dim DSN As OleDbConnection =  New OleDbConnection(szDSN)
  Dim xs As XmlSerializer =  New XmlSerializer((New _
```

```
    DataSet).GetType())
    Dim ds As DataSet =  New DataSet()
    DSN.Open()
    Dim odbc As OleDbCommand =  New OleDbCommand(tbSQL.Text,DSN)
    Dim odda As OleDbDataAdapter =  New OleDbDataAdapter(odbc) _
      odda.Fill(ds,"sql")
    Dim tw As TextWriter =  New StreamWriter("c:\sql.xml")
    xs.Serialize(tw, ds)
    tw.Close()
    DSN.Close()
    Dim notUsed As Object =  Nothing
    WebBrowser.Navigate("c:\sql.xml")
  End Sub
```

Note: The dataset is shallowly serialized. This does not cause a problem because there are no private members of interest in the dataset object.

Please note that the above example assumes that you have used Microsoft Access rather than SQL Server and that the database was saved to c:\purchaseOrder.mdb. If you have used SQL Server, then you must change the

Figure 2.6
Serialization from an SQL query.

szDSN string to "Provider=sqloledb;Network Library=DBMSSOCN;Data-Source=<IP>,1433;Initial Catalog=<database>;UserID=;Password=<password>;", where <IP>, <database>, and <password> are substituted as necessary.

To test this application, run it from Visual Studio .NET, enter an SQL statement in the box provided (e.g., "select * from company"), and press the Query button. XML should appear in the browser window that represents the set of data returned, as shown in Figure 2.6.

2.3   Conclusion

This chapter has introduced the concept of streams. These are used heavily throughout the remainder of this book.

Serialization was also explored and can clearly be seen as a powerful tool that can be implemented in only a few lines of code. It certainly is a must have for any object-oriented distributed application.

To conclude the chapter, a brief introduction to databases was given. This provides a rudimentary grounding in using either SQL Server or Microsoft Access in your .NET applications.

Chapter 3 deals with sockets, the .NET implementation of the fundamental Internet protocols, TCP/IP and UDP.

Working with Sockets

3.1   Introduction

This chapter explains the most important aspect of network programming, the socket. It is essential to fully understand how to use sockets in .NET before proceeding to the following chapters. Examples in this chapter will enable the user to send files and messages over the Internet, using simple network applications.

Two socket-level protocols are described in this chapter. Both protocols are demonstrated as a pair of applications—one client, one server. This follows the classic client/server model, which is prevalent in most distributed applications. The chapter follows this structure, describing the client first, followed immediately by an implementation of the server.

3.2   What is a socket?

A socket is an object that represents a low-level access point to the IP stack. This socket can be open or closed or one of a set number of intermediate states. A socket can send and receive data down this connection. Data is generally sent in blocks of a few kilobytes at a time for efficiency; each of these blocks is called a *packet*.

Table 3.1   *Well-known port numbers .*

Port Number	Protocol
20	FTP data
21	FTP control

Table 3.1   *Well-known port numbers (continued).*

Port Number	Protocol
25	SMTP (email, outgoing)
53	DNS
80	HTTP (Web)
110	POP3 (email, incoming)
143	IMAP (email, incoming)

Source: *www.iana.org/assignments/port-numbers.txt.*

All packets that travel on the Internet must use the Internet protocol. This means that the source IP address, destination address must be included in the packet. Most packets also contain a port number. A port is simply a number between 1 and 65,535 that is used to differentiate higher protocols, such as email or FTP (Table 3.1). Ports are important when it comes to programming your own network applications because no two applications can use the same port. It is recommended that experimental programs use port numbers above 1024.

Packets that contain port numbers come in two flavors: UDP and TCP/IP. UDP has lower latency than TCP/IP, especially on startup. Where data integrity is not of the utmost concern, UDP can prove easier to use than TCP, but it should never be used where data integrity is more important than performance; however, data sent via UDP can sometimes arrive in the wrong order and be effectively useless to the receiver. TCP/IP is more complex than UDP and has generally longer latencies, but it does guarantee that data does not become corrupted when traveling over the Internet. TCP is ideal for file transfer, where a corrupt file is more unacceptable than a slow download; however, it is unsuited to Internet radio, where the odd sound out of place is more acceptable than long gaps of silence.

3.3   Creating a simple "hello world" application

This program will send the words "hello world" over a network. It consists of two executables, one a client, the other a server. These two programs could be physically separated by thousands of kilometers, but as long as the IP addresses of both computers are known, the principle still works.

In this example, the data will be sent using UDP. This means that the words "hello world" will be bundled up with information that will be used by IP routers to ensure that the data can travel anywhere it wishes in the world. UDP data is not bundled with headers that track message integrity or security. Furthermore, the receiving end is not obliged to reply to the sender with acknowledgments as each packet arrives. The elimination of this requirement allows UDP data to travel with much lower latency than TCP. UDP is useful for small payload transfers, where all of the data to be sent can be contained within one network packet. If there is only one packet, the out-of-sequence problems associated with UDP do not apply; therefore, UDP is the underlying protocol behind DNS.

3.3.1   Writing a simple UDP client

To get started, open Visual Studio .NET, click New Project, then click Visual C# projects, and then Windows Application. Set the name to "UDP Client" and press OK. You could alternately click Visual Basic .NET projects and follow the code labeled VB.NET in the examples.

Now, design the form as shown in Figure 3.1. Name the button button1 and the textbox tbHost.

Click the button and type in the source code as follows:

C#

```
private void button1_Click(object sender, System.EventArgs e)
{
  UdpClient udpClient = new UdpClient();
  udpClient.Connect(tbHost.Text, 8080);
  Byte[] sendBytes = Encoding.ASCII.GetBytes("Hello World?");
    udpClient.Send(sendBytes, sendBytes.Length);
}
```

VB.NET

```
Private sub button1_Click(sender as object, e as _
System.EventArgs) Handles button1.Click
  Dim udpClient as new UdpClient()
  udpClient.Connect(tbHost.Text, 8080)
  Dim sendBytes as Byte()
  sendBytes = Encoding.ASCII.GetBytes("Hello World?")
    udpClient.Send(sendBytes, sendBytes.Length)
End sub
```

Figure 3.1
*UDP client
application.*

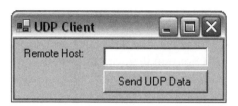

From the code, we can see that the first task is creating a UDP Client object. This is a socket that can send UDP packets. A port number is chosen arbitrarily. Here, the port number 8080 is used, simply because it is easy to remember and it is not in the first 1024 port numbers, which are reserved for special use by IANA.

The first argument in the Connect method indicates where any data should be sent. Here, I have used tbHost.Text (i.e., whatever is typed into the textbox). If you have access to only one computer, you would type localhost into this window; otherwise, if you are using two computers, type the IP address of the server.

You also need to include some assemblies by adding these lines to just under the lock of the using statements at the top of the code:

C#

```
using System.Net;
using System.Net.Sockets;
using System.Text;
using System.IO;
```

VB.NET

```
imports System.Net
imports System.Net.Sockets
imports System.Text
imports System.IO
```

Now, press F5 to compile and run the application. You should see your application resembling Figure 3.1.

Table 3.2 shows the significant methods and properties for UdpClient.

3.3.2   **Writing a simple UDP server**

The purpose of the UDP server is to detect incoming data sent from the UDP client. Any new data will be displayed in a list box.

Table 3.2   *Significant members of the UdpClient class.*

Method or Property	Purpose
Constructor	Initializes a new instance of the UdpClient class. For client UDP applications, this is used as new UdpClient (string,int); for servers use new UdpClient(int).
Close()	Closes the UDP connection.
DropMulticastGroup()	Leaves a multicast group.
JoinMulticastGroup()	Adds a UdpClient to a multicast group. This may be invoked thus: JoinMulticastGroup(IPAddress).
Receive()	Returns a UDP datagram that was sent by a remote host. This may be invoked thus: Receive(ref IPEndPoint). Returns Byte[].
Send()	Sends a UDP datagram to a remote host. This may be invoked thus Send(byte[], int).
Active	Gets or sets a value indicating whether a connection to a remote host has been made. Returns Bool
Client	Gets or sets the underlying network sockets. Returns Socket.

As before, create a new C# project, but with a new user interface, as shown below. The list box should be named lbConnections.

A key feature of servers is multithreading (i.e., they can handle hundreds of simultaneous requests). In this case, our server must have at least two threads: one handles incoming UDP data, and the main thread of execution may continue to maintain the user interface, so that it does not appear hung. The details of threading are not within the scope of this book.

First, we write the UDP data handling thread:

C#

```
public void serverThread()
{
UdpClient udpClient = new UdpClient(8080);
while(true)
{
  IPEndPoint RemoteIpEndPoint = new IPEndPoint(IPAddress.Any,
```

```
    0);
  Byte[] receiveBytes = udpClient.Receive(ref
RemoteIpEndPoint);
  string returnData = Encoding.ASCII.GetString(receiveBytes);
  lbConnections.Items.Add(
   RemoteIpEndPoint.Address.ToString() + ":" +
returnData.ToString()
  );
 }
}
```

VB.NET

```
Public Sub serverThread()
 Dim udpClient as new UdpClient(8080)
 While true
  Dim RemoteIpEndPoint as new IPEndPoint(IPAddress.Any, 0)
  Dim receiveBytes as Byte()
  receiveBytes = udpClient.Receive(RemoteIpEndPoint)
  Dim returnData As String = _
  Encoding.ASCII.GetString(receiveBytes)
  lbConnections.Items.Add _
  RemoteIpEndPoint.Address.ToString() + ":" + _
  returnData.ToString()
 Wend
End Sub
```

Again, we use the UdpClient object. Its constructor indicates that it should be bound to port 8080, like in the client. The Receive method is blocking (i.e., the thread does not continue until UDP data is received). In a real-world application, suitable timeout mechanisms should be in place because UDP does not guarantee packet delivery. Once received, the data is in byte array format, which is then converted to a string and displayed on-screen in the form *source address: data*.

There is then the matter of actually invoking the serverThread method asynchronously, such that the blocking method, Receive, does not hang the application. This is solved using threads as follows:

C#

```
private void Form1_Load(object sender, System.EventArgs e)
{
```

```
    Thread thdUDPServer = new Thread(new
ThreadStart(serverThread));
    thdUDPServer.Start();
}
```

VB.NET

```
Private Sub Form1_Load(ByVal sender As System.Object, _
    ByVal e As System.EventArgs) Handles MyBase.Load
 Dim thdUDPServer = new Thread(new ThreadStart(AddressOf _
    serverThread))
 thdUDPServer.Start()
End Sub
```

To finish off, the following assemblies are to be added:

C#

```
using System.Threading;
using System.Net;
using System.Net.Sockets;
using System.Text;
```

VB.NET

```
imports System.Threading
imports System.Net
imports System.Net.Sockets
imports System.Text
```

Figure 3.2
*UDP Server
application.*

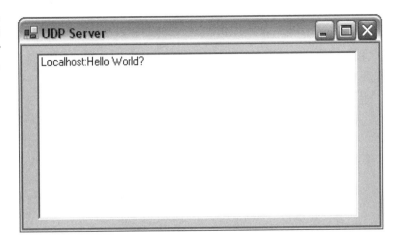

To test this application, execute it from Visual Studio .NET. On the same computer, open the UDP client and execute it. Type `localhost` into the textbox and press the button on the UDP client. A message "Localhost:Hello World?" should appear, such as shown in Figure 3.2.

If you have a second PC, get its IP address and install the server on this second PC and execute it. Again open the client, but type the IP address into the textbox. When you press the button on the client, the server should display the "Hello World" message. Voilà! You have used .NET to send data across a network.

3.4   Using TCP/IP to transfer files

Most networked applications use TCP/IP because there is no risk of data becoming corrupted while traveling over the Internet. It is said to be connection oriented; that is, both client and server after a setup phase treat a set of IP packets as being sent along a virtual channel, allowing for data that is too large to fit into a single IP packet to be sent and for retransmission to occur when packets are lost.

This sample application will allow you to send any file from one computer to another. Again, it is client/server based, so you will need either two computers or to run both the client and server on the same computer.

3.4.1   Writing a simple TCP/IP client

Create a new project as usual, and design a form as shown in Figure 3.3. Name the Send button `btnSend`, the Browse button `btnBrowse`, the File textbox `tbFilename`, and the Server textbox `tbServer`. Also add an Open File Dialog control named `openFileDialog`.

Click on the Browse button and add the following code:

Figure 3.3
*TCP client
application.*

C#

```
private void btnBrowse_Click(object sender,
System.EventArgs e)
  {
    openFileDialog.ShowDialog();
    tbFilename.Text = openFileDialog.FileName;
  }
```

VB.NET

```
Private Sub btnBrowse_Click(ByVal sender As _
    System.Object, ByVal e As System.EventArgs) _
    HandlesbtnBrowse.Click
  openFileDialog.ShowDialog()
  tbFilename.Text = openFileDialog.FileName
end sub
```

This code opens the default file open dialog box. If the user does not select a file, openFileDialog.Filename will return an empty string.

Click on the Send button and add the following code:

C#

```
private void btnSend_Click(object sender, System.EventArgs e)
  {
    Stream fileStream = File.OpenRead(tbFilename.Text);
    // Alocate memory space for the file
    byte[] fileBuffer = new byte[fileStream.Length];
    fileStream.Read(fileBuffer, 0, (int)fileStream.Length);
    // Open a TCP/IP Connection and send the data
   TcpClient clientSocket = new TcpClient(tbServer.Text,8080);
   NetworkStream networkStream =  clientSocket.GetStream();
    networkStream.Write(fileBuffer,0,fileBuffer.GetLength(0));
    networkStream.Close();
  }
```

VB.NET

```
Private Sub btnSend_Click(ByVal sender As System.Object, _
ByVal e As System.EventArgs) Handles btnSend.Click
  Dim filebuffer As Byte()
    Dim fileStream As Stream
    fileStream = File.OpenRead(tbFilename.Text)
```

```
' Alocate memory space for the file
ReDim filebuffer(fileStream.Length)
fileStream.Read(filebuffer, 0, fileStream.Length)
' Open a TCP/IP Connection and send the data
Dim clientSocket As New TcpClient(tbServer.Text, 8080)
Dim networkStream As NetworkStream
networkStream = clientSocket.GetStream()
networkStream.Write(filebuffer, 0, fileStream.Length)
end sub
```

The above code reads in a file and sends it over a network connection. To read in a file, a stream for this file is created by passing the filename to the OpenRead method. This stream is read into the file buffer array. An alternate means of reading this file would be to pass the file stream as a parameter to the constructor of a StreamReader, then to call the ReadToEnd method, although this approach would only be useful for text-only files.

It then opens a TCP/IP connection with the server on port 8080, as specified in tbServer.Text. The TcpClient constructor is blocking, in that code execution will not continue until a connection is established. If a connection cannot be established, a SocketException will be thrown: "No connection could be made because the target machine actively refused it." As usual, the following assemblies are added:

C#

```
using System.Threading;
using System.Net;
using System.Net.Sockets;
using System.Text;
using System.IO;
```

VB.NET

```
imports System.Threading
imports System.Net
imports System.Net.Sockets
imports System.Text
imports System.IO
```

Table 3.3 shows the significant methods and properties for TcpClient.

Table 3.3   *Significant methods and properties of TcpClient.*

Method or Property	Purpose
Constructor	Initializes a new instance of the `TcpClient` class. It may be used thus: `new TcpClient(string,Int)`.
NoDelay	When set to `true`, it increases efficiency if your application only transmits small amounts of data in bursts. Returns `Bool`.
ReceiveBufferSize	Gets or sets the size of the receive buffer. Returns `Int`.
SendBufferSize	Gets or sets the size of the send buffer. Returns `Int`.
SendTimeout	Gets or sets the amount of time a `TcpClient` will wait to receive confirmation after you initiate a send. Returns `Int`.
Close()	Closes the TCP connection.
Connect()	Connects the client to a remote TCP host using the specified host name and port number. It may be invoked thus: `Connect(string,Int)`.
GetStream()	Returns the stream used to send and receive data. Returns `NetworkStream`.

3.4.2   Writing a simple TCP/IP server

Open a new project as before, and design a user interface as depicted in Figure 3.4. The label should be named `lblStatus`, and the list box, `lbConnections`.

Like the UDP server in a preceding example, the TCP server is multi-threaded. In this case, three threads are used: the main thread maintains the user interface, a second thread listens for connections, and a third thread handles the connections.

One socket is required for each connection and will remain loaded in memory until the connection is closed. These sockets need to be stored in an ArrayList rather than a standard array because it is impossible to predict how many connections will be received.

To start, declare a global `ArrayList` variable:

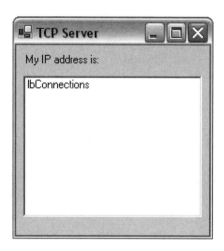

Figure 3.4
*TCP Server
application.*

C#
```
public class Form1 : System.Windows.Forms.Form
{
    private ArrayList alSockets;
    ...
```

VB.NET
```
Public Class Form1 Inherits System.Windows.Forms.Form
    private alSockets as ArrayList
    ...
```

Because any client wishing to connect to this server would need to know its IP address, it is helpful to display this on-screen. This is a cosmetic feature, but it may come in handy in other applications. In order to retrieve the local IP address, we call the static method Dns.GetHostByName. This returns an IPHostEntry object, which is a collection of IP addresses, to accommodate multihomed computers, which many are. Element zero in this array is commonly the external IP address for the computer.

The Form1_Load method displays the local IP address on the form and starts the thread that will wait for incoming connections. If the listenerThread method were to be called directly, the program would become unresponsive and appear to hang, while the socket waited on incoming connections. This effect is avoided by executing the listenerThread method in a separate thread of execution, which can block without adversely affecting the user interface.

C#

```csharp
private void Form1_Load(object sender, System.EventArgs e)
{
 IPHostEntry IPHost = Dns.GetHostByName(Dns.GetHostName());

  lblStatus.Text = "My IP address is " +
IPHost.AddressList[0].ToString();
  alSockets = new ArrayList();
  Thread thdListener = new Thread(new
ThreadStart(listenerThread));
  thdListener.Start();
}
```

VB.NET

```vbnet
Private Sub Form1_Load(ByVal sender As System.Object, _
   ByVal e As System.EventArgs) Handles MyBase.Load
   Dim IPHost as IPHostEntry
   IPHost = Dns.GetHostByName(Dns.GetHostName())
   lblStatus.Text = "My IP address is " + _
   IPHost.AddressList(0).ToString()
   alSockets = new ArrayList()
   Dim thdListener As New Thread(New ThreadStart _
   (AddressOf listenerThread))
   thdListener.Start()
End Sub
```

The `listenerThread` method's function is to wait indefinitely for TCP connections on port 8080 and then to redelegate the work of handling these requests to the `handlerThread` method. This function also reports the source of the connections.

This time, the reason for redelegating work to a thread is not to maintain the responsiveness of the user interface, but rather to ensure that the application will continue to listen for new connections while it is handling a previous client. The new thread will be required to have access to the socket that is dealing with the current client. Otherwise, there would be no means of returning data.

This thread will block on the call to `AcceptSocket`. Execution will not continue until an incoming connection has been detected; when it has, a new socket is created and dedicated to handling this particular client. Once this socket has established a connection, the socket is placed on top of the alSockets array list to await pickup by the handler thread.

It may seem unusual that the socket is not passed directly to the thread. This is because it is not valid to specify parameters when defining the starting point of a thread, for example, making an erroneous statement such as

```
New ThreadStart(AddressOf handlerThread(Parameter))
```

Therefore, another means of passing parameters to threads is required. In this example, a public array list of sockets is used, where the top-most entry is used by the newest thread, and so forth. Another common technique for passing parameters to threads is to encapsulate the thread's methods in a separate class, with public variables acting as parameters. When a new instance of this class is created, it can be passed to the `ThreadStart` constructor.

Once the socket has been added to the array list, the handler thread is invoked, and this thread continues to listen for incoming connections.

Note: You may notice a port number added to the end of the source IP address. This is an internally negotiated port number used by TCP/IP. More details on this topic can be found in Chapter 13.

C#

```csharp
public void listenerThread()
{
  TcpListener tcpListener = new TcpListener(8080);
  tcpListener.Start();
  while(true)
  {
    Socket handlerSocket = tcpListener.AcceptSocket();
    if (handlerSocket.Connected)
    {
     lbConnections.Items.Add(
      handlerSocket.RemoteEndPoint.ToString() + " connected."
     );
     lock (this)
     {
      alSockets.Add(handlerSocket);
     }
     ThreadStart thdstHandler = new
```

```
    ThreadStart(handlerThread);
    Thread thdHandler = new Thread(thdstHandler);
    thdHandler.Start();
   }
  }
 }
```

VB.NET

```
Public sub listenerThread()
  Dim tcpListener as new TcpListener(8080)
  Dim handlerSocket as Socket
  Dim thdstHandler as ThreadStart
  Dim thdHandler as Thread
  tcpListener.Start()
  do
    handlerSocket = tcpListener.AcceptSocket()
    if handlerSocket.Connected then
      lbConnections.Items.Add( _
      handlerSocket.RemoteEndPoint.ToString() + _
      "connected.")
      SyncLock (Me)
        alSockets.Add(handlerSocket)
      end SyncLock
      thdstHandler = New ThreadStart(AddressOf _
      handlerThread)
      thdHandler = New Thread(thdstHandler)
      thdHandler.Start()
    end if
  Loop
End sub
```

The remainder of the work is carried out in the handlerThread method. This function finds the last used socket and then retrieves the stream from this socket. An array is allocated to the same size as the stream, and once the stream is fully received, its contents are copied into this array.

Once the connection closes, the data is written to file at c:\my documents\upload.txt. It is important to have the lock() keyword around the lines of code associated with file access; otherwise, if two concurrent connections try to access the same file, the program will crash. The contents of the file are then displayed in the list box on-screen. The socket is then set to null to remove it from memory. If this point were omitted, the array list would quickly fill with sockets that had lost connection with their clients.

Note that the constructor for `TcpListener` that takes only a single `int` for a port number is now obsolete. To stop the compiler complaining about this line of code, simply call the constructor thus:

```
new TcpListener(IPAddress.Any,8080)
```

C#

```
public void handlerThread()
{
 Socket handlerSocket = (Socket)alSockets[alSockets.Count-1];
 NetworkStream networkStream = new
 NetworkStream(handlerSocket);
    int thisRead=0;
    int blockSize=1024;
    Byte[] dataByte = new Byte[blockSize];
    lock(this)
    {
     // Only one process can access
     // the same file at any given time

     Stream fileStream = File.OpenWrite("c:\\my documents\
     \upload.txt");
     while(true)
     {
      thisRead=networkStream.Read(dataByte,0,blockSize);
      fileStream.Write(dataByte,0,thisRead);
      if (thisRead==0) break;
     }
     fileStream.Close();
    }
    lbConnections.Items.Add("File Written");
    handlerSocket = null;
   }
```

VB.NET

```
     Public Sub handlerThread()
        Dim handlerSocket As Socket
        handlerSocket = alSockets(alSockets.Count - 1)
```

```
Dim networkStream As NetworkStream = New _
    NetworkStream(handlerSocket)
Dim blockSize As Int16 = 1024
Dim thisRead As Int16
Dim dataByte(blockSize) As Byte
SyncLock Me
' Only one process can access the
' same file at any given time
Dim fileStream As Stream
    fileStream = File.OpenWrite("c:\upload.txt")
    While (True)
        thisRead = networkStream.Read(dataByte, _
            0, blockSize)
        fileStream.Write(dataByte, 0, dataByte.Length)
        If thisRead = 0 Then Exit While
    End While
    fileStream.Close()
End SyncLock
lbConnections.Items.Add("File Written")
handlerSocket = Nothing
End Sub
```

As before, add the namespace references to the head of the code:

C#

```
using System.Threading;
using System.Net;
using System.Net.Sockets;
using System.Text;
using System.IO;
```

VB.NET

```
imports System.Threading
imports System.Net
imports System.Net.Sockets
imports System.Text
imports System.IO
```

To test the application, run the server application, and take note of the IP address displayed. Then, run the client application. Type the IP address into the box provided. Click on browse to select a file. Press send to transfer the file. A file will soon appear on the server at `c:\my documents\upload.txt`, which is an exact copy of the file that was located on the client.

To further demonstrate this principle, you can use a telnet program to write text to `c:\upload.txt` remotely.

On Windows 95, 98, or ME machines, click Start→Run, then type `Telnet`. Click Connect→Remote System. Type the server IP address into the host name textbox, and type 8080 into the port textbox. Press Connect. Type some text into the window, and when finished, press Connect, Disconnect. A file will soon appear on the server at `c:\my documents\ upload.txt`.

On Windows NT, 2000, and XP machines, click Start→Run, then type `Telnet`. Type `Open 127.0.0.1 8080`. Replace 127.0.0.1 with the IP address of your server, if you have two computers. Type some text into the window, and when finished, close the window. A file will soon appear on the server at `c:\upload.txt`.

Table 3.4 *Significant members of the TcpListener class.*

Method or Property	Purpose
`Constructor`	Initializes a new instance of the `TcpListenerClient` class. It may be used thus: `new TcpListener(int)`.
`LocalEndpoint`	Gets the underlying `EndPoint` of the current `TcpListener`. Returns `EndPoint`.
`AcceptSocket()`	Accepts a pending connection request. Returns `Socket`.
`AcceptTcpClient()`	Accepts a pending connection request. Returns `TcpClient`.
`Pending()`	Determines if there are pending connection requests. Returns `Bool`.
`Start()`	Starts listening to network requests.
`Stop()`	Closes the listener.
`Active`	Gets a value that indicates whether `TcpListener` is actively listening for client connections. Returns `Bool`.
`Server`	Gets the underlying network socket. Returns `Socket`.

Ways have already been developed to send files through the Internet. Anybody who has ever written a Web site would be familiar with programs such as cuteFTP and smartFTP, which do exactly what was demonstrated in the previous example, albeit with a much more flexible interface.

It is rarely a good idea to try to reinvent the wheel and develop a new way to send data through the Internet. The global standardization of protocols has made the Internet what it is today.

Table 3.4 shows the significant methods and properties for TcpListener.

3.5   Debugging network code

Network connections can and do break, and other applications may be already using the ports you want to use. It is therefore foolhardy to assume that a call to a Connect or Listen method will always succeed. For this reason, the try/catch construct should be employed as demonstrated below:

C#

```
try
{
 serverSocket.Bind(ipepServer);
 serverSocket.Listen(-1);
}
catch(SocketException e)
{
 MessageBox.Show(e.Message);
}
catch(Exception e)
{
 MessageBox.Show(e.Message);
 Application.Exit();
}
```

VB.NET

```
try
 serverSocket.Bind(ipepServer)
 serverSocket.Listen(-1)
catch e as SocketException
 MsgBox(e.Message)
Catch e as Exception
 MsgBox(e.Message)
```

```
Application.Exit()
End try
```

Another type of problem that plagues network applications is scalability. This is where the software cannot cope with a large number of sequential or concurrent connections, or both. To discover scalability problems, you can either repetitively hit the Connect and Send buttons on your client or write a stress test program to do this for you over long periods. The program may run out of memory if sockets are not set to `null` after use, or it may crash because of simultaneous access to a limited resource, or start dropping connections, or work perfectly.

To locate problems in multithreaded applications, tracing statements are invaluable. A good mechanism for doing this is the `System.Diagnostics.Trace` class or simple `Console.WriteLine` statements at the entrance and exit of methods. Once the problem has been located, placing `Lock` statements around non-thread-safe code usually aids system stability; however, placing a `Lock` clause around a blocking statement may cause your application to hang.

When developing an application that interfaces with a third-party distributed application, it is sometimes quite difficult to see exactly what is being sent between client and server. This matter can be further complicated if the protocol is proprietary, with little or no technical information.

Many protocols are inherently text based and were originally designed for users to access by typing the commands directly into the server, rather than using a GUI. Nowadays, nobody would have the patience to upload a file via FTP by typing the FTP commands directly into the server, but because Internet standards are somewhat immortal, these old systems have remained.

This rather arcane way of accessing Web-based services may no longer be relevant to the end-user, but it is a godsend to the developer. Say, for example, you are developing a program that is designed to interface an IMAP (email) server. If the program is not receiving emails, after you've meticulously implemented the protocol as per RFC spec, you can always open up telnet and go through the paces of receiving an email by typing text into telnet. If you can re-create the error manually, it should help solve the problem from a programmatic perspective. This approach would not work with binary protocols such as Distributed Common Object Model (DCOM).

Figure 3.5
Netstat *utility.*

If you are working with an unofficial or proprietary protocol, there may be little chance you can guess how it works. The first step in approaching any such protocol is to determine on which port it is operating. A useful tool in doing this is netstat. To see it in action, open the command prompt and type netstat (Figure 3.5).

This lists all of the current outgoing and incoming connections to your computer at that time, along with the port in use. To isolate the port used by any particular application, use the process of elimination. If you turn off all nonessential network services apart from the application that you are trying to analyze, take note of the list of ports, then turn off the application, and compare the new list with the old list; whatever port is missing is the application's port.

Knowing the port number is only one step toward tapping into a protocol. To see exactly what bits and bytes are being sent between the two applications, you can use one of the example protocol analyzer programs described in Chapter 13 or a ready-made application such as Trace Plus from *www.sstinc.com.*

3.6   Socket-level networking in .NET

It is often necessary to understand network code written by other developers in order to debug it or adapt it to your own application. After all, no program is ever written without referring to some existing code.

This book will consistently use the most concise code possible, but it is important to realize that there are many techniques to implement networked applications in .NET. It is equally important to be able to understand and recognize these techniques when they are used in code written by other developers.

The most important class in .NET networking is the Socket class. This can be used for either TCP/IP or UDP as either a client or server; however, it requires the help of the Dns class to resolve IP addresses and is quite difficult to use. Three other classes exist, which are simpler to use, but less flexible: TcpListener, TcpClient, and UdpClient. To illustrate the differences between the two techniques, listed below is code that demonstrates how a socket can be made to listen for incoming connections on port 8080 and display any received data on screen.

The example below shows how to create a single-threaded TCP server using only the Socket class. Begin a new project in Visual Studio .NET. Drag a textbox onto the form, named tbStatus, which has its multiline property set to true. Also add a button, named btnListen. Click on this button and add the following code:

C#

```
private void btnListen_Click(object sender, System.EventArgs e)
{
  int bytesReceived = 0;
  byte[] recv = new byte[1];
  Socket clientSocket;
  Socket listenerSocket = new Socket(
        AddressFamily.InterNetwork,
        SocketType.Stream,
        ProtocolType.Tcp
        );
  IPHostEntry IPHost = Dns.GetHostByName(Dns.GetHostName());
  IPEndPoint ipepServer = new
  IPEndPoint(IPHost.AddressList[0],8080);
  listenerSocket.Bind(ipepServer);
  listenerSocket.Listen(-1);
  clientSocket = listenerSocket.Accept();
  if (clientSocket.Connected)
  {
    do
    {
      bytesReceived = clientSocket.Receive(recv);
      tbStatus.Text += Encoding.ASCII.GetString(recv);
    }
```

```
        while (bytesReceived!=0);
   }
}
```

VB.NET

```
Private  Sub btnListen_Click(ByVal sender As Object, _
ByVal e As System.EventArgs)
  Dim bytesReceived As Integer = 0
    Dim recv() As Byte = New Byte(1) {}
    Dim clientSocket As Socket
    Dim listenerSocket As New Socket( _
          AddressFamily.InterNetwork, _
          SocketType.Stream, _
          ProtocolType.Tcp)
    Dim IPHost As IPHostEntry = _
    Dns.GetHostByName(Dns.GetHostName())
    Dim ipepServer As IPEndPoint = New _
    IPEndPoint(IPHost.AddressList(0), 8080)
    listenerSocket.Bind(ipepServer)
    listenerSocket.Listen(-1)
    clientSocket = listenerSocket.Accept()
    If clientSocket.Connected Then
       Do
           bytesReceived = clientSocket.Receive(recv)
           tbStatus.Text += Encoding.ASCII.GetString(recv)
       Loop While bytesReceived <> 0
    End If
End Sub
```

So far, the sockets we have dealt with have been abstracted to perform specific tasks, and as such provide specialized methods that make the coding easier. The generic socket object can be either a server or client.

The listener socket is created with a constructor that is passed three parameters: addressing scheme, socket type, and protocol type.

Table 3.5 shows supported addressing schemes.

Most of these addressing schemes would rarely be used in a modern Windows environment, but they could be used when interfacing to mini-computers or legacy systems.

Table 3.6 shows upported protocol types.

Table 3.5   *Addressing schemes supported by Socket .*

Addressing scheme	Usage
`AddressFamily.AppleTalk`	AppleTalk address, used for communications with Apple Macintosh computers.
`AddressFamily.Atm`	Native asynchronous transfer mode (ATM) services address.
`AddressFamily.Banyan`	Banyan VINES (Virtual Networking System) address.
`AddressFamily.Ccitt`	Addresses for protocols such as X.25.
`AddressFamily.Chaos`	Address for CHAOS protocols, in format 007.*x.y.z.*
`AddressFamily.Cluster`	Address for Microsoft cluster products, such as MSCS.
`AddressFamily.DataKit`	Address for Datakit protocols, such as the universal receiver protocol.
`AddressFamily.DataLink`	Direct data-link (MAC) interface address.
`AddressFamily.DecNet`	DECnet address, designed for DEC minicomputers.
`AddressFamily.Ecma`	European Computer Manufacturers Association (ECMA) address, used for circuit-switched call control.
`AddressFamily.FireFox`	FireFox address, runs over TCP 1689.
`AddressFamily.HyperChannel`	NSC hyperchannel address, defined in RFC 1044.
`AddressFamily.Ieee12844`	IEEE 1284.4 workgroup address, commonly known as DOT4 and used by HP printers.
`AddressFamily.ImpLink`	ARPANET interface message processor (IMP) address.
`AddressFamily.InterNetwork`	IPv4 address, most commonly used for Internet transfers.
`AddressFamily.InterNetworkV6`	IPv6 address, used for the next version of IP.
`AddressFamily.Ipx`	Internetwork packet exchange (IPX) address.

Table 3.5   *Addressing schemes supported by Socket (continued).*

Addressing scheme	Usage
`AddressFamily.Irda`	Infrared data association address.
`AddressFamily.Iso`	Address for ISO protocols, such as ISO-IP.
`AddressFamily.Lat`	Local area transport protocol address, used with DEC minicomputers.
`AddressFamily.Max`	MAX address.
`AddressFamily.NetBios`	NetBios address, used for Windows file and printer sharing.
`AddressFamily.NetworkDesigners`	Address for Network Designers OSI gateway-enabled protocols.
`AddressFamily.NS`	Address for Xerox NS protocols, such as IDP.
`AddressFamily.Pup`	Address for PARC universal packet (PUP) protocols.
`AddressFamily.Sna`	IBM Systems Network Architecture address.
`AddressFamily.Unix`	UNIX local-to-host address.
`AddressFamily.VoiceView`	VoiceView address, used in voice and data telephony.

Table 3.6   *Protocol types supported by socket .*

Addressing scheme	Usage
`ProtocolType.Ggp`	Gateway to gateway protocol (GGP), used for interrouter communications
`ProtocolType.Icmp`	Internet control message protocol (ICMP), also known as Ping and used to report network errors
`ProtocolType.Idp`	Internet datagram protocol (IDP), the underlying transport for Xerox networking protocols
`ProtocolType.Igmp`	Internet group management protocol (IGMP), used in multicasting

Table 3.6   *Protocol types supported by socket (continued).*

Addressing scheme	Usage
ProtocolType.IP	Internet protocol (IP), the underlying transport for all communications on the Internet
ProtocolType.Ipx	Internetwork packet exchange (IPX), Novell's implementation of IDP
ProtocolType.ND	Specifies an unofficial protocol named net disk (ND)
ProtocolType.Pup	PARC universal packet (PUP) protocol, a predecessor of routing information protocol (RIP)
ProtocolType.Raw	Raw socket data; excludes frame headers
ProtocolType.Spx	Sequential packet exchange (SPX), Novell's transport layer protocol that provides a packet delivery service
ProtocolType.SpxII	Sequential packet exchange 2 (SPX2), a more modern implementation of SPX
ProtocolType.Tcp	Transmission control protocol (TCP), the most common protocol for Internet data transfer
ProtocolType.Udp	User datagram protocol (UDP), used for high-speed, low-integrity data transfers on the Internet

The next section of code following the socket constructor is used to resolve the local IP address of the computer. Using the same construct as before, Dns.GetHostByName returns an IPHostEntry object. Element number 0 of the AddressList array is then assumed to be the external address.

An IPEndPoint object is created from the local IP address and the port number 8080. The listener socket is then bound to the endpoint. The socket does not start listening until the Listen method is called. The parameter specifies the number of clients to keep on hold at any one time; -1 indicates an indefinite holding time.

As before, when the Accept method is called, execution stops until a connection request is received. Once a connection request is received, a new socket dedicated to this client is returned. Once a connection has been established, the socket will read incoming data one byte at a time and append it to the textbox tbStatus. When the Receive method returns 0, the remote end will have closed the connection. Because this example does not use threading, it cannot handle more than one client at a time and will appear to hang during operation.

To complete the program, you will also require the following namespaces:

C#

```
using System.Text;
using System.Net.Sockets;
using System.Net;
```

VB.NET

```
Imports System.Text
Imports System.Net.Sockets
Imports System.Net
```

To test this application, run it from Visual Studio .NET. Press the listen button. At this point, the application will become unresponsive and appear to hang. Open telnet on the local machine with the following command:

```
telnet localhost 8080
```

Type some text, and then quit telnet. You should see that text on the application window, as depicted in Figure 3.6.

Most networked applications deal with the interchange of commands and data between client and server. Because TCP/IP requires connections to be explicitly opened and closed, it is possible to locate where networking code starts by searching for phrases such as "new TcpListener" or "Listen" for servers, and "new TcpClient" or "Connect" for clients.

It is both unprofessional and irritating to users if your application becomes unresponsive during normal operation. To avoid this problem, you could use threading, as was demonstrated in examples earlier in this chapter; however, another technique is sometimes employed. Asynchronous sockets are arguably more complicated than threading, but can sometimes offer higher performance when you are handling a large number of concurrent connections. Asynchronous operation is mapped to low-level I/O completion ports in the operating system.

Figure 3.6
TCP server using
socket-level code.

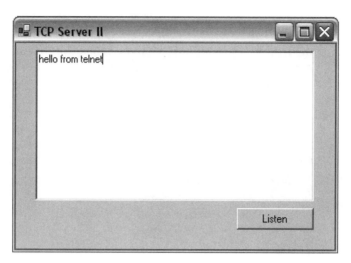

The following code modifies the above example such that it does not become unresponsive when waiting for incoming requests or data. Reopen the previous example in Visual Studio .NET, and add the following public variables directly inside the Form class:

C#

```
private AsyncCallback acceptCallBack;
private AsyncCallback receiveCallBack;
public Socket listenerSocket;
public Socket clientSocket;
public byte[] recv;
```

VB.NET

```
Private acceptCallBack As AsyncCallback
Private receiveCallBack As AsyncCallback
Public listenerSocket As Socket
Public clientSocket As Socket
Public recv() As Byte
```

These variables need to be accessible to any function within the form because server operation is split between three functions: btnListen_Click uses a socket to listen on port 8080; acceptHandler accepts incoming connections; and receiveHandler handles incoming data.

Double-click on the Listen button, and replace the code with the following code:

C#

```csharp
private void btnListen_Click(object sender, System.EventArgs
e)
{
  acceptCallBack = new AsyncCallback(acceptHandler);
  listenerSocket = new Socket(
    AddressFamily.InterNetwork,
    SocketType.Stream,
    ProtocolType.Tcp
    );
  IPHostEntry IPHost = Dns.GetHostByName(Dns.GetHostName());
  IPEndPoint ipepServer = new
IPEndPoint(IPHost.AddressList[0],8080);
  listenerSocket.Bind(ipepServer);
  listenerSocket.Listen(-1);
  listenerSocket.BeginAccept(acceptCallBack,null);
}
```

VB.NET

```vbnet
Private  Sub btnListen_Click(ByVal sender As Object, _
   ByVal e As System.EventArgs)
   acceptCallBack = New AsyncCallback(AddressOf _
   acceptHandler)
   Dim listenerSocket As Socket = New Socket( _
                   AddressFamily.InterNetwork, _
                   SocketType.Stream, _
                   ProtocolType.Tcp _
                   )
   Dim IPHost As IPHostEntry = _
   Dns.GetHostByName(Dns.GetHostName())
   Dim ipepServer As IPEndPoint = New _
       IPEndPoint(IPHost.AddressList(0), 8080)
   listenerSocket.Bind(ipepServer)
   listenerSocket.Listen(-1)
   listenerSocket.BeginAccept(acceptCallBack, Nothing)
End Sub
```

Instead of calling Listen on the socket, BeginListen is called. By doing this, the function will return immediately, and .NET knows that if an incoming connection appears on the port, the function acceptHandler is to be called. The second parameter passed to BeginAccept is Nothing, or null because no extra information needs to be passed to the callback function once it is called.

Now, add the callback function to handle incoming connections:

C#

```
public void acceptHandler(IAsyncResult asyncResult)
{
  receiveCallBack = new AsyncCallback(receiveHandler);
  clientSocket = listenerSocket.EndAccept(asyncResult);
  recv = new byte[1];
  clientSocket.BeginReceive(recv,0,1,
  SocketFlags.None,receiveCallBack,null);
}
```

VB.NET

```
Public Sub acceptHandler(ByVal asyncResult As IAsyncResult)
  receiveCallBack = New AsyncCallback(receiveHandler)
  clientSocket = listenerSocket.EndAccept(asyncResult)
  recv = New Byte(1) {}
  clientSocket.BeginReceive(recv,0,1, _
  SocketFlags.None,receiveCallBack,Nothing)
End Sub
```

The EndAccept method returns the same socket as would be created by the Accept method; however, EndAccept is nonblocking and will return immediately, unlike Accept.

Just as incoming connections are asynchronous by nature, incoming data also arrives asynchronously. If the connection is held open for longer than a few seconds, users will begin to notice that the application has become unresponsive; therefore, a second asynchronous call is used here. Instead of calling Receive, BeginReceive is called on the socket. This is passed an array buffer, which it populates asynchronously as data arrives. Again, an AsyncCallback object is passed to it because this object contains the reference to the callback function: receiveHandler.

Now, add the callback function to handle incoming data:

C#

```
public void receiveHandler(IAsyncResult asyncResult)
{
```

```
int bytesReceived = 0;
bytesReceived = clientSocket.EndReceive(asyncResult);
if (bytesReceived != 0)
{
  tbStatus.Text += Encoding.UTF8.GetString(recv);
  recv = new byte[1];
  clientSocket.BeginReceive(recv,0,1,
    SocketFlags.None,receiveCallBack,null);
}
}
```

VB.NET

```
Public  Sub receiveHandler(ByVal asyncResult As _
IAsyncResult)
  Dim bytesReceived As Integer =  0
  bytesReceived = clientSocket.EndReceive(asyncResult)
  if bytesReceived <> 0 then
    tbStatus.Text += Encoding.UTF8.GetString(recv)
    recv = New Byte(1) {}
    clientSocket.BeginReceive(recv,0,1, _
      SocketFlags.None,receiveCallBack,Nothing)
  End if
End Sub
```

In this example, the array buffer is only one byte long, so this function will be called every time one byte of data appears on port 8080. This function is also called when the connection closes, but in this case, the number returned from `EndReceive` is 0. If data is received, the asynchronous read must be continued by calling `BeginReceive` again.

To complete the program, you will also require the following namespaces:

C#

```
using System.Text;
using System.Net.Sockets;
using System.Net;
```

VB.NET

```
Imports System.Text
Imports System.Net.Sockets
Imports System.Net
```

Test the application in the same way as before. This time, you will notice that the application does not become unresponsive once the Listen button is pressed.

3.7   Conclusion

Socket-level programming is the foundation of all network programming. This chapter should provide enough information to assist you in implementing any TCP- or UDP-based protocol, proprietary or otherwise.

Not all network protocols need to be coded at the socket level; extensive support for HTTP is provided through classes provided by the .NET framework. Leveraging this ready-made functionality can cut down on the development time required for socket-level implementation.

The next chapter takes a detailed look at HTTP and how to write programs in .NET that communicate with Web servers.

4

HTTP: Communicating with Web Servers

4.1   Introduction

This chapter demonstrates how to pull data from the Web and use it within your own applications. As mentioned in Chapter 1, Web pages are hosted on computers that run Web server software such as Microsoft Internet Information Services (IIS) or Apache. Hypertext transfer protocol (HTTP) is used to communicate with these applications and retrieve Web sites.

There are many reasons why an application may interact with a Web site, such as the following:

- To check for updates and to download patches and upgrades
- To retrieve information on data that changes from hour to hour (e.g., shared values, currency conversion rates, weather)
- To automatically query data from services operated by third parties (e.g., zip code lookup, phone directories, language translation services)
- To build a search engine
- To cache Web pages for faster access or to act as a proxy

The first half of this chapter describes how to send and receive data to web servers. This includes an example of how to manipulate the HTML data received from the web server. The chapter is concluded with an implementation of a custom web server, which could be used instead of IIS.

4.1.1 **Data mining**

Data mining is where an application downloads a Web page and extracts specific information from it automatically. It generally refers to the retrieval of large amounts of data from Web pages that were never designed for automated reading.

A sample application could be a TV guide program that would download scheduling information from TV Web sites and store it in a database for quick reference.

Note: You should always check with Web site administrators whether they permit data mining on their sites because it may infringe copyright or put excessive load on their servers. Unauthorized data mining can result in a Web administrator blocking your IP address or worse!

In order to extract useful data from this HTML, you will need to be well acquainted with the language and good at spotting the patterns of HTML that contain the data required; however, several good commercial products aid developers with data mining from HTML pages, and home-brewed solutions are not always the best idea.

4.2   **HTTP**

HTTP operates on TCP/IP port 80 and is described definitively in RFC 2616. The protocol is quite straightforward. The client opens TCP port 80 to a server, the client sends an HTTP request, the server sends back an HTTP response, and the server closes the TCP connection.

4.2.1 **The HTTP request**

The simplest HTTP request is as follows:

```
GET /
<enter><enter>
```

Tip: On some servers, it is necessary to specify the DNS name of the server in the GET request.

This request will instruct the server to return the default Web page; however, HTTP requests are generally more complex, such as the following:

```
GET / HTTP/1.1
Accept: image/gif, image/x-xbitmap, image/jpeg, image/pjpeg,
application/vnd.ms-powerpoint, application/vnd.ms-excel,
application/msword, */*
Accept-Language: en-gb
Accept-Encoding: gzip, deflate
User-Agent: Mozilla/4.0 (compatible; MSIE 6.0; Windows NT
5.1; .NET CLR 1.0.3705)
Host: 127.0.0.1:90
Connection: Keep-Alive
```

This tells the server several things about the client, such as the type of browser and what sort of data the browser can render.

Table 4.1 shows a complete list of standard HTTP request headers are as follows:

Table 4.1   *Standard HTTP request headers .*

HTTP header	Meaning
Accept	Used to specify which media (MIME) types are acceptable for the response. The type `*/*` indicates all media types and `type/*` indicates all subtypes of that type. In the example above, `application/msword` indicates that the browser can display Word documents.
Accept-Charset	Used to specify which character sets are acceptable in the response. In the case where a client issues `Accept-Charset: iso-8859-5`, the server should be aware that the client cannot render Japanese (Unicode) characters.
Accept-Encoding	Used to specify if the client can handle compressed data. In the above example, the browser is capable of interpreting GZIP compressed data.
Accept-Language	Used to indicate the language preference of the user. This can be used to estimate the geographic location of a client; `en-gb` in the above example may indicate that the client is from the United Kingdom.

Table 4.1   *Standard HTTP request headers (continued).*

HTTP header	Meaning
Authorization	Used to provide authentication between clients and servers. Refer to RFC 2617 or Chapter 9 for more details.
Host	Host indicates the intended server IP address as typed in at the client. This could differ from the actual destination IP address if the request were to go via a proxy. The host address `127.0.0.1:90` in the above example indicates that the client was on the same computer as the server, which was running on port 90.
If-Modified-Since	Indicates that the page is not to be returned if it has not been changed since a certain date. This permits a caching mechanism to work effectively. An example is `If-Modified-Since: Sat, 29 Oct 1994 19:43:31 GMT`.
Proxy-Authorization	This provides for authentication between clients and proxies. Refer to RFC 2617 or Chapter 9 for more details.
Range	This provides for a mechanism to retrieve a section of a Web page by specifying which ranges of bytes the server should return; this may not be implemented on all servers. An example is `bytes=500-600,601-999`.
Referer	This indicates the last page the client had visited before going to this specific URL. An example is `Referer: http://www.w3.org/index.html`. (The misspelling of *"referrer"* is not a typing mistake!)
TE	Transfer encoding (TE) indicates which extension transfer encoding it can accept in the response and if it can accept trailer fields in a chunked transfer encoding.
User-Agent	Indicates the type of device the client is running from. In the above example, the browser was Internet Explorer 6.
Content-Type	Used in POST requests. It indicates the MIME type of the posted data, which is usually `application/x-www-form-urlencoded`.
Content-Length	Used in POST requests. It indicates the length of the data immediately following the double line.

> **Note:** Device-specific HTTP request headers are prefixed with "x-".

GET and POST are the most common HTTP commands. There are others, such as HEAD, OPTIONS, PUT, DELETE, and TRACE, and interested readers can refer to RFC 2616 for information on these HTTP commands.

Web developers may be familiar with GET and POST from the HTML form tag, which takes the form:

```
<form name="myForm" action="someDynamicPage" method="POST">
```

The difference from a user's point of view is that form parameters do not appear in the URL bar of the browser when submitting this form. These parameters are contained in the region immediately following the double-line feed. A POST request resembles the following:

```
POST / HTTP/1.1
Content-Type: application/x-www-form-urlencoded
Content-Length: 17


myField=some+text
```

4.2.2   The HTTP response

When the server receives an HTTP request, it retrieves the requested page and returns it along with an HTTP header. This is known as the HTTP response.

A sample HTTP response is as follows:

```
HTTP/1.1 200 OK
Server: Microsoft-IIS/5.1
Date: Sun, 05 Jan 2003 20:59:47 GMT
Connection: Keep-Alive
Content-Length: 25
Content-Type: text/html
Set-Cookie: ASPSESSIONIDQGGQQFCO=MEPLJPHDAGAEHENKAHIHGHGH;
path=/
Cache-control: private

This is a test html page!
```

Table 4.2   *Standard HTTP request headers.*

HTTP request header	Meaning
ETag	The entity tag is used in conjunction with the If-suffixed HTTP requests. Servers rarely return it.
Location	It is used in redirects, where the browser is requested to load a different page. Used in conjunction with HTTP 3xx responses.
Proxy-Authenticate	This provides for authentication between clients and proxies. Refer to RFC 2617 Section 14.33 or Chapter 9 for more details.
Server	Indicates the server version and vendor. In the above example, the server was IIS running on Windows XP.
WWW-Authenticate	This provides for authentication between clients and proxies. Refer to RFC 2617 Section 14.47 or Chapter 9 for more details.
Content-Type	Indicates the MIME type of the content returned. In the above example, the type is HTML
Content-Length	Indicates the amount of data following the double-line feed. The server will close the connection once it has sent all of the data; therefore, it is not always necessary to process this command.
Set-Cookie	A cookie is a small file that resides on the client. A cookie has a name and value. In the above example, the cookie name is ASPSESSIONIDQGGQQFCO.

The client would display the message "This is a test html page!" on screen in response to this command.

Table 4.3   *HTTP response codes .*

HTTP response code range	Meaning
100–199	Informational: Request was received; continuing the process.
200–299	Success: The action was successfully received, understood, and accepted.
300–399	Redirection: Further action must be taken in order to complete the request.

Table 4.3 *HTTP response codes (continued).*

HTTP response code range	Meaning
400–499	Redirection: Further action must be taken in order to complete the request.
500–599	Server error: The server failed to fulfill an apparently valid request.

Every HTTP response has a response code. In the above example, the response code was 200. This number is followed by some human-readable text (i.e., OK).

The response codes fall into five main categories shown in Table 4.3.

4.2.3 MIME types

Multipart Internet mail extensions (MIME) types are a means of describing the type of data, such that another computer will know how to handle the data and how to display it effectively to the user.

To illustrate the example, if you changed the extension of a JPEG image (.JPG) to .TXT, and clicked on it, you would see a jumble of strange characters, not the image. This is because Windows contains a mapping from file extension to file type, and .JPG and .TXT are mapped to different file types: image/jpeg for .JPG and text/plain for .TXT.

To find an MIME type for a particular file, such as .mp3, you can open the registry editor by clicking on Start > Run, then typing REGEDIT. Then click on HKEY_CLASSES_ROOT, scroll down to .mp3, and the MIME type is written next to Content Type.

Note: Not all file types have a MIME type (e.g., .hlp help files).

4.2.4 System.Web

One of the most common uses of HTTP within applications is the ability to download the HTML content of a page into a string. The following application demonstrates this concept.

It is certainly possible to implement HTTP at the socket level, but there is a wealth of objects ready for use in HTTP client applications, and it makes little sense to reinvent the wheel. The HTTP server in the next section is implemented using HTTPWebReqest.

Start a new project in Visual Studio .NET, and drag on two textboxes, tbResult and tbUrl. TbResults should be set with multiline=true. A button, btnCapture, should also be added. Click on the Capture button, and enter the following code:

C#

```
private void btnCapture_Click(object sender, System.EventArgs
e)
{
  tbResult.Text = getHTTP(tbUrl.Text);
}
```

VB.NET

```
Private Sub btnCapture_Click(ByVal sender As Object, _
  ByVal e As System.EventArgs) Handles btnCapture.Click
  tbResult.Text = getHTTP(tbUrl.Text)
End Sub
```

Then implement the getHTTP function:

C#

```
public string getHTTP(string szURL)
{
  HttpWebRequest   httpRequest;
  HttpWebResponse httpResponse;
  string           bodyText = "";
  Stream           responseStream;
  Byte[] RecvBytes = new Byte[Byte.MaxValue];
  Int32 bytes;
  httpRequest = (HttpWebRequest) WebRequest.Create(szURL);
  httpResponse = (HttpWebResponse) httpRequest.GetResponse();
  responseStream = httpResponse.GetResponseStream();
  while(true)
  {
   bytes = responseStream.Read(RecvBytes,
   0,RecvBytes.Length);
   if (bytes<=0) break;
   bodyText += System.Text.Encoding.UTF8.GetString(RecvBytes,
   0, bytes);
```

```
      }
      return bodyText;
   }
```

VB.NET

```
Public Function getHTTP(ByVal szURL As String) As String
   Dim httprequest As HttpWebRequest
   Dim httpresponse As HttpWebResponse
   Dim bodytext As String = ""
   Dim responsestream As Stream
   Dim bytes As Int32
   Dim RecvBytes(Byte.MaxValue) As Byte
   httprequest = CType(WebRequest.Create(szURL), _
   HttpWebRequest)
   httpresponse = CType(httprequest.GetResponse(), _
   HttpWebResponse)
   responsestream = httpresponse.GetResponseStream()
   Do While (True)
    bytes = responsestream.Read(RecvBytes, 0, _
    RecvBytes.Length)
    If bytes <= 0 Then Exit Do
    bodytext += System.Text.Encoding.UTF8.GetString _
    (RecvBytes, 0, bytes)
   Loop
   Return bodytext
End Function
```

Taking a closer look at this code, it should be relatively easy to identify how it operates. The first action taken as this code is executed is that a static method on the WebRequest class is called and passed the string szURL as a parameter. This creates a webRequest object that can be cast to an HttpWebRequest object, which will handle outgoing HTTP connections.

Once we have an HttpWebRequest object, we can then send the HTTP request to the server and start receiving data back from the server by calling the GetResponse method. The return value is then cast to an HttpWebResponse object, which is then held in the httPresponse variable.

A response from a Web server is asynchronous by nature, so it is natural to create a stream from this returning data and read it in as it becomes available. To do this, we can create a stream by calling the GetResponseStream method. Once the stream is obtained, we can read bytes from it in chunks of 256 bytes (`byte.Max`). Reading data in chunks improves performance. The chunk size can be arbitrarily chosen, but 256 is efficient.

The code sits in an infinite loop until all of the incoming data is received. In a production environment, therefore, this type of action should be contained within a separate thread. Once we have a string containing all of the HTML, we can simply dump it to screen. No other processing is required. You will also need some extra namespaces:

C#

```
using System.Net;
using System.IO;
```

VB.NET

```
Imports System.Net
Imports System.IO
```

To test the application, run it from Visual Studio, type in a Web site address (not forgetting the http:// prefix), and press Capture. The HTML source will appear in the body (Figure 4.1).

This is a very simple HTTP client, with no error handling, and is single threaded; however, it should suffice for simpler applications.

Figure 4.1
*HTTP client
application.*

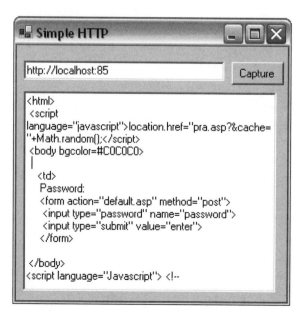

Table 4.4 *Significant members of the HttpWebResponse class.*

Method or property	Meaning
ContentEncoding	Gets the method used to encode the body of the. response. Returns `String`.
ContentLength	Gets the length of the content returned by the request. Returns `Long`.
ContentType	Gets the content type of the response. Returns `String`.
Cookies	Gets or sets the cookies associated with this request. May be used thus: `Cookies["name"].ToString()`.
Headers	Gets the headers associated with this response from the server. May be invoked thus: `Headers["Content-Type"].ToString()`.
ResponseUri	Gets the URI of the Internet resource that responded to the request. May be invoked thus: `RequestURI.ToString()`.
Server	Gets the name of the server that sent the response. Returns `String`.
StatusCode	Gets the status of the response. Returns the `HttpStatusCode` enumerated type. The `StatusDescription` returns a descriptive `String`.
GetResponseHeader	Gets the specified header contents that were returned with the response. Returns `String`.
GetResponseStream	Gets the stream used to read the body of the response. No asynchronous variant. Returns `stream`.

Table 4.4 shows the significant methods of `HttpWebResponse`.

4.2.5 Posting data

Many dynamic Web sites contain forms for login details, search criteria, or similar data. These forms are usually submitted via the POST method. This poses a problem, however, for any application that needs to query a page that lies behind such a form because you cannot specify posted data in the URL line.

First, prepare a page that handles POST requests. In this case, type the following lines into a file called postTest.aspx in c:\inetpub\wwwroot (your HTTP root):

ASP.NET

```
<%@ Page language="c#" Debug="true"%>
<script language="C#" runat="server">
  public void Page_Load(Object sender, EventArgs E)
  {
   if (Request.Form["tbPost"]!=null)
   {
    Response.Write(Request.Form["tbPost"].ToString());
   }
  }
</script>

<form method="post">
 <input type="text" name="tbpost">
 <input type="submit">
</form>
```

ASP.NET is a vast subject that lies outside the scope of this book; however, for the sake of explaining the above example, a quick introduction is necessary. ASP.NET is an extension to IIS that enables .NET code to be executed on receipt of requests for Web pages. This also provides means for .NET code to dynamically generate responses to clients in the form of HTML, viewable on Web browsers.

Incoming requests and outgoing data are mapped to objects in .NET, which can easily be read and manipulated. The most fundamental of these objects are the Request and Response objects. The Request object encapsulates the data sent from the Web browser to the server; of its properties, two of the most important are the Form and QueryString collections. The Form collection reads data sent from the client via the POST method, whereas the QueryString collection reads data sent from the client via the GET method.

The Response object places data on the outgoing HTTP stream to be sent to the client. One of its most important methods is Write. This method is passed a string that will be rendered as HTML on the client.

One of the features that makes ASP.NET more powerful than its predecessor, classic ASP, is its ability to model HTML elements as objects, not merely as input and output streams. For example, an input box would be typically written in ASP.NET as `<ASP:TEXTBOX id="tbText" runat="server"/>`, and the properties of this textbox could then be modified from code by accessing the `tbText` object. In classic ASP, the only way to achieve such an effect would be to include code within the textbox declaration, such as `<input type="text" <%=someCode%>>`, which is less desirable because functional code is intermixed with HTML.

ASP.NET provides better performance than classic ASP because it is compiled on first access (in-line model) or precompiled (code-behind model). It also leverages the .NET framework, which is much richer than the scripting languages available to ASP.

The example above is appropriate for demonstrating the posting method. Every Web scripting language handles posted data in much the same way, so the technique is applicable to interfacing with any Web form.

Web scripting languages share a common feature: some sections of the page are rendered on the browser screen as HTML, and some are processed by the server and not displayed on the client. In the example, anything marked `runat="server"` or prefixed `<%` will be processed by the server.

When the user presses the submit button (`<input type="submit">`), the browser packages any user-entered data that was contained within the `<form>` tags and passes it back to the server as a POST request.

The server parses out the data in the POST request once it is received. The server-side script can retrieve this data by accessing the `Request.Form` collection. The `Response.Write` command prints this data back out to the browser.

To try the page out, open a browser and point it at *http://localhost/post-Test.aspx*; type something into the textbox, and press Submit. Then you will see the page refresh, and the text you typed appears above the form.

Reopen the previous example and add a new textbox named `tbPost`. Click on the Capture button and modify the code as follows:

C#

```csharp
private void btnCapture_Click(object sender, System.EventArgs e)
{
    tbPost.Text = HttpUtility.UrlEncode(tbPost.Text);
    tbResult.Text =
getHTTP(tbUrl.Text,"tbPost="+tbPost.Text);
}
```

VB.NET

```
Private Sub btnCapture_Click(ByVal sender As Object, _
ByVal e As System.EventArgs) Handles btnCapture.Click
    tbPost.Text = HttpUtility.UrlEncode(tbPost.Text)
    tbResult.Text = getHTTP(tbUrl.Text,"tbPost="+tbPost.Text)
End Sub
```

The reason for the call to `HttpUtility.UrlEncode` is to convert the text entered by the user into a string that is safe for transport by HTTP. This means the removal of white space (spaces are converted to "+") and the conversion of nonalphanumeric characters, which is a requirement of the HTTP protocol.

Once the data to post is encoded, it can be passed to the `getHTTP` function, which is described below. It is a modified version of the code previously listed.

C#

```
public string getHTTP(string szURL,string szPost)
{
    HttpWebRequest   httprequest;
    HttpWebResponse  httpresponse;
    StreamReader     bodyreader;
    string           bodytext = "";
    Stream           responsestream;
    Stream           requestStream;

    httprequest = (HttpWebRequest) WebRequest.Create(szURL);
    httprequest.Method = "POST";
    httprequest.ContentType =
    "application/x-www-form-urlencoded";
    httprequest.ContentLength = szPost.Length;
    requestStream = httprequest.GetRequestStream();
    requestStream.Write(Encoding.ASCII.GetBytes(szPost),0,
    szPost.Length);
    requestStream.Close();
    httpresponse = (HttpWebResponse) httprequest.GetResponse();
    responsestream = httpresponse.GetResponseStream();
    bodyreader = new StreamReader(responsestream);
    bodytext = bodyreader.ReadToEnd();
    return bodytext;
}
```

VB.NET

```
Public Function getHTTP(ByVal szURL As String, _
ByVal szPost As String) As String
    Dim httprequest As HttpWebRequest
    Dim httpresponse As HttpWebResponse
    Dim bodyreader As StreamReader
    Dim bodytext As String =  ""
    Dim responsestream As Stream
    Dim requestStream As Stream

    httprequest = CType(WebRequest.Create(szURL), _
    HttpWebRequest)
    httprequest.Method = "POST"
    httprequest.ContentType = _
    "application/x-www-form-urlencoded"
    httprequest.ContentLength = szPost.Length
    requestStream = httprequest.GetRequestStream()
    requestStream.Write(Encoding.ASCII.GetBytes(szPost), _
    0,szPost.Length)
    requestStream.Close()
    httpresponse = CType(httprequest.GetResponse(), _
    HttpWebResponse)
    responsestream = httpresponse.GetResponseStream()
    bodyreader = New StreamReader(responsestream)
    bodytext = bodyreader.ReadToEnd()
    Return bodytext
End Function
```

This differs from the code to simply retrieve a Web page in that once the HttpWebRequest has been created, several parameters are set such that the request also includes the posted data. The chunked reader loop is also replaced with the ReadToEnd() method of StreamReader. This method may be elegant, but it is not compatible with binary data.

The three settings that need to be changed are the request method, content type, and content length. The request method is usually GET but now must be set to POST. The content type should be set to the MIME type application/x-www-form-urlencoded, although this is not strictly necessary. The content length is simply the length of the data being posted, including the variable names, and after URL encoding.

Figure 4.2
Visual Studio
.NET, Add
Reference dialog.

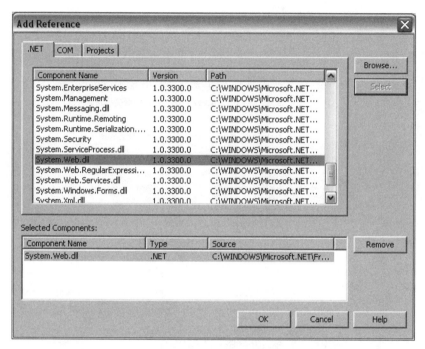

The data to be posted must then be sent to the server using the `Write` method on the request stream. Once the request has been created, it is simply a matter of receiving the stream from the remote server and reading to the end of the stream.

Finally, we need namespaces for the `HttpUtility` and `Encoding` objects. You will need to make a reference to `System.Web.dll` by selecting Project→ Add Reference, as shown in Figure 4.2.

C#

```
using System.Web;
using System.Text;
using System.IO;
using System.Net;
```

VB.NET

```
Imports System.Web
Imports System.Text
Imports System.IO
Imports System.Net
```

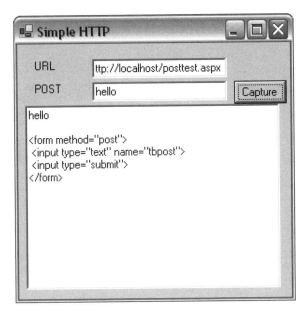

Figure 4.3
*HTTP client
application with
POST facility.*

To test the application, run it through Visual Studio .NET, enter *http://
localhost/postTest.aspx* into the URL textbox, and add some other text into
the POST textbox. When you press Capture, you will see that the posted
text appears as part of the Web page (Figure 4.3).

Table 4.5 shows the significant members of `HttpWebRequest`.

Table 4.5 *Significant members of HttpWebRequest .*

Method or Property	Meaning
`Accept`	Gets or sets the value of the `Accept` HTTP header. Returns `String`.
`AllowAutoRedirect`	Gets or sets a Boolean value that indicates whether the request should follow redirection (3xx) responses.
`ContentLength`	Gets or sets the `Content-length` HTTP header.
`ContentType`	Gets or sets the value of the `Content-type` HTTP header.
`CookieContainer`	Gets or sets the cookies associated with the request. May be invoked thus: `CookieContainer.getCookies["name"].ToString()`.

Table 4.5   *Significant members of HttpWebRequest (continued).*

Method or Property	Meaning
`Headers`	Gets a collection of strings that are contained in the HTTP header. May be invoked thus: `Headers["Content-Type"].ToString()`.
`Method`	Gets or sets the method for the request. Can be set to `GET, HEAD, POST, PUT, DELETE, TRACE,` or `OPTIONS`.
`Proxy`	Gets or sets proxy information for the request. Returns `WebProxy`.
`Referer`	Gets or sets the value of the `Referer` HTTP header. Returns `String`.
`RequestUri`	Gets the original URI of the request. Address is the URI after redirections. May be invoked thus: `RequestURI.ToString()`.
`Timeout`	Gets or sets the time-out value. May be invoked thus `Timeout=(int) new TimeSpan(0,0,30).TotalMilliseconds`.
`TransferEncoding`	Gets or sets the value of the `Transfer-encoding` HTTP header. Returns `String`.
`UserAgent`	Gets or sets the value of the `User-agent` HTTP header. Returns `String`.
`GetResponse`	Returns a `webResponse` from an Internet resource. Its asynchronous variant is `BeginGetResponse` and `EndGetResponse`.

4.2.6 A note on cookies

HTTP does not maintain state information. It is therefore difficult to differentiate between two users accessing a server or one user making two requests. From the server's point of view, it is possible for both users to have the same IP address (e.g., if they are both going through the same proxy server). If the service being accessed contained personal information, the user to whom this data pertains is legally entitled to view this data, but other users should not be allowed access.

In this situation, the client side of the connection needs to differentiate itself from other clients. This can be done in several ways, but for Web sites, cookies are the best solution.

Cookies are small files stored in `c:\windows\cookies` (depending on your Windows installation). They are placed there in one of two ways: by the JavaScript `document.cookie` object, or by the `set-cookie` header in HTTP requests. These cookies remain on the client's machine for a set time and can be retrieved in JavaScript or in HTTP responses.

Cookies are supported in .NET via the `HttpWebResponse.Cookies` and the `HttpWebRequest.CookieContainer` objects.

Cookies are domain specific; therefore, a cookie stored on *www.library.com* cannot be retrieved by *www.bookshop.com*. In circumstances where both sites are affiliated with each other, the two sites might need to share session state information. In this example, it would be advantageous for *bookshop.com* to know a user's reading preferences, so that it could advertise the most relevant titles.

The trick to copying cookies across domains is to convert the cookies into text, pass the text between the servers, and pass the cookies back to the client from the foreign server. .NET offers a facility to serialize cookies, which is ideal for the purpose.

4.2.7   A WYSIWYG editor

WYSIWYG (what you see is what you get) is a term used to describe Web and graphics editors that enable you to naturally manipulate graphical output, without having to be concerned with the underlying code. This feature is a handy way to let users be more creative in the type of textual messages or documents they create, without requiring them to take a crash course in HTML.

Internet Explorer can run in a special design mode, which is acceptable as a WYSIWYG editor. The trick to accessing design mode in Internet Explorer is simply to set the property `WebBrowser.Document.designMode` to `On`. Users can type directly into the Internet Explorer window and use well-known shortcut keys to format text (e.g., Ctrl + B, Bold; Ctrl + I, Italic; Ctrl + U, Underline). By right-clicking on Internet Explorer in design mode, a user can include images, add hyperlinks, and switch to browser mode. When an image is included in the design view, it can be moved and scaled by clicking and dragging on the edge of the image.

More advanced features can be accessed via Internet Explorer's `execCommand` function. Only `FontName`, `FontSize`, and `ForeColor` are used in the following sample program, but here is a list of the commands used by Internet Explorer.

Table 4.6   *Parameters of Internet Explorer's execCommand function .*

Command	Meaning
Bold	Inserts a <B> tag in HTML
Copy	Copies text into the clipboard
Paste	Pastes text from the clipboard
InsertUnorderedList	Creates a bulleted list, <UL> in HTML
Indent	Tabulates text farther right on the page
Outdent	Retabulates text left on the page
Italic	Inserts an <I> tag in HTML
Underline	Inserts an <U> tag in HTML
CreateLink	Creates a hyperlink to another Web page
UnLink	Removes a hyperlink from text
FontName	Sets the font family of a piece of text
FontSize	Sets the font size of a piece of text
CreateBookmark	Creates a bookmark on a piece of text
ForeColor	Sets the color of the selected text
SelectAll	Is equivalent to pressing CTRL + A
JustifyLeft	Moves all text as far left as space allows
JustifyRight	Moves all text as far right as space allows
JustifyCenter	Moves all selected text as close to the center as possible
SaveAs	Saves the page to disk

Other functionality not included in this list can be implemented by dynamically modifying the underlying HTML.

To start coding this application, open a new project in Visual Studio .NET. Add a reference to Microsoft.mshtml by clicking Project→Add Reference. Scroll down the list until you find Microsoft.mshtml, highlight it, and press OK. If you have not already done so from Chapter 1's example, add Internet Explorer to the toolbox. To do this, right-click on the toolbox and select Customize Toolbox. Scroll down the list under the COM components tab until you see Microsoft Web Browser. Check the box opposite it, and press OK.

Draw a Tab control on the form named `tabControl`. Click on the `tabPages` property in the properties window and add two tab pages, labeled Preview and HTML. Draw the Microsoft Web Browser control onto the preview tab page and name the control `WebBrowser`. Add three buttons to the Preview tab page, named `btnViewHTML`, `btnFont`, and `btnColor`. In the HTML tab page, add a textbox named `tbHTML`, and set its `multiline` property to `true`. Also add a button to the HTML tab page named `btnPreview`. Drag a Color Dialog control onto the form, and name it `colorDialog`. Drag a Font Dialog control onto the form and name it `fontDialog`.

Double-click on the form, and add the following code:

C#

```
private void Form1_Load(object sender, System.EventArgs e)
{
  object any = null;
  object url = "about:blank";
  WebBrowser.Navigate2(ref url,ref any,ref any,ref any,ref
any);
  Application.DoEvents();
  ((HTMLDocument)WebBrowser.Document).designMode="On";
}
```

VB.NET

```
Private  Sub Form1_Load(ByVal sender As Object, _
ByVal e As System.EventArgs)
  Dim url As Object =  "about:blank"
  WebBrowser.Navigate2( url)
  Application.DoEvents()
  (CType(WebBrowser.Document, HTMLDocument)).designMode="On"
End Sub
```

In order to access the HTML contained within the Web browser page, it must first point to a valid URL that contains some HTML source. In this case, the URL `about:blank` is used. This page contains nothing more than `<HTML></HTML>`, but is sufficient for the needs of this application. The `DoEvents` method releases a little processor time to allow the Web browser to load this page. The `Document` property of the Web browser contains the object model for the page, but it must first be cast to an `HTMLDocument` object to be of use. The `designMode` property of Internet Explorer is then set to `On` to enable WYSIWYG editing.

Click on the view HTML button on the Preview tab page and enter the following code:

C#

```csharp
private void btnViewHTML_Click(object sender,
System.EventArgs e)
{
  tbHTML.Text=(
  (HTMLDocument)WebBrowser.Document).body.innerHTML;
}
```

VB.NET

```vbnet
Private  Sub btnViewHTML_Click(ByVal sender As Object, _
  ByVal e As System.EventArgs)
  tbHTML.Text= _
  (CType(WebBrowser.Document, HTMLDocument)).body.innerHTML
End Sub
```

This button extracts the HTML from the Web Browser control and places it into the HTML-viewer textbox. Again, the `Document` property must be cast to an `HTMLDocument` object in order to access the page object model. In this case, the `body.innerHTML` property contains the page source. If you required the page source less the HTML tags, then `body.innerText` would be of interest.

Click on the corresponding Preview button on the HTML tab page, and enter the following code:

C#

```csharp
private void btnPreview_Click(object sender, System.EventArgs
e)
{
  ((HTMLDocument)WebBrowser.Document).body.innerHTML=
  tbHTML.Text;
}
```

VB.NET

```vbnet
Private Sub btnPreview_Click(ByVal sender As Object, _
ByVal e As System.EventArgs)
  (CType(WebBrowser.Document, _
  HTMLDocument)).body.innerHTML=tbHTML.Text
End Sub
```

This code simply performs the reverse of the preceding code, replacing the HTML behind the Web browser with the HTML typed into the text-box.

Click on the Font button on the Preview tab page, and enter the following code:

C#

```
private void btnFont_Click(object sender, System.EventArgs e)
{
  fontDialog.ShowDialog();
  HTMLDocument doc = (HTMLDocument)WebBrowser.Document;
  object selection= doc.selection.createRange();
  doc.execCommand("FontName",false,
  fontDialog.Font.FontFamily.Name);
  doc.execCommand("FontSize",false,fontDialog.Font.Size);
  ((IHTMLTxtRange)selection).select();
}
```

VB.NET

```
Private  Sub btnFont_Click(ByVal sender As Object, _
 ByVal e As System.EventArgs)
  fontDialog.ShowDialog()
  Dim doc As HTMLDocument = CType(WebBrowser.Document, _
  HTMLDocument)
  Dim selection As Object =  doc.selection.createRange()
  doc.execCommand("FontName",False,fontDialog.Font. _
  FontFamily.Name)
  doc.execCommand("FontSize",False,fontDialog.Font.Size)
  (CType(selection, IHTMLTxtRange)).select()
End Sub
```

Pressing the Font button will bring up the standard font dialog box (Figure 4.4), which allows the user to select any font held on the system and its size. Other properties that may be available on this screen, such as subscript, strikethrough, and so on, are not reflected in the WYSIWYG editor. This works by first capturing a reference to any selected text on the screen using the `selection.createRange()` method. The `execCommand` method is called twice, first to apply the font family to the selected text and then the font size. The selection is then cast to an `IHTMLTxtRange` interface, which exposes the `select` method and commits the changes to memory.

Figure 4.4
*Font-chooser dialog
box.*

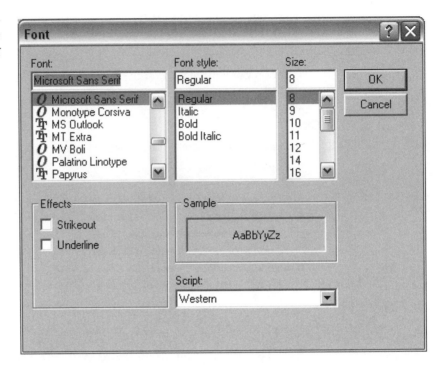

Now click on the Color button on the Preview tab page, and enter the
following code:

C#

```
private void btnColor_Click(object sender, System.EventArgs
e)
{
  colorDialog.ShowDialog();
  string colorCode = "#" +
      toHex(colorDialog.Color.R) +
      toHex(colorDialog.Color.G) +
      toHex(colorDialog.Color.B);
  HTMLDocument doc = (HTMLDocument)WebBrowser.Document;
  object selection = doc.selection.createRange();
  doc.execCommand("ForeColor",false,colorCode);
  ((IHTMLTxtRange)selection).select();
}
```

VB.NET

```
Private  Sub btnColor_Click(ByVal sender As Object, _
```

```
    ByVal e As System.EventArgs)
    colorDialog.ShowDialog()
    String colorCode = "#" + _
        toHex(colorDialog.Color.R) + _
        toHex(colorDialog.Color.G) + _
        toHex(colorDialog.Color.B)
    Dim doc As HTMLDocument = CType(WebBrowser.Document, _
    HTMLDocument)
    Dim selection As Object = doc.selection.createRange()
    doc.execCommand("ForeColor",False,colorCode)
    (CType(selection, IHTMLTxtRange)).select()
End Sub
```

Pressing the Color button brings up the standard Color dialog box (Figure 4.5). When a color is chosen, the selected color is applied to any selected text. This code brings up the Color dialog box by calling the Show-Dialog method. The color returned can be expressed in terms of its red (R), green (G), and blue (B) constituents. These values are in decimal format, in the range 0 (least intense) to 255 (most intense). HTML expresses colors in the form #RRGGBB, where RR, GG, and BB are hexadecimal equivalents

Figure 4.5
Color-picker dialog box.

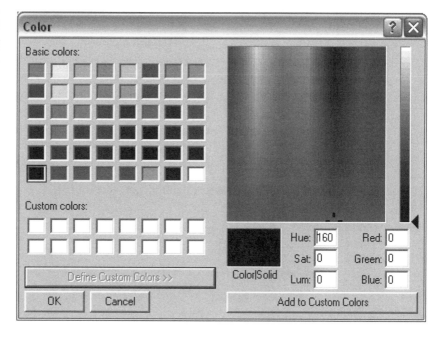

of the R, G, and B values. To give a few examples, #FF0000 is bright red, #FFFFFF is white, and #000000 is black.

Once again, a handle to the selected text is obtained in the same way as before. The execCommand method is called and passed ForeColor, along with the HTML color code. The selected text is cast to an IHTMLTxtRange interface and committed to memory with the Select method as before.

The above code calls the function toHex to convert the numeric values returned from the colorDialog control to hexadecimal values, which are required by Internet Explorer. Enter the following code:

C#

```csharp
public string toHex(int digit)
{
  string hexDigit = digit.ToString("X");
  if (hexDigit.length == 1){
  hexDigit = "0" + hexDigit;
  }
  return hexDigit;
}
```

VB.NET

```vbnet
Public Function toHex(ByVal number As Integer) As String
    Dim hexByte As String
    hexByte = Hex(number).ToString()
    If hexByte.Length = 1 Then
        hexByte = "0" & hexByte
    End If
    Return hexByte
 End Function
```

Finally, the relevant namespaces are required:

C#

```csharp
using mshtml;
```

VB.NET

```vbnet
Imports mshtml
```

Figure 4.6
HTML editor
application.

To test this application, run it from Visual Studio .NET. Type into the Web Browser control under the Preview tab. Press the Font button to change the style and size of any text that is selected. Press the Color button to change the color of selected text. You can insert images by right-clicking and selecting Insert image (special thanks to Bella for posing for this photograph!). Press the view HTML button, then switch to the HTML tab page to view the autogenerated HTML (Figure 4.6).

4.3   Web servers

One may ask why you should develop a server in .NET when IIS is freely available. An in-house-developed server has some advantages, such as the following:

- Web server can be installed as part of an application, without requiring the user to install IIS manually from the Windows installation CD.

- IIS will not install on the Windows XP Home Edition, which constitutes a significant portion of Windows users.

4.3.1 Implementing a Web server

Start a new Visual Studio .NET project as usual. Draw two textboxes,
tbPath and tbPort, onto the form, followed by a button, btnStart, and a
list box named lbConnections, which has its view set to list.

At the heart of an HTTP server is a TCP server, and you may notice an
overlap of code between this example and the TCP server in the previous
chapter. The server has to be multithreaded, so the first step is to declare an
Array List of sockets:

C#

```
public class Form1 : System.Windows.Forms.Form
{
  private ArrayList alSockets;
  ...
```

VB.NET

```
Public Class Form1 Inherits System.Windows.Forms.Form

    Private alSockets As ArrayList
  ...
```

Every HTTP server has an HTTP root, which is a path to a folder on
your hard disk from which the server will retrieve Web pages. IIS has a
default HTTP root of c:\inetpub\wwwroot; in this case, we shall use the
path in which the application is saved.

To obtain the application path, we can use Application.Executable-
Path, which returns not only the path but also the filename, and thus we
can trim off all characters after the last backslash.

C#

```
private void Form1_Load(object sender, System.EventArgs e)
{
  tbPath.Text = Application.ExecutablePath;
  // trim off filename, to get the path
  tbPath.Text =
  tbPath.Text.Substring(0,tbPath.Text.LastIndexOf("\\"));
}
```

VB.NET

```
Private  Sub Form1_Load(ByVal sender As Object, _
ByVal e As System.EventArgs)
  tbPath.Text = Application.ExecutablePath
  ' trim off filename, to get the path
  tbPath.Text = _
  tbPath.Text.Substring(0,tbPath.Text.LastIndexOf("\"))
End Sub
```

Clicking the Start button will initialize the Array List of sockets and start the main server thread. Click btnStart:

C#

```
private void btnStart_Click(object sender, System.EventArgs e)
{
  alSockets = new ArrayList();
  Thread thdListener =
  new Thread(new ThreadStart(listenerThread));
  thdListener.Start();
}
```

VB.NET

```
Private  Sub btnStart_Click(ByVal sender As Object, _
 ByVal e As System.EventArgs)
  alSockets = New ArrayList()
  Dim thdListener As Thread =  New Thread(New _
  ThreadStart( AddressOf listenerThread))
  thdListener.Start()
End Sub
```

The listenerThread function manages new incoming connections, allocating each new connection to a new thread, where the client's requests will be handled.

HTTP operates over port 80, but if any other application is using port 80 at the same time (such as IIS), the code will crash. Therefore, the port for this server is configurable. The first step is to start the TcpListener on the port specified in tbPort.Text.

This thread runs in an infinite loop, constantly blocking on the AcceptSocket method. Once the socket is connected, some text is written to the screen, and a new thread calls the handlerSocket function.

The reason for the   lock(this) command is that handlerSocket
retrieves the socket by reading the last entry in ArrayList. In the case where
two connections arrive simultaneously, two entries will be written to
ArrayList, and one of the calls to handlerSocket will use the wrong
socket. Lock ensures that the spawning of the new thread cannot happen at
the same time as the acceptance of a new socket.

C#

```csharp
public void listenerThread()
{
  int port =0;
  port = Convert.ToInt16(tbPort.Text);
  TcpListener tcpListener = new TcpListener(port);
  tcpListener.Start();
  while(true)
  {
    Socket handlerSocket = tcpListener.AcceptSocket();
    if (handlerSocket.Connected)
    {
    lbConnections.Items.Add(
    handlerSocket.RemoteEndPoint.ToString() + " connected."
    );
    lock(this)
    {
     alSockets.Add(handlerSocket);
     ThreadStart thdstHandler = new
     ThreadStart(handlerThread);
     Thread thdHandler = new Thread(thdstHandler);
     thdHandler.Start();
    }
   }
  }
}
```

VB.NET

```vbnet
Public  Sub listenerThread()
  Dim port As Integer = 0
  port = Convert.ToInt16(tbPort.Text)
  Dim tcpListener As TcpListener =  New TcpListener(port)
  tcpListener.Start()
  do
```

```
        Dim handlerSocket As Socket =  tcpListener.AcceptSocket()
        If handlerSocket.Connected = true then
          lbConnections.Items.Add( _
          handlerSocket.RemoteEndPoint.ToString() + " _
          connected.")
          syncLock(me)
            alSockets.Add(handlerSocket)
            Dim thdstHandler As ThreadStart =  New  _
              ThreadStart(AddressOf handlerThread)
            Dim thdHandler As Thread =  New  _
              Thread(thdstHandler)
            thdHandler.Start()
          end syncLock
        end if
      loop
    End sub
```

The `handlerThread` function is where HTTP is implemented, albeit minimally. Taking a closer look at the code should better explain what is happening here.

The first task this thread must perform, before it can communicate with the client to which it has been allocated, is to retrieve a socket from the top of the public `ArrayList`. Once this socket has been obtained, it can then create a stream to this client by passing the socket to the constructor of a `NetworkStream`.

To make processing of the stream easier, a `StreamReader` is used to read one line from the incoming `NetworkStream`. This line is assumed to be:

```
GET <some URL path> HTTP/1.1
```

HTTP posts will be handled identically to HTTP gets. Because this server has no support for server-side scripting, there is no use for anything else in the HTTP POST data, or anything else in the HTTP Request header for that matter.

Assuming that the HTTP request is properly formatted, we can extract the requested page URL from this line by splitting it into an array of strings (verbs[ ]), delimited by the space character.

The next task is to convert a URL path into a physical path on the local hard drive. This involves four steps:

1.   Converting forward slashes to backslashes

2.   Trimming off any query string (i.e., everything after the question mark)

3.   Appending a default page, if none is specified; in this case, "index.htm"

4.   Prefixing the URL path with the HTTP root

Once the physical path is resolved, it can be read from disk and sent out on the network stream. It is reported on screen, and then the socket is closed. This server does not return any HTTP headers, which means the client will have to determine how to display the data being sent to it.

C#

```csharp
public void handlerThread()
{
  Socket handlerSocket = (
  Socket)alSockets[alSockets.Count-1];
  String streamData = "";
  String filename = "";
  String[] verbs;
  StreamReader    quickRead;
  NetworkStream networkStream =
  new NetworkStream(handlerSocket);
  quickRead = new StreamReader(networkStream);
  streamData = quickRead.ReadLine();
  verbs = streamData.Split(" ".ToCharArray());
  // Assume verbs[0]=GET
  filename = verbs[1].Replace("/","\\");
  if (filename.IndexOf("?")!=-1)
  {
    // Trim of anything after a question mark (Querystring)
    filename = filename.Substring(0,filename.IndexOf("?"));
  }

  if (filename.EndsWith("\\"))
  {
    // Add a default page if not specified
    filename+="index.htm";
  }
```

```
        filename = tbPath.Text + filename;
        FileStream  fs = new FileStream(filename,
        FileMode.OpenOrCreate);
        fs.Seek(0, SeekOrigin.Begin);
        byte[] fileContents= new byte[fs.Length];
        fs.Read(fileContents, 0, (int)fs.Length);
        fs.Close();

        // optional: modify fileContents to include HTTP header.

        handlerSocket.Send(fileContents);
        lbConnections.Items.Add(filename);
        handlerSocket.Close();
    }
```

VB.NET

```
Public  Sub handlerThread()
  Dim handlerSocket As Socket = _
  CType(alSockets(alSockets.Count-1), Socket)
  Dim streamData As String =  ""
  Dim filename As String =  ""
  Dim verbs() As String
  Dim quickRead As StreamReader
  Dim networkStream As NetworkStream = New _
  NetworkStream(handlerSocket)
  quickRead = New StreamReader(networkStream)
  streamData = quickRead.ReadLine()
  verbs = streamData.Split(" ".ToCharArray())
  ' Assume verbs[0]=GET
  filename = verbs(1).Replace("/","\\")
  If filename.IndexOf("?")<>-1 Then
    ' Trim of anything after a question mark (Querystring)
    filename = filename.Substring(0,filename.IndexOf("?"))
  End If

  If filename.EndsWith("\\") Then
    ' Add a default page if not specified
    filename+="index.htm"
  End If
  filename = tbPath.Text + filename
  Dim fs As FileStream =  New _
```

```
FileStream(filename,FileMode.OpenOrCreate)
fs.Seek(0, SeekOrigin.Begin)
Dim fileContents() As Byte =  New Byte(fs.Length) {}
fs.Read(fileContents, 0, CType(fs.Length, Integer))
fs.Close()
' optional: modify fileContents to include HTTP header.
handlerSocket.Send(fileContents)
lbConnections.Items.Add(filename)
handlerSocket.Close()
End Sub
```

Most modern browsers can determine how best to display the data being sent to them, without the need for Content-Type headers. For instance, Internet Explorer can tell the difference between JPEG image data and HTML by looking for the standard JPEG header in the received data; however, this system is not perfect.

A simple example is the difference between how XML is rendered on a browser window and how HTML is displayed. Without the Content-Type header, Internet Explorer will mistake all XML (excluding the <?xml?> tag) as HTML. You can see this by viewing a simple XML file containing the text <a><b/></a> through this server.

And, the usual namespaces are thrown in:

C#

```
using System.Threading;
using System.Net;
using System.Net.Sockets;
using System.Text;
using System.IO;
```

VB.NET

```
Imports System.Threading
Imports System.Net
Imports System.Net.Sockets
Imports System.Text
Imports System.IO
```

To test the server, you will need a simple HTML page. Save the following text as index.htm in the same folder where the executable is built (the HTTP root).

```
HTML
<html>
 Hello world!
</html>
```

Run the server from Visual Studio .NET, change the port to 90 if you are running IIS, and press Start. Open a browser and type in `http://localhost:90`. `Localhost` should be replaced by the IP address of the server, if you are running the server on a second computer (Figure 4.7).

As mentioned previously, the server does not return HTTP headers. It is worthwhile to extend the example to include one of the more important headers, `Content-Type`, to save data from being misinterpreted at the client.

Figure 4.7
HTTP server
application.

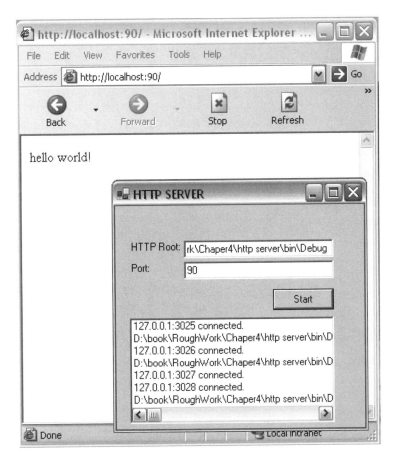

First, implement a new function called `getMime()`. This will retrieve a file's MIME type from the computer's registry from its file extension:

C#

```
public string getMime(string filename)
{
  FileInfo thisFile = new FileInfo(filename);
  RegistryKey key = Registry.ClassesRoot;
  key = key.OpenSubKey(thisFile.Extension);
  return key.GetValue("Content Type").ToString();
}
```

VB.NET

```
Public Function getMime(ByVal filename As String) As String
  Dim thisFile As FileInfo =  New FileInfo(filename)
  Dim key As RegistryKey =  Registry.ClassesRoot
  key = key.OpenSubKey(thisFile.Extension)
  Return key.GetValue("Content Type").ToString()
End Function
```

If you have never used Windows registry before, this code may need a little explaining. The Windows registry is a repository for information that holds the vast amount of settings and preferences that keep Windows ticking over. You can view and edit the registry using Registry Editor (Figure 4.8); start this by clicking Start→Run and typing `regedit` or `regedt32`.

To view MIME types that correspond with file type extensions, click on HKEY_CLASSES_ROOT, scroll down to the file extension in question, and look at the `Content Type` key on the right-hand side of the screen.

Figure 4.8
Registry Editor utility.

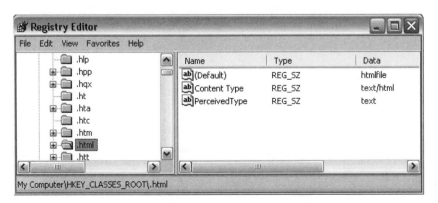

This data is accessed programmatically by first extracting the file type extension using the `Extension` property of a `FileInfo` object. The first step in drilling down through the registry data is to open the root key. In this case, it is `Registry.ClassesRoot`.

The `.html` subkey is then opened using the `openSubKey` method. Finally, the `Content Type` value is retrieved using the `getValue` statement and returned as a string to the calling function.

Now the final call to the `Send` method must be replaced by a slightly more elaborate sending procedure, which issues correct HTTP headers:

C#

```
handlerSocket.Send(fileContents);
```

VB.NET

```
handlerSocket.Send(fileContents)
```

These become:

C#

```
string responseString = "HTTP/1.1 200 OK\r\nContent-Type: " +
        getMime(filename) + "\r\n\r\n";
System.Collections.ArrayList al = new ArrayList();
al.AddRange(Encoding.ASCII.GetBytes(responseString));
al.AddRange(fileContents);
handlerSocket.Send((byte[])al.ToArray((new
byte()).GetType()));
```

VB.NET

```
Dim responseString As String
responseString = "HTTP/1.1 200 OK" + vbCrLf + _
"Content-Type: " + getMime(filename) + vbCrLf + vbCrLf
Dim al As System.Collections.ArrayList = New ArrayList
al.AddRange(Encoding.ASCII.GetBytes(responseString))
al.AddRange(fileContents)
handlerSocket.Send(CType( _
al.ToArray((New Byte).GetType()), Byte()))
```

Finally, to support the registry access functionality, we need to include an extra namespace:

C#

```
using Microsoft.Win32;
```

VB.NET

```
Imports Microsoft.Win32
```

To demonstrate the difference this makes to running the server, create two files, test.txt and test.xml, both containing the text <a><b/></a>. Save them both in the HTTP root of your server and type in *http:localhost/test.xml* and *http:localhost/test.txt*. You will notice that test.xml will be rendered as a collapsible tree, and the text file will be shown as a series of characters.

4.4 System.Net.HttpWebListener

In .NET 2 Whidbey, a more elegant solution for implementing Web servers exists, namely the HttpWebListener class. This class leverages the Http.sys driver (where available) to deliver unprecedented performance, and integrates many features, such as SSL encryption and authentication, which would be difficult to develop from the ground up.

The HttpWebListener class consists of the significant methods and properties shown in Table 4.7.

Table 4.7 *Significant members of the HttpWebListener class .*

Method or Property	Description
Abort / Close	Destroys the request queue.
AddPrefix	Adds a prefix to the Web listener.
BeginGetRequest	Awaits a client request asynchronously. Returns IasyncResult.
EndGetRequest	Handles client request. Returns ListenerWebRequest.
GetPrefixes	Retrieves all handled prefixes. Returns String[ ]v.
GetRequest	Awaits a client request synchronously. Returns ListenerWebRequest.
RemoveAll	Removes all prefixes.
RemovePrefix	Removes a specified prefix.

Table 4.7 *Significant members of the HttpWebListener class (continued).*

Method or Property	Description
`Start`	Starts the Web server.
`Stop`	Stops the Web server.
`AuthenticationScheme`	Sets the means by which the server authenticates clients. Returns `AuthenticationScheme` (i.e., Basic, Digest, NTLM).
`IsListening`	Determines if the server is running. Returns **Boolean**.
`Realm string`	If Basic or Digest authentication schemes are selected, gets the realm directive. Returns `String`.

The `ListenerWebRequest` returned by `GetRequest` contains the significant methods and properties shown in Table 4.8.

Table 4.8

Method or Property	Description
`Abort / Close`	Closes the client connection.
`GetRequestStream`	Retrieves a reference to the stream sent from the client. Returns `Stream`.
`GetResponse`	Retrieves a reference to the response to be sent to the client. Returns `ListenerWebResponse`.
`Accept`	Gets the **Accept** HTTP header sent in the client request. Returns `String`.
`ClientCertificate`	Gets the digital certificate sent with the client request. Returns `X509Certificate`.
`ClientCertificateError`	Determines if any errors were present in the client certificate. Returns `int32`.
`Connection`	Gets the **Connection** HTTP header sent in the client request. Returns `String`.
`ContentLength`	Gets the length of any data posted in the client request. Returns `int64`.
`ContentType`	Gets the **ContentType** HTTP header sent in the client request. Returns `String`.

Table 4.8

Expect	Gets the **Expect** HTTP header sent in the client request. Returns `String`.
HasEntityBody	Determines if the client request had an `Entity` body. Returns `Boolean`.
Headers	Gets a reference to the set of HTTP headers sent from the client. Returns `WebHeaderCollection`.
Host	Gets the `Host` HTTP header sent in the client request. Returns `String`.
Identity	Determines the identity credentials in the client request. Returns `Identity`.
IfModifiedSince	Gets the **IfModifiedSince** header sent in the client request. Returns `DateTime`.
KeepAlive Boolean	Determines if the client sent `Connection: Keep-Alive` in its request. Returns `Boolean`.
LocalEndPoint	Determines the local logical endpoint of the communication. Returns `IPEndPoint`.
Method	Gets the HTTP send method (i.e., `GET`, `POST`) in the client request. Returns `String`.
ProtocolVersion	Determines the HTTP version used by the client. Returns `Version`.
RawUri	Gets the URI requested by the client. Returns `String`.
Referer	Gets the **Referer** HTTP header sent in the client request. Returns `String`.
RemoteEndPoint	Determines the remote logical endpoint of the communication. Returns `IPEndPoint`.
RequestUri	Gets the URI requested by the client. Returns `Uri`.
UserAgent	Gets the `UserAgent` HTTP header sent in the client request. Returns `String`.

The `ListenerWebResponse` returned by `GetResponse` contains the significant methods and properties listed in Table 4.9.

Table 4.9

Method or Property	Description
`Abort / Close`	Disconnects the client.
`GetResponseStream`	Retrieves a reference to the stream to be returned to the client. Returns `Stream`.
`ContentLength`	Sets the length of data to be sent back to the client. Returns `int64`.
`ContentType`	Sets the `ContentType` HTTP header to be sent back the client. Returns `String`.
`Date`	Sets the `Date` HTTP header to be sent back to the client. Returns `DateTime`.
`EntityDelimitation`	Determines how the response content should be delimited (i.e., `ContentLength`, `Chunked`, `Raw`). Returns `EntityDelimitation`.
`Headers`	Retrieves a reference to the HTTP headers to be sent back to the client. Returns `WebHeaderCollection`.
`KeepAlive`	Determines if `Connection: Keep-Alive` should be set in the HTTP headers returned to the client. Returns `Boolean`.
`LastModified`	Sets the `LastModified` HTTP header to be sent back to the client. Returns `DateTime`.
`ProtocolVersion`	Sets the HTTP protocol version to be used in communicating with the client. Returns `Version`.
`RawHeaders`	Retrieves a reference to the HTTP headers to be sent back to the client. Returns `Byte[ ]`.
`Request`	Retrieves a reference to the request that initiated the response. Returns `ListenerWebRequest`.
`Server`	Sets the `Server` HTTP header to be sent back to the client. Returns `String`.
`StatusCode`	Sets the HTTP status code to be sent to the client. Returns `httpstatuscode` (e.g., `OK`, `Moved`, `NotFound`).
`StatusDescription`	Sets the HTTP status description to be sent to the client. Returns `String`.

4.5   **Mobile Web browsers**

Not all HTTP clients are PCs. Many people use their mobile phones to access the Internet. Some applications are infinitely more useful when available wirelessly. Even though mobile phones ferry data in a totally different way from wired networks, a wireless application protocol (WAP) phone will communicate via a WAP gateway, which converts mobile phone signals into TCP/IP and accesses servers in much the same way as browsers.

WAP runs over HTTP and wireless transfer protocol (WTP), with a few extra headers thrown into the HTTP request. The following is a sample HTTP request generated by a WAP phone:

```
GET / HTTP/1.1
Accept-Charset: ISO-8859-1
Accept-Language: en
Content-Type: application/x-www-form-urlencoded
x-up-subno: Fiach_hop
x-upfax-accepts: none
x-up-uplink: none
x-up-devcap-smartdialing: 1
x-up-devcap-screendepth: 1
x-up-devcap-iscolor: 0
x-up-devcap-immed-alert: 1
x-up-devcap-numsoftkeys: 3
x-up-devcap-screenchars: 15,4
Accept: application/x-hdmlc, application/x-up-alert,
application/x-up-cacheop, application/x-up-device,
application/x-up-digestentry, text/x-hdml;version=3.1, text/
x-hdml;version=3.0, text/x-hdml;version=2.0, text/x-wap.wml,
text/vnd.wap.wml, */*, image/bmp, text/html
User-Agent: UP.Browser/3.1-ALAV UP.Link/3.2
Host: 127.0.0.1:50
```

Note: x-up-subno is set to the computer username followed by the computer name.

WAP clients and PC browsers differ most in the response. WAP clients cannot read HTML and use a simpler language, wireless markup language (WML), which has a MIME type text/vnd.wap.wml.

A minimal page in WML is as follows:

```
WML
<!DOCTYPE wml PUBLIC "-//WAPFORUM//DTD WML 1.1//EN"
        "http://www.wapforum.org/DTD/wml_1.1.xml">
<wml>
 <card>
  <p align="left">
   <b>Title</b><br/>
    body
  </p>
 </card>
</wml>
```

To view this page on a WAP phone, save the above text to `index.wml`. Ensure that the MIME type is registered on your computer by adding a registry key to `HKEY_CLASSES_ROOT\.wml` named `Content Type` with the value `text/vnd.wap.wml`.

Run the server as described in the previous section, and copy `index.wml` into the HTTP root as displayed. Ensure that your computer is online and has an externally visible IP address. Connect your mobile phone to the Internet and type your IP address into it, followed by `/index.wml` (Figure 4.9).

Note: If you do not have a WAP phone, you can use a WAP emulator such as the UP.SDK from *www.openwave.com*.

Not all wireless HTTP clients read WML. A competing technology, iMode, which is the most widely used technology in Asia, offers a similar, yet incompatible, system. iMode reads compact HTML (cHTML), which is a stripped-down version of the language with features such as frames, tables, and even JPEG images explicitly unsupported; however, iMode has

Figure 4.9
Sample WML page.

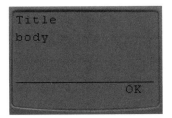

good support for Unicode and can adequately display many Web pages designed for PCs.

An iMode browser can be recognized by the word DoCoMo in the user agent HTTP request header.

4.5.1   Mobile Web SDK

When implementing WAP compatibility in a Web application, it is worth considering the .NET Mobile Web SDK. This enables you to develop applications for WAP in the same way as an ASP.NET Web application. Therefore, there is no need to learn WML.

Note: Utilities are available to convert HTML to WML on-the-fly, but the .NET Mobile Web SDK is freely available.

A sample page could be as follows:

ASP.NET

```
<%@ Page Inherits="System.Mobile.UI.MobilePage" language="c#"
%>
<%@ Register TagPrefix="mobile" Namespace="System.Mobile.UI"
%>
<mobile:Form runat="server">
<mobile:Label runat="server">
 Hello world!
</mobile:Label>
</mobile:Form>
```

To try this page out, save it as mobile.aspx in your IIS root (usually c:\ inetpub\wwwroot). Ensure that your computer is online and has an externally visible IP address. Connect your mobile phone to the Internet, and type your IP address into it, followed by /mobile.aspx.

4.6   Conclusion

This chapter should have provided enough information to link your .NET application into data from the Web, to illustrate the point that HTTP is not only used for Web browsing and the WAP.

The next chapter deals with sending and receiving email from .NET applications.

5

SMTP and POP3: Communicating with email Servers

5.1   Introduction

More emails are sent every day than postal mail. Why? Because email is cheap, informal, fast, and can be picked up at the receiver's convenience. Emails can be automatically generated and sent, making them ideal for automated status notification. One day, you may receive an email from your home sprinkler system saying simply, "Your house is on fire."

After reading this chapter you will be able to send and receive emails from your .NET applications. These features can be useful for customer support systems, collaborative personnel management, and many other types of applications.

This chapter begins by describing how emails can be constructed and sent, using either a socket-level approach, or by using in-built .NET classes. Immediately following that, is a description on how emails may be received, again, by either using a socket level approach, or a higher-level methodology, leveraging Microsoft Outlook.

5.2   Sending an email

Every email must have a destination email address. An email address takes the following form:

```
<Username>@<domain name>
```

The domain name in an email address generally does not include the "www" prefix, which is common for Web site addresses. Despite that, the domain name is globally recognized under the DNS system. The username is recognized only by the recipient mail server.

Emails are not immediately delivered to the recipient; instead, they are initially sent to your ISP's or company's mail server. From there, they are forwarded to the recipient's mail server or held for a period of time until the recipient's mail server accepts the email. Emails are sent using the simple mail transfer protocol (SMTP), which is described in detail later.

In order to determine the recipient's mail server, a DNS mail exchange (MX) query is issued to the local DNS server for that domain name. That computer will then return details of where the server or servers that handle incoming mail are located.

Note: Most ISPs have only one incoming mail server, but Hotmail.com has more than 10 mail servers.

You will always be told the IP address of your SMTP server. Unfortunately, you cannot use an SMTP server from another ISP because it will block you with an error message such as "Relaying denied."

Microsoft virtual SMTP server is available for most versions of Windows and generally appears under IIS when installed.

5.3   SMTP

SMTP is used to send, but not receive, emails. Every mail server in the world must conform to the SMTP standard in order to send emails reliably regardless of destination. The definitive guide to SMTP is held by the Internet Engineering Task Force (IETF) under RFC 821 at *www.ietf.org/rfc/rfc0821.txt.*

The definitive guides to most major protocols are held at the IETF. They are free to download and should be consulted when you are developing network applications that are designed to work with preexisting or third-party clients or servers.

SMTP is not a difficult protocol to implement from the ground up; however, it is natively supported from .NET and, thus, would be a waste of time to redevelop. Also, many commercial email components are available, which can be imported into your application. One of the most popular is AspEmail from Persits Software. The demo version of this component is adequate for most applications.

5.3.1 Implementing SMTP

SMTP operates on TCP port 25. Before sitting down to code, you should first find out the IP address of your ISP's SMTP server. In the examples below, the SMTP server smtp.ntlworld.com is used. You should replace this with your own SMTP server, or the examples will not work.

SMTP was originally designed for UNIX users and has a command-line-type feel to it, although the commands are issued over a network connection, rather than a keyboard.

A good way to test the protocol is to open telnet by clicking Start→Run and type telnet. In Windows NT, 2000, and XP, type o smtp.ntl-world.com 25. In prior versions of Windows, click File→Connect, and then type smtp.ntlworld.com into the connection box and 25 into the port box. Then press Connect.

Once the client establishes a TCP connection to the server on port 25, the server will always reply with 220 <some greeting message><enter>. A number is always included at the start of every server response. Any number beginning with 5 is an error and should be dealt with; everything else can be ignored.

The client must then send a greeting back to the server. This is merely a formality and does not contain any useful information. The format is HELLO server <enter>, and the server should reply with 250 server <enter>.

The next step is to send a contact email address for the sender. This is sent in the format MAIL FROM:<email address><enter>. The server should reply 250 OK<enter>.

Following that, the recipient must be indicated. To do this, RCPT TO:<email address><enter> is used. The server should reply 250 OK<enter>.

To create the body of the email, the client sends the command DATA<enter>. To this the server should reply 354 <some instructions><enter>.

The client can then send as much text as required to make up the body of the email. It is recommended to split the mail over several lines because of restrictions in some mail servers. To indicate the end of the mail body, send <enter>.<enter>. The server should reply 250 OK<enter>.

At this point, it is possible simply to close the TCP connection, but it is recommended to send QUIT<enter>. The following passage shows the chain of events between client and server when an email is sent from *smith@usc-*

isif.arpa to *jones@bbn-unix.arpa.* "S" indicates a transmission from server to client, and "C" indicates a client-to-server transaction.

```
S: 220 Simple Mail Transfer Service
C: HELO SERVER
S: 250 SERVER
C: MAIL FROM:<Smith@USC-ISIF.ARPA>
S: 250 OK
C: RCPT TO:<Jones@BBN-UNIX.ARPA>
S: 250 OK
C: DATA
C: 354 Start mail input; end with <CRLF>.<CRLF>
C: Dear sir
C:  Please give me a call to discuss your offer
C: .
S: 250 OK
C: QUIT
S: 221 CLOSED
```

Example: Complaints department SMTP server

If you ever work in the complaints department of a company, this application will make your life a lot easier. It mimics the communications an SMTP server would make, but it thoughtfully ignores the email content, saving you a lot of stress.

Of course, a real application would be to have it log the emails to a database, but, for the sake of clarity, that feature is not included in this example. Possible derivations of this project could be an email proxy server, which could filter emails for viruses, and so forth.

Start a C# or VB.NET Windows form project as usual, and drag a textbox onto the form. Call it `tbStatus`, and set `multiline` to `true`.

To start with, we must import all of the namespaces we intend to use in this application. Put this code at the beginning of the program:

C#

```
using System.Threading;
using System.Net;
using System.Net.Sockets;
using System.Text;
```

VB.NET

```
Imports System.Threading
Imports System.Net
Imports System.Net.Sockets
Imports System.Text
```

For simplicity, this server will be single threaded. The thread that listens for incoming connections runs in the background and starts when the form loads. This means that, although the program won't hang waiting for connections, it can only handle one email at a time.

C#

```
private void Form1_Load(object sender, System.EventArgs e)
{
  Thread thdSMTPServer = new Thread(new
  ThreadStart(serverThread));
  thdSMTPServer.Start();
}
```

VB.NET

```
Private Sub Form1_Load(ByVal sender As System.Object, _
 ByVal e As System.EventArgs) Handles MyBase.Load
        Dim thdSMTPServer As Thread
        thdSMTPServer = New Thread(New ThreadStart( _
          AddressOf serverThread))
        thdSMTPServer.Start()
End Sub
```

This thread provides the functionality to receive emails sent via SMTP. It listens on port 25 and blocks until an incoming connection is detected. This connection is accepted, and a 250 hello<enter> reply is sent back to the client. Note that here it is possible to use ASCII.GetBytes because SMTP is a text-based protocol, and binary content is not sent at this level.

The function socketReadLine is not defined yet, but its purpose is to store incoming data in a string until the termination character(s) is found.

Data returned from the client is displayed in tbStatus, but no other processing takes place.

C#

```
public void serverThread()
```

```
{
Byte[] sendBytes;
TcpListener tcpListener = new TcpListener(25);
tcpListener.Start();
while(true)
{
 Socket handlerSocket = tcpListener.AcceptSocket();
 if (handlerSocket.Connected)
 {
  // Reply 250 hello
  sendBytes = Encoding.ASCII.GetBytes("250 hello\n");
  handlerSocket.Send(sendBytes,0,
  sendBytes.Length,SocketFlags.None);
  // Wait for enter (hello)
  tbStatus.Text += socketReadLine(handlerSocket,"\n");
  // Reply 250 ok
  sendBytes = Encoding.ASCII.GetBytes("250 ok\n");
  handlerSocket.Send(sendBytes,0,
  sendBytes.Length,SocketFlags.None);
  // Wait for enter (mail from)
  tbStatus.Text += socketReadLine(handlerSocket,"\n");
  // Reply 250 ok
  sendBytes = Encoding.ASCII.GetBytes("250 ok\n");
  handlerSocket.Send(sendBytes,0,
  sendBytes.Length,SocketFlags.None);
  // Wait for enter (rcpt to)
  tbStatus.Text += socketReadLine(handlerSocket,"\n");
  // Reply 250 ok
  sendBytes = Encoding.ASCII.GetBytes("250 ok\n");
  handlerSocket.Send(sendBytes,0,
  sendBytes.Length,SocketFlags.None);
  // Wait for enter (data)
  tbStatus.Text += socketReadLine(handlerSocket,"\n");
  // Reply 354
  sendBytes = Encoding.ASCII.GetBytes("354 proceed\n");
  handlerSocket.Send(sendBytes,0,
  sendBytes.Length,SocketFlags.None);
  // Wait for enter.enter (email body)
  tbStatus.Text += socketReadLine(handlerSocket,
  "\r\n.\r\n");
  // Reply 221 close
```

```
        sendBytes = Encoding.ASCII.GetBytes("221 close\n");
        handlerSocket.Send(sendBytes,0,
        sendBytes.Length,SocketFlags.None);
        handlerSocket.Close();
      }
    }
  }
```

VB.NET

```
Public Sub serverThread()
 Dim sendBytes As Byte()
 Dim tcpListener As New TcpListener(25)
 Dim handlerSocket As Socket
 tcpListener.Start()
 Do
  handlerSocket = tcpListener.AcceptSocket()
  If handlerSocket.Connected = True Then
   ' Reply 250 hello
   sendBytes = Encoding.ASCII.GetBytes("250 hello" + vbCrLf)
   handlerSocket.Send(sendBytes, 0, sendBytes.Length, _
   SocketFlags.None)
   ' Wait for enter (hello)
   tbStatus.Text += socketReadLine(handlerSocket, vbCrLf)
   ' Reply 250 ok
   sendBytes = Encoding.ASCII.GetBytes("250 ok" + vbCrLf)
   handlerSocket.Send(sendBytes, 0, sendBytes.Length, _
   SocketFlags.None)
   ' Wait for enter (mail from)
   tbStatus.Text += socketReadLine(handlerSocket, vbCrLf)
   ' Reply 250 ok
   sendBytes = Encoding.ASCII.GetBytes("250 ok" + vbCrLf)
   handlerSocket.Send(sendBytes, 0, sendBytes.Length, _
   SocketFlags.None)
   ' Wait for enter (rcpt to)
   tbStatus.Text += socketReadLine(handlerSocket, vbCrLf)
   ' Reply 250 ok
   sendBytes = Encoding.ASCII.GetBytes("250 ok" + vbCrLf)
   handlerSocket.Send(sendBytes, 0, sendBytes.Length, _
   SocketFlags.None)
   ' Wait for enter (data)
   tbStatus.Text += socketReadLine(handlerSocket, vbCrLf)
```

```
  ' Reply 354
  sendBytes = Encoding.ASCII.GetBytes("354 proceed" + _
  vbCrLf)
  handlerSocket.Send(sendBytes, 0, sendBytes.Length, _
  SocketFlags.None)
  ' Wait for enter.enter (email body)
  tbStatus.Text += socketReadLine(handlerSocket, _
  vbCrLf + "." + vbCrLf)
  ' Reply 221 close
  sendBytes = Encoding.ASCII.GetBytes("221 close" + vbCrLf)
  handlerSocket.Send(sendBytes, 0, sendBytes.Length, _
  SocketFlags.None)
  handlerSocket.Close()
  End If
 Loop
End Sub
```

This thread starts by listening on port 25 for incoming connections. The thread blocks on the call to AcceptSocket() and waits indefinitely until a connection arrives. Once a connection arrives, it is stored in a socket object named handlerSocket. Once the connection is established, the server immediately responds with 250 hello. The server then waits for the client to respond. In response to every command sent by the client, the server responds with 250 ok. The client is then expected to send a mail from command, and the server will wait until the client does so. Once the server has replied, it will wait for a rcpt to command and finally a data command. The server will read in data from the socket until the end-of-message marker (a period on a line by itself) appears. The server then prompts the client to close the connection before closing the connection itself.

The socketReadLine function is called many times from serverThread. It takes a socket and a terminator string as parameters. Again, it reads in from the network stream one byte at a time and builds up the streamData string. If the terminator string appears in the streamData string, or if ReadByte fails because of a network error, then the function returns.

C#

```
public String socketReadLine(Socket socket,String terminator)
{
  int lastRead=0;
  String streamData = "";
  NetworkStream networkStream = new NetworkStream(socket);
```

```
    do
    {
      lastRead = networkStream.ReadByte();
      if (lastRead==-1) break;
      streamData+=(Convert.ToChar(lastRead));
      if (streamData.EndsWith(terminator)) break;
    }
    while(true);
    return streamData;
}
```

VB.NET

```
Public Function socketReadLine(ByVal socket As Socket, _
ByVal terminator As String) As String
 Dim lastRead As Int16
 Dim streamData As String
 Dim networkStream As New NetworkStream(socket)
 Do
   lastRead = networkStream.ReadByte()
   If lastRead = -1 Then Exit Do
   streamData += (Convert.ToChar(lastRead))
   If streamData.EndsWith(terminator) Then Exit Do
 Loop
 Return streamData
End Function
```

The socketReadLine function may look a little verbose, especially because the StreamReader already has a ReadLine method; however, this function is designed to be generic enough such that it can detect both new-line (\n or vbcrlf) message terminators and end-of-message markers (a period on a line by itself). This function creates a NetworkStream to the socket and then reads from the stream one byte at a time, appending the byte to a string, which is returned once the message terminator has been found.

Before running this example, ensure that no other SMTP server is running at the same time. You can check for the default virtual SMTP server by opening IIS from Administrative Tools and expanding your local computer name from within the console. You can stop the SMTP server (if it is installed) by right-clicking on its icon and selecting stop.

Figure 5.1
*Microsoft Outlook,
new account.*

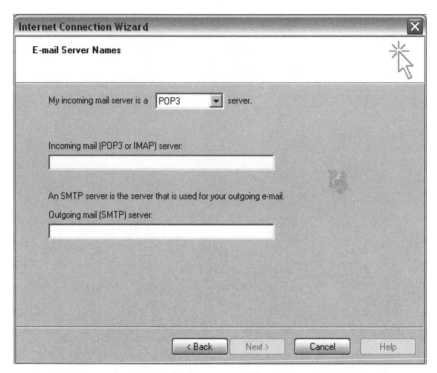

To test this example, run it from Visual Studio .NET. Then open an email program (e.g., Microsoft Outlook). Press Tools→Accounts (Figure 5.1), then click Add→Mail, and click Next twice.

Type anything in the POP3 box, and type the IP address of the computer on which you are running the SMTP Server, or 127.0.0.1 if you only have one computer. Keep pressing Next until you arrive back at the previous screen.

Create a new email as usual, and select your new account to send from. On Outlook, this is selected from an arrow to the right of the Send button; on Outlook Express, this is selected from a drop-down list in the "to" field. Now press Send.

You will see the raw TCP data written as text in the application's window, as shown in Figure 5.2.

5.4   Post office protocol 3

Post office protocol 3 (POP3) is used to receive, but not send, emails. Every ISP has a POP3 server, and many Web hosting companies offer access to a

Figure 5.2
*SMTP server
application.*

POP3 server to provide personalized email addresses such as *joeDoe@example.com* (fictitious). POP3 is described definitively in RFC 1939, which is downloadable at *www.ietf.org/rfc/rfc1939.txt* and operates on TCP port 110.

POP3 is used to store emails on behalf of users. Users can then download these emails selectively from the server. Some service providers limit the amount of space devoted to any one user on a POP3 server. Therefore, POP3 also facilitates message deletion.

Again, before rushing into implementing POP3, be aware that there are alternatives; for instance, you can use Microsoft Exchange as a POP3 server, and commercial components by IP*Works or SoftArtisans can be used as POP3 clients.

5.4.1 Implementing POP3

Like SMTP, POP3 is a command-line-based protocol, where each line is terminated with a line-feed (<enter>) character. For variable length lines, the command is terminated by <enter>.<enter> as in SMTP.

When the server is operating normally, each line will start with +OK. If an error occurs, the line begins with –ERR *<some explanation>*. Once the client establishes a TCP connection to the server on port 110, the server will always reply with +OK *<some greeting message>*<enter>.

To access a mailbox, the client must authenticate itself with a username and password. The client sends USER *<username>*<enter>. The server then replies with +OK <welcome><enter>. The password is sent as USER *<password>*<enter> with the same response from the server.

To get summary information about the mailbox, the command STAT<enter> is issued. To this the server will reply +OK *<number of messages>* *<total size>*<enter>. Unlike the previous messages, where the text after the +OK could be ignored, here it must be read and stored for future use.

To read back an email, the client sends the RETR *<number>* command; Number must be between 1 and the number received in response to the STAT command. The server will respond +OK *<some message>*<enter>*<mail body>*<enter>.<enter>. The only piece of important information is the mail body; everything else can be ignored.

To delete emails, the client sends the DELE *<number>* command. The server will respond +OK *<some message>*<enter>. At this point, it is possible simply to close the TCP connection, but it is recommended to send QUIT<enter>.

To illustrate the protocol more simply, the following text shows the chain of events that occur between a POP3 server and client. As before, "S" indicates a transmission from server to client, and "C" indicates a client-to-server transaction. Here, user Bob is checking his emails, when he receives two messages from Alice and Terry.

```
S:     +OK POP3 server ready
C:     USER bob
S:     +OK user valid
C:     PASS secret
S:     +OK pass valid
C:     STAT
S:     +OK 2 170
C:     RETR 1
S:     +OK 120 octets
S:     hello, how are you bob?, haven't seen you in
S:     ages, any chance you could give me a call
S:     sometime? I'd love to see you. Alice
S:     .
C:     DELE 1
S:     +OK message 1 deleted
```

```
C:      RETR 2
S:      +OK 50 octets
S:      Hi bob, I got the order of 500 widgets placed
S:      with Acme. Terry
S:      .
C:      DELE 2
S:      +OK message 2 deleted
C:      QUIT
S:      +OK
```

This transcript has been simplified for reasons of clarity. Modern mail messages contain headers, including the subject, date, natural names of the sender and recipient, and technical information concerning what software was used to send the email and how it was relayed.

This is a message header sent from *fiach_reid@hotmail.com* to *fiach@eircom.net*.

```
Return-Path: <fiach_reid@hotmail.com>
Delivered-To: eircom.net-fiach@eircom.net
Received: (vpopmail 31497 invoked by uid 16); 11 Jan 2004
21:51:58 +0000
Received: (qmail 31491 messnum 229855 invoked from
network[64.4.19.76/law12-f76.law12.hotmail.com]); 11 Jan 2004
21:51:57 -0000
Received: from law12-f76.law12.hotmail.com (HELO hotmail.com)
(64.4.19.76)
  by mail09.svc.cra.dublin.eircom.net (qp 31491) with SMTP;
11 Jan 2004 21:51:57 -0000
Received: from mail pickup service by hotmail.com with
Microsoft SMTPSVC;
    Sun, 11 Jan 2004 13:51:56 -0800
Received: from 195.92.168.176 by lw12fd.law12.hotmail.msn.com
with HTTP;
  Sun, 11 Jan 2004 21:51:56 GMT
X-Originating-IP: [195.92.168.176]
X-Originating-Email: [fiach_reid@hotmail.com]
X-Sender: fiach_reid@hotmail.com
From: "Fiach Reid" <fiach_reid@hotmail.com>
To: fiach@eircom.net
Bcc:
Subject: test message
```

```
Date: Sun, 11 Jan 2004 21:51:56 +0000
Mime-Version: 1.0
Status:  U
X-UIDL:
1073857917.31497.mail09.svc.cra.dublin.eircom.net,S=1118
Content-Type: text/plain; format=flowed
Message-ID: <Law12-F76F1HkikieqX000054e5@hotmail.com>
X-OriginalArrivalTime: 11 Jan 2004 21:51:56.0469 (UTC)
FILETIME=[21BF7650:01C3D88D]
```

Two line-feed characters separate the message header from the body.

Example: POP3 client SPAM filter

SPAM is the term used for mass, unsolicited email. These emails are sometimes accompanied by attached viruses, which can be accidentally opened by unwitting users. This application could be used to safely delete emails containing message fragments indicative of a SPAM email; in this case, the string "free money."

This simple program scans your mailbox for emails containing the text "free money" and deletes them. This is obviously overly simplistic, but the example is here for illustration, not practicality.

The first step is to draw the user interface; you will need three textboxes, labeled `tbServer`, `tbUsername`, and `tbPassword`. Another textbox is required, named `tbStatus`; this textbox should be set with `multiline` to true. Finally, place a button on the form, and call it `btnClean`.

First, import the required namespaces:

C#

```
using System.Threading;
using System.Net;
using System.Net.Sockets;
using System.Text;
using System.IO;
```

VB.NET

```
Imports System.Threading
Imports System.Net
Imports System.Net.Sockets
Imports System.Text
Imports System.IO
```

Double-click on the Clean button and type the following code:

C#

```csharp
private void btnClean_Click(object sender, System.EventArgs
e)
{
 TcpClient clientSocket = new TcpClient(tbServer.Text,110);

  NetworkStream NetStrm = clientSocket.GetStream();
  StreamReader RdStrm= new StreamReader(NetStrm);
  tbStatus.Text += RdStrm.ReadLine();

  sendPOP3cmd("USER "+ tbUsername.Text + "\r\n",NetStrm);
  sendPOP3cmd("PASS "+ tbPassword.Text+ "\r\n",NetStrm);
  string Data = sendPOP3cmd("STAT\r\n",NetStrm);

  string[] BreakDown = Data.Split(" ".ToCharArray());
  int messageCount = Convert.ToInt16(BreakDown[1]);

  for (int i=1;i<= messageCount;i++)
  {
  StringBuilder message = new StringBuilder("");
  Data = "RETR " + Convert.ToString(i) + "\r\n";
  byte[] szData=
  System.Text.Encoding.ASCII.GetBytes(Data.ToCharArray());
  NetStrm.Write(szData,0,szData.Length);
  string szTemp = RdStrm.ReadLine();
  while(szTemp!=".")
  {
    message.Append(szTemp);
    tbStatus.Text += szTemp+"\r\n";
    szTemp = RdStrm.ReadLine();
  }
  if (message.ToString().IndexOf("free money")>0)
  {
    sendPOP3cmd("DELE " + Convert.ToString(i) +
    "\r\n",NetStrm);
  }
  }
  clientSocket.Close();
}
```

VB.NET

```
Private Sub btnClean_Click(ByVal sender As System.Object, _
ByVal e As System.EventArgs) Handles _
btnClean.Click
 Dim clientSocket As TcpClient
 Dim NetStrm As NetworkStream
 Dim RdStrm As StreamReader
 Dim Data As String
 Dim BreakDown() As String
 Dim messageCount As Int16
 Dim message As StringBuilder
 Dim szData() As Byte
 Dim i As Int16
 Dim szTemp As String
 clientSocket = New TcpClient(tbServer.Text, 110)
 NetStrm = clientSocket.GetStream()
 RdStrm = New StreamReader(NetStrm)
 tbStatus.Text += RdStrm.ReadLine()
 sendPOP3cmd("USER " + tbUsername.Text + vbCrLf, NetStrm)
 sendPOP3cmd("PASS " + tbPassword.Text + vbCrLf, NetStrm)
 Data = sendPOP3cmd("STAT" + vbCrLf, NetStrm)
 BreakDown = Data.Split(" ".ToCharArray())
 messageCount = Convert.ToInt16(BreakDown(1))
 For i = 1 To messageCount
  message = New StringBuilder("")
  Data = "RETR " + Convert.ToString(i) + vbCrLf
  szData = _
  System.Text.Encoding.ASCII.GetBytes(Data.ToCharArray())
  NetStrm.Write(szData, 0, szData.Length)
  szTemp = RdStrm.ReadLine()
  Do While szTemp <> "."
   message.Append(szTemp)
   tbStatus.Text += szTemp + vbCrLf
   szTemp = RdStrm.ReadLine()
  Loop
  If message.ToString().IndexOf("free money") > 0 Then
   sendPOP3cmd("DELE " + Convert.ToString(i) + vbCrLf, _
   NetStrm)
  End If
 Next i
 clientSocket.Close()
End Sub
```

Note that the `sendPOP3cmd` function is not yet implemented.

This piece of code uses a different method from the code for the SMTP server to read in lines of data from the network. In this case, the `ReadLine` method is used for single-line responses and an iterative loop reads multiple-line responses. The chain of events is that the client reads the welcome message from the server, then sends the USER and PASS commands. After it issues the STAT command, the server stores the response in `Data`.

`Data` is in the format +OK n1 n2, where n1 is the number of messages and n2 is the total size of the messages. To extract n1 from this string, it is split into an array of strings, delimited by the space character. The second element in this array is now n1.

The program then loops through the messages, issuing the RETR command for each one. The contents of the messages returned are built up using a `stringBuilder` object, rather than a string, for performance purposes. When it reaches a message that has the string "free money" contained within it, it issues the DELE command.

This code implements the `sendPOP3cmd` function:

C#

```
public string sendPOP3cmd(string cmd,NetworkStream NetStrm)
{
  byte[] szData;
  string returnedData = "";
  StreamReader RdStrm= new StreamReader(NetStrm);
  szData =
System.Text.Encoding.ASCII.GetBytes(cmd.ToCharArray());
  NetStrm.Write(szData,0,szData.Length);
  returnedData = RdStrm.ReadLine();
  tbStatus.Text += cmd + "\r\n" + returnedData + "\r\n";
  return returnedData;
}
```

VB.NET

```
Public Function sendPOP3cmd(ByVal cmd As String, _
ByVal NetStrm As NetworkStream) As String
  Dim szData() As Byte
  Dim returnedData As String
  Dim RdStrm As StreamReader
  RdStrm = New StreamReader(NetStrm)
  szData = _
```

```
      System.Text.Encoding.ASCII.GetBytes(cmd.ToCharArray())
      NetStrm.Write(szData, 0, szData.Length)
      returnedData = RdStrm.ReadLine()
      tbStatus.Text += cmd + vbCrLf + returnedData + vbCrLf
      Return returnedData
  End Function
```

It sends the specified command to the POP3 server and reads back data until it encounters the end-of-line marker \r\n or vbCrLf. The data that is read back is displayed on screen and returned to the calling function.

To test this application, run it from Visual Studio .NET. Type your POP3 server's IP address into the field provided. You will also need to provide your email account username and password.

Using your email program, send an email to yourself with the words "free money" in the subject line. Press Send. Now press Clean out. If you scroll the text to the bottom, you will see the POP3 command DELE, signifying that the email was deleted as shown in Figure 5.3.

5.5   System.Web.Mail

There is a built-in mechanism for Windows 2000 and later to send emails. This is called CDOSYS (Microsoft Collaboration Data Objects for Win-

Figure 5.3
*POP3 client
application.*

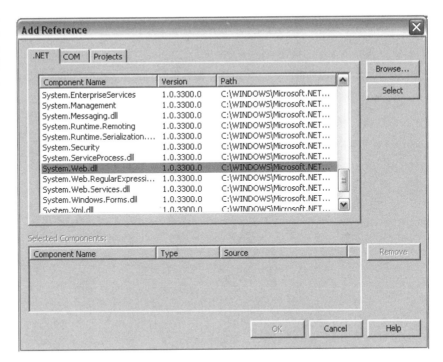

Figure 5.4
Visual Studio .NET, Add Reference.

dows 2000). It is much simpler than implementing SMTP, especially where attachments and rich-text emails are involved; however, CDOSYS can only provide functionality for the client side of the email service.

The following example shows how to send a simple email from *source@here.com* to *destination@there.com* via the SMTP server *smtp.ntl-world.com* (change this to your own SMTP server).

You must first make a reference to `System.Web.dll` before you can import the `System.Web.Mail` namespace. This DLL is a .NET assembly, not .COM. To do so, click Project→Add Reference, and then click on the DLL (Figure 5.4).

With that, you can draw your GUI. Drag three textboxes onto the form, name them `tbTo`, `tbFrom`, and `tbServer`. Drag another textbox onto the form, name it `tbMessage`, and set `multiline` to `true`. Finally, place a button on the form, and name it `btnSend`.

C#

```
using System.Web.Mail;
```

VB.NET

```
Imports System.Web.Mail
```

Now click on the Send button and type in the following code:

C#

```
private void btnSend_Click(object sender, System.EventArgs e)
{
        MailMessage email = new MailMessage();
        email.From = tbFrom.Text;
        email.To = tbTo.Text;
        email.Subject = "email from .NET";
        email.Body = tbMessage.Text;
        SmtpMail.SmtpServer = tbServer.Text;
        SmtpMail.Send(email);
}
```

VB.NET

```
Private Sub btnSend_Click(ByVal sender As System.Object, _
ByVal e As System.EventArgs) Handles btnSend.Click
        Dim email As New MailMessage()
        With email
            .From = tbFrom.Text
            .To = tbTo.Text
            .Subject = "email from .NET"
            .Body = tbMessage.Text
        End With
        SmtpMail.SmtpServer = tbServer.Text
        SmtpMail.Send(email)
End Sub
```

This code simply sets the various properties of a MailMessage object and passes it to the SmtpMail object. To test the application, run it from Visual Studio .NET. Fill in your own email address in the "To:" field, your SMTP server in the "Server" field, and then fill in whatever you wish in the other fields and press Send. A few moments later, check your email, and you should have received the message (Figure 5.5).

Figure 5.5
*SMTP client
application.*

5.5.1 Attachments

To elaborate on this example, let's add an attachment box and change the
format to HTML. Drag in the Open File Dialog control, name it
ofdAttachment, and then add in a textbox, tbAttachment, and a button,
btnAttachment.

Click on the Browse button and type the following code:

C#

```
private void btnBrowse_Click(object sender, System.EventArgs
e)
{
        ofdAttachment.ShowDialog();
        tbAttachment.Text = ofdAttachment.FileName;
}
```

VB.NET

```
Sub btnBrowse_Click(ByVal sender As System.Object, _
  ByVal e As System.EventArgs) Handles btnBrowse.Click
        ofdAttachment.ShowDialog()
        tbAttachment.Text = ofdAttachment.FileName
End Sub
```

Click on the Send button, and modify the code as follows:

C#

```csharp
private void btnSend_Click(object sender, System.EventArgs e)
{
        MailMessage email = new MailMessage();
        MailAttachment fileAttachment=new
        MailAttachment(tbAttachment.Text);
        email.Priority = MailPriority.High;
        email.BodyFormat = MailFormat.Html;
        email.From = tbFrom.Text;
        email.To = tbTo.Text;
        email.Subject = "email from .NET";
        email.Body = tbMessage.Text;
        email.Attachments.Add(fileAttachment);
        SmtpMail.SmtpServer = tbServer.Text;
        SmtpMail.Send(email);
}
```

VB.NET

```vbnet
Private Sub btnSend_Click(ByVal sender As System.Object, _
ByVal e As System.EventArgs) Handles btnSend.Click
        Dim email As New MailMessage()
        Dim fileAttachment As New _
        MailAttachment(tbAttachment.Text)

        With email
            .Priority = MailPriority.High
            .BodyFormat = MailFormat.Html
            .From = tbFrom.Text
            .To = tbTo.Text
            .Subject = "email from .NET"
            .Body = "<html>" + tbMessage.Text + "</html>"
            .Attachments.Add(fileAttachment)
        End With

        SmtpMail.SmtpServer = tbServer.Text
        SmtpMail.Send(email)
    End Sub
```

5.5.2   Images

Anyone who is familiar with HTML will instantly notice a snag here. On a Web site, if you want to display an image, you use a piece of HTML such as `<img src="picture.jpg">`; however, where can HTML in an email body look for images?

First, use the following HTML to represent an in-line picture in an email, `<img src="cid:picture1">`, and then, before calling the `send` method on the `system.web.mail.mailmessage` object, call the following:

```
attachInlineFile("c:\picture.jpg", "", "picture1")
```

where `c:\picture.jpg` is the image you wish to display.

5.6   Mail application programming interface

Microsoft Outlook provides an interface to applications to access emails stored within its message store. This interface is called the mail application programming interface (MAPI), and it's based on legacy COM interfaces, but nevertheless can still be accessed from .NET.

The following example lists the subject lines of all the emails in your Outlook inbox.

Start a new project as usual, draw a list view onto the form, and name it `lvOutlook`. Set the view to `Details`, and create two column headers labeled `From` and `Subject`. Click on the Project→Add Reference. Click COM, scroll down the list, and select Microsoft Outlook 10.0 Object Library, and then click Select.

Note: You do not need to have version 10.0 of the Microsoft Outlook Object Library; this demonstration program will work fine with older versions.

Add the following code:

C#

```
private void Form1_Load(object sender, System.EventArgs e)
{
        ListViewItem liEmail;
        Outlook.Application  App;
```

```
        Outlook.MailItem Msg;
        Outlook.NameSpace NS;
        Outlook.MAPIFolder Inbox;
        Outlook.Items Items;
        int I;

        App = new Outlook.Application();
        NS= App.GetNamespace("mapi");
        Inbox = NS.GetDefaultFolder
        (Outlook.OlDefaultFolders.olFolderInbox);
        Items = Inbox.Items;
        for (I=1;I<Items.Count;I++)
        {
            Msg = (Outlook.MailItem)Items.Item(I);
            liEmail = lvOutlook.Items.Add(Msg.SenderName);
            liEmail.SubItems.Add(Msg.Subject);
        }
    }
```

VB.NET

```
Private Sub Form1_Load(ByVal sender As System.Object, _
ByVal e As System.EventArgs) Handles MyBase.Load

        Dim liEmail As ListViewItem
        Dim App As Outlook.Application
        Dim Msg As Outlook.MailItem
        Dim NS As Outlook.NameSpace
        Dim Inbox As Outlook.MAPIFolder
        Dim Items As Outlook.Items
        Dim i As Integer

        App = New Outlook.Application()
        NS= App.GetNamespace("mapi")
        Inbox = NS.GetDefaultFolder _
        (Outlook.OlDefaultFolders.olFolderInbox)
        Items = Inbox.Items
        For i = 1 To Items.Count
            Msg = Items.Item(i)
            liEmail = lvOutlook.Items.Add(Msg.SenderName)
            liEmail.SubItems.Add(Msg.Subject)
        Next
    End Sub
```

The procedure for receiving emails from outlook via MAPI is relatively straightforward; however, the MAPI interface is huge and offers an extremely flexible means of leveraging Outlook's functionality. In the above example, a new instance of Outlook Express is created, and a handle to MAPI is obtained using the `GetNamespace()` method. The inbox folder is then picked up and its contents examined by iterating through its `Items` collection. Here, only two pieces of information are extracted from each email: the name of the sender and the message subject (Figure 5.6).

This application may take a few seconds to start because Microsoft Outlook must start when the `Outlook.Application()` object is created.

It is good programming practice to set these types of objects to `nothing` or `null` after use to prevent hidden instances of Outlook hogging system resources.

You will note in the above example that some sender names are fully qualified email addresses, whereas some are aliases. To specify email addresses only, the following command should be used in preference to the `SenderName` property:

```
Msg.Recipients(1).Address
```

Figure 5.6
*MAPI client
application.*

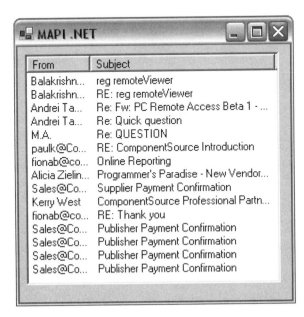

5.6.1 **Accessing the address book**

MAPI can be used to access most features of Microsoft Outlook, some of which may be useful for developers working on plug-in applications for Outlook.

The address book can be accessed via the `AddressLists` collection in the MAPI namespace (`NS` in the example above). Each element in the collection contains an `AddressEntries` collection. Each entry in the latter collection contains a `Name` and `Address` property that can be used to extract email addresses and proper names from the Outlook address book.

To create an application that reads the Outlook address book, reopen the example shown above and alter the column headers to read `Alias` and `email address`. Now click on the form and enter the following code:

C#

```
private void Form1_Load(object sender, System.EventArgs e)
{
ListViewItem liEmail;
Outlook.Application  App;
Outlook.NameSpace NS;

App = new Outlook.Application();
NS= App.GetNamespace("mapi");
int ListsIndexer;
int EntriesIndexer;
Outlook.AddressList CurrentList;
Outlook.AddressEntry CurrentEntry;

for(ListsIndexer = 1;
ListsIndexer<=NS.AddressLists.Count;ListsIndexer++)
{
 CurrentList = NS.AddressLists.Item(ListsIndexer);
 for(EntriesIndexer=1;
     EntriesIndexer<=CurrentList.AddressEntries.Count;
     EntriesIndexer++)
 {
 CurrentEntry =
 CurrentList.AddressEntries.Item(EntriesIndexer);
 liEmail = lvOutlook.Items.Add(CurrentEntry.Name);
 liEmail.SubItems.Add(CurrentEntry.Address);
 }
```

```
    }
    }
```

VB.NET

```
Private Sub Form1_Load(ByVal sender As System.Object, _
 ByVal e As System.EventArgs) Handles MyBase.Load
 Dim liEmail As ListViewItem
 lvOutlook.View = View.Details

 Dim App As Outlook.Application = New Outlook.Application()
 Dim NS As Outlook.NameSpace = App.GetNamespace("mapi")
 Dim ListsIndexer As Integer
 Dim EntriesIndexer As Integer
 Dim CurrentList As Outlook.AddressList
 Dim CurrentEntry As Outlook.AddressEntry

 For ListsIndexer = 1 To NS.AddressLists.Count
  CurrentList = NS.AddressLists.Item(ListsIndexer)
  For EntriesIndexer = 1 To CurrentList.AddressEntries.Count
   CurrentEntry = _
CurrentList.AddressEntries.Item(EntriesIndexer)
   liEmail = lvOutlook.Items.Add(CurrentEntry.Name)
   liEmail.SubItems.Add(CurrentEntry.Address)
  Next
 Next
End Sub
```

To test this code, first check that there are entries in the Outlook address book by pressing Tools→Address Book in Outlook. If there are no entries, add one by pressing the New→New Contact button. Now run the above application from Visual Studio .NET, and the contact's name and email address will appear as shown in Figure 5.7.

Figure 5.7
*MAPI address book
application.*

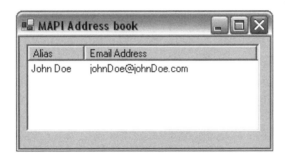

5.6.2 IMAP

The Internet message access protocol (IMAP) runs over port 143 and is described definitively in RFC 1730.

Although SMTP and POP3 are the de facto standards for email communication on the Internet, they are both very simple protocols, and some contenders exist for their place on people's desktops. IMAP is a competing technology for POP3. IMAP is much more richly featured than POP3, but for some reason it is less popular.

Messages stored in an IMAP server can be marked as being answered, flagged, deleted, seen, draft, or recent (fetch only). In POP3, a message is either stored or not deleted. These flags help manage an IMAP account over multiple clients. If a single POP3 account is accessed by numerous clients, it is difficult to keep track of who has seen or sent what.

The protocol itself is line-based, similar to the POP3 protocol. It uses a more complicated, but flexible syntax. Following is an overview of the protocol. It is recommended that you review RFC 1730 for a definitive guide to IMAP.

To access a mailbox, the client must authenticate itself with a username and password. The client sends `login <username> <password>`, to which the server replies with `OK LOGIN completed`, assuming the username and password are correct.

To get summary information about the mailbox, the command `select inbox` is issued. To this the server replies `* <number of messages> EXISTS`.

To read back an email, the client sends the `fetch <number> full` command; `number` must be between 1 and the number received in response to the `select inbox` command. The server responds with the message body in RFC 822 format, followed by an end-of-message marker, `OK FETCH completed`.

To delete emails, the client sends the `store <number> +flags \deleted` command. The server responds with `OK +FLAGS completed`.

To illustrate the protocol more simply, the following text shows the chain of events that occurs between an IMAP server and client. As before, "S" indicates a transmission from server to client, and "C" indicates a client-to-server transaction. Here, user Marc is checking his emails, when he receives 18 new messages. One of these emails is from Terry Gray, which he deletes after reading the subject line.

```
S:    * OK IMAP4 Service Ready
C:    a001 login marc secret
S:    a001 OK LOGIN completed
C:    a002 select inbox
S:    * 18 EXISTS
S:    * FLAGS (\Answered \Flagged \Deleted \Seen
      \Draft)
S:    * 2 RECENT
S:    * OK [UNSEEN 17] Message 17 is the first
      unseen message
S:    * OK [UIDVALIDITY 3857529045] UIDs valid
S:    a002 OK [READ-WRITE] SELECT completed
C:    a004 fetch 12 rfc822.header
S:    * 12 FETCH (RFC822.HEADER {346}
S:    Date: Wed, 14 Jul 1993 02:23:25 -0700 (PDT)
S:    From: Terry Gray <gray@cac.washington.edu>
S:    Subject: IMAP4 WG mtg summary and minutes
S:    To: imap@cac.washington.edu
S:    cc: minutes@CNRI.Reston.VA.US, John Klensin
      <KLENSIN@INFOODS.MIT.EDU>
S:    Message-Id: <B27397-
      0100000@cac.washington.edu>
S:    MIME-Version: 1.0
S:    Content-Type: TEXT/PLAIN; CHARSET=US-ASCII
S:    )
S:    a004 OK FETCH completed
C:    a005 store 12 +flags \deleted
S:    * 12 FETCH (FLAGS (\Seen \Deleted))
S:    a005 OK +FLAGS completed
C:    a006 logout
S:    * BYE IMAP4 server terminating connection
S:    a006 OK LOGOUT completed
```

Because of its low prevalence in everyday computing, a full implementation of IMAP is not included here.

5.6.3   Network news transfer protocol

The network news transfer protocol (NNTP) runs over port 119 and is described definitively in RFC 977.

This protocol is used for efficient management of mailing lists and is gradually becoming obsolete and being replaced by email-based systems. It is based on the idea that many users can send and receive undirected email, which is sorted into subjects of interest.

Two basic tasks can be performed with NNTP: reading postings and creating new postings. To read posts from a newsgroup, a client connects to the news server and retrieves a list of newsgroups by using the LIST command. To select a group, the client issues the GROUP command followed by the group name. The server response to this command includes the number of messages stored for that group. To download one of these messages, the client sends the STAT command, followed by the message number. To view the downloaded message, the client can use either the HEAD or BODY command.

To better explain the procedure, in this example a client wishes to view message number 10,110 in a group named net.unix-wizards. As before, "S" indicates a transmission from server to client, and "C" indicates a client-to-server transaction:

```
S:      200 wombatvax news server ready - posting ok
C:      LIST
S:      215 list of newsgroups follows
S:      net.wombats 00543 00501 y
S:      net.unix-wizards 10125 10011 y
        (more information here)
S:      net.idiots 00100 00001 n
S:      .
C:      GROUP net.unix-wizards
S:      211 104 10011 10125 net.unix-wizards group
        Selected (there are 104 articles on file,
        from 10011 to 10125)
C:      STAT 10110
S:      223 10110 <23445@sdcsvax.ARPA> article
        retrieved - statistics only (article 10110
        selected, its message-id is
        <23445@sdcsvax.ARPA>)
C:      BODY
S:      222 10110 <23445@sdcsvax.ARPA> article
        retrieved – body follows (body text here)
S:      .
```

The second operation that can be performed through NNTP is posting to newsgroups. Not all newsgroups allow this function, but for those that do, this is the procedure. Here the user is posting a message to a server named BANZAIVAX:

```
S:      200 BANZAIVAX news server ready, posting
        allowed.
C:      POST
S:      340 Continue posting; Period on a line by
        itself to end
C:      (transmits news article in RFC850 format)
C:      .
S:      240 Article posted successfully.
C:      QUIT
S:      205 BANZAIVAX closing connection.  Goodbye.
```

5.7   Conclusion

This chapter has explained how to send and receive emails from your .NET application, either from high-level code or socket-level operations. This chapter outlined the key facets of SMTP and POP3, in summary:

■ SMTP is used to send emails from client to server.

■ POP3 is used to receive emails from server to client.

■ POP3 can be used to delete emails from the server once received.

Chapter 12 deals with the issue of determining mail exchange servers from domain names. This helps improve the performance of email-driven applications.

The next chapter deals with the file transfer protocol (FTP). This is the de facto standard for transferring files over the Internet and is well worth knowing about.

6

FTP: Communicating with File Servers

6.1   Background

Anybody with experience in Web design knows that in order to put the site "live," the Web page files need to be sent to a Web server provided by your hosting company or ISP. Most people never get to see the physical machine that their Web site is hosted on, and their only contact with it is through a file transfer protocol, or FTP, program such as cuteFTP or smartFTP.

FTP is the most common cross-platform file transfer mechanism between computers over the Internet. FTP software is freely available for all major operating systems, including Windows, UNIX, and Mac OS X. This cross-platform interoperability is very important for Web site development because most Web designers work on Windows and most Web servers run from UNIX, Linux, and Netware OS.

FTP as defined in RFC 1350 supersedes an older protocol known as trivial file transfer protocol (TFTP). This system is very seldom used on the Internet, but it can be used for procedures such as diskless booting on a network. It has no authentication facilities.

6.2   Microsoft file sharing

A competing technology developed by Microsoft is the Common Internet File (CIF) system. This is the native file-sharing protocol of Windows 2000 and XP. It is an extension of the earlier server message block (SMB) protocol used in prior versions of Windows. It is used to provide for the network drive functionality and print sharing. It is more secure than FTP, because of NTLM encryption, and generally faster; however, non-Windows implementations are not commonplace, but do exist for VMS and

UNIX. The protocol is largely proprietary, which is often a deterrent to non-Microsoft developers.

Windows file sharing is most commonplace within office networks, where many employees share a printer or a central repository for files. From a programmer's perspective, it is an ideal technology to use as a once-off solution at a company where all of the system users would be on the same internal network. If, for instance, an architecture firm were looking for a central repository for drawings, network share would be ideal because it requires no programming. The equivalent system using FTP would be slower, more awkward, and less secure; however, if the same firm wanted to share drawings with other firms, then FTP would be more suitable because of its interoperability and ease of deployment on Internet (rather than intranet) environments.

The terms *NETBIOS* and *NETBEUI* are the more correct names for Microsoft file and print sharing. A flavor of NETBIOS, NBT runs over IP, but all other forms are not based on IP addresses; they use NETBIOS hostnames. These hostnames are resolved into physical addresses in one of four ways. They can broadcast the request on the network (B-Node). Alternately, they may query a WINS server (P-Node). Using a combination of these methods, by broadcasting before querying, is M-Node operation, and the reverse is H-Node operation.

6.3   Netware file sharing

This is somewhat of a dinosaur of file-transfer mechanisms, but it regularly appears in networks that have been in place for decades. It is, however, one of the fastest file transfer protocols over internal networks. It is built on top of the Internetworking packet exchange / Sequenced Packet Exchange (IPX/SPX) protocols and is thus nonroutable. Translators are available to convert these packets to TCP/IP, but the performance factor is lost.

The Netware system (also referred to as *IntranetWare*) is centered on a central Netware server. This server runs the Novell operating system, which is started from a bootstrap DOS application. The server hosts the Netware directory service (NDS), which is used to control authentication and privileges. Older Novell servers (3.x) use a bindery instead of NDS. The difference between the two systems is that the NDS is a relational database and can replicate among other servers, whereas the bindery cannot.

Novell clients are available for almost any platform, from DOS and Windows to Macintosh and UNIX. The clients locate the server by using the Novell core protocol (NCP). When a remote file server is found, it is mapped to a local drive on the client's machine.

There is no native support for interoperating with Netware in .NET, and it is no small undertaking to integrate a .NET application with a Novell network. If you have to do so, look at the DOS command-line interfaces to the network, or failing that, try interfacing at the IPX level using raw sockets.

6.4   An overview of FTP

FTP operates on two ports: 21, the control socket, and a data socket, which can exist on port 20 or some other, high port. The definitive description of the protocol is found in RFC 959 at *www.ietf.org/rfc/rfc959.txt.*

Like the email protocols, the commands that flow between client and server are quite human readable and are broken up into lines, like English text; however, it is not feasible to upload or download files using FTP through telnet. If, however, you require a simple batch program to perform a routine upload of files to an FTP server, it may save time to look at the FTP.exe utility.

The FTP utility is a DOS-based program with a command-line interface. It can, however, accept script files with the —s command-line parameter, such that it can run autonomously. To try this utility, create a file named `script.ftp` containing the following text:

```
open www.eej.ulst.ac.uk
anonymous
me@myemail.com
cd lib
get libtermcap.so.2.0.8
quit
```

This FTP script file will open a connection to a server named *www.eej.ulst.ac.uk.* Log in anonymously, navigate to the `lib` folder, and download a file named `libtermcap.so.2.0.8`, and then exit. The downloaded file will be stored in the current local directory.

To run the script as shown in Figure 6.1, go to the command prompt, navigate to the location where `script.ftp` was saved, and then type the following keywords:

```
ftp —s:script.ftp
```

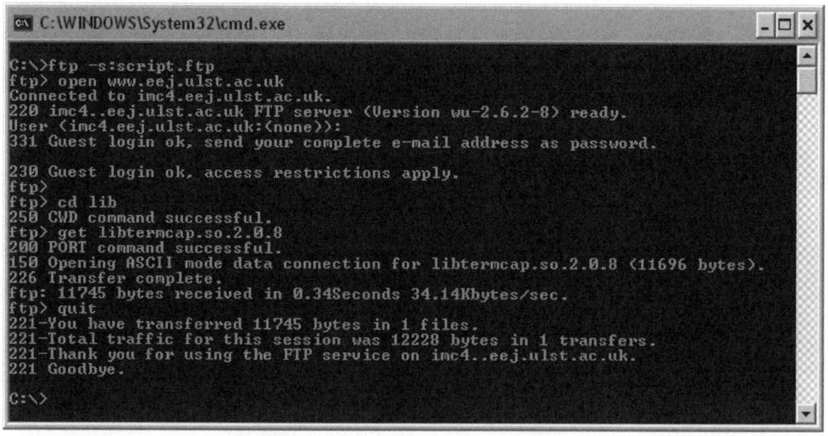

Figure 6.1
FTP MS-DOS
utility.

```
C:\WINDOWS\System32\cmd.exe                                          _ □ ×

C:\>ftp -s:script.ftp
ftp> open www.eej.ulst.ac.uk
Connected to imc4.eej.ulst.ac.uk.
220 imc4..eej.ulst.ac.uk FTP server (Version wu-2.6.2-8) ready.
User (imc4.eej.ulst.ac.uk:(none)):
331 Guest login ok, send your complete e-mail address as password.

230 Guest login ok, access restrictions apply.
ftp>
ftp> cd lib
250 CWD command successful.
ftp> get libtermcap.so.2.0.8
200 PORT command successful.
150 Opening ASCII mode data connection for libtermcap.so.2.0.8 (11696 bytes).
226 Transfer complete.
ftp: 11745 bytes received in 0.34Seconds 34.14Kbytes/sec.
ftp> quit
221-You have transferred 11745 bytes in 1 files.
221-Total traffic for this session was 12228 bytes in 1 transfers.
221-Thank you for using the FTP service on imc4..eej.ulst.ac.uk.
221 Goodbye.

C:\>
```

The technique of using the FTP utility is not the best-practice means of transferring files, but it is a simple and straightforward way to perform routine uploads when aesthetics and performance are not important. To leverage FTP from within a .NET application properly, it is necessary to be well-acquainted with the FTP protocol at a socket level, which is not all that dissimilar to learning to use the FTP utility command-line interface.

The FTP protocol facilitates more than uploading and downloading: It must also be able to accommodate all manner of file-manipulation tasks. This includes deleting, renaming, and navigating through folders. You cannot, however, edit the contents of files using FTP, unless you replace them completely.

Commands issued from client to server take the form

```
<keyword> <parameter> <enter>
```

Commands from server to client take the form:

```
<status code> <human and/or computer readable message>
<enter>
```

Table 6.1 lists the main groups for status codes.

When you open an FTP connection to a server using an FTP client, you sometimes will be shown the raw data being sent to and from the server on the command socket. The text may resemble the following:

Table 6.1   *FTP status codes.*

Status code range	Meaning
1xx	Positive preliminary reply. The command has begun on the server.
2xx	Positive completion reply. The command has been completed successfully.
3xx	Positive intermediate reply. The command has been accepted, but no action has been taken.
4xx	Transient negative completion reply. The command has been denied, but can be reissued later.
5xx	Permanent negative completion reply. The command has been denied and should not be reissued.

```
220 Serv-U FTP-Server v2.5k for WinSock ready...
    USER secret
331 User name okay, need password.
    PASS (hidden)
230 User logged in, proceed.
    PWD
257 "/" is current directory.
    TYPE A
200 Type set to A.
    PASV
227 Entering Passive Mode (212,17,38,3,11,144)
    LIST -aL
150 Opening ASCII mode data connection for /bin/ls.
226 Transfer complete.
```

This is a dump of the traffic on the command port. The data port is not shown.

6.4.1   How FTP uses ports

In the email protocols, sections of data of variable length (i.e., emails) could be suffixed with <enter>.<enter> to mark the end of the data. If this character sequence is detected within the body of the email, it could be removed before sending without any real degradation of the legibility of the email; however, in FTP, an executable file could quite easily have this sequence of characters embedded within it, and the removal of those characters could cause the file to corrupt.

To avoid this problem, port 21 is used to send and receive commands and responses, each terminated by an <enter>. When variable length data is sent between client and server, such as files or directory listings, a temporary connection is opened on port 20, the data is transferred, and the port is closed again. In most real-world FTP client implementations, however, the FTP client may be behind a firewall, so the server should do all the serving and the client should do all the requesting.

Passive-mode FTP is where the client instructs the server to listen on a port other than the default data port. The client will then connect to this port and use it for uploading and downloading as usual.

The response to the PASV command will always include a bracketed list of six numbers separated by commas. The first four digit groups represent the IP address of the server, and the final two groups represent the port the server is listening on for its data connection.

In the previous example, the four digits are 212,17,38,3,11,144. This means that the server is located at IP address 212.17.38.3 and listening on port 2960 (11 × 256 + 144).

The server will begin listening on the port as soon as it receives the PASV command. It will return a 227 message to indicate that it has begun listening on this port. Once the client connects to this port, the server will return a 150 message. If the client does not connect to the port in a timely fashion (a few seconds), the server will issue a 425 timeout message. The server will send the requested data on that port and close the connection once all of the data is sent, and then issue a 226 message.

The same process happens in reverse when uploading to the server. In this case, the PASV command is issued, and the client connects to the port specified by the server. The client then places the contents of the file on the new socket and closes the connection once the file is sent.

6.4.2   The FTP handshake

In the same way, FTP uses a basic authentication mechanism: It accepts a username and password in plain text, which can be seen by anyone using a protocol analyzer at any point between the client and the server. FTP over SSL is recommended when a Web site carries information of substantial value.

An FTP server may allow anonymous access. This is where the username is set to anonymous and the password can be anything. This is the default setup of the Microsoft FTP service.

When you connect to an FTP server on port 21, the server will respond as follows:

```
220 <some message><enter>
```

Using the same format as the POP3 handshake, the next commands to send are USER and PASS (in that order). The USER command is of this format:

```
USER <username><enter>
```

The server will generally respond with 331 and request a password, whether there is any record of that user on the system or not. This is to make brute-force attacks more difficult.

```
331 <some message><enter>
```

The PASS command must then be sent:

```
PASS <password><enter>
```

The server will either respond with a 530 message for a failed login or 230 for a successful login.

```
230 <some message><enter>
```

At this point, the user should have access to the FTP server. Depending on the privileges set on the FTP server, the user will be able to read or write operations within a limited section of the remote computer's disk drives.

Some FTP servers will disconnect inactive users to save resources. Therefore, a periodic NOOP command will keep the FTP server from closing the connection. A NOOP command has no effect on the server beyond this task.

```
NOOP<enter>
```

```
200 <message><enter>
```

To close the connection, the client may simply close the underlying TCP connection, or issue a QUIT command as follows:

```
QUIT<enter>
221 <message><enter>
```

6.4.3 Navigating folders

In order to navigate around a remote computer's file system, you need to know what files and subfolders are contained within each folder.

Like files, this data is returned on the data socket. The process for receiving folder listings is as follows:

- Client issues LIST command.

- Server waits for data socket to be created. A timeout will occur with a 425 response. Otherwise, a 125 response is received.

- Server transfers file data, as illustrated below.

- Server closes data connection and issues a 226 response on the control socket.

On the Windows FTP service, the default directory listing style is DOS. A listing would resemble the following:

```
01-18-03   03:22PM                    0 ge.bmp
01-18-03   11:40PM                  733 Project1.vbp
01-18-03   05:00PM                 2498 Readme.txt
01-18-03   03:40PM      <DIR>           wat
```

The five columns are last modified date, time, folder or file, size, and name, respectively.

For UNIX FTP servers, the directory listing style is in this format:

```
d---rw-rw-    1 user    group       0 Jan 18  2003 .
d---rw-rw-    1 user    group       0 Jan 18  2003 ..
----rw-rw-    1 user    group       0 Jan 18 15:22 ge.bmp
```

```
----rw-rw-   1 user   group      733 Jan 18 23:40 Project1.vbp
----rw-rw-   1 user   group     2498 Jan 18 17:00 Readme.txt
d---rw-rw-   1 user   group        0 Jan 18  2003 wat
```

> **Note:** The Cerberus FTP server for Windows (*www.cerberusftp.com*) will also return file data in a UNIX format. The directory listing style is interchangeable in IIS.

This is an unfortunate lack of standardization, but something that developers must be aware of. A quick-and-dirty approach is to read the last word at the end of each line and assume it to be a file if there is a period in it.

A more foolproof implementation is to issue a SYST command to the server and read the response, either 215 UNIX*<version><enter>* or 215 Windows*<version><enter>*. Alternately, the NLST command may be used to receive a list of files (only) from the server.

The folder system in FTP is navigated in much the same way as in DOS. To move to a subfolder, the client issues CWD */<folder name><enter>*, to which the server replies 250 for success or 550 for failure. To move to the parent folder, the client issues CDUP.

To retrieve the current folder, the client may issue PWD, to which the server replies:

```
257 "<folder name>"<message><enter>
```

6.4.4 FTP command reference

Following is a comprehensive list of FTP commands as would be issued by a client.

Table 6.2   *FTP commands .*

FTP Command	Action
RETR	Downloads
STOR	Uploads
STOU	Uploads, where the server chooses the name of the remote file; this name is specified in the 250 response

Table 6.2   *FTP commands (continued).*

FTP Command	Action
APPE	Appends
REST	Restarts file transfer at a specified position
RNFR	Renames a file (RNFR *<old name>*); must be followed by RNTO
RNTO	Renames a file (RNTO *<new name>*); must be preceded by RNFR
ABOR	Aborts the current data transfer
DELE	Deletes the specified file
RMD	Deletes the specified folder
MKD	Creates a new folder
PWD	Responds with the current working directory
LIST	Responds with the contents of the current working directory in human-readable format
NLST	Responds with a list of files in the current working directory
SITE	Provides proprietary FTP services
SYST	Responds with the name of the operating system (or the OS being emulated)
STAT	Responds with the status of a data transfer
HELP	Responds with human-readable text with information about the server
NOOP	No effect
USER	Specifies the username of the user
PASS	Specifies the password of the user
TYPE	Indicates the format of the data, either A for ASCII, E for EBCDIC, I for Binary, or L n to select a custom byte size (where *n* is the length of the byte)

6.4.5   Implementing FTP

To access an FTP server, you need to know its IP address and have a username and password with it. Most ISPs provide you with a small amount of Web space on their servers when you sign up, and you should be able to get these details if you call your ISP.

Figure 6.2
Windows: Add or
remove components
for IIS.

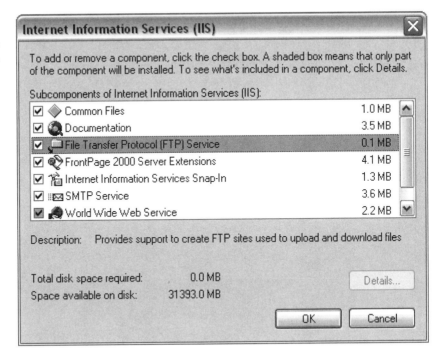

Some versions of Windows come with an option to install an FTP server. Click Control Panel→Add/Remove Programs→Add or Remove Windows Components→Internet Information Services→Details→FTP Service (Figure 6.2).

To administer the FTP server once it is installed, click Control Panel→Administrative Tools→Internet Information Services→FTP Site→Default FTP site. Then right-click and go to Properties.

Click on the Home Directory tab (Figure 6.3). This is where you can set the FTP site directory path, which is where uploaded FTP files are stored on your local hard disk. For the purposes of the code examples in this chapter, you should check both the read and write options.

To test out your FTP server, type *ftp://localhost* into Internet Explorer. You can download various FTP clients from the Internet (e.g., smartFTP, *www.smartftp.com*, or cuteFTP, *www.globalscape.com*).

Figure 6.3
*FTP site
administration.*

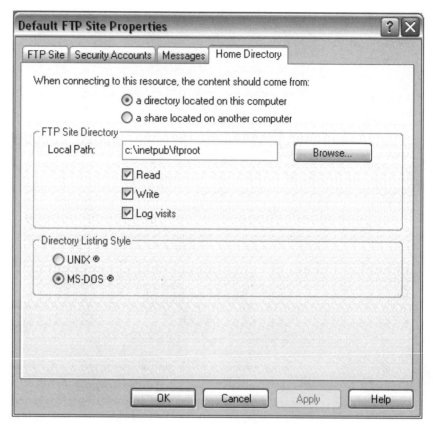

6.4.6 Implementing FTP with the Internet Transfer Control

A full implementation of FTP is quite an undertaking. It may be worthwhile to consider the Microsoft Internet Transfer Control if you need to perform this task. It is a legacy COM control (and thus carries a lot of overhead for .NET applications). Native .NET components are available commercially from Dart and IP*Works.

Having said that, for many applications you don't need an all-singing, all-dancing implementation of FTP to get your job done. If you are writing a feature to an application to perform a scheduled upload of files to a server, you probably don't want to confuse the user with details of the remote computer's directory structure. All you may need is a few lines of code to transfer the file to a predetermined location.

Create a new Windows application project in Visual Studio .NET as usual, and draw two textboxes, one named tbServer and the other tbFile.

Add two buttons, btnBrowse and btnUpload. You will also require an Open File Dialog control named openFileDialog.

Click on the Browse button, and add the following code:

C#

```csharp
private void btnBrowse_Click(object sender, System.EventArgs
e)
{
  openfileDialog.ShowDialog();
  tbFile.Text = openfileDialog.FileName;
}
```

VB.NET

```vbnet
Private  Sub btnBrowse_Click(ByVal sender As Object, _
 ByVal e As System.EventArgs) Handles btnBrowse.Click
  openfileDialog.ShowDialog()
  tbFile.Text = openfileDialog.FileName
End Sub
```

Now, double-click on the Upload button, and add this code:

C#

```csharp
private void btnUpload_Click(object sender, System.EventArgs
e)
{
  FileInfo thisFile = new FileInfo(tbFile.Text);
  Type ITC;
  object[] parameter= new object[2];
  object ITCObject;

  ITC = Type.GetTypeFromProgID("InetCtls.Inet");
  ITCObject = Activator.CreateInstance(ITC);
  parameter[0] = (string)tbServer.Text;
  parameter[1] = (string)"PUT " + thisFile.FullName + " /" +
                   thisFile.Name;
  ITC.InvokeMember("execute", BindingFlags.InvokeMethod,
                   null, ITCObject, parameter);
}
```

VB.NET

```
Private Sub btnUpload_Click(ByVal sender As Object, _
  ByVal e As System.EventArgs) Handles btnUpload.Click
    Dim thisFile As FileInfo = New FileInfo(tbFile.Text)
      Dim ITC As Type
      Dim parameter() As Object = New Object(1) {}
      Dim ITCObject As Object

      ITC = Type.GetTypeFromProgID("InetCtls.Inet")
      ITCObject = Activator.CreateInstance(ITC)

      parameter(0) = CType(tbServer.Text, String)
      parameter(1) = CType("PUT " + thisFile.FullName + _
        " /" + thisFile.Name, String)
      ITC.InvokeMember("execute", BindingFlags.InvokeMethod, _
        Nothing, ITCObject, parameter)
    End Sub
```

As mentioned earlier, the Internet Transfer Control (ITC) is a legacy COM control rather than a native .NET control. In Chapter 1, the Internet Explorer component (which was also COM) was used as part of an application to form a custom Web browser. This time, instead of including the COM control in the project by right-clicking on the toolbox and adding it there, we call the COM control directly through code.

This is slightly more complex, but offers the advantage of late binding (i.e., the object is loaded at run time rather than compile time). This gives the benefit of fault tolerance; in case the external COM control is accidentally deleted, the host application will still operate, albeit with degraded functionality. Late binding does incur a performance penalty because the code will need to determine the object's supported methods and types at run time by interrogating the object's IDispatch interface. The environment would already know the object's interface if it had been early bound. Late binding is not strictly required for use with the ITC, but it is useful to learn new techniques.

Every COM control has a unique programmatic ID, or ProgID. This string is stored in the registry and is in the format *<project name>.<Class name>.<version>*. In this instance, the programmatic ID is InetCtls.Inet, with no version number.

The Activator creates an instance of the class at run time. At design time, there is no way of knowing the methods and properties of the object;

therefore, the return value is of the generic `object` type. In order to call methods on an object that has unknown type (at design time at least), we use the `InvokeMember` method.

In order to invoke the `execute` method on the object and pass two parameters to it, we need first to define the two parameters. The first is the FTP address to which the object will connect. The second is the FTP command that the object will execute on the server. These two parameters are cast to strings and stored in an array. Finally, the `InvokeMember` method is called, passing the method name as the first parameter and the parameters to be sent to the COM control as the last parameter.

You will also need the relevant namespaces:

C#

```
using System.IO;
using System.Reflection;
using System.Threading;
```

VB.NET

```
Imports System.IO
Imports System.Reflection
Imports System.Threading
```

To test this piece of code, first ensure that your FTP server is running. After you have checked this, run the application from Visual Studio .NET. Type the IP address, username, and password into the Server textbox in the standard URL format (i.e., *ftp://username:password@myserver.com*). Choose a file from your hard disk by pressing the Browse button, then press Upload (Figure 6.4). Now check your FTP root to ensure that the file is there.

Figure 6.4
FTP client using COM.

Table 6.3 *FTP command usage.*

FTP command	Action
DIR /*anyFolder*	Retrieves the directory listing tree from the specified folder at the remote machine; listing can be retrieved using the GetChunk method
CD *anyFolder*	Moves to the specified folder on the remote machine
CDUP	Moves to the parent folder (if one exists) on the remote machine
GET *anyFolder/anyFile.txt* c:\ *anyFile.txt*	Downloads a remote file to a local file
PUT c:*anyFile.txt anyFolder*/ *anyFile.txt*	Uploads a local file to a remote file
MKDIR /*anyFolderName*	Creates a directory on the remote machine
RMDIR *anyFolderName*	Removes a directory from the remote machine
RENAME *oldFileName.txt newFileName.txt*	Changes the name of a file on the remote machine
SIZE /*anyFile.txt*	Retrieves the size of a specified file
QUIT	Closes the connection to the FTP server

There is an important limitation in the ITC; that is that the file must be in the old DOS 8.3 format, where c:\program files\myile.txt becomes c:\progra~1\myfile.txt. Please note that you must have write access to the root of the FTP server; otherwise, the code example will not work.

The second parameter passed to the execute method of the ITC determines the action to be performed on the remote FTP server. Table 6.3 lists the possible actions.

6.4.7 A more substantial implementation of FTP

The ITC has several limitations, contains quite a few well-known bugs, and is far from being a high-performance implementation. Furthermore, it is not native to .NET, and many software houses will demand that a .NET project is 100% managed code.

By following the code on the next few pages, you will have a full-fledged FTP client, with the ability to browse a remote file system, upload, and download.

Start a new project in Visual Studio .NET and add two forms, `frmLogon` and `frmMain`. On the Logon form, draw four textboxes: `tbServer`, `tbUsername`, `tbPassword`, and `tbStatus`. The latter should be set with `multiline=true` and greyed out appropriately. A button, `btnLogon`, should also be added.

On the Main form, draw two list boxes: `lbFiles` and `lbFolders`. Add a textbox named `tbStatus` in the same style as in the Logon form. Add three buttons: `btnUpload`, `btnDownload`, and `btnRoot`. Also add an File Open Dialog control named `OpenFileDialog` and a Save File Dialog control named `SaveFileDialog`.

In the Main form, add a few public variables:

C#

```
public frmLogon LogonForm = new frmLogon();
public NetworkStream NetStrm;
public string RemotePath = "";
public string server = "";
```

VB.NET

```
Public LogonForm As frmLogon = New frmLogon()
Public NetStrm As NetworkStream
Public RemotePath As String = ""
Public server As String = ""
```

In the Logon form, add the following public variable:

C#

```
public frmMain MainForm;
```

VB.NET

```
Public MainForm as frmMain
```

The call to new `frmLogon()` does not make the Logon form visible; instead, it is used to help ensure that only one instance of the Logon form occurs. The `NetworkStream` variable is used to represent the command socket connection. The data connection is less permanent and does not need to be defined globally. The two strings maintain information about where the server is and what the working folder is on the server.

Double-click on the Main form and add these lines:

C#

```csharp
private void frmMain_Load(object sender, System.EventArgs e)
{
  LogonForm.MainForm = this;
  LogonForm.Visible = true;
}
```

VB.NET

```vbnet
Private  Sub frmMain_Load(ByVal sender As Object, _
ByVal e As System.EventArgs)
  LogonForm.MainForm = Me
  LogonForm.Visible = True
End Sub
```

This shows the Logon form and provides a means for the Logon form to call public methods on this particular instance of the Main form.

On the Logon from, comment out the Dispose method to ensure that it cannot be deleted from memory unless the Main form is closed. You may need to expand the "Windows Form Designer generated code" region to view this method.

C#

```csharp
protected override void Dispose( bool disposing )
{ }
```

VB.NET

```vbnet
Protected Overrides  Sub Dispose(ByVal disposing As Boolean)
End Sub
```

On the logon form, click on the Logon button, and enter the following code:

C#

```csharp
private void btnLogon_Click(object sender, System.EventArgs
e)
```

```
{
  TcpClient clientSocket = new TcpClient(tbServer.Text,21);

  MainForm.NetStrm = clientSocket.GetStream();
  StreamReader RdStrm= new StreamReader(MainForm.NetStrm);
  tbStatus.Text = RdStrm.ReadLine();

  tbStatus.Text = MainForm.sendFTPcmd("USER "+
  tbUsername.Text + "\r\n");
  tbStatus.Text = MainForm.sendFTPcmd("PASS "+
  tbPassword.Text+ "\r\n");

  if (tbStatus.Text.Substring(0,3)!="230")
  {
    MessageBox.Show ("Failed to log in");
  }
  else
  {
    MainForm.server = tbServer.Text;
    MainForm.getRemoteFolders();
    MainForm.Text += "[logged in]";
    Visible=false;
  }
}
```

VB.NET

```
Private  Sub btnLogon_Click(ByVal sender As Object, _
ByVal e As System.EventArgs)  Handles btnLogon.Click
  Dim clientSocket As TcpClient =  New _
  TcpClient(tbServer.Text,21)
  MainForm.NetStrm = clientSocket.GetStream()
  Dim RdStrm As StreamReader =  New _
  StreamReader(MainForm.NetStrm)
  tbStatus.Text = RdStrm.ReadLine()

  tbStatus.Text = MainForm.sendFTPcmd("USER "+ _
  tbUsername.Text + vbcrlf)
  tbStatus.Text = MainForm.sendFTPcmd("PASS "+ _
  tbPassword.Text+ vbcrlf)
  If tbStatus.Text.Substring(0,3)<>"230" Then
    MessageBox.Show ("Failed to log in")
```

```
     Else
        MainForm.server = tbServer.Text
        MainForm.getRemoteFolders()
        MainForm.Text += "[logged in]"
        Visible=False
     End If
  End Sub
```

This code opens a TCP connection to the FTP server on port 21. Once
the connection has been made, a stream to the remote host is established.
This stream is then extended through a StreamReader. The welcome message from the server is read in and displayed on-screen.

The program then attempts to log in using the username and password
supplied. If the FTP server responds with a 230 message, then a message
box is displayed. Otherwise, the getRemoteFolders() method is called on
the main form, a "Logged in" message appears in the form caption, and the
logon form disappears.

The function sendFTPcmd() has not yet been implemented, so insert
this code into the Main form:

C#

```csharp
public string sendFTPcmd(string cmd)
{
   byte[] szData;
   string returnedData = "";
   StreamReader RdStrm= new StreamReader(NetStrm);
   szData = Encoding.ASCII.GetBytes(cmd.ToCharArray());
   NetStrm.Write(szData,0,szData.Length);
   tbStatus.Text += "\r\nSent:" + cmd;
   returnedData = RdStrm.ReadLine();
   tbStatus.Text += "\r\nRcvd:" + returnedData;
   return returnedData;
}
```

VB.NET

```vbnet
Public Function sendFTPcmd(ByVal cmd As String) As String
   Dim szData() As Byte
   Dim ReturnedData As String =   ""
   Dim RdStrm As StreamReader =  New StreamReader(NetStrm)
   szData = Encoding.ASCII.GetBytes(cmd.ToCharArray())
```

```
    NetStrm.Write(szData,0,szData.Length)
    tbStatus.Text += vbcrlf +"Sent:" + cmd
    ReturnedData = RdStrm.ReadLine()
    tbStatus.Text += vbcrlf +"Rcvd:" + ReturnedData
    Return ReturnedData
End Function
```

This code sends a string on the command socket via the public `NetworkStream NetStrm`. This stream is passed to the constructor of a `StreamReader` to facilitate easier reading of the stream. The string passed into the function is converted to a character array and sent over the wire using the `Write` method. The outgoing command is printed on screen. The `StreamReader` reads incoming data up to the end-of-line character and then displays this on-screen. Finally, the data received is returned to the calling function.

As seen earlier, when the Logon button is pressed, a call is made to `getRemoteFolders()`. We can now implement this in the Main form:

C#

```csharp
public void getRemoteFolders()
{
  string[] filesAndFolders;
  string fileOrFolder;
  string folderList="";
  int lastSpace=0;
  folderList =
  Encoding.ASCII.GetString(sendPassiveFTPcmd("LIST\r\n"));
  lbFiles.Items.Clear();
  lbFolders.Items.Clear();
  filesAndFolders = folderList.Split("\n".ToCharArray());
  for(int i=0;i<filesAndFolders.GetUpperBound(0);i++)
  {
    if (filesAndFolders[i].StartsWith("-") ||
    filesAndFolders[i].StartsWith("d"))
    {
      lastSpace=59; // UNIX format
    }
    else
    {
      lastSpace=39; // DOS format
    }
```

```
      fileOrFolder =  filesAndFolders[i].Substring(lastSpace);
      if (fileOrFolder.IndexOf(".")!=-1)
      {
        lbFiles.Items.Add(fileOrFolder.Trim());
      }
      else
      {
        lbFolders.Items.Add(fileOrFolder.Trim());
      }
   }
}
```

VB.NET

```
Public  Sub getRemoteFolders()
  Dim filesAndFolders() As String
  Dim fileOrFolder As String
  Dim folderList As String = ""
  Dim lastSpace As Integer = 0
  folderList = Encoding.ASCII.GetString(sendPassiveFTPcmd _
    ("LIST" + vbCrLf))
  lbFiles.Items.Clear()
  lbFolders.Items.Clear()
  filesAndFolders = folderList.Split(vbCr.ToCharArray())
  Dim i As Integer
  For i = 0 To filesAndFolders.GetUpperBound(0) - 1
    If filesAndFolders(i).StartsWith("-") Or _
    filesAndFolders(i).StartsWith("d") Then
      lastSpace = 59 ' UNIX format
    Else
      lastSpace = 39 ' DOS format
    End If
    fileOrFolder = filesAndFolders(i).Substring(lastSpace)
    If fileOrFolder.IndexOf(".") <> -1 Then
      lbFiles.Items.Add(fileOrFolder.Trim())
    Else
      lbFolders.Items.Add(fileOrFolder.Trim())
    End If
  Next
End Sub
```

This uses the quick-and-dirty method of pulling file and folder details out of the file data received from the FTP server. It issues the LIST FTP command via a passive connection. The passive connection is required because the data returned could potentially be quite large and contains many lines of information.

The data returned is then split into lines by delimiting the string by the end-of-line character and applying the split method. Going through these lines one by one, everything is stripped off that precedes the final space. If the remaining string contains a period, then it is added to the file list; if not, it is added to the folder list.

In order to receive data from a passive connection, we need to implement the sendPassiveFTPcmd() function:

C#

```
public byte[] sendPassiveFTPcmd(string cmd)
{
  byte[] szData;
  System.Collections.ArrayList al = new ArrayList();
  byte[] RecvBytes = new byte[Byte.MaxValue];
  Int32 bytes;
  Int32 totalLength=0;
  szData =
  System.Text.Encoding.ASCII.GetBytes(cmd.ToCharArray());
  NetworkStream passiveConnection;
  passiveConnection = createPassiveConnection();
  tbStatus.Text += "\r\nSent:" + cmd;
  StreamReader commandStream= new StreamReader(NetStrm);
  NetStrm.Write(szData,0,szData.Length);
  while(true)
  {
    bytes = passiveConnection.Read(RecvBytes,
    0,RecvBytes.Length);
    if (bytes<=0) break;
    totalLength += bytes;
    al.AddRange(RecvBytes);
  }
  al = al.GetRange(0,totalLength);
  tbStatus.Text+="\r\nRcvd:"+commandStream.ReadLine(); // 125
  tbStatus.Text+="\r\nRcvd:"+commandStream.ReadLine(); // 226
  return (byte[])al.ToArray((new byte()).GetType());
}
```

VB.NET

```
Public Function sendPassiveFTPcmd(ByVal cmd As String) _
As Byte()
  Dim szData() As Byte
  Dim al As New System.Collections.ArrayList
  Dim bytes As Int32
  Dim RecvBytes(Byte.MaxValue) As Byte
  szData = _
  System.Text.Encoding.ASCII.GetBytes(cmd.ToCharArray())
  Dim totalLength As Int32 = 0
  Dim passiveConnection As NetworkStream
  passiveConnection = createPassiveConnection()
  tbStatus.Text += vbCrLf + "Sent:" + cmd
  Dim commandStream As StreamReader = New _
  StreamReader(NetStrm)
  NetStrm.Write(szData, 0, szData.Length)
  Do While (True)
    bytes = passiveConnection.Read(RecvBytes, 0, _
    RecvBytes.Length)
    If bytes <= 0 Then Exit Do
    totalLength += bytes
    al.AddRange(RecvBytes)
  Loop
  al = al.GetRange(0, totalLength)
  tbStatus.Text += vbCrLf + "Rcvd:" + _
  commandStream.ReadLine() ' 125
  tbStatus.Text += vbCrLf + "Rcvd:" + _
  commandStream.ReadLine() ' 226
  Return CType(al.ToArray((New Byte).GetType()), Byte())
End Function
```

This code requests a passive connection to the server via the createPassiveConnection() function. It then sends the string on the command socket, and then reads everything sent on the passive connection until the server closes it. This data is then returned to the calling function. Any data sent back on the command socket is more or less ignored, apart from some on-screen reporting.

The next step is to implement the createPassiveConnection() function:

C#

```csharp
private NetworkStream createPassiveConnection()
{
  string[] commaSeperatedValues;
  int highByte =0;
  int lowByte =0;
  int passivePort =0;
  string response="";
  response = sendFTPcmd("PASV\r\n");
  // 227 Entering Passive Mode (127,0,0,1,4,147).
  commaSeperatedValues = response.Split(",".ToCharArray());
  highByte = Convert.ToInt16(commaSeperatedValues[4]) * 256;
  commaSeperatedValues[5] =
  commaSeperatedValues[5].Substring(0,
  commaSeperatedValues[5].IndexOf(")"));
  lowByte = Convert.ToInt16(commaSeperatedValues[5]);
  passivePort = lowByte + highByte;
  TcpClient clientSocket = new TcpClient(server,passivePort);
  NetworkStream pasvStrm = clientSocket.GetStream();
  return pasvStrm;
}
```

VB.NET

```vbnet
Private Function createPassiveConnection() As NetworkStream
  Dim commaSeperatedValues() As String
  Dim highByte As Integer = 0
  Dim lowByte As Integer = 0
  Dim passivePort As Integer = 0
  Dim response As String = ""
  response = sendFTPcmd("PASV"+vbCrLf)
  ' 227 Entering Passive Mode (127,0,0,1,4,147).
  commaSeperatedValues = response.Split(",".ToCharArray())
  highByte = Convert.ToInt16(commaSeperatedValues(4)) * 256
  commaSeperatedValues(5) = _
  commaSeperatedValues(5).Substring(0, _
  commaSeperatedValues(5).IndexOf(")"))
  lowByte = Convert.ToInt16(commaSeperatedValues(5))
  passivePort = lowByte + highByte
  Dim clientSocket As TcpClient= New _
  TcpClient(server,passivePort)
  Dim pasvStrm As NetworkStream=clientSocket.GetStream()
```

```
    Return pasvStrm
End Function
```

This function issues a PASV command on the command socket to the server. The received data should resemble the following:

```
227 Entering Passive Mode (127,0,0,1,4,147)
```

The final two numbers indicate the port number of the socket that the server has just begun to listen on. In this case, it is 1171 (4 × 256 + 147). To extract these numbers, the string is first split into smaller strings, which are divided up using the comma character in the Split method.

The low-order byte of the new port number is followed by a closed bracket. This bracket must be stripped off before it will convert to an integer. To do this, the IndexOf method locates the superfluous bracket, and Substring removes everything following the final digit.

Once the passive port has been determined, the function then opens a TCP connection to the server on this port. The resultant NertworkStream is sent back to the calling function.

At this point, you can compile and run the code from Visual Studio .NET and check that you can log onto any FTP server and view the root directory listing. The next step is to add the folder-browsing capabilities. We can implement the event that is fired when a user clicks on a folder in the folder list. Click on the folder list, and type this code:

C#

```csharp
private void lbFolders_SelectedIndexChanged(object sender,
System.EventArgs e)
{
  RemotePath += "/" + lbFolders.SelectedItem.ToString();
  sendFTPcmd("CWD /" + RemotePath +"\r\n");
  getRemoteFolders();
}
```

VB.NET

```vbnet
Private  Sub lbFolders_SelectedIndexChanged(ByVal _
sender As Object, ByVal e As System.EventArgs) Handles _
 lbFolders.SelectedIndexChanged
  RemotePath += "/" + lbFolders.SelectedItem.ToString()
```

```
      sendFTPcmd("CWD /" + RemotePath + vbcrlf)
      getRemoteFolders()
   End Sub
```

The purpose of building up the `RemotePath` variable is that when the next list of folders is shown, the application must remember that each listing corresponds to `/folder/subfolder` rather than `/subfolder`. The folder and file lists are refreshed once the operation is complete. We could, of course, have used the PWD command to get the path from the server, but it is probably easier and quicker to store this information locally. To instruct the FTP server to move to a working directory, the CWD command is used.

This gives a user the means to drill down directories, but no means of returning back up. In this case, we can double-click on `btnRoot`:

C#

```csharp
private void btnRoot_Click(object sender, System.EventArgs e)
{
  RemotePath = "/";
  sendFTPcmd("CWD /\r\n");
  getRemoteFolders();
}
```

VB.NET

```vb
Private  Sub btnRoot_Click(ByVal sender As Object, _
ByVal e As System.EventArgs)
  RemotePath = "/"
  sendFTPcmd("CWD /" + vbcrlf)
  getRemoteFolders()
End Sub
```

This resets the working folder to the root and sends a command to the FTP server to return to the FTP root. It then refreshes the file and folder lists. Again, the CWD command is issued to instruct the FTP server to move working folders.

Now, to implement the core purpose of this application, double-click the Upload button:

C#

```csharp
private void btnUpload_Click(object sender, System.EventArgs
  e)
```

```csharp
{
  openFileDialog.ShowDialog();
  NetworkStream passiveConnection;
  FileInfo fileParse = new FileInfo(openFileDialog.FileName);
  FileStream fs = new
  FileStream(openFileDialog.FileName,FileMode.Open);
  byte[] fileData = new byte[fs.Length];
  fs.Read(fileData,0,(int)fs.Length);
  passiveConnection = createPassiveConnection();
  string cmd = "STOR " + fileParse.Name + "\r\n";
  tbStatus.Text += "\r\nSent:" + cmd;
  string response = sendFTPcmd(cmd);
  tbStatus.Text += "\r\nRcvd:" + response;
  passiveConnection.Write(fileData,0,(int)fs.Length);
  passiveConnection.Close();
  MessageBox.Show("Uploaded");
  tbStatus.Text += "\r\nRcvd:" + new
  StreamReader(NetStrm).ReadLine();  getRemoteFolders();
}
```

VB.NET

```vbnet
Private  Sub btnUpload_Click(ByVal sender As Object, _
ByVal e As System.EventArgs)
  openFileDialog.ShowDialog()
  Dim passiveConnection As NetworkStream
  Dim fileParse As FileInfo = New _
  FileInfo(openFileDialog.FileName)
  Dim fs As New FileStream(openFileDialog.FileName, _
  FileMode.Open)
  Dim fileData(fs.Length) As Byte
  fs.Read(fileData, 0, fs.Length)
  passiveConnection = createPassiveConnection()
  Dim cmd As String = "STOR " + fileParse.Name + vbCrLf
  tbStatus.Text += vbCrLf + "Sent:" + cmd
  Dim response As String = sendFTPcmd(cmd)
  tbStatus.Text += vbCrLf + "Rcvd:" + response
  passiveConnection.Write(fileData, 0, fs.Length)
  passiveConnection.Close()
  MessageBox.Show("Uploaded")
  tbStatus.Text += vbCrLf + "Rcvd:" + New _
  StreamReader(NetStrm).ReadLine()
  getRemoteFolders()
End Sub
```

This function opens the standard File Open dialog and then reads the contents of the specified file into a string by passing the filename to a `StreamReader`, and reading to the end of the file while storing the data in the `fileData` string.

A passive connection is then opened to the server, and a `STOR` command is issued on the command socket. Once the server has responded to the `STOR` command, the file contents are placed on the passive connection. Once all of the data is sent, the connection is closed. A message is displayed on screen, and the file and folder list is refreshed.

Note that you do not have to pass the local path of the file to the FTP server because the file will be stored in the current working folder. The file-name, minus its path, is obtained from the `FileName` property of the `FileInfo` class.

Finally, the download functionality can be implemented by clicking on the Download button:

C#

```csharp
private void btnDownload_Click(object sender,
System.EventArgs e)
{
  byte[] fileData;
  saveFileDialog.ShowDialog();
  fileData = sendPassiveFTPcmd(
        "RETR " + lbFiles.SelectedItem.ToString()+ "\r\n");
  FileStream fs = new FileStream(
          saveFileDialog.FileName,FileMode.CreateNew);
  fs.Write(fileData,0,fileData.Length);
  fs.Close();
  MessageBox.Show("Downloaded");
}
```

VB.NET

```vbnet
Private  Sub btnDownload_Click(ByVal sender As Object, _
 ByVal e As System.EventArgs)
  Dim fileData As Byte()
  saveFileDialog.ShowDialog()
  fileData = sendPassiveFTPcmd( _
    "RETR " + lbFiles.SelectedItem.ToString() + vbCrLf)
  Dim fs As FileStream = New FileStream( _
    saveFileDialog.FileName, FileMode.CreateNew)
```

```
    fs.Write(fileData, 0, fileData.Length)
    fs.Close()
    MessageBox.Show("Downloaded")
End Sub
```

This event opens the standard File Save dialog window. The file to be downloaded is the one that is currently selected in the files list. A RETR command is issued via a passive connection. The returned data is the contents of the remote file. In order to write this data to the local disk, a new FileStream is created. The FileStream constructor includes the name of the local file. The data to be written to disk is converted from a string into a byte array and then passed to the write method of the stream. A message is shown to signify the end of the operation.

Add these namespaces to both forms, and we're ready to go:

C#

```
using System.Net;
using System.Net.Sockets;
using System.Text;
using System.IO;
```

VB.NET

```
Imports System.Net
Imports System.Net.Sockets
Imports System.Text
Imports System.IO
```

To test the application, ensure that you have an FTP server running, and then execute the application from Visual Studio .NET. Note that when compiling this application, if you are prompted for "Sub Main" (VB.NET),

Figure 6.5
FTP client Logon dialog.

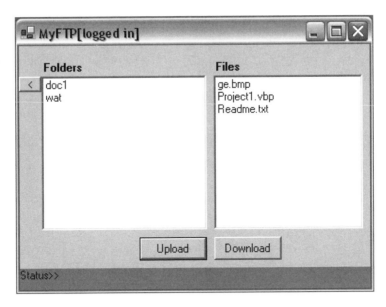

Figure 6.6
FTP client file-management dialog.

please select the Main form for this purpose. When the application is running, you may enter your FTP account details into the Logon window (Figure 6.5) and press Logon.

On the next screen (Figure 6.6), you can navigate around the remote computer's file system by clicking on the folder names in the list provided. To return to where you started, press the root button.

To upload a file, click Upload, then select a file. Wait until you receive a message box, and then you should see the file in the files list. To download a file, click on a file in the files list, and then press Save. Choose a destination for the file (e.g., the desktop). When you press OK, wait until you see a message box, and then you should see the file on the desktop.

6.4.8 FTP support in .NET 2.0

In the .NET Framework version 2.0 (Whidbey), FTP support is included in the `WebClient` class, thus negating the need to use either socket-level programming or COM objects. The following code illustrates the simplicity of this new feature:

C#

```
public void downloadFile()
{
 string filename = "ftp://ms.com/files/dotnetfx.exe";
 WebClient client = new WebClient();
```

```
client.DownloadFile(filename,"dotnetfx.exe");
}
```

VB.NET

```
Sub downloadFile()
 Dim Filename as String = "ftp://ms.com/file/dotnetfx.exe"
 Dim client as new WebClient
 Client.DownloadFile(filename,"dotnetfx.exe")
End sub
```

6.5　Conclusion

This chapter gave a brief overview of Microsoft file sharing and two implementations of FTP clients in .NET: one for a five-minute solution and one as a substantial, flexible implementation of the protocol.

The next chapter deals with the practical issues faced by developers working with real-world networks. It is designed to help solve network problems for individual scenarios and provide tips and tricks to keep your software from crashing on unusual network setups.

7

Securing a Network: Firewalls, Proxy Servers, and Routers

7.1   Introduction

This chapter deals with the practical issues of setting up a network and network architecture in general. Knowing how networks differ from a programmatic perspective can help fix a lot of network-application-related bugs. Furthermore, basic working knowledge of network setup is essential in the day-to-day life of many developers.

This chapter is structured in two sections. The first section explains how to create a network from autonomous, stand-alone machines. Immediately following that is a discussion of common devices that form gateways between your network and the Internet. These gateway devices can often create problems for your software by imposing their own restrictions and regulations. By being able to detect and work around these problems, your application will be more stable in a mass-market environment.

7.1.1   Building a network from scratch

If you are developing a point-of-sale system for a supermarket, each terminal will need to communicate with a central server to consolidate the day's takings and process stock levels. This is not easily achievable without a network. In many cases, you can't just give a shopkeeper a CD and expect him to figure out how to get every computer in his business tied to a single network.

Choosing a topology

If you have only two computers that you want to network, and there is no need for a third, then the most economic solution is a unshielded twisted pair (UTP) crossover cable (not UTP patch cable). This can be used to link two computers directly.

There are three main types of physical connections in modern networking: UTP, BNC, and wireless. The latter uses radio waves to transmit data between terminals, whereas the other two systems use wired connections.

The benefits of a wireless network are quite readily apparent. Users can move within the radius of the transmitter and maintain a connection to the Internet; however, wireless networks are slower than their wired counterparts. For instance, a typical network card can support a 100-Mbps connection, whereas the equivalent wireless card will operate at 11 or 54 Mbps, and the actual throughput may only be a fraction of that. A network cable can easily stretch for 100 meters, but wireless hubs have a radius substantially smaller than that. Wireless networks are more expensive but are similar in architecture to a UTP network.

The differences between UTP and BNC are most apparent in the type of cable used to connect the computers. UTP cable resembles a phone line, only thinner, whereas BNC is coaxial, like a television cable. BNC plugs are circular, whereas UTP plugs (RJ45 connectors) are rectangular.

UTP is laid out in a star topology, where each computer has a dedicated line to its nearest hub or router. In smaller networks, one of the computers on the network uses a modem (or other device) to connect to the ISP. Every other machine on the network then shares this Internet connection. On larger networks, a router connects directly to a line provided by the service provider. This arrangement provides better performance because the router helps steer the data, as well as being dedicated to the task of providing a network connection; however, it adds extra cost to the network.

BNC is laid out in a bus topology. This is where all computers on the network share a single line of communications. In a BNC network, each computer has a T-shaped connection attached to its network card. At each end of the wire is a terminator. BNC is rare nowadays, and it is more common to use either UTP or wireless.

Other networks, based on Universal Serial Bus (USB) and serial connections, are available, but they should be avoided because of possible interoperability problems.

Setting up a network

When building a UTP network, ensure that each computer is wired to a hub, and make sure the hub is powered. In a BNC network, each computer is connected to its neighbor, and a BNC terminator should be affixed to the end of the wire.

Users will expect a file-sharing mechanism on the network, so you should provide this from the outset. To provide this mechanism, you have to choose a unique name for each computer on the network. To name a computer on Windows 2000, right-click My Computer→Properties→Network Identification, and select Properties. On Windows XP, right-click My Computer→Properties→Computer Name→Change (Figure 7.1).

Enter in a computer name, and if required, a workgroup. Then press OK. You may need to restart the computer for these changes to take effect.

You will need to bind some protocols and services to your new network card. To do this in Windows 2000, right-click My Network Places→Properties→Local Area Connection→Properties. On Windows XP, click Control Panel→Network Connections→Local Area Connection.

In this box, you need to see three things: Client for Microsoft Networks, File and Printer Sharing for Microsoft Networks, and Internet Protocol (TCP/IP). If any of these is missing, press the Install button.

Figure 7.1
Windows,
Computer Name
Changes Dialog.

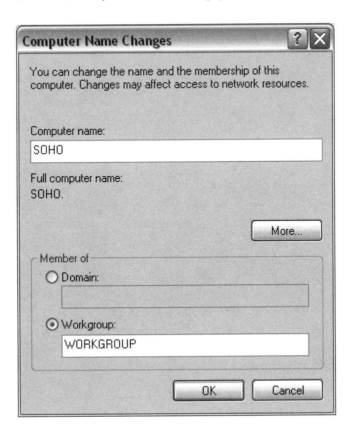

The next task is to set up the TCP/IP settings for the computer. To open the dialog box, highlight Internet Protocol (TCP/IP) and click Properties.

If this computer is part of a larger network, there may be a DHCP server on the network, which automatically assigns IP addresses. In this case, choose the options "Obtain an IP address automatically" and "Obtain DNS server address automatically." Otherwise, set the fields manually.

You have to set the IP addresses as nonpublic addresses, and each computer must be assigned a unique IP address. A series of IP addresses could be 10.0.0.1, 10.0.0.2, 10.0.0.3, and so on. The subnet mask should be 255.255.255.0. Press OK to save the settings.

To share a folder, right-click on the folder, click Properties→Sharing. Click on Share this folder (on Windows XP, you will need to click on a disclaimer message, "If you understand the risk but still want to share the contents of this folder").

Note: If you intend to accept Windows 9x clients, you will need to have a guest account on your system.

To limit remote users' access to your files on Windows 2000, click Permissions. On the next window you can grant and revoke read, write, and change permissions to any or all users on the network. On Windows XP, this has been simplified to a checkbox, "Allow network users to change my files."

Another useful feature of networks is the ability to remotely print documents. This section assumes that you have a printer attached to a computer on your network. On Windows 2000, click Start→Settings→Printers. On Windows XP, press Start→Control Panel→Printers and Faxes. Right-click on a printer that you would like to share, and select the Sharing option. Then select Shared As, enter a unique name, and a descriptive name for the printer. You can set the level of control users will have over the printer from the Security tab. Press OK to complete the process.

How to set up a virtual private network

A virtual private network (VPN) is used to give a remote client secure access to a LAN. The remote client will have transparent (albeit, slower) access to the LAN and will be able to share files and use remote printers, and so forth.

A VPN operates over the point-to-point tunneling protocol (PPTP) or layer 2 tunneling protocol (L2TP). The local traffic is layered on top of this to support true transparency and support for nonroutable protocols such as IPX.

A VPN has some advantages over dial-in connections to a network. These are security, where every transmission is encrypted, and transparency, because the client can retain its own IP address.

To become a VPN client, on Windows 2000, click Start→Settings→ Network Connections, and then click New Connection wizard. On Windows XP, click Start→Control Panel→Network Connections→Create a New Connection→Next.

Click on "Connect to a private network through the Internet" on Windows 2000 or "Connect to the network at my workplace," then Virtual Private Network Connection on Windows XP.

When prompted, type in the IP address of the VPN gateway. This should be as supplied by the administrator of the VPN. Press Finish to finalize the settings.

7.2   Building an enterprise network

Up to now, private IP addresses have been mentioned in passing, more by way of highlighting the fact that they exist, how to recognize them, and how to understand their limitations. In enterprise networks, it is unfeasible to supply every user with a separate direct connection to the Internet. It is normal to channel each user's network connection to a gateway, and from here, a direct connection to the Internet exists.

The term *gateway* is generic. It simply means the device that is connected to both the internal network and the Internet. This can be either a computer or a stand-alone device. Both proxies and routers can function as a gateway. A proxy would be in the form of software running on a computer, and a router being a stand-alone device. A router is always preferable to a proxy in every respect, apart from cost.

7.2.1   Routers

If you have inherited a network running a proxy server that is experiencing performance problems or on which users are finding it difficult to run certain applications, then you should consider using a router instead of a proxy server.

A router is generally a piece of hardware. It performs minimal processing of packets. This means that a router can operate at speeds far exceeding those of a proxy server. It also steers packets in the right direction, instead of blindly sending them out to the next router up the chain. Furthermore, its presence is much more transparent to clients, and it has much higher resiliency.

If you look at the rear panel of a router, you will see several LAN connections: one marked WAN, a power lead, and possibly a serial connection. To wire one up, you connect the WAN port to the cable provided by your ISP. Each LAN port can be connected to a computer, or hub. You need to obtain the following information from your ISP:

- What fixed IP address to use, or whether to obtain one via DHCP
- The IP address of the default gateway
- What subnet mask to use
- The primary and secondary DNS

Each computer behind the router must then set its default gateway and DNS servers to the IP address of the gateway and set the IP addresses to private addresses.

7.2.2   Firewalls

A good analogy for a firewall is a switchboard operator for a company. If an unsolicited salesperson rings, chances are the operator will not forward the call through; however, if an employee makes an outgoing call to the salesperson, the operator will not block the call. Calls made from employees within the company go through the switchboard, so the caller ID that appears on the recipient's phone will be that of the switchboard rather than the direct line.

A firewall performs this function, only at very high speeds, either in software or hardware. It is possible to buy stand-alone firewalls, but every modern router will contain some sort of firewall (sometimes referred to as *packet filtering*). A firewall can also come in the guise of software.

In Administrative Tools→Services, you will see the Internet Connection Firewall (ICF) service. You can press Start to enable this service. This will suffice to protect a single computer from the ravages of the Internet. There is no need to use this service if your local gateway uses a firewall.

Proxies

Proxies should only be considered when you have no budget to develop a network or only two or three computers require an Internet connection. Proxies will slow down your Internet connection considerably.

First, if you expect to have multiple users sharing an Internet connection, you will need something more than a dial-up connection. ISDN would be the minimum, with DSL being a preferred option. You will have already created your LAN, with one computer equipped with a DSL modem of some description. This computer runs the proxy server software.

All other computers on the network have to use this computer as a via point to request Web pages and so forth. This means that every Internet-connecting program needs to know the IP address of the proxy. In Internet Explorer, this is set from Tools→Internet Options→Connections→LAN Settings→Use a proxy server.

Proxies come in two flavors: application proxies and circuit-level proxies. Application proxies normally accept only one protocol, such as HTTP. Circuit-level proxies can accept any protocol over IP. The most popular circuit-level proxy is known as SOCKS; a popular HTTP proxy is Wingate (www.wingate.com).

Some applications will only work with an HTTP proxy or SOCKS. It is generally a case of determining which applications you need to use and getting a proxy server to suit.

The SOCKS protocol is defined in RFC 1928. In order to use a SOCKS proxy, the client must first authenticate itself. This consists of an initial short (3-byte) negotiation followed by a vendor-specific subnegotiation. Once the client is authenticated, a packet to the outside world can be sent when preceded by a short (10-byte) header. This header includes the port and IP address of the destination. Responses are tagged with the same header, only reversed.

Network address translators

All gateways perform some sort of network address translation, or NAT. For simplicity's sake, any device that implements NAT will also be referred to as a NAT. A NAT rewrites the IP header of packets leaving the network with a new, public IP address. When the response packet returns, the NAT will have remembered what computer had originally issued the request and rewrite the IP header with the appropriate private IP address.

A proxy server, although it can provide HTTP requests that emanate from a different IP address than the source, is not considered to implement NAT. This is because the input is different from the output in more ways than just the IP address. More specifically, a proxy server expects a header in the data sent to it to indicate the destination host and port. True NAT devices do not require this identification. When configuring a computer to use a NAT, it is only necessary to change the gateway and DNS settings (under TCP/IP settings) to allow all applications to communicate transparently through the NAT. With a proxy, there is no such global setting, and each application has to be configured independently.

NAT was developed by Cisco, but it is now an Internet standard (RFC 1631). Several different translations can be performed on network addresses, which can be used to provide more flexible gateways to the Internet. Not all gateway devices support the full range of NAT operations.

Static NAT is where every private IP address has its own corresponding public IP address. This means that each computer is distinguishable from the outside world, yet not necessarily accessible.

Dynamic NAT is where every private IP address is mapped to a unique public IP address, although not always the same one every time.

Overloading is the most common form of NAT (sometimes called *port address translation*). It maps every private IP address to a single public IP, but differentiates the connections by placing them on different local ports (multiplexing).

Overlapping is used when two LANs with different subnets are joined together. Every private IP on one network is mapped to a unique private IP on the second network, and vice versa. Overlapping can be done by using static or dynamic NAT. The latter is a more complex undertaking.

When there is a mixture of public and private IP addresses on the stub domain (a private LAN), the NAT will not perform any translation on public IP addresses, but the packets still pass through the device.

As mentioned previously, a NAT needs to store information about what packets it has sent out, so that it can appropriately return the replies. In dynamic NAT, an IP address mapping cannot change midway through a TCP/IP session. Therefore, a NAT also needs to store which TCP/IP session is mapped to each IP address. Because a computer can theoretically maintain a TCP/IP session on each port, a network of 100 computers could maintain 6 million concurrent sessions.

The number of clients a router can process should be stated by the manufacturer; however, as a rough estimate, every entry in the NAT translation table is 160 bytes long; therefore a router with 2 Mb of RAM could handle about 12,000 sessions, which is more than enough for any office network.

A device that implements NAT will probably also include some sort of packet filtering and logging to compliment it. After all, what is the point of providing the ultimate network if the users spend all of their time browsing pornographic Web sites (unless of course you're in that industry)? Filtering can block various destination addresses, port numbers, and so forth. Logging will record packets entering and leaving the router, but not the internal nonroutable traffic. On large networks, a packet analyzer will have difficulty recording the activities of 100 users who all decide to ghost their machines at once.

Note: Ghost is a product developed by Symantec that can replicate hard disks over a network http://www.symantec.com/ghost/.

Even with its complexity, NAT eases system administration (e.g., if your server goes down, and you can't get physical access to it). You can use the remote-access facility that comes standard on most routers to change the inbound mapping to point to the IP address of a server that you do have access to, and the problem will be solved, for Internet clients anyway.

In order to provide a backup Internet connection, you will require a second router. This router ensures that outgoing traffic to the backup ISP will be appropriately mapped. Providing both routers are interconnected, when one ISP fails, the other router will take all of the traffic from the other, and will do so without any human intervention. This type of arrangement is known as a *multihomed network*. This is made possible because of the various ways routers interoperate. They use the interborder gateway protocol (IGBP) to talk to each other inside a LAN and the exterior gateway protocol (EGP) to communicate with the ISP's routers.

A piece of NAT software named Sygate is freely available, but hardware implementations are recommended

7.3   Tunneling out of an enterprise network

If your customer already has a functioning network, but your software doesn't work on it, you can't ignore the problem, or you will lose the sale.

There are always two ways to fix a problem: address it or avoid it. Both methods are equally valid and equally applicable to different situations. Take the situation where a teleconferencing application does not operate behind a firewall. You can either move the server outside the firewall, set up port forwarding to tunnel through the firewall (or router), or bounce data off a proxy server to avoid the firewall. The first two options may involve you going on-site to fix the problem, whereas the latter involves renting a dedicated server and doing some programming.

Proxy tunneling

If you write an application for the mass market, you have to bear in mind that not all software users will have either direct or transparent connections to the Internet. In some cases, users may access the Internet via a proxy. Unfortunately, there is no foolproof means of detecting if a proxy is in use on a network, where it is, or what type it is.

Unlike routers, proxies are not transparent to clients. You will need to modify your code to account for a proxy. If you are using the `HTTPWebRequest` and are trying to navigate an application proxy, then this is relatively straightforward:

C#

```
WebProxy myProxy= new WebProxy("proxyserver",8080);
myProxy.BypassProxyOnLocal = true;
String url = "http://www.yahoo.com";
HttpWebRequest request =
(HttpWebRequest)HttpWebRequest.Create(url);
request.Proxy = myProxy;
```

VB.NET

```
Dim myProxy As WebProxy = New WebProxy("proxyserver", 8080)
myProxy.BypassProxyOnLocal = True
Dim url As String = "http://www.yahoo.com"
Dim request As HttpWebRequest = _
CType(HttpWebRequest.Create(url), _
  HttpWebRequest)
request.Proxy = myProxy
```

Note that the above code requires the `System.Net` namespace.

Firewall tunneling

If a firewall is in place that blocks all ports, then you could make changes to the firewall to allow access on your requested port. Firewalls are generally accessed either through a Web interface (*http://192.168.1.1* or similar) or via a serial connection. You will need to have the manual and passwords close at hand. Some routers offer port forwarding to bypass firewalls. This is where the data directed at the router's IP address on a specified port is forwarded to a specified internal IP address. The process is transparent to both ends of the connection.

Finally, if you have no access to the firewall, or you want to provide a user-friendly solution, you can bounce data from a proxy. This is where the machine behind the firewall opens a steady TCP and connects to a proxy machine, which is outside of the firewall, and the proxy allows the client to connect to it. Data from the client to the proxy is forwarded via the previously opened connection. This is the technique used by Instant Messenger applications. A coded example of this solution is provided at the end of this chapter.

7.4   Avoiding the networking pitfalls

Prevention is always better than cure. If you are releasing a product into the wild, it is almost certain that some user will have such an unusual network configuration that your software won't work. To them, their network isn't unusual, and in fact a hundred other users out there have the same problem, but they didn't bother to tell you that your software doesn't work.

Port conflict

If your software can't start on its default port, it should move to another port, or at least prompt the user to enter a new port. If you don't provide this function, you will encounter one of two problems: (1) users will inevitably run software that uses the same port as yours and that they don't want to stop using, or (2) firewalls may already be set up to allow traffic through some ports; even if your customer doesn't use a firewall, their ISP might.

The client who is waiting to connect to your software will need to know that it has moved port. You could simply display a message box and ask the user to type in the new port, or you could use a DNS request (Chapter 12) to tell users which ports the server is listening on and connect to each in turn. Generally, this approach is overkill.

Tip: It is possible to force sockets to listen on an occupied port, by setting the reuse-address option thus: `Socket.SetSocketOption(SocketOption-Level.Socket, SocketOptionName.ReuseAddress,1)`. This approach is not recommended as it may cause undefined behavior.

Dynamic IP addresses

Another problem that is regularly encountered is dynamic IP addresses. This is where the IP address of the computer changes every time it goes online. Left unchecked, many applications will grab the local IP address when the application starts and assume that is will remain static for the life-time of the application. When users have dial-up connections, they could obtain five different IP addresses in the space of an hour under normal usage (signing on and off the Internet). This situation poses a problem for server applications because there is no way a client can know where it should connect. This can be solved either on a case-by-case basis or by host-ing an IP tracking mechanism.

Software such as "no-IP" can be used to map a dynamic IP address to a DNS name. The process of using this software is relatively straightforward, but it may be unfeasible to request software users to use this product to solve the dynamic IP address issue. The alternative is to have the computer periodically post its IP address to a server, whereupon the server will store the IP address, along with a timestamp and a human-readable identifier. Clients can look this up and connect to the dynamic IP address. The time-stamp ensures that offline computers will be deleted from the listing.

When posting an IP address, care must be taken to ensure that the IP is valid for the Internet. A LAN IP such as 192.168.0.1 is no good to a client on the other side of the world.

7.4.1 Firewall tunneling

If you sell firewalls for a living, look away now because this section describes how to tunnel files (or any other data) through a firewall, in either direc-tion, rendering the whole purpose of a firewall defunct. If you are develop-ing a peer-to-peer application for the open market, however, this information opens up a whole new customer base.

To best illustrate the concept of firewall tunneling, let's look at an anal-ogy: Imagine two prisoners, one in Alcatraz and another in the Bastille. They can both make one phone call, but obviously, neither is allowed to receive calls. The prisoner in Alcatraz knows an escape route from the Bastille, which he wants to tell his partner in crime. How does he send the message? The prisoner in Alcatraz phones his friend's home answering machine and leaves a message of where the escape route is located. The prisoner in the Bastille then makes his call to his own answering machine, where he hears the message and uses the information to escape.

The same technique is used to tunnel though firewalls. One user sends data to a publicly accessible server with a header indicating from whom the data came and who the intended recipient is. The recipient is constantly polling this server, querying it for any new messages. Once the data has been posted up to the server, the recipient can then download it and instruct the server to remove its copy.

The system could be implemented roughly by simply using an email account. Both computers would poll it using POP3 and post new messages using SMTP. Otherwise, Microsoft Message Queue (MSMQ) server (see Chapter 15) could be used for the same purpose.

Peer-to-peer architecture

Peer-to-peer (P2P) is a way of structuring distributed applications such that the individual nodes have symmetric roles. Rather than being divided into clients and servers, each with distinct roles (such as Web clients versus Web servers), in P2P applications a node may act as both a client and a server. P2P systems are generally deployable in an ad hoc fashion, without requiring centralized management or control. They can be highly autonomous and can lend themselves to anonymity.

In order to function correctly, each node on a P2P network must know the location of at least one other node. In some implementations, a node could contact an indexing server, which would return a list of other nodes on the P2P network. The benefit of P2P networks is that they are fault tolerant (i.e., there is no single point of failure), and the network can continue to operate smoothly even if several nodes are missing. Furthermore, the combined processing power and storage available across a multitude of nodes can greatly exceed what is practical to combine into one central server computer. Famous P2P software includes Napster and Kazaa.

7.5   Conclusion

This chapter should contain enough information to enable anyone to develop a simple LAN. More importantly, it illustrates network peculiarities of which a developer must be aware when developing distributed applications for enterprise environments.

With this information, it should be possible to develop an approach that will render the low-level network implementation details (such as private and dynamic IP addresses) transparent to higher-level processes.

The next chapter deals with data encryption and security. It explains how the industry-standard encryption mechanisms work and how they can be proclaimed to be "unbreakable."

8

Protecting Data: Encryption

8.1   Introduction

Without encryption, it is easy for anyone with access to a computer between you and the receiver to view transmitted data while it is in transit. In fact, this book includes a chapter that describes how to monitor network traffic at the packet level. This network traffic could include confidential or privileged information that you transmit from your computer.

Security is paramount in financial transactions and many other types of information exchange with an associated dollar value. It is vitall that privileged information remain in the hands of its rightful owners and not stray into the hands of hackers, or worse, the public domain.

This chapter is divided into three sections. The first section describes how encrypted data is cracked and how to recognize weak encryption, which effectively makes your data less secure than plain text. The second section describes asymmetric encryption, which is most applicable for securing data in transit. The chapter concludes with a discussion on symmetric encryption, which is ideal for use in conjunction with other types of encryption for added performance and security.

8.2   Cryptanalysis

In order to appreciate fully what cryptography is, it is necessary to understand the difference between good and bad encryption. When encryption techniques are used incorrectly, they are worse than having no encryption at all because system users will mistakenly trust the encryption, when it is not secure at all. This section should plainly demonstrate how to recognize weak encryption and how simply it can be broken.

Any encryption algorithm that substitutes one character for another can be broken without knowing the key or even the mechanism by which the text was encrypted. The process is known as *frequency analysis*.

The most common character used in English text is the space character (ASCII code 32). After that comes the letter "e," then "t," right down to "z," the least common.

The complete list is:

```
(space)etaoinshrdlcumwfgypbvkjxqz
```

In ciphers, where each letter is substituted by another letter, the frequency of its occurrence is similar to that of plain English.

For instance, a piece of text was taken randomly out of a text file and encrypted. The resultant cipher text was:

```
v`z/bnv/a`{/c`na/}ja{/cjn|j/cjak/`}/`{gj}xf|j/{}na|ij}/{gj/
`{gj}/bjkfzb/{`/na`{gj}/z|j}/jwlj {/n|/ n}{/`i/{gj/ j}bnaja{/
{}na|ij}/n|/ }`yfkjk/nm`yj/`i/{gj/|`i{xn}j/ }`kzl{
```

The most common character is "/," so we can assume that it is the space character. After that, "j" can be assumed to be "e," and so on down to "z." The result seems more like a human language, but only a few English words can be seen (e.g., "not," "the," "to").

```
fou cif not moin aent meise mend oa otheagwse tainsrea the
othea cedwuc to inothea usea ebpelt is liat or the leacinent
tainsrea is laoywded ivoye or the sortgiae laodupt
```

Looking through the text, a few words would make sense if one letter were changed. Because character substitution ciphers must have one-to-one mapping between characters, if one letter is changed, then the letter it is changed to must also be substituted.

We can therefore make three assumptions:

1.   othea → other: a = r, r = ?

2.   o? → on, of: Assume "not" is correct, r = f, f = ?

3.   ?ou → you: f = y, "y" doesn't appear in cipher text

This process can be iterated several times. Each step makes the cipher text more legible.

```
you ciy not moin rent meise mend or othergwse trinsfer the
other cedwuc to inother user ebpelt is lirt of the lercinent
trinsfer is lroywded ivoye of the softgire lrodupt
```

1.   trinsfer → transfer: i = a

2.   softgare → software: g = w, w = ?

3.   otherw?se → otherwise: w = I

```
you cay not moan rent mease mend or otherwise transfer the
other cediuc to another user ebpelt as lart of the lercanent
transfer as lroyided avoye of the software lrodupt
```

1.   cediuc → medium: c = m

2.   ?ermanent → permanent: l = p, p =?

3.   mease → lease: m = l

```
you may not loan rent lease lend or otherwise transfer the
other medium to another user eb?ept as part of the permanent
transfer as proyided avoye of the software produ?t
```

1.   produ?t → product: p = c

2.   ebcept → except: b = x

3.   proyided → provided: y = v

4.   avove → above: v = b

Voilà! The message has been decrypted.

```
you may not loan rent lease lend or otherwise transfer the
other medium to another user except as part of the permanent
transfer as provided above of the software product
```

Frequency analysis software can be programmed to run without any human intervention and could easily recognize and decrypt files or network data that was encrypted with any of the ciphers mentioned to date. If the message had not been in English, or was audio data rather than text, this approach would not have worked.

8.3   Terminology

Cryptography carries with it a vast amount of jargon, some of which is unavoidable when discussing the subject.

- *Plain text* is digital information that is unencrypted.

- *Cipher text* is digital information that has been encrypted.

- A *key* is a piece of digital data that is used by a computer program to convert plain text, to cipher text or vice versa.

- A *cryptographic algorithm*, or *cipher*, is a prescribed algorithm for converting plain text into cipher text and back again, using a key.

- *Strength* is the measure of the difficulty a hacker would have converting cipher text to plain text without having access to the key.

8.4   Asymmetric encryption

If you imagine a padlock, it consists of a bolt, a key, and a locking mechanism. Each padlock is unique. They all have different keys and different locking mechanisms. The way these padlocks are made in the factory, it is impossible to guess the shape of the key by simply looking at the locking mechanism. It is possible to close the bolt on the padlock without having a key. This makes it much more secure than the previous encryption methods described, which would be more akin to a combination lock, where the combination needs to be set when inserting the bolt into the lock.

Now imagine three people: a tourist, a travel agent, and a thief. The tourist wants to send $1,000 to the travel agent, but if the thief gets to the key before the travel agent, he will steal the money. If the tourist were to put the money in a box and then lock it, the travel agent would not have a way to reopen the box if she did not have the key. If the key were to be sent, the thief would surely steal the key and the money before anyone knew what had happened.

The solution is that the tourist asks the travel agent to send him an open padlock and keep the key. The tourist then puts the money in the box, locks it, and sends it back. The travel agent still has the key, so she can open the box and bank the money. The thief may have seen the padlock, and may even have been able to examine the locking mechanism, but he could not open it.

In this case, the padlock key is called the *private key*, and the locking mechanism is the *public key*. In computing, the padlocks become one-way mathematical equations, and the keys become numbers.

An example of a one-way mathematical equation is as follows:

A prime number is a number that is divisible only by itself and 1 (e.g., 13). Given a number *z*, which is a product of two prime numbers *x* and *y*, determine the values of *x* and *y*, where neither *x* nor *y* is equal to 1.

For example, what two numbers multiply to give 22,321?

To solve this problem by hand, you could multiply every prime number between 1 and 149 (square root of 22,321). Other techniques to factor large primes exist, but this would take a computer merely seconds to do; however, if the number to be factored was in the order of billions, it no longer remains feasible for desktop PCs to solve.

The Rivest-Shamir-Adleman (RSA) is quite slow in comparison to most of the shared key (symmetrical) encryption technologies available. In a system using a combination of public key and shared key, overall encryption speed can be increased.

If a message is encrypted with the Triple Data Encryption Standard (3DES), then the key is encrypted with RSA. The same level of security is offered, but with a much faster execution.

8.5   Using RSA as asymmetric encryption

RSA (Rivest Shamir Adleman, named after its inventors) is implemented in the `RSACryptoServiceProvider` class. It generates public and private keys on instantiation; encryption and decryption are performed from the `Encrypt` and `Decrypt` methods. Keys are stored in XML format.

Start a new project in Visual Studio .NET. Add two textboxes: `tbWork-ing` and `tbStatus`. The latter should be set with `MultiLine` to `True`. Add two more buttons: `btnEncrypt` and `btnDecrypt`. To further assist code development, we will encapsulate the core cryptographic functions in a class. Therefore, add a new class to your project named `clsCryptography`.

First, the `Cryptography` class has to implement both encryption and decryption. The cryptographic framework works from byte arrays primarily, so the functions will accept and return byte arrays. As mentioned earlier, RSA is asymmetric, so it uses two keys, which happen to be stored in XML (string) format.

Open `clsCryptography` and enter the following code:

C#

```csharp
namespace rsa
{
  public class clsCryptography
  {
    private RSACryptoServiceProvider RSA;
    public string PublicKey;
    public string PrivateKey;
    public byte[] Encrypt(byte[] Data, string PublicKeyIn)
    {
      RSA.FromXmlString(PublicKeyIn);
      return RSA.Encrypt(Data, false);
    }
    public byte[] Decrypt(byte[] Data, string PrivateKeyIn)
    {
      RSA.FromXmlString(PrivateKeyIn);
      return RSA.Decrypt(Data, false);
    }
  }
}
```

VB.NET

```vbnet
Namespace rsa
  Public Class clsCryptography
    Private RSA As RSACryptoServiceProvider
    Public PublicKey As String
    Public PrivateKey As String

    Public function Encrypt(Data as byte(),PublicKeyIn as _
    string) as Byte()
      RSA.FromXmlString(PublicKeyIn)
```

```
      Return RSA.Encrypt(Data,False)
  End function

  Public Function Decrypt(Data as byte(),PrivateKeyIn as_
  string) as Byte()
    RSA.FromXmlString(PrivateKeyIn)
    Return RSA.Decrypt(Data,False)
  End Function


 End Class
End Namespace
```

RSA cryptography is of little value if we have no keys to work from. These keys should be generated when the class is created, so we insert this code as the constructor of clsCryptography:

C#

```
public clsCryptography()
{
  CspParameters cspParams = new CspParameters();
  cspParams.Flags = CspProviderFlags.UseMachineKeyStore;
  RSA = new RSACryptoServiceProvider(cspParams);
  PublicKey = RSA.ToXmlString(false);
  PrivateKey = RSA.ToXmlString(true);
}
```

VB.NET

```
Public Sub New()
  Dim cspParams As CspParameters = New CspParameters()
  cspParams.Flags = CspProviderFlags.UseMachineKeyStore
  RSA = New RSACryptoServiceProvider(cspParams)
  PublicKey = RSA.ToXmlString(False)
  PrivateKey = RSA.ToXmlString(True)
End Sub
```

The Boolean parameter sent to ToXmlString indicates whether the private key should be included in the XML output.

The following namespaces must be added to the clsCryptography class:

C#

```
using System;
using System.Security.Cryptography;
```

VB.NET

```
imports System
imports System.Security.Cryptography
```

Open the application, go to the point in the code directly after the constructor of the form, and enter some private variables:

C#

```
public class Form1 : System.Windows.Forms.Form
{
  private rsa.clsCryptography clsRSA = new
  rsa.clsCryptography();
  private byte[] Decrypted;
  private byte[] Encrypted;
  ...
```

VB.NET

```
Public Class Form1
  Inherits System.Windows.Forms.Form
  Private clsRSA As clsCryptography =  New clsCryptography()
  Private Decrypted() As Byte
  Private Encrypted() As Byte
```

To display the generated keys on-screen, we append the XML to the status textbox at startup:

C#

```
private void Form1_Load(object sender, System.EventArgs e)
{
   tbStatus.Text += "Private key is:\r\n" + clsRSA.PrivateKey
+ "\r\n";
   tbStatus.Text += "Public key is:\r\n" + clsRSA.PublicKey +
"\r\n";
}
```

VB.NET

```
Private  Sub Form1_Load(ByVal sender As Object, ByVal e _
As System.EventArgs)
   tbStatus.Text += "Private key is:"
   tbStatus.Text += clsRSA.PrivateKey + vbcrlf
   tbStatus.Text += "Public key is:" + vbcrlf
   tbStatus.Text += clsRSA.PublicKey + vbcrlf
End Sub
```

To encrypt the text, we convert it to a byte array and pass it to the
clsCryptography class; the process is similar with decryption. Click on the
two buttons in turn and add the following code:

C#

```
private void btnEncrypt_Click(object sender, System.EventArgs
e)
{
  byte[] PlainText =
  System.Text.Encoding.ASCII.GetBytes(tbWorking.Text);
  Encrypted = clsRSA.Encrypt(PlainText, clsRSA.PublicKey);
  tbWorking.Text =
  System.Text.Encoding.ASCII.GetString(Encrypted);
}

private void btnDecrypt_Click(object sender, System.EventArgs e)
{
  Decrypted = clsRSA.Decrypt(Encrypted,
  clsRSA.PrivateKey);
  tbWorking.Text =
  System.Text.Encoding.ASCII.GetString(Decrypted);
}
```

VB.NET

```
Private  Sub btnEncrypt_Click(ByVal sender As Object, _
 ByVal e As System.EventArgs)
  Dim PlainText() As Byte = _
  System.Text.Encoding.Encoding.ASCII.GetBytes _
      (tbWorking.Text)
  Encrypted = clsRSA.Encrypt(PlainText, _
      clsRSA.PublicKey)
  tbWorking.Text = _
```

```
       System.Text.Encoding.ASCII.GetString(Encrypted)
  End Sub


  Private  Sub btnDecrypt_Click(ByVal sender As Object, _
    ByVal e As System.EventArgs)
    Decrypted = clsRSA.Decrypt(Encrypted, clsRSA.PrivateKey)
    tbWorking.Text = _
    System.Text.Encoding.ASCII.GetString(Decrypted)
  End Sub
```

No additional namespaces are required.

To test the application, run it from Visual Studio .NET. Type something into the box provided and press Encrypt (Figure 8.1). The text should change into an unrecognizable series of characters. Pressing Decrypt will revert this back to plain text again.

8.6   Symmetric encryption

Symmetric encryption is when the same key is used for encryption and decryption. It is commonly used in conjunction with asymmetric encryption for performance purposes. When used on its own, it is important that the key never travel on an insecure channel and that is be delivered by hand to the receiver on physical media, such as a disk or smart card. It is not suitable for network use by itself; however, asymmetric encryption can provide a means to deliver these keys on a secure channel and, therefore, makes symmetric encryption viable for networked applications.

Symmetric encryption is, however, suitable for securing software and databases because the administrator can hold this key on a disk in a secure location. Without the key, symmetric algorithms are actually more difficult to break than RSA for the same key size.

8.6.1   Using 3DES as symmetric encryption

A famous author, Simon Singh, once offered $15,000 to crack a short passage of text encrypted with 3DES. One year later, a Swedish team managed to crack the message and claimed the prize. Unbeknown to Simon Singh at the time, the message had actually been singleDES and thus substantially less secure. 3DES remains one of the world's unbroken cryptographic algorithms.

Figure 8.1
Asymmetric
encryption
application.

Create an application in Visual Studio .NET as usual, and draw a text-box, `tbFile`. Include three buttons named `btnEncrypt`, `btnDecrypt`, and `btnBrowse`. You will also require an Open File Dialog control named `open-FileDialog`.

Directly following the class definition, add a public `DESCryptoService-Provider` object as follows:

C#

```
public class Form1 : System.Windows.Forms.Form
{
   private DESCryptoServiceProvider des;
```

VB.NET

```
Public Class Form1
   Inherits System.Windows.Forms.Form
   Private des As DESCryptoServiceProvider
```

This public object will contain the symmetric keys required to encrypt and decrypt files. In this application, the keys are not saved to disk; they are only stored within this object.

Click on the Browse button and enter the following code:

C#

```
private void btnBrowse_Click(object sender,
```

```
System.EventArgs e)
{
  openFileDialog.ShowDialog();
  tbFile.Text  = openFileDialog.FileName;
}
```

VB.NET

```
Private  Sub btnBrowse_Click(ByVal sender As Object, _
ByVal e As System.EventArgs)
openFileDialog.ShowDialog()
tbFile.Text  = openFileDialog.FileName
End Sub
```

This code is pretty self-explanatory. It opens the standard File Open dialog window and displays the filename of the selected file in the tbFile textbox.

Click on the Encrypt button and enter the following code:

C#

```
private void btnEncrypt_Click(object sender,
System.EventArgs e)
{
  string encFile = tbFile.Text + ".enc";
  FileStream fs = new FileStream(encFile, FileMode.Create,
    FileAccess.Write);
  StreamReader sr = new StreamReader(tbFile.Text);
    string strinput = (sr).ReadToEnd();
    sr.Close();

        byte[] bytearrayinput  =
        Encoding.Default.GetBytes(strinput);
        des = new DESCryptoServiceProvider();
        ICryptoTransform desencrypt =
        des.CreateEncryptor();
        CryptoStream cryptostream =
        new CryptoStream(fs, desencrypt,
        CryptoStreamMode.Write);
        cryptostream.Write(bytearrayinput, 0,
        bytearrayinput.Length);
        cryptostream.Close();
```

```
        fs.Close();
        MessageBox.Show("encrypted");

    }
```

VB.NET

```
Private Sub btnEncrypt_Click(ByVal sender As _
System.Object, ByVal e As System.EventArgs) _
Handles btnEncrypt.Click
        Dim encFile As String = tbFile.Text + ".enc"
        Dim fs As FileStream = New FileStream(encFile, _
            FileMode.Create,FileAccess.Write)
        Dim sr As StreamReader = New _
            StreamReader(tbFile.Text)
        Dim strinput As String = (sr).ReadToEnd()
        sr.Close()
        Dim bytearrayinput() As Byte = _
            Encoding.Default.GetBytes(strinput)
        des = New DESCryptoServiceProvider
        Dim desencrypt As ICryptoTransform = _
            des.CreateEncryptor()
        Dim CryptoStream As CryptoStream = _
            New CryptoStream(fs, desencrypt, _
            CryptoStreamMode.Write)
        cryptostream.Write(bytearrayinput, 0, _
            bytearrayinput.Length)
        cryptostream.Close()
        fs.Close()
        MessageBox.Show("encrypted")
    End Sub
```

The encryption procedure consists of several steps. The first step is where an output file is prepared. The output file has the same name as the input file, except that the extension .enc is appended to the end of the file-name. The input file is then read in from memory by passing the filename as a parameter to the constructor of a StreamReader object and calling the ReadToEnd method to pull in the file contents to a string. This string is then converted to a byte array.

The next step in the encryption process is the application of DES. Here the public DES variable is instantiated. At this point, a unique symmetric key is generated within the DESCryptoServiceProvider class. The encryption mechanism works as a stream. As with most value-added streams, an existing stream is passed to the constructor of the new stream. In this case, the output file stream is the underlying stream used by the cryptographic stream. This stream then processes and writes out the byte array read in from the input file using the `Write` method. The stream is then closed, and a message is shown on the screen.

Now double-click on the Decrypt button, and enter the following code:

C#

```csharp
private void btnDecrypt_Click(object sender, System.EventArgs e)
{
    FileStream fsread = new FileStream(tbFile.Text,
    FileMode.Open, FileAccess.Read);
    ICryptoTransform desdecrypt = des.CreateDecryptor();
    CryptoStream cryptostreamDecr = new CryptoStream(fsread,
    desdecrypt, CryptoStreamMode.Read);
    string decryptedFile = new StreamReader(
        cryptostreamDecr).ReadToEnd();
    FileInfo fi = new FileInfo(tbFile.Text);
    string origionalFile = tbFile.Text.Substring(0,
        tbFile.Text.Length - fi.Extension.Length);
    StreamWriter fileWriter = new
        StreamWriter(origionalFile);
    fileWriter.Write(decryptedFile);
    fileWriter.Close();
    MessageBox.Show("decrypted");
}
```

VB.NET

```vbnet
Private Sub btnDecrypt_Click(ByVal sender As _
System.Object, ByVal e As System.EventArgs) Handles _
btnDecrypt.Click
Dim fsread As FileStream = _
    New FileStream(tbFile.Text, _
    FileMode.Open, FileAccess.Read)
    Dim desdecrypt As ICryptoTransform = _
        des.CreateDecryptor()
    Dim cryptostreamDecr As CryptoStream = _
        New CryptoStream(fsread, _
        desdecrypt, CryptoStreamMode.Read)
    Dim decryptedFile As String = New _
        StreamReader(cryptostreamDecr).ReadToEnd()
```

```
Dim fi As FileInfo = New FileInfo(tbFile.Text)
Dim origionalFile As String = _
    tbFile.Text.Substring(0,tbFile.Text.Length _
        - fi.Extension.Length)
Dim fileWriter As StreamWriter = New _
    StreamWriter(origionalFile)
fileWriter.Write(decryptedFile)
fileWriter.Close()
MessageBox.Show("decrypted")
End Sub
```

The decryption process is a little easier because our symmetric key is already generated. Three streams are used to decrypt the file on disk. The first stream is a `FileStream` that reads the cipher text from the file on disk. The crypto stream is created from our public `des` variable, which would have been previously instantiated in the encryption process. The `FileStream` is passed as a parameter to the constructor of the crypto stream, which decrypts the data from the stream. To extract the data quickly from the crypto stream, a `StreamReader` is used, which uses the `ReadToEnd` method to pull the decrypted data into a string.

Finally, using a bit of string manipulation, the `.enc` extension is removed from the filename, and a `StreamWriter` dumps the string containing the decrypted data to disk. This stream is then closed, and a message is displayed on-screen.

As usual, the following namespaces are required:

C#

```
using System.IO;
using System.Text;
using System.Security.Cryptography;
```

VB.NET

```
Imports System.IO
Imports System.Text
Imports System.Security.Cryptography
```

To test this application, run it from Visual Studio .NET. Press Browse and locate a file on your hard disk. Press the Encrypt button, and press OK when the message box appears. You will notice that a new file has been created with the extension `.enc`. If you open this file in Notepad, it will appear

Figure 8.2
*Symmetric
encryption
application.*

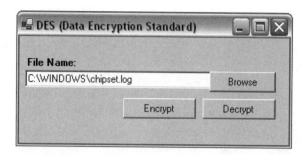

to be garbage. If you wish, you can delete or move the original file. Press the Browse button again, and select the `.enc` file (Figure 8.2). When the message box appears, you will notice that the original file has been re-created.

8.7 Piracy protection

Software is expensive to create, but costs virtually nothing to duplicate. People generally have few qualms about sharing a CD filled with copyrighted material with anyone who they believe will find it useful. To the software producer, this can be considered a lost sale.

The most common form of software piracy is a CD-R with the license code scribbled across the front. The only real way to guarantee that the same license code cannot be used on multiple machines is to track these codes from a central server.

A common way to generate license codes is to choose a large random number (a), and increment it with a multiple of a smaller random number (b). This number would generally be encrypted so that it is not easily memorable. A key that the user enters (c) can be deemed to be valid if

```
(c - a) mod b = 0
```

Your software can broadcast this key on the local network or a central server to ensure uniqueness of the key. It is difficult for an attacker to determine a second valid key from c if a and b are sufficiently large.

An other way to protect software is if your software generates a large random number (n) at the time of purchase. This number can be encrypted by your private key to produce a second number (m) and returned to your software. If m, decrypted with the public key, is n, then the key is valid. Because n is random, m is not valid for any other copy of the software.

Hackers can also use programs to cycle automatically through millions of key combinations by simulating a user typing into your "enter license key" window. For this reason, you should have your software close after 3 failed attempts to enter the license key and delete itself after 100 failed attempts.

Beyond license fraud, there are people who make a hobby out of disassembling executable files and disabling piracy protection. There is no surefire way to defeat this type of attack, but it can be made difficult by duplicating the piracy protection code several times throughout the application.

8.8   Conclusion

This chapter has introduced the concept of data encryption in .NET with both asymmetric and symmetric forms. Also covered was the basic theory behind cryptographic systems and cryptanalysis.

It cannot be stressed enough that you are more likely to get a faster, simpler, stronger, and sometimes even more interoperable method when using the standard encryption mechanisms used in .NET as compared to home-grown encryption algorithms.

The next chapter deals with authentication, the science of knowing with whom you are dealing.

9

Controlling User Access: Authentication and Authorization

9.1   Introduction

Until now, we have assumed that hackers use network-sniffing software to intercept confidential data; however, there is as much danger in forged or spoofed data. Chapter 5 on SMTP/POP3 demonstrates how the sender can specify the originating email address arbitrarily, making it easy to send an email that appears to have come from someone else's account. One can imagine the havoc this would cause if a student were to send an email purporting to be from a professor saying, "All lectures have been canceled. You can all go home now, and we've decided to give you all an A+ on your exams."

This chapter deals with the tricky issue of confirming that a client is who he says he is and that no fraudulent activity is taking place. Authentication systems must be able to validate supplied credentials securely against trusted sources and also to ensure that the message has not been tampered with in transit.

This chapter is structured in four distinct sections. The first section deals with Microsoft authentication systems, such as NTLM and .NET Passport. This is followed by a discussion on techniques to detect data tampering. The chapter continues with an explanation of secure sockets layer (SSL), one of the most common security mechanisms for data delivered via Web sites. The chapter concludes with coverage of some other related authentication technologies, such as .NET permissions and legacy authentication schemes.

9.2   Authentication techniques

To guarantee the identity of a client, you need to trust one piece of information that is unique to that client and that cannot easily be determined or faked (e.g., IP address, Windows username/password, or some other credential). Authentication systems prevent the masquerading of credentials, but they cannot protect against a careless user compromising the security of a Windows password.

Several different types of authentications are applicable to different scenarios. If you are developing a solution for an ISP, then the chances are the ISP can be sure which client base has what IP address and, thus, can use IP addresses as credentials. When developing a Windows-only intranet application, you can trust Windows logins. Internet service developers may use a combination of the IIS authentication options or a custom username and password system.

The most basic form of authentication is IP address validation, where access to information is granted only if the IP address of the client is within a given range. This scheme is used by ISPs to limit access to technical support to current customers. They can do this because their customers will have IP addresses in the range that was assigned to the ISP. IP spoofing would defeat form of authentication, but this is not an easy undertaking. Only a select few determined hackers are capable of carrying it off.

9.2.1   IIS authentication

Although this book focuses on stand-alone software, using IIS as a server is always an option not to be dismissed lightly. This approach does remove some of the flexibility from the system, and it becomes necessary to use the encryption and authentication mechanisms that Microsoft provides, rather than proprietary protocols. IIS5 provides five kinds of authentication: anonymous, basic, NT challenge/response (NTLM, standard for Windows 9x and NT), Integrated Windows (Kerberos, standard for Windows 2000 and XP), and digest. The latter two options are not available on IIS4. Each kind of authentication offers varying degrees of interoperability and security.

The most basic form of IIS authentication, if it has a right to be called authentication, is anonymous. This is where the clients do not have to supply any credentials and are automatically granted IUSR (guest) privileges. This allows them to read and write files, but not to generate any graphical interface or access certain API functions.

One step above this is basic authentication. This forces the client to supply credentials in base64 (basically, clear text). This system is completely interoperable between browsers, but offers very little security; however, when combined with SSL, this is a secure solution.

Moving toward the Microsoft world, we have NT challenge/response, or NTLM. This is quite secure and cannot be broken without significant effort, but it can be hacked by a determined individual. NTLM is supported on IIS4 and all versions of Internet Explorer. The credentials supplied by the client will have to match those of a local account on the server.

Digest authentication was introduced in IIS5. There has not been widely publicized case of any hacker breaking digest encryption. It is compatible with most versions of Internet Explorer. Again, the credentials supplied by the client will have to match those of a local account on the server.

Kerberos provides one of the highest levels of security for authentication available over the Internet. It requires access to a domain controller and works only on IIS5 and recent versions of Internet Explorer.

To access authentication options on IIS, click Start→Control Panel→Administrative Tools→Internet Information Services. Right-click on the server in question, and click Properties. Select the Directory Security tab and press Edit (Figure 9.1).

The screen in Figure 9.1 shows the authentication options for IIS. In this case, the lowest form of security is selected as the default. Options

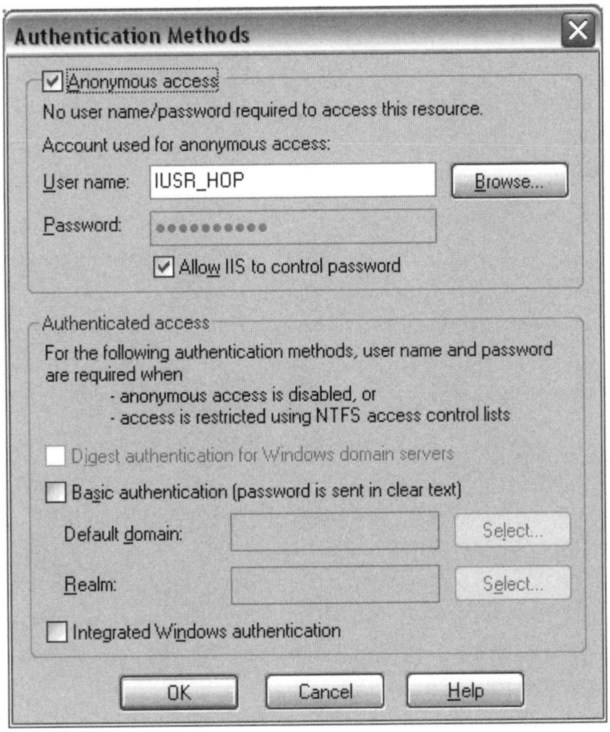

Figure 9.1
IIS authentication dialog.

exist to upgrade this to basic authentication or NTLM. The option for digest authentication is not enabled here because this particular server has no access to a domain controller.

Apart from the security versus interoperability trade-off, there is also a security versus performance trade-off. On a benchmark computer (Pentium 3, 450 MHz, 128 Mb RAM), each of the preceding authentication systems was tested for performance in a high-load environment.

When accepting anonymous connections, the computer handled 860 requests per second. With basic authentication, the computer handled 780 requests per second, proving to be the fastest authentication mechanism, albeit with little security. NTLM incurred an additional overhead, reducing the overall speed to 99 requests per second. Digest authentication clocked in at 96 requests per second. With Kerberos authentication, the computer could handle only 55 requests per second. Finally, with full-blown SSL, the server dropped as low as a mere 2 requests per second.

9.3   Microsoft .NET Passport authentication

Passport authentication is where users can be identified by their Hotmail email addresses. Other passport-supporting email accounts do exist, but Hotmail is the most prevalent. This form of authentication is not meant to secure international fund transfers, but it certainly suffices for personal communications. The advantage of passport over in-house-developed systems is that many people already have a Hotmail email address, and thus do not have to reregister their details.

Passport authentication is used primarily for Web sites, but can also be applied to applications, MSN Messenger being a good example. The online help for .NET Passport is centered on Web site development, but it is possible to implement a proxy service built as a programmatically accessible Web site that your application could connect to. This could then be used to obtain personal details from a user-supplied passport.

Passports are available in two flavors: preproduction and production. Preproduction passports are free, but only a limited amount of personal information can be extracted from a passport. Production passports are not free, and Microsoft will inspect your site or application before you are granted a production passport. You do, however, get the benefit of being able to read full personal details from visitors' passports. Furthermore, a preproduction passport does not have the functionality to perform a sign-out operation.

The first step in implementing .NET Passport–enabled software is to obtain what is known as a site ID. This is simply a number, which is given to you when you register your details with Microsoft .NET Services Manager. On *www.netservicesmanager.com*, click Applications→Create Application, and then fill in all of the necessary fields.

Once you have a site ID, you can download the Passport SDK from *www.microsoft.com/net/services/passport/developer.asp*. This SDK should be installed on the server on which you intend to deploy the Web site, or the proxy server that is to provide passport services to the .NET-enabled stand-alone applications.

The final step is to download a private key that is to be installed on the deployment server. This can be downloaded under Manage Applications, in .NET Services Manager. The key comes in the form of an executable, which must be run from the command prompt as follows:

```
Partner###_#.exe /addkey
Partner###_#.exe /makecurrent /t 0
```

Where ####_# differs for different installations and site IDs. At this point, you may then run the passport administration utility (Figure 9.2).

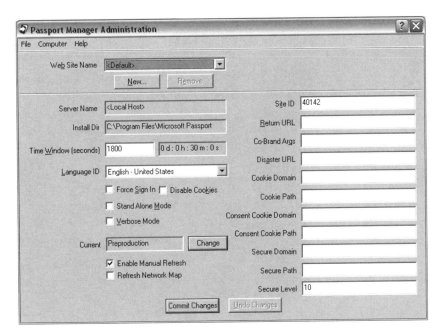

Figure 9.2
.NET Passport Manager Administration dialog.

Figure 9.3
*.NET Passport test
page.*

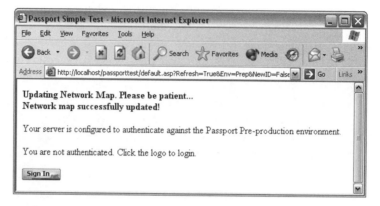

Enter your site ID in the space provided. Then press the Commit Changes button.

To test the system, start and stop IIS using Computer Management, or the IIS snap-in, then press Refresh Network Map, and Commit Changes again. You should see the following Web site appear: *http:/localhost/passport-test/*, as shown in Figure 9.3.

Pressing the Sign-In button will bring you to a cobranded login page for Passport. On successful login, the browser will display the URL that was specified during the site ID signup procedure

9.4   Hashing information

Hashing is a one-way algorithm in which data can be converted to a hash value, but a hash value cannot be converted back to meaningful data. It is used in conjunction with encryption to ensure that messages are not tampered with in transit. Modern hashing systems include Message Digest (MD5) and Secure Hash Algorithm (SHA-1).

When a hash value is produced from a block of plain text, it should be computationally difficult to generate a different block of text that would yield the same hash value. A standard property of hashing algorithms is that a small change in the input text creates a large change in the hash value. Hash algorithms always produce output values with the same length, regardless of the amount of input text.

In practice, a hash value is generated for a given message, and then the message and the hash code are encrypted together. When the message is decrypted, a hash must match that of the message; otherwise, it may have been tampered with. Even though it would be impossible for a hacker to read this encrypted message in transit, it would be possible for him to alter the contents of the transmission, which could result in misinterpreted communications.

Another useful application of hashing is the secure storage of usernames and passwords. If an application stores username and password pairs in a database, it is easy for a professional hacker to access this database and read them off. If the password is hashed, the hacker cannot tell what the original password was. When the legitimate user enters a password into your application, the entered password will be hashed, and if it matches the value in the database, then the user is granted access.

This may pose a problem if the user forgets a password because the application cannot determine the original password from the hash. A system should be in place to replace passwords from an administrator's account. More importantly, if the hacker can guess the hashing algorithm used, he could generate a hashed password, replace the existing one, and gain access. For this reason, where data integrity can be compromised, the hashing procedure should be combined with another form of encryption such as 3DES.

Hashing can also be used to prevent unauthorized data mining of online services. If you provide an Internet-based service that is accessed via a custom-made client (e.g., a DLL that provides currency conversion based on live exchange rates, or whatever), and you want only paying customers to access the service, the last thing you want is a competitor to use a packet-sniffing tool to determine what data you are sending to the server and create a product that uses your service without paying you. The obvious solution is to use asymmetric encryption; however, let us imagine that performance is the overriding factor, and asymmetric encryption would cause an unacceptable processing overhead.

A keyed hash (or a hash of the payload with an appended secret string of characters) of the data included in the header creates only a small overhead, but it makes the header impossible to re-create without knowing the hash key. This affords no security against your competitors' reading what is being sent back and forth to your server, but it prevents them from generating their own client; however, you should take care that the client cannot be disassembled to view this key easily. A tool such as Dotfuscator (www.preemptive.com)can be used to obfuscate the code and help hide this key from prying eyes.

A real-world example of this system in use is the Google toolbar. This utility can display Google's page rank for any given Web page. Google does not want people to be able to data-mine these values using automatic processes, so the request that the toolbar component makes to the Google server contains a keyed hash code for the Web site in question. It is difficult to predict this hash code, and requests made without this code return an error. Full-blown asymmetric encryption was not used in this case because it would have created unacceptable overhead for the servers to return data that is basically available to anyone.

9.4.1 Hashing algorithms

.NET provides support for two hashing algorithms: Secure Hash Algorithm, or SHA, and Message Digest, or MD5 in the classes `SHA1Managed` and `MD5CryptoServiceProvider`, respectively.

SHA is specified by the secure hash standard (SHS). The hash is generated from 64-byte blocks, which are transformed by a combination of one-way operations and a function of previous block transforms. The specification for SHA is widely available and can be implemented easily in any other language, so it is suitable for use on solutions with clients written in other languages or on other platforms. The specification is available in RFC 3174 (*ftp://ftp.rfc-editor.org/in-notes/rfc3174.txt*).

Hashing algorithms do not involve the same high-level mathematics as RSA or elliptic curve encryption. This is not to say that it is advisable to try to develop your own hashing algorithm. Breeds of algorithms that are similar in function to hashing are cyclic redundancy check (CRC) functions. CRC functions provide a fixed-length checksum for any given input. Although these may be one-way functions and provide generally higher throughput than hashing algorithms, they do not afford the same level of security.

There are four different variations of the SHA available for use in .NET: `SHA1Managed` (20-byte hash), `SHA256Managed` (32-byte hash), `SHA384Managed` (48-byte hash), and `SHA512Managed` (64-byte hash). The longer the hash, the more difficult it is for a hacker to create a new message with the same hash, although a longer hash may contain more information about the original message. In either case, SHA1 should be sufficient.

9.4.2 Using SHA

Create a new Windows application in Visual Studio .NET as usual, and draw two textboxes on the form named `tbPlaintext` and `tbHashed`. A button named `btnHash` is also needed. Click on the button and enter the following code:

C#

```
private void btnHash_Click(object sender, System.EventArgs e)
{
  byte[]  entered =
  Encoding.ASCII.GetBytes(tbPlaintext.Text);
  byte [] hash = new SHA1Managed().ComputeHash(entered);
  tbHashed.Text = Encoding.ASCII.GetString(hash);
}
```

VB.NET

```
Private  Sub btnHash_Click(ByVal sender As Object, _
  ByVal e As System.EventArgs)
  Dim entered() As Byte = _
  Encoding.ASCII.GetBytes(tbPlainText.Text)
  Dim hash() As Byte = New _
  SHA1Managed().ComputeHash(entered)
  tbHashed.Text = Encoding.ASCII.GetString(hash)
End Sub
```

This code converts the text entered in tbPlainText into a byte array, and then passes this byte array to the ComputeHash method of the SHA1Managed class. The hash code is generated by an instance of this SHA1Mananged class. By substituting SHA1Managed with SHA512Managed or even MD5cryptoServiceProvider, the hashing will take place using that algorithm instead of SHA1.

You will also require the relevant namespaces:

C#

```
using System.Text;
using System.Security.Cryptography;
```

VB.NET

```
Imports System.Text
Imports System.Security.Cryptography
```

To test this, run it from Visual Studio .NET, type some text into the textbox provided, and press the button. A fixed-length hash will appear in the second textbox as shown in Figure 9.4. A small change in the plain text will cause a large change in the hash value, which will always remain the same length.

Figure 9.4
*Secure hashing
application.*

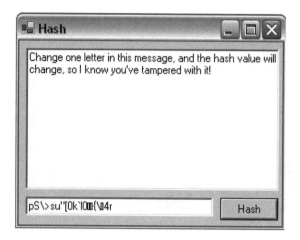

Figure 9.4
*Secure hashing
application.*

9.5   SSL

The most common form of security used over the Internet is secure sockets layer, or SSL. SSL is a secure stream protocol, which uses both symmetric and asymmetric encryption, combined with digital certificates to provide authentication. Digital certificates can be bought from a certificate authority (CA) such as Thawte or Verisign. In order to buy a certificate, you need to prove your identity beyond doubt, which may involve providing a letter from your bank manager or the articles of association for your company. The certificate contains details of your server's DNS name and your organization, and it is encrypted by the CA's private key. The public key for every CA is installed in every browser, so anyone on the Internet can be sure that your company, and no one else, operates the machine that serves the page they are looking at. Furthermore, all data sent between client and server is encrypted with RSA.

SSL is defined in RFC 2660. The most common use for SSL is securing Web pages, but it can be equally applied to email, FTP, or news. HTTP over SSL (HTTPS) operates on port 443; SMTP over SSL (SSMTP) operates on port 465; and NNTP over SSL (SNNTP) operates on port 563.

9.6   Certificates

SSL provides end-to-end encryption and authentication. Whenever a browser views a secure Web site, a padlock appears in the status bar. Clicking this icon will authenticate the server as belonging to a particular company, in a specific location. This is achieved by using server certificates.

A certificate has to be issued by a CA in order to be globally accepted. It is possible to create self-signed certificates, but these would generally be deemed trustworthy only within your organization. A digital certificate signed by XYZ Corporation would be trusted by employees of XYZ, but probably wouldn't be trusted by the general public.

The most common form of digital certificate is known as X.509. This is an international standard maintained by the IETF Public Key Infrastructure (PKIX) working group. X.509 comes in three versions: v1, v2, and v3. Version 3 is the most commonly used form. The certificate comprises various fields that identify the holder, the issuer, and the certificate itself:

- *Serial number:* The unique serial number on every certificate created by an issuer

- *Signature:* Identifies the makeup of the certificate, represented by an object identifier (OID).

- *Validity period:* The date at which the certificate becomes and ceases to be valid

- *Subject:* The owner of the private key

- *Public key:* The key that will decrypt the certificate hash

- *Signed hash:* The hash of the certificate encrypted with the private key of the CA

The subject has several predefined fields (Table 9.1), some of which are standard, but there are no strict guidelines as to what can or cannot be included in the subject line.

The certificate is not encrypted, but its contents are held in either Base64 or Distinguished Encoding Rules (DER). This is to facilitate transmission over plain-text email and to make it more difficult to sniff certificates from the network.

Some common myths about certificates should be mentioned in this context. Contrary to popular belief, certificates are not only used for Web page authentication; they can also be used in email (S/MIME) and general-purpose data (IPSec). Another common fallacy is that the private key should be kept in the HTTP root of the server it authenticates. This is akin to leaving the house keys under the doormat. The private key should never be transmitted over the Internet because if it is lost, it will need to be reissued. The issuer generally does not retain private keys for customers.

Table 9.1   *Standard subject markers for digital certificates.*

Subject Marker	Meaning
C	Country
SP	State/province
S	State
L	Locality
O	Organization
OU	Organizational unit
CN	Common name
E	Email

9.7   Server certificates

If you ever enter your credit card details into a Web site, the first thing you should look for is the padlock icon in the bottom right-hand corner of the browser. This icon not only means that the communications with the remote site are secure, but also that you can click on this icon and assure yourself that the company with which you are dealing is the owner of the Web site you are viewing.

Server certificates for real-world Web sites need to be obtained from a CA. For development purposes, however, it is possible to make self-signed certificates. A useful utility for creating self-signed certificates is IBM Key-Man (*www.alphaworks.ibm.com/tech/keyman*). You could also use Keytool, which is part of the Java SDK from Sun, but this utility doesn't have a GUI and is more awkward to use.

The steps to enable HTTPS using a self-signed certificate and IBM Key-Man on IIS are as follows:

1.   Click Control Panel→Administrative Tools→Internet Information Services.

2.   Expand the tree, and right-click Default Web Site, then click Properties.

3.   Select the Directory Security tab, then click Server Certificate→Next→Create a new certificate.

4. Select Prepare a request now, then fill in your details on each page, pressing the Next button when complete. The default location for the certificate request file is `c:\certreq.txt`.

5. Install IBM KeyMan, and run it from Start→Programs→IBM KeyMan→KeyMan.

6. Select Create New, then PKCS #12 Token, then the tick icon.

7. Select Actions→Generate Key, then click the tick icon to accept the default RSA 1024bit security.

8. Select Actions→Create Certificate→Self-Signed certificate, then fill in your details in the space provided. Press the tick icon twice to proceed.

9. Select Actions→Create Certificate→Sign a PCKS #10 request, then enter `c:\certreq.txt` into the box provided and press the tick icon.

10. Select a location to save the certificate. You should use the `.cer` extension for your file.

11. Going back to the directory security settings for IIS, select Server Certificate, press Next, then click Process the pending request.

12. Enter the path of the `.cer` file produced by KeyMan. Then press Next and then Finish.

13. You can now test HTTPS on your local server, by entering *https://localhost* in your browser. You will receive a warning saying that "The security certificate was issued by a company you have not chosen to trust." This is because it was signed by yourself, not a CA. Pressing Yes on this warning will allow you to proceed.

9.8 Client certificates

Whereas server certificates authenticate a Web site to a browser, a client certificate authenticates a browser to a server. Client certificates are only used for maximum-security Web sites, such as online business banking. Client certificates are available free of charge from Thawte. They are used to send and receive encrypted emails and to authenticate your email address to recipients. You will need to have a passport or social security number to receive a client certificate.

A basic client certificate only authenticates the email address, not the person who sent the email. To get your name on the certificate, you need to

Figure 9.5
*Internet Explorer
Certificates dialog.*

have a bank manager or attorney vouch for your identity. The rest of this section assumes that you have, at this point, received a client certificate from Thawte.

To view the client certificates installed on your system, open Internet Explorer. Click on Tools→Internet Options→Content→Certificates (Figure 9.5).

Clicking on View→Details→Subject on this screen will show which email address this certificate authenticates. Pressing Export will produce an X.509 (.cer) file, which is used in the next example program.

9.8.1 Microsoft Certificate Services

As mentioned earlier, you cannot download a software package that will create globally acceptable X.509 certificates on the fly because the certificate issuer needs to be trusted in order for the certificate to be meaningful. Certificate issuers are to legally required enforce policies and have their private key fully insured against theft.

Organizations may require internal security (e.g., in a university, the servers that hold student grade information would need to be authenticated, to ensure that a student is not using a "poisoned" DNS server to impersonate one of the servers). In this scenario, it might be expensive to buy certificates for every server, and there is no need for people from outside the campus to access the servers, let alone trust them. This is where Microsoft Certificate Services (MSCS) is used.

MSCS runs on Windows 2000 and can generate X.509 certificates in PKCS #7 format from PKCS #10 certificate requests. MSCS can run as either a root CA or subordinate CA and can optionally hold certificates in the active directory. When used in conjunction with the active directory, MSCS will use this as its certificate revocation list (CRL).

A CRL is a publicly accessible list of serial numbers of certificates that have been compromised or have been shown to have been fraudulently acquired. Verisign holds its CRL at *http://crl.versign.com.*

9.8.2 Reading certificates

Certificates can be read using the `X509Certificate` class (Table 9.2) in .NET.

Table 9.2 *Significant methods and properties of X.509 certificates .*

Method or Property	Description
GetCertHashString	Returns the hash value for the certificate as a hexadecimal string
GetEffectiveDateString	Returns the effective date of this certificate
GetExpirationDateString	Returns the expiration date of this certificate
GetFormat	Returns the name of the format of this certificate
GetIssuerName	Returns the name of the certification authority that issued the certificate
GetKeyAlgorithm	Returns the key algorithm information for this certificate
GetKeyAlgorithmParameters	Returns the key algorithm parameters for this certificate
GetName	Returns the name of the principal to which the certificate was issued

Table 9.2 *Significant methods and properties of X.509 certificates (continued).*

Method or Property	Description
GetPublicKeyString	Returns the public key for the certificate
GetRawCertDataString	Returns the raw data for the entire certificate
GetSerialNumberString	Returns the serial number of the certificate

To write a short .NET application to read certificate files, create a new project in Visual Studio .NET. Draw two textboxes named tbCertFile and tbDetails. Add two buttons, btnBrowse and btnExamine. You will also require a File Open Dialog control named openFileDialog.

Click on the Browse button and add the following code:

C#

```
private void btnBrowse_Click(object sender, System.EventArgs
e)
{
  openFileDialog.ShowDialog();
  tbCertFile.Text = openFileDialog.FileName;
}
```

VB.NET

```
Private Sub btnBrowse_Click(ByVal sender As System.Object, _
  ByVal e As System.EventArgs) Handles btnBrowse.Click
    openFileDialog.ShowDialog()
    tbCertFile.Text = openFileDialog.FileName
End Sub
```

Once we have the name of the certificate file, we can use an X.509certificate object to decrypt the file and extract some pertinent information.

Now click on the Examine button and enter the following code:

C#

```
private void btnExamine_Click(object sender, System.EventArgs e)
{
 X509Certificate x509 =
 X509Certificate.CreateFromCertFile(tbCertFile.Text);
```

```
   tbDetails.Text = x509.GetName();
   tbDetails.Text += x509.GetIssuerName();
}
```

VB.NET

```
Private Sub btnExamine_Click(ByVal sender As _
System.Object, ByVal e As System.EventArgs) _
Handles btnExamine.Click
  Dim x509 As X509Certificate
  x509 = X509Certificate.CreateFromCertFile(tbCertFile.Text)
  tbDetails.Text = x509.GetName()
  tbDetails.Text += x509.GetIssuerName()
End Sub
```

You will also need to include the relevant namespace:

C#

```
using System.Security.Cryptography.X509Certificates;
```

VB.NET

```
Imports System.Security.Cryptography.X509Certificates
```

Figure 9.6
*Digital certificate
reader application.*

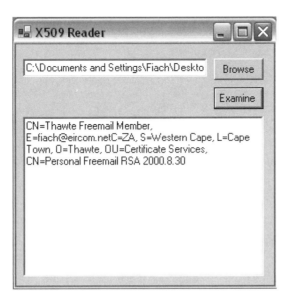

To test the application, run it from Visual Studio .NET. Click Browse, and locate your `.cer` file on disk, which you have previously exported from Internet Explorer. Press Examine, and you should see information about the issuer and the certificate owner, as is shown in Figure 9.6.

9.9   Permissions in .NET

Any programmer familiar with Java will know about the sandbox imposed on applets. This protects client computers from accidentally executing Java code that could potentially damage that computer. The restrictions include file reading and writing and connecting to a computer other than the one that the applet was downloaded from.

.NET offers the same sandbox architecture, which provides users with a facility to execute untrustworthy code without risking damage to their computers. There are several levels of sandbox, from trusted local computer to potentially dangerous code downloaded from an unknown site on the Internet.

Although there is no widespread usage of .NET applets running inside Web pages, there will be in the future. At present, the most significant impact the .NET sandbox will have on code is when a program is executed directly from a network share. This type of application deployment could be used on a corporate intranet, where a small application is executed from a central server at every login to record employees' working practices and the like.

Code running from network shares is restricted in several ways. It cannot write arbitrarily to the local hard disk, but it can use an unlimited amount of isolated storage space on the local computer or the network share from which it was executed. Because unmanaged code cannot be governed by .NET, any assembly operating within a sandbox cannot make a call to unmanaged code. This includes any use of legacy COM controls or Windows API functions. Restrictions also apply to reading environment variables, performing reflection, and accessing the event log.

To view or edit the run-time security policy in .NET, you can access this from Control Panel→Administrative Tools→Microsoft .NET Framework Configuration. Then click Runtime Security Policy (Figure 9.7).

The `System.Security.Permissions` namespace offers facilities to check permissions programmatically and impose further restrictions on the code. There seem to be very few circumstances in which it would be necessary to impose further restrictions on an intranet application.

Figure 9.7
*.NET permission
configuration
utility.*

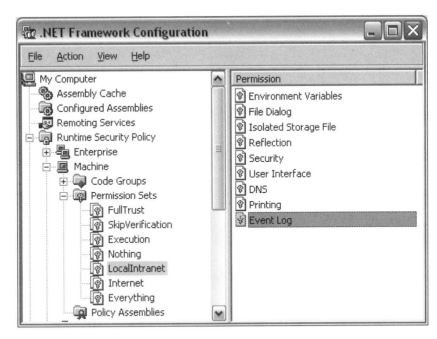

An interesting feature of code access security in .NET is the isolated storage feature. This is one idea that was not adapted from Java, unlike so many other features of .NET. This feature enables applications deployed over an intranet or other semitrusted source to read and write a limited amount of data to the host computers. If the application could read and write arbitrarily, the privilege could be exploited maliciously to read your personal emails, but isolated storage is a clever solution to this problem.

Isolated storage, as the name suggests, is where a small amount of hard disk space (10 Kb) is allocated to any particular application originating from a trusted Internet site. The folder where this data is placed is well away from the system folders and anything else that may contain user data. Each application is allocated its own folder and space such that untrusted applications cannot read each other's data. The amount of isolated storage allocated to any particular application is configurable. This can prevent rogue applications from hogging too much disk space. Intranet-originating applications are allocated unlimited isolated storage.

To use isolated storage from within a .NET application, obtain an `Iso-latedStorageFile` object and then create a stream to it. This stream can then be used in the same way as a `FileStream`.

C#

```
IsolatedStorageFile IsolatedStore;
IsolatedStorageFileStream IsolatedStream;
IsolatedStore =
IsolatedStorageFile.GetStore(IsolatedStorageScope.Assembly,
    null,null);
IsolatedStream = new IsolatedStorageFileStream("data.txt",
    FileMode.CreateNew, IsolatedStore);
```

VB.NET

```
Dim IsolatedStore as IsolatedStorageFile
Dim IsolatedStream as IsolatedStorageFileStream
IsolatedStore = IsolatedStorageFile.GetStore _
    (IsolatedStorageScope.Assembly, _
    Nothing,Nothing)
IsolatedStream = New IsolatedStorageFileStream _
    ("data.txt", FileMode.CreateNew, IsolatedStore)
```

Access to isolated storage in the case described above would be allocated on a per-assembly basis. Isolated storage can also be allocated on a per-user basis, per–domain name basis (for Internet code), or a combination of the above.

9.10 Financial network security

If a hacker were to break into an e-commerce site successfully and capture someone's credit card number, some unfortunate person would get stung financially; however, if the same thing happened on an interbank network, a country's economy could be ruined overnight. Banks and financial institutions use a diverse array of cryptography and authentication systems, which are not accessible to the general public.

The threat to security so far has been pictured as a lone hacker trying to steal credit cards; however, a rogue nation or terrorist organization could use a network of supercomputers to bring down a large national bank in order to cripple a country's economy.

Most banks use private leased lines between their branches so that the confidential information does not come into contact with the public phone network. ATMs usually employ VPN links to the bank. ATMs are limited to a maximum value of transactions they can perform, so it would be impossible to use one rogue VPN connection to drain a bank of its capital.

When a bank needs to communicate with a second financial institution overseas to perform, it must use the public phone network. Where communications between two banks happen on a daily basis, a private virtual circuit (PVC) is set up between the two banks. This reduces the amount of foreign data on the line, but neither bank actually owns the telecom connection. The communication will be very strongly encrypted in one of two main formats: ISO 8730 or SWIFT.

9.10.1 X.25

Many financial protocols run over X.25 packet layer protocol rather than IP. This offers no inherent security above the fact that it isn't IP. X.25 was developed by the CCITT in 1978 and is in widespread use on banking networks. Like the OSI model, it uses encapsulation, where low-level details such as packet framing are not of concern at the implementation level. It supports many of the features of TCP/IP, such as connection orientation and data integrity provided by high-level data link control/Link access procedure balanced (HDLC/LAPB). Supported speeds are from 300 bps to 2.04 Mbps, on packets up to 1,024 bytes.

Routing on X.25 is extensive, with support for both shared virtual circuits and PVCs. Up to 200 virtual circuits can be supported on one X.25 line. A network has to be designed to support X.25 data. In situations where X.25 must travel over an IP network, LAPB can be replaced by TCP/IP. Cisco IOS software or TCP X.25 gateways have the capability to do this, as described in RFC 1613.

9.10.2 ISO 8730

Although less common than SWIFT, this format is used frequently for interbank transfers. It uses symmetric keys with ISO 8732 / ANSI X9.17 key distribution. The key distribution center (KDC) would be run by one or the other of the banks, or a trusted third party.

An ISO 8730 message can be hashed in one of two ways: a hash can be taken of (1) the entire message, or (2) only of the details that are crucial to the purpose of the message. In any case, every message must include the date on which the MAC was created. Out-of-date messages can therefore be discarded. This date value must be hashed regardless of the mode of operation. Hashed fields throughout the message are clearly delimited thus:

QD<*date*>DQ: The date the MAC was created

QK<*key*>QK: The authentication key used by the recipient

QX<*message ID*>XQ: A unique number for that day and key

QT<*transaction detail*>TQ: Details of the transaction amount, currency, identification of the parties, and the date

MQ<*hash*>MQ: The hash itself, being eight bytes long, separated by a space

9.10.3 SWIFT

The Society for Worldwide Interbank Financial Telecommunications (SWIFT) network caters to 7,000 financial institutions in almost 200 countries around the world. It is based in Belgium, Holland, and the United States. To access the SWIFT network, dedicated terminals are required, each with SWIFT-accredited software.

Communications can be made using either X.25 or Secure IP Network (SIPN). Connections to the SWIFT point of presence (POP) are made with leased lines or dedicated ISDN links. An API is available from SWIFT to communicate on this network, but accreditation must be sought before any transactions are made using any in-house software.

SWIFT is not solely concerned with electronic fund transfers. The pre-defined communications on SWIFT are customer transfers, bank-to-bank instructions, foreign exchange and derivatives, documentary collections, securities, syndicated loans, precious metals, travelers checks, documentary credits, statements, advice, and general messages.

When a transaction involves two currencies, control of the debit and credit is designated to the bank at which the transaction currency is local tender. When only one currency is involved, a third-party clearinghouse or other financial institution carries out the control of the debit and credit.

9.10.4 Corporate transactions

When a bank has a large corporation as a client, it will expect to process many highly sensitive transactions with them on a daily basis. Some of these transactions will be on a par with interbank transfers and, thus, must be afforded the same level of security.

The Comité Français d'Organisation et de Normalisation Bancaires (CFONB) designed a secure file-transfer mechanism named ETEBAC 5.

This mechanism was designed specifically for client–bank transactions and is widely used in France and elsewhere.

A common system for corporate transactions in the United Kingdom is the Bankers Automated Clearing Service (BACS). This is used when a company performs an electronic fund transfer (EFT) to pay an employee's salary or wishes to process a direct debit. The BACS can process anywhere up to 60 million transactions per day, for more than 40,000 customers. It is accessed remotely via the BACSTEL service during office hours. BACSTEL runs over X.25, but an IP version of BACSTEL is set to replace this standard.

9.11 Conclusion

This chapter has looked at the mechanisms for guaranteeing the identity of network clients over the Web and on Microsoft networks. The structure and use of digital certificates in a distributed environment were discussed. Extending the topic to real-world scenarios, we looked at how banks use authentication to transfer billions of dollars safely across phone lines.

Sample code was provided to demonstrate how to process a credit card payment securely over an SSL connection. This type of facility is commonplace in most e-commerce solutions, point-of-sale systems, and many other software products.

The next chapter introduces the concept of application scalability (i.e., how software performs under heavy usage and when designed to run reliably for long periods).

10

Programming for Scalability

10.1 Introduction

Providing software that lets people do their jobs is *usability*; providing software that lets 10,000 people do their jobs is *scalability*. The term *scalability* encompasses many facets of software. It means stability, reliability, and efficient use of one or more computer resources. The goal of a scalable system is that it must be available for use at all times and remain highly responsive regardless of how many people use the system.

Scalability, with respect to software architectures, has also come to mean extensibility and modularity. This simply means that when a software system needs to scale upward in complexity, it does not need to be overhauled with each addition. In the following pages, you will learn about both aspects of scalability.

The first half of this chapter deals with scalable architecture design. This is most largely applicable when a distributed service requires more than one server and the system-performance-to-hardware-cost ratio is of paramount importance. This is followed by some hands-on code examples of how to provide added scalability to your application, such as load balancing and efficient thread management.

10.2 Case study: The Google search engine

Google.com is certainly the Internet's largest search engine. It serves 200 million requests per day and runs from more than 15,000 servers distributed worldwide. It is arguably one of the most scalable Internet services ever provided to the general public.

Each server that Google uses is no more powerful than the average desktop PC. Granted, each server crashes every so often, and they are prone to hardware failure, but a complex software failover system is employed by Google to account for server crashes seamlessly. This means that even if a hundred servers crashed at the same time, the service would still be available and in working order.

The rationale behind using a large number of bog-standard PCs rather than a few state-of-the-art servers is simple: cost per performance. It is possible to buy servers with 8 CPUs, 64-Gb memory, and 8 Tb of disk space, but these cost roughly three times the price of a rack of 88 dual-processor machines with 2-Gb memory and 80-Gb disk space. The high-end server would serve a single client four times faster than the rack of slower computers, but the rack could serve 22 times as many of concurrent users as the high-end server. That's scalability.

It is not the case, however, to say that one server handles one user's request. If this were the case, each computer would have to trawl through thousands of terabytes of data looking for a search term. It would take weeks to return a single query. Instead, the servers are divided into six different groups—Web servers, document servers, index servers, spell check servers, advertisement servers, and Googlebot servers—each performing its own task.

Google uses a sophisticated DNS system to select the most appropriate Web server for its visitors. This DNS system can automatically redirect visitors to the geographically closest data center. This is why, for instance, if you type *www.google.com* in Switzerland, you will be directed to *www.google.ch*, which is located in Zurich. But if you type *www.google.com* in California, you will be directed to their data center in Santa Clara. The DNS system also accounts for server load and may redirect to different centers in the event of high congestion.

When the request arrives at the data center, it goes through a hardware load balancer that selects one from a cluster of available Web servers to handle the request. These Web servers' sole function is to prepare and serve the HTML to the client; they do not perform the actual search. The search task is delegated to a cluster of index servers, which lie behind the Web servers.

An index server cluster comprises hundreds of computers, each holding a subset (or shard) of a multiterabyte database. Many computers may hold identical subsets of the same database in case of a hardware failure on one of the index servers. The index itself is a list of correlated words and terms with a list of document IDs and a relevancy rating for each match. A document ID is a reference to a Web page or other Google-readable media (e.g., PDF, DOC). The order of results returned by the index depends on the combined relevancy rating of the search terms and the page rank of the document ID. The page rank is a gauge of site popularity measured as a sum of the popularity of the sites linking to it. Other factors also affect page rank, such as the number of links leaving the site, the structure of internal links, and so forth.

Google's document servers contain cached copies of virtually the entire World Wide Web on their hard drives. Each data center would have its own document server cluster, and each document server cluster would need to hold at least two copies of the Web, in order to provide redundancy in case of server failure. But document servers are not merely data warehouses. They also perform retrieval of the page title and keyword-in-context snippet from the document ID provided by the index servers.

As the search is running, the peripheral systems also add their content to the page as the search is in progress. This includes the spell check and the advertisements. Once all elements of the page are together, the page is shipped off to the visitor, all in less than a second.

Google also employs another breed of software, a spider named Googlebot. This piece of software, running on thousands of PCs simultaneously, trawls the Web continuously, completing a full round-trip in approximately one month. Googlebot requests pages in an ordered fashion, following links to a set depth, storing the content in the document servers and updating the index servers with updated document IDs, relevancy ratings, and page rank values. Another spider named Fastbot crawls the Web on a more regular basis, sometimes in less than a week. It only visits sites with a high page rank and those that are frequently updated.

The Google architecture is one of the best in the world and is the pinnacle of scalability; however, for .NET developers, there is a slight twist in the tail. Google can afford to buy 15,000 servers by cutting down on licensing costs. This means that they use Linux, not Windows. Unfortunately, Linux isn't exactly home turf for .NET, but there is an open-source project called MONO, which aims to provide a C# compiler for Linux (see *www.go-mono.com*).

10.3 Replication and redundancy

Keeping a backup system ready for instant deployment is *redundancy*; keeping the backup system identical to the live system is *replication*. When dealing with a high-availability Internet-based service, it is important to keep more than one copy of critical systems. Thus, in the event of software or hardware failure, an identical copy of the software can take the place of the failed module.

Backup systems do not need to be kept on separate machines. You can use redundant hard drives using a redundant array of inexpensive disks (RAID) array. This is where the file system is stored on several physical hard disks. If one disk fails, then the other disks take over, with no loss of data. Many computers can read from a RAID array at once but only one computer can write at the same time (known as "shared nothing"). Of course, it's not just hard disks that fail. If a computer fails, another must take over in the same way.

Providing redundancy among computers is the task of a *load balancer*, a piece of hardware or software that delegates client requests among multiple servers. In order to provide redundancy, the load balancer must be able to recognize a crashed computer or one that is unable to respond in a timely fashion. A full discussion of load balancers is included later in this chapter.

Replication provides the means by which a backup system can remain identical to the live system. If replication did not occur, data on the backup system could become so out-of-date that it would be worthless if set live. Replication is built into Microsoft SQL, accessible under the replication folder in Enterprise Manager. SQL replication works by relaying update, insert, and delete statements from one server to another. Changes made while the other server is down are queued until the server goes live again.

10.4 Scalable network applications

Server-side applications are often required to operate with full efficiency under extreme load. *Efficiency*, in this sense, relates to both the throughput of the server and the number of clients it can handle. In some cases, it is common to deny new clients to conserve resources for existing clients.

The key to providing scalable network applications is to keep threading as efficient as possible. In many examples in this book, a new thread is created for each new client that connects to the server. This approach, although simple, is not ideal. The underlying management of a single thread consumes far more memory and processor time than a socket.

In benchmarking tests, a simple echo server, running on a Pentium IV 1.7 GHz with 768-Mb memory, was connected to three clients: a Pentium II 233 MHz with 128-Mb memory, a Pentium II 350 MHz with 128-Mb memory, and an Itanium 733 MHz with 1-Gb memory. This semitypical arrangement demonstrated that using the approach outlined above, the server could only serve 1,008 connections before it reached an internal thread creation limit. The maximum throughput was 2 Mbps. When a further 12,000 connections were attempted and rejected, the throughput keeled off to a mere 404 Kbps.

The server, although having adequate memory and CPU time resources to handle the additional clients, was unable to because it could not create any further threads as thread creations and destructions were taking up all of the CPU resources. To better manage thread creation, a technique known as *thread pooling* (demonstrated later in this chapter) can be employed. When thread pooling was applied to the echo server example, the server performed somewhat better. With 12,000 client connections, the server handled each one without fail. The throughput was 1.8 Mbps, vastly outperforming the software in the previous example, which obtained only 0.4 Mbps at the same CPU load. As a further 49,000 clients connected, however, the server began to drop 0.6% of the connections. At the same time, the CPU usage reached 95% of its peak capacity. At this load, the combined throughput was 3.8 Mbps.

Thread pooling unarguably provides a scalability bonus, but it is not acceptable to consume 95% of server resources just doing socket I/O, especially when other applications must also use the computer. In order to beef up the server, the threading model should be abandoned completely, in favor of I/O completion ports (see Chapter 3). This methodology uses asynchronous callbacks that are managed at the operating system level.

By modifying the above example to use I/O completion ports rather than thread pools, the server once again handled 12,000 clients without fail; however, this time the throughput was an impressive 5 Mbps. When the load was pushed to 50,000 clients, the server handled these connections virtually flawlessly and maintained a healthy throughput of 4.3 Mbps. The CPU usage at this load was 65%, which could have permitted other applications to run on the same server without conflicts.

In the thread-pool and completion-port models, the memory usage at 50,000 connections was more than 240 Mb, including non-paged-pool usage at more than 145 Mb. If the server had less than this available in physical memory, the result would have been substantially worse.

10.5 **Future proofing**

Scalability can also apply to the ability of an application to evolve gracefully to meet future demands without major overhaul. When software is first designed, the primary goal is to hit all of the customer's requirements or to meet the perceived needs of a typical end-user. After rollout of the product, it may address these requirements perfectly. Once the market demands some major change to the application, the program has to scale to meet the new demands without massive recoding.

This connotation of scalability is not the focus of the chapter, but some of the following tips may help create a future-proof application:

- Use classes instead of basic types for variables that represent elements within your software that may grow in complexity. This ensures that functions accept these variables because parameters will not need to be changed as dramatically in the future.

- Keep culture-specific strings in a resource file; if the software is ever localized for a different language, this will reduce the change impact.

- Keep abreast of modern technologies. It may soon be a requirement of network applications to be IPv6 compliant.

- Provide a means to update your software automatically post deployment.

The key to architectural scalability is to make everything configurable and to assume nothing of the deployment environment.

10.6 Thread pooling

Every computer has a limit to the number of threads it can process at one time. Depending on the resources consumed by each thread, this number could be quite low. When given the choice either to guarantee your software to handle a set number of clients or to "max out" the computer's resources and risk a system crash, choose the first option: thread pooling.

Threads can improve the responsiveness of applications, where each thread consumes less than 100% processor time. Multitasking operating systems share the available CPU resources among the running threads by quickly switching between them to give the impression that they are all running in parallel. This switching, which may occur up to 60 times per second, incurs some small switching cost, which can become prohibitive if the number of threads becomes too large. Threads that are blocked waiting for some event do not, however, consume CPU resources while they wait, but they still consume some kernel memory resources. The optimum number of threads for any given application is system dependent. A thread pool is useful at finding this optimum number of threads to use.

To give some perspective on the effect of unpooled threading, examine the code below:

C#

```
public static void IncrementThread()
{
  while(true)
  {
    myIncrementor++;
    long ticks = DateTime.Now.Ticks - startTime.Ticks;
    lock (this)
    {
      lblIPS.Text = "Increments per second:" +
      (myIncrementor / ticks) * 10000000;
    }
  }
}
```

VB.NET

```
Public Shared Sub IncrementThread()
 Dim ticks as long
 Do
  MyIncrementor = MyIncrementor+1
  Ticks = DateTime.Now.Ticks - startTime.Ticks
  SyncLock(me)
   lblIPS.Text = "Increments per second:" + _
      (myIncrementor / ticks) * 10000000
  End synclock
 Loop
End Sub
```

This code adds one to a public variable named MyIncrementor. It then takes an accurate reading of system time, before updating the screen to show the level of increments per second. The SyncLock or Lock statement is used to ensure that no two threads attempt to update the screen at the same time because this causes unpredictable results. The results shown on-screen should not be used as a measure of how quickly the computer can perform subtraction because most of the processor time is actually spent showing the results!

When this thread was instantiated on its own, it operated at a speed of 235 increments per second; however, when this thread was instantiated 1,000 times and ran concurrently, the threads consumed more than 60 Mb of memory stack frame, which on some older computers would go directly to a paging file on disk, creating a systemwide loss of performance. In a group of 1,000 threads, the overall performance was a mere 98 increments per second, meaning that a single thread could take more than 10 seconds to iterate through one `while` loop. The test machine was a 333 MHz Pentium III with 128 Mb of RAM.

With a thread pool, the optimal number of threads on this particular computer was found to be 25, which gave an overall operating speed of 402 increments per second, with a slightly modified `Incrementer-Thread()` routine.

10.6.1 Implementing a thread pool

Thread pools are used constantly in servers, where a reliable service must be provided regardless of load. This sample application is a simply a benchmarking utility, but with experimentation it could be adapted for any purpose.

Create a new project in Visual Studio .NET and drop in two labels: `lblThreads` and `lblIPS`. The thread pool will be populated with threads as soon as the form loads. The exact time at which the form starts is stored in a public variable named `startTime`. Every thread then adds one to a public variable named `myIncrementor`, which helps gauge overall performance. Both of these are included in the code directly after the class declaration:

C#

```
public class Form1 : System.Windows.Forms.Form
{
  public  double myIncrementor;
  public  DateTime startTime;
  ...
```

VB.NET

```
Public Class Form1
   Inherits System.Windows.Forms.Form
   Public myIncrementor As Double
   Public startTime As DateTime
   ...
```

To populate the thread pool, a check is made to see how many threads should run together concurrently. That number of threads is then added to the thread pool. There is no problem in adding more than the recommended number of threads to the pool because the surplus threads will not execute until another thread has finished. In this case, the threads run in an infinite loop; therefore, no surplus threads would ever execute.

Double-click on the form and add the following code:

C#

```csharp
private void Form1_Load(object sender, System.EventArgs e)
{
  int workerThreads=0;
  int IOThreads=0;
  ThreadPool.GetMaxThreads(out workerThreads,out IOThreads);
  lblThreads.Text = "Threads: " + workerThreads;
  for (int threads=0;threads<workerThreads;threads++)
  {
    ThreadPool.QueueUserWorkItem(new
    WaitCallback(Increment),this);
  }
  startTime = DateTime.Now;
}
```

VB.NET

```vbnet
Private  Sub Form1_Load(ByVal sender As Object, _
ByVal e As System.EventArgs)
  Dim workerThreads As Integer = 0
  Dim IOThreads As Integer = 0
  ThreadPool.GetMaxThreads(workerThreads, IOThreads)
  lblThreads.Text = "Threads: " & workerThreads
  Dim threads As Integer = 0
  For threads = 1 To workerThreads
  ThreadPool.QueueUserWorkItem(New WaitCallback _
    (AddressOf Increment), Me)
  Next
  startTime = DateTime.Now
End Sub
```

This code first obtains the default number of threads that can run concurrently on the local machine using the `GetMaxThreads` method. It then displays this value on-screen before creating and running these threads.

There can only be one thread pool in an application, so only static methods are called on the thread pool. The most important method is `QueueUserWorkItem`. The first parameter of this method is the function (delegate) to be called, and the second parameter (which is optional) is the object that is to be passed to the new thread. The `Increment` function is then implemented thus:

C#

```csharp
public void Increment()
{
 while(true)
 {
  myIncrementor++;
  long ticks = DateTime.Now.Ticks - startTime.Ticks;
  lock (this)
  {
   lblIPS.Text = "Increments per second:"+
   (myIncrementor/ticks) * 10000000;
  }
 }
}
```

VB.NET

```vbnet
Public Sub Increment()
  Dim ticks As Long
  Do
    myIncrementor = myIncrementor + 1
    ticks = DateTime.Now.Ticks - startTime.Ticks
    SyncLock (Me)
      lblIPS.Text = "Increments per second:" & _
      (myIncrementor / ticks) * 10000000
    End SyncLock
  Loop
End Sub
```

Figure 10.1
*Thread pool sample
application.*

The `lock` (or `syncLock`) is required for application stability. If two threads repeatedly access the same user interface element at the same time, the application's UI becomes unresponsive.

Finally, the threading namespace is required:

C#

```
using System.Threading;
```

VB.NET

```
imports System.Threading
```

To test the application, run it from Visual Studio .NET and wait for a minute or two for the increments-per-second value to settle on a number (Figure 10.1). You can experiment with this application and see how performance increases and decreases under certain conditions, such as running several applications or running with low memory.

10.7 Avoiding deadlocks

Deadlocks are the computing equivalent of a Catch-22 situation. Imagine an application that retrieves data from a Web site and stores it in a database. Users can use this application to query from either the database or the Web site. These three tasks would be implemented as separate threads, and for whatever reason, no two threads can access the Web site or the database at the same time.

The first thread would be:

- Wait for access to the Web site.
- Restrict other threads' access to the Web site.
- Wait for access to the database.

- Restrict other threads' access to the database.

- Draw down the data, and write it to the database.

- Relinquish the restriction on the database and Web site.

The second thread would be:

- Wait for access to the database.

- Restrict other threads' access to the database.

- Read from the database.

- Execute thread three, and wait for its completion.

- Relinquish the restriction on the database.

The third thread would be:

- Wait for access to the Web site.

- Restrict other threads' access to the Web site.

- Read from the Web site.

- Relinquish the restriction on the Web site.

Any thread running on its own will complete without any errors; however, if thread 2 is at the point of reading from the database, while thread 1 is waiting for access to the database, the threads will hang. Thread 3 will never complete because thread 1 will never get access to the database until thread 2 is satisfied that thread 3 is complete.

A deadlock could have been avoided by relinquishing the database restriction before executing thread 3, or in several different ways, but the problem with deadlocks is spotting them and redesigning the threading structure to avoid the bug.

10.8 Load balancing

Load balancing is a means of dividing workload among multiple servers by forwarding only a percentage of requests to each server. The simplest way of doing this is DNS round-robin, which is where a DNS server contains multiple entries for the same IP address. So when a client requests a DNS, it will receive one of a number of IP addresses to connect to. This approach has one major drawback in that if one of your servers crashes, 50% of your clients will receive no data. The same effect can be achieved on the client side, where the application will connect to an alternative IP address if one server fails to return data. Of course, this would be a nightmare scenario if you deploy a thousand kiosks, only to find a week later that your service provider had gone bust and you were issued new IP addresses. If you work by DNS names, you will have to wait 24 hours for the propagation to take place.

Computers can change their IP addresses by themselves, by simply returning a different response when they receive an ARP request. There is no programmatic control over the ARP table in Windows computers, but you can use specially designed load-balancing software, such as Microsoft Network Load Balancing Service (NLBS), which ships with the Windows 2000 advanced server. This allows many computers to operate from the same IP address. By way of checking the status of services such as IIS on each computer in a cluster, every other computer can elect to exclude that computer from the cluster until it fixes itself, or a technician does so. The computers do not actually use the same IP address; in truth, the IP addresses are interchanged to create the same effect.

NLBS is suitable for small clusters of four or five servers, but for high-end server farms from between 10 and 8,000 computers, the ideal solution is a hardware virtual server, such as Cisco's Local Director. This machine sits between the router and the server farm. All requests to it are fed directly to one of the 8,000 computers sitting behind it, provided that that server is listening on port 80.

None of the above solutions—DNS round-robin, Cisco Local Director, or Microsoft NLBS—can provide the flexibility of custom load balancing. NLBS, for instance, routes requests only on the basis of a percentage of the client requests they will receive. So if you have multiple servers with different hardware configurations, it's your responsibility to estimate each system's performance compared to the others. Therefore, if you wanted to route a percentage of requests based on actual server CPU usage, you couldn't achieve this with NLBS alone.

There are two ways of providing custom load balancing, either through hardware or software. A hardware solution can be achieved with a little imagination and a router. Most routers are configurable via a Web interface or serial connection. Therefore, a computer can configure its own router either through an RS232 connection (briefly described in Chapter 4) or by using HTTP. Each computer can periodically connect to the router and set up port forwarding so that incoming requests come to it rather than the other machine. The hardware characteristics of the router may determine how quickly port forwarding can be switched between computers and how requests are handled during settings changes. This method may require some experimentation, but it could be a cheap solution to load balancing, or at least to graceful failover.

Custom software load balancers are applicable in systems where the time to process each client request is substantially greater than the time to move the data across the network. For these systems, it is worth considering using a second server to share the processing load. You could program the clients to connect to switch intermittently between servers, but this may not always be possible if the client software is already deployed. A software load balancer would inevitably incur an overhead, which in some cases could be more than the time saved by relieving server load. Therefore, this solution may not be ideal in all situations.

This implementation of a software load balancer behaves a little like a proxy server. It accepts requests from the Internet and relays them to a server of its choosing. The relayed requests must have their HOST header changed to reflect the new target. Otherwise, the server may reject the request. The load balancer can relay requests based on any criteria, such as server CPU load, memory usage, or any other factor. It could also be used to control failover, where if one server fails, the load balancer could automatically redirect traffic to the remaining operational servers. In this case, a simple round-robin approach is used.

The example program balances load among three mirrored HTTP servers: *uk.php.net, ca.php.net, and ca2.php.net.* Requests from users are directed initially to the load-balancing server and are then channeled to one of these servers, with the response returned to the user. Note that this approach does not take advantage of any geographic proximity the user may have to the Web servers because all traffic is channeled through the load balancer.

To create this application, start a new project in Microsoft Visual Studio .NET. Draw a textbox on the form, named tbStatus. It should be set with multiline to true.

Add two public variables at the top of the Form class as shown. The port variable is used to hold the TCP port on which the load balancer will listen. The site variable is used to hold a number indicating the next available Web server.

C#

```
public class Form1 : System.Windows.Forms.Form
```

```
{
   public int port;
   public int site;
```

VB.NET

```
Public Class Form1
 Inherits System.Windows.Forms.Form
     Public port As Integer
     Public Shadows site As Integer
```

When the application starts, it will immediately run a thread that will wait indefinitely for external TCP connections. This code is placed into the form's Load event:

C#

```
private void Form1_Load(object sender, System.EventArgs e)
{
   Thread thread = new Thread(new
   ThreadStart(ListenerThread));
   thread.Start();
}
```

VB.NET

```
Private Sub Form1_Load(ByVal sender As System.Object, _
 ByVal e As System.EventArgs) Handles MyBase.Load
 Dim thread As Thread = New Thread(New ThreadStart( _
     AddressOf ListenerThread))
 thread.Start()
End Sub
```

The ListenerThread works by listening on port 8889 and waiting on connections. When it receives a connection, it instantiates a new instance of the WebProxy class and starts its run method in a new thread. It sets the class's clientSocket and UserInterface properties so that the WebProxy instance can reference the form and the socket containing the client request.

C#

```
public void ListenerThread()
{
```

```
    port = 8889;
    TcpListener tcplistener = new TcpListener(port);
    reportMessage("Listening on port " + port);
    tcplistener.Start();
    while(true)
    {
      WebProxy webproxy = new WebProxy();
      webproxy.UserInterface = this;
      webproxy.clientSocket = tcplistener.AcceptSocket();
      reportMessage("New client");
      Thread thread = new
        Thread(new ThreadStart(webproxy.run));
      thread.Start();
    }
}
```

VB.NET

```
Public Sub ListenerThread()
  port = 8889
  Dim tcplistener As TcpListener = New TcpListener(port)
  reportMessage("Listening on port " + port.ToString())
  tcplistener.Start()
  Do
    Dim webproxy As WebProxy = New WebProxy
    webproxy.UserInterface = Me
    webproxy.clientSocket = tcplistener.AcceptSocket()
    reportMessage("New client")
    Dim thread As Thread = New Thread(New ThreadStart( _
      AddressOf webproxy.run))
    thread.Start()
  Loop
End Sub
```

A utility function that is used throughout the application is reportMessage. Its function is to display messages in the textbox and scroll the textbox automatically, so that the user can see the newest messages as they arrive.

C#

```
public void reportMessage(string msg)
{
  lock(this)
```

```
    {
      tbStatus.Text += msg + "\r\n";
      tbStatus.SelectionStart = tbStatus.Text.Length;
      tbStatus.ScrollToCaret();
    }
  }
```

VB.NET

```
Public Sub reportMessage(ByVal msg As String)
  SyncLock Me
    tbStatus.Text += msg + vbCrLf
    tbStatus.SelectionStart = tbStatus.Text.Length
    tbStatus.ScrollToCaret()
  End SyncLock
End Sub
```

The core algorithm of the load balancer is held in the getMirror function. This method simply returns a URL based on the site variable. More
complex load-balancing techniques could be implemented within this function if required.

C#

```
public string getMirror()
{
  string Mirror = "";
  switch(site)
  {
    case 0:
     Mirror="uk.php.net";
     site++;
     break;
    case 1:
     Mirror="ca.php.net";
     site++;
     break;
    case 2:
     Mirror="ca2.php.net";
     site=0;
     break;
  }
  return Mirror;
}
```

VB.NET

```
Public Function getMirror() As String
  Dim Mirror As String = ""
  Select Case site
  Case 0
    Mirror = "uk.php.net"
    site = site + 1
  Case 1
    Mirror = "ca.php.net"
    site = site + 1
  Case 2
    Mirror = "ca2.php.net"
    site = 0
  End Select
  Return Mirror
End Function
```

The next step is to develop the WebProxy class. This class contains two public variables and two functions. Create the class thus:

C#

```
public class WebProxy
{
  public Socket clientSocket;
  public Form1 UserInterface;
}
```

VB.NET

```
Public Class WebProxy
    Public clientSocket As Socket
    Public UserInterface As Form1
End Class
```

The entry point to the class is the run method. This method reads 1,024 (or fewer) bytes from the HTTP request. It is assumed that the HTTP request is less than 1 Kb in size, in ASCII format, and that it can be received in one Receive operation. The next step is to remove the HOST HTTP header and replace it with a HOST header pointing to the server returned by getMirror. Having done this, it passes control to relayTCP to complete the task of transferring data from user to Web server.

C#

```csharp
public void run()
{
  string sURL = UserInterface.getMirror();
  byte[] readIn = new byte[1024];
  int bytes = clientSocket.Receive(readIn);
  string clientmessage = Encoding.ASCII.GetString(readIn);
  clientmessage = clientmessage.Substring(0,bytes);
  int posHost = clientmessage.IndexOf("Host:");
  int posEndOfLine = clientmessage.IndexOf("\r\n",posHost);
  clientmessage =
    clientmessage.Remove(posHost,posEndOfLine-posHost);
  clientmessage =
    clientmessage.Insert(posHost,"Host: "+ sURL);
  readIn = Encoding.ASCII.GetBytes(clientmessage);
  if(bytes == 0) return;
  UserInterface.reportMessage("Connection from:" +
    clientSocket.RemoteEndPoint + "\r\n");
  UserInterface.reportMessage
    ("Connecting to Site:" +  sURL + "\r\n");
  relayTCP(sURL,80,clientmessage);
  clientSocket.Close();
}
```

VB.NET

```vbnet
Public Sub run()
  Dim sURL As String = UserInterface.getMirror()
  Dim readIn() As Byte = New Byte(1024) {}
  Dim bytes As Integer = clientSocket.Receive(readIn)
  Dim clientmessage As String = _
  Encoding.ASCII.GetString(readIn)
  clientmessage = clientmessage.Substring(0, bytes)
  Dim posHost As Integer = clientmessage.IndexOf("Host:")
  Dim posEndOfLine As Integer = clientmessage.IndexOf _
    (vbCrLf, posHost)
  clientmessage = clientmessage.Remove(posHost, _
    posEndOfLine - posHost)
  clientmessage = clientmessage.Insert(posHost, _
    "Host: " + sURL)
  readIn = Encoding.ASCII.GetBytes(clientmessage)
  If bytes = 0 Then Return
```

```
  UserInterface.reportMessage("Connection from:" + _
      clientSocket.RemoteEndPoint.ToString())
  UserInterface.reportMessage("Connecting to Site:" + sURL)
  relayTCP(sURL, 80, clientmessage)
  clientSocket.Close()
End Sub
```

The data transfer takes place on relayTCP. It opens a TCP connection to the Web server on port 80 and then sends it the modified HTTP header sent from the user. Immediately after the data is sent, it goes into a loop, reading 256-byte chunks of data from the Web server and sending it back to the client. If at any point it encounters an error, or the data flow comes to an end, the loop is broken and the function returns.

C#

```
public void relayTCP(string host,int port,string cmd)
{
  byte[] szData;
  byte[] RecvBytes = new byte[Byte.MaxValue];
  Int32 bytes;
  TcpClient TcpClientSocket = new TcpClient(host,port);
  NetworkStream NetStrm = TcpClientSocket.GetStream();
  szData =
  System.Text.Encoding.ASCII.GetBytes(cmd.ToCharArray());
  NetStrm.Write(szData,0,szData.Length);
  while(true)
  {
    try
    {
      bytes = NetStrm.Read(RecvBytes, 0,RecvBytes.Length);
      clientSocket.Send(RecvBytes,bytes,SocketFlags.None);
      if (bytes<=0) break;
    }
    catch
    {
      UserInterface.reportMessage("Failed connect");
      break;
    }
  }
}
```

VB.NET

```
Public Sub relayTCP(ByVal host As String, ByVal port _
    As Integer, ByVal cmd As String)
  Dim szData() As Byte
  Dim RecvBytes() As Byte = New Byte(Byte.MaxValue) {}
  Dim bytes As Int32
  Dim TcpClientSocket As TcpClient = New TcpClient(host, port)
  Dim NetStrm As NetworkStream = TcpClientSocket.GetStream()
  szData = _
    System.Text.Encoding.ASCII.GetBytes(cmd.ToCharArray())
  NetStrm.Write(szData, 0, szData.Length)
  While True
    Try
      bytes = NetStrm.Read(RecvBytes, 0, RecvBytes.Length)
      clientSocket.Send(RecvBytes, bytes, SocketFlags.None)
      If bytes <= 0 Then Exit While
    Catch
      UserInterface.reportMessage("Failed connect")
      Exit While
    End Try
  End While
End Sub
```

As usual, some standard namespaces are added to the head of the code:

C#

```
using System.Net;
using System.Net.Sockets;
using System.Text;
using System.IO;
using System.Threading;
```

VB.NET

```
Imports System.Net
Imports System.Net.Sockets
Imports System.Text
Imports System.IO
Imports System.Threading
```

To test the application, run it from Visual Studio .NET, and then open a browser on *http://localhost:8889;* you will see that the Web site is loaded

Figure 10.2
*HTTP load-
balancing
application.*

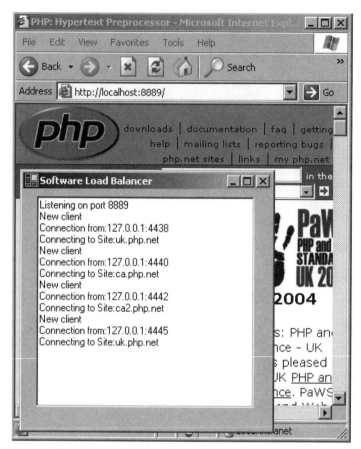

from all three servers. In this case, data transfer consumes most of the site's
loading time, so there would be little performance gain, but it should serve
as an example (Figure 10.2).

10.9 Conclusion

Scalability problems generally only start appearing once a product has
rolled out into full-scale production. At this stage in the life cycle, making
modifications to the software becomes a logistical nightmare. Any changes
to the software will necessarily have to be backwards compatible with older
versions of the product.

Many software packages now include an autoupdater, which accommo-
dates postdeployment updates; however, the best solution is to address scal-

ability issues at the design phase, rather than ending up with a dozen versions of your product and the server downtime caused by implementing updates.

The next chapter deals with network performance, including techniques such as compression and multicast.

Optimizing Bandwidth Utilization

11.1 Introduction

You can't always expect your customer to have the same bandwidth as your office LAN. Huge numbers of people still use modem connections, and some use mobile GPRS devices with even lower connection speeds.

These customers will only buy your software if it works at a speed that is at least usable and does not frustrate them. Online services with slow loading times will infuriate casual Web users and drive away potential customers. Conversely, people will pay more for better performance. To give an example, VNC (*www.realvnc.com*) is free, under general public license (GPL), whereas client licenses for Microsoft Terminal Services (MTS) are certainly not free. Both pieces of software allow you to control another computer remotely, but many people still opt for MTS. Why? Performance. MTS provides more fluid control over the remote computer than VNC over the same bandwidth.

This chapter is largely devoted to two different performance-enhancing techniques. The first section of the chapter covers a technology known as *multicast*, the ability to send one piece of data to more than one recipient simultaneously. The second section deals with data compression and decompression. This is the ability to convert a block of data into a smaller block of data and then return this to either an exact or near copy of the original data.

11.2 Tricks and tips to increase performance

Performance increases can often be made by simple changes to how data is moved between client and server. In some cases, these techniques may not be applicable; however when used correctly, each of the following methods will help keep your data moving quickly.

11.2.1   Caching

Caching can increase network performance by storing frequently accessed static data in a location that provides faster data return than the normal access time for the static data. It is important that all three of the following criteria are met:

- *The data must be frequently accessed.* There is no point in storing large datasets in memory or on disk when only one client will ever request it, once.

- *The data must not change as often as it is requested.* The data should remain static for long periods, or else clients will receive outdated data.

- *The access time for cached data must be substantially faster than the access time to receive the data directly.* It would defeat the purpose if a client were denied access to the data from its source and instead was redirected to a caching server that had to reprocess the data.

Data can be cached at any point between the client and server. *Server-side caches* can protect against out-of-date data, but they are slower than client-side caches. *Client caches* are very fast because the data is read from disk, not the network, but they are prone to out-of-date data. *Proxy caches* are a combination of the two. They can refresh their cache regularly when idle and can serve data faster because they will be on a local connection to the client. Old data on a proxy can be frustrating for a user because it is awkward to flush the cache of a proxy server manually.

Server caching can be extremely useful when data on the server needs to be processed before it can be sent to clients. A prime example of this is that when an ASP.NET page is uploaded to a server, it must be compiled before generating content that is sent to the client. It is extremely wasteful to have the server recompile the page every time it is requested, so the compiled version is held in a server-side cache.

When a site consists of mainly static content, it is possible to cache a compressed version of each of the pages to be delivered because most browsers can dynamically decompress content in the right format. Therefore, instead of sending the original version of each page, a compressed version could be sent. When the content is dynamic, it is possible to utilize on-the-fly compression from server-accelerator products such as Xcache and Pipeboost.

Caching introduces the problem of change monitoring, so that the cached data reflects the live data as accurately as possible. Where the data is in the form of files on disk, one of the simplest mechanisms is to compare the "date modified" field against the cached data. Above that, hashing could be used to monitor changes within datasets or other content.

Within the environment of a single Web site or application, caching can be controlled and predicted quite easily, except when the content to be served could come from arbitrary sources. This situation might arise in a generic caching proxy server, where content could come from anywhere on the Internet. In this case, the proxy must make an educated assessment about whether pages should be cached locally or not.

The proxy would need to hold an internal table, which could record all requests made to it from clients. The proxy would need to store the full HTTP request because many sites behave differently depending on what cookies and so forth are sent by the client. Along with the requests, the proxy would need to be able to count the number of identical requests and how recently they were made. The proxy should also keep checksums (or hashes) of the data returned from the server relative to each request. With this information, the proxy can determine if the content is too dynamic to cache. With that said, even the most static and frequently accessed sites change sometimes. The proxy could, during lull periods, check some of the currently cached Web sites against the live versions and update the cache accordingly.

11.2.2 Keep-alive connections

Even though most Web pages contain many different images that all come from the same server, some older (HTTP 1.0) clients create new HTTP connections for each of the images. This is wasteful because the first HTTP connection is sufficient to send all of the images. Luckily, most browsers and servers are capable of handling HTTP 1.1 persistent connections. A client can request that a server keep a TCP connection open by specifying `Connection: Keep-Alive` in the HTTP header.

Netscape pioneered a technology that could send many disparate forms of data through the same HTTP connection. This system was called "server push" and could provide for simple video streaming in the days before Windows media. Server push was never adopted by Microsoft, and unfortunately it is not supported by Internet Explorer, but it is still available in Netscape Navigator.

When a TCP connection opens and closes, several handshake packets are sent back and forth between the client and server, which can waste up to one second per connection for modem users. If you are developing a proprietary protocol that involves multiple sequential requests and responses between client and server, you should always aim to keep the TCP connection open for as long as possible, rather than repeatedly opening and closing it with every request.

The whole handshake latency issue can be avoided completely by using a non-connection-oriented protocol such as UDP. As mentioned in Chapter 3, however, data integrity is endangered when transmitted over UDP. Some protocols such as real-time streaming protocol (RTSP, defined in RFC 2326) use a combination of TCP and UDP to achieve a compromise between speed and reliability.

11.2.3 Progressive downloads

When most of a file is downloaded, the client should be able to begin to use the data. The obvious applications are audio and video, where users can begin to see and hear the video clip before it is fully downloaded. The same technique is applicable in many scenarios. For instance, if product listings are being displayed as they are retrieved, a user could interrupt the process once the desired product is shown and proceed with the purchase.

Image formats such as JPEG and GIF come in a progressive version, which renders them as full-size images very soon after the first few hundred bytes are received. Subsequent bytes form a more distinct and higher-quality image. This technique is known as *interlacing*. Its equivalent in an online catalog application would be where product names and prices download first, followed by the images of the various products.

11.2.4 Tweaking settings

Windows is optimized by default for use on Ethernets, so where a production application is being rolled out to a client base using modems, ISDN, or DSL, some system tweaking can be done to help Windows manage the connection more efficiently and, ultimately, to increase overall network performance. Because these settings are systemwide, however, these changes should only be applied when the end-customer has given your software permission to do so.

The TCP/IP settings are held in the registry at

```
HKEY_LOCAL_MACHINE\SYSTEM\CurrentControlSet\Services\Tcpip\
Parameters
```

Under this location, various parameters can be seen, such as default name servers and gateways, which would otherwise be inaccessible programmatically. Not all of these parameters would already be present in the registry by default, but they could be added when required.

The first system tweak is the TCP window size, which can be set at the following registry location:

```
HKLM\SYSTEM\CurrentControlSet\Services\Tcpip\Parameters\
GlobalMaxTcpWindowSize
```

The TCP window specifies the number of bytes that a sending computer can transmit without receiving an ACK. The recommended value is 256,960. Other values to try are 372,300, 186,880, 93,440, 64,240, and 32,120. The valid range is from the maximum segment size (MSS) to 2^{30}. For best results, the size has to be a multiple of MSS lower than 65,535 times a scale factor that's a power of 2. The MSS is generally roughly equal to the maximum transmission unit (MTU), as described later. This tweak reduces protocol overhead by eliminating part of the safety net and trimming some of the time involved in the turnaround of an ACK.

`TcpWindowSize` can also exist under `\Parameters\Interface\`. If the setting is added at this location, it overrides the global setting. When the window size is less than 64K, the `Tcp1323Opts` setting should be applied as detailed below:

```
HKLM\SYSTEM\CurrentControlSet\Services\Tcpip\Parameters\
Tcp1323Opts
```

"Tcp1323" refers to RFC 1323, a proposal to add timestamps to packets to aid out-of-order deliveries. Removing timestamps shaves off 12 bytes per TCP/IP packet, but reduces reliability over bad connections. It also affects TCP window scaling, as mentioned above. Zero is the recommended option for higher performance. Set the size to one to include window-scaling features and three to apply the timestamp. This setting is particularly risky and should not be tampered with without great care.

The issue of packets with a time-to-live (TTL) value is discussed again in the multicast section in this chapter, where it is of particular importance. The setting can be applied on a systemwide level at this registry location:

```
HKLM\SYSTEM\CurrentControlSet\Services\Tcpip\Parameters\
DefaultTTL
```

The TTL of a packet is a measure of how many routers a packet will travel through before being discarded. An excessively high TTL (e.g., 255) will cause delays, especially over bad links. A low TTL will cause some packets to be discarded before they reach their destination. The recommended value is 64.

The MTU is the maximum size of any packet sent over the wire. If it is set too high, lost packets will take longer to retransmit and may get fragmented. If the MTU is set too low, data becomes swamped with overhead and takes longer to send. Ethernet connections use a default of 1,500 bytes per packet; ADSL uses 1,492 bytes per packet; and FDDI uses 8,000 bytes per packet. The MTU value can be left as the default or can be negotiated at startup. The registry key in question is

```
HKLM\SYSTEM\CurrentControlSet\Services\Tcpip\Parameters\
EnablePMTUDiscovery
```

The recommended value is one. This will make the computer negotiate with the NIC miniport driver for the best value for MTU on initial transmission. This may cause a slow startup effect, but it will ultimately be beneficial if there should be little packet loss and the data being transferred is large.

Ideally, every piece of datagram being sent should be the size of the MTU. If it is any larger than the MTU, the datagram will fragment, which takes computing time and increases the risk of datagram loss. This setting is highly recommended for modem users:

```
HKLM\SYSTEM\CurrentControlSet\Services\Tcpip\Parameters\
EnablePMTUBHDetect
```

The recommended setting is zero. Setting this parameter to one (True) enables "black hole" routers to be detected; however, it also increases the maximum number of retransmissions for a given TCP data segment. A black hole router is one that fails to deliver packets and does not report the failure to the sender with an ICMP message. If black hole routers are not an issue on the network, they can be ignored.

```
HKLM\SYSTEM\CurrentControlSet\Services\Tcpip\Parameters\
SackOpts
```

The recommended setting is one. This enables Selective Acknowledgement (SACK) to take place, which can improve performance where window sizes are low.

```
HKLM\SYSTEM\CurrentControlSet\Services\Tcpip\Parameters\
TcpMaxDupAcks
```

The recommended value is two. The parameter determines the number of duplicate acknowledgments that must be received for the same sequence number of sent data before "fast retransmit" is triggered to resend the segment that has been dropped in transit. This setting is of particular importance on links where a high potential for packet loss exists.

Moving outside the low-level TCP nuts and bolts, a setting can improve the performance of outgoing HTTP connections. These settings can speed up activities such as Web browsing:

```
HKEY_USERS\.DEFAULT\Software\Microsoft\Windows\
CurrentVersion\Internet Settings\
"MaxConnectionsPerServer"=dword:00000020
"MaxConnectionsPer1_0Server"=dword:00000020
```

```
HKEY_CURRENT_USER\Software\Microsoft\Windows\CurrentVersion\
Internet Settings\
"MaxConnectionsPerServer"=dword:00000020
"MaxConnectionsPer1_0Server"=dword:00000020
```

This setting actually increases the number of concurrent outgoing connections that can be made from the same client to the one server. This is a (small) violation of the HTTP standard and can put undue strain on some Web servers, but the bottom line is, if it makes your application run faster, who cares?

11.3 **Multicast UDP**

Multicasting is where a message can travel to more than one destination at the same time. This can provide significant increases in efficiency where there is more than one recipient of the data being sent. It is ideally suited to networks where all clients and servers are on the same LAN, and it is routable on the Internet, but is only supported by some service providers.

The first audio multicast took place in 1992, followed one year later by the first video multicast. Nowadays, multicast UDP is used in products such as Symantec Ghost to provide remote software installations on multiple hosts simultaneously. It is also used to broadcast video footage of popular events over the Internet.

11.3.1 **Multicast basics**

From a programmer's perspective, the difference between point-to-point UDP and multicast UDP is minimal. In .NET, we use the UDPClient object and call the JoinMulticastGroup() method, passing to it a multicast IP address. We can then send and receive packets using the same methods as we would with a standard UDP connection.

A multicast IP address is one that lies in the range 224.0.0.0 to 239.255.255.255. Unfortunately, you can't pick any multicast IP address arbitrarily because there are some restrictions. The IANA controls multicast IP addresses, so you should consult RFC 3171 and the IANA Web site for a definitive list. Never use a multicast IP address that is already assigned to a well-known purpose, such as the following:

- *224.0.0.0 to 224.0.0.255:* The Local Network Control Block is non-routable and cannot travel over the Internet. These addresses have well-known purposes (e.g., DHCP is on address 224.0.0.12).

- *224.0.1.0 to 224.0.1.255:* The Internetwork Control Block is routable, but these addresses have special uses. Network time protocol (NTP) is on address 224.0.1.1, and WINS is on address 224.0.1.24.

- *239.0.0.0 to 239.255.255.255:* The scope-relative addresses are not routable, but they have no special purpose and can be used freely for experimental purposes.

It is possible to request a globally unique multicast IP address from the IANA. Initially, you should use an experimental multicast address such as 234.5.6.11 or obtain a leased multicast address from multicast address dynamic client allocation protocol (MADCAP), as defined in RFC 2730.

If other people are using the same multicast address as you, you may receive stray packets that could corrupt the data you are trying to transmit. If you are broadcasting exclusively to a LAN, use a scope-relative address.

When broadcasting on a WAN (but not the Internet), you can limit the TTL of the packet to less than 63. TTL prevents a packet from being routed indefinitely. Every hop decreases the TTL by one. When the TTL reaches zero, the packet is discarded. This can confine a packet to a geographic area and also prevents multicast avalanches, which occur when packets are replicated exponentially and end up clogging routers all over the Internet.

11.3.2 Multicast routing

Multicast UDP may be the first non-P2P protocol to be accessible programmatically, but there is nothing new in protocols that broadcast rather than going from A to B. Routing protocols such as RIP and OSPF do not have set endpoints; rather, they percolate through networks in all directions at once. In fact, it would be a paradox if a routing protocol needed to be routed from point to point. The technique is not limited to routing protocols (e.g., BOOTP [bootstrap] and ARP are other examples of nondirectional protocols).

The biggest limitation of network broadcasts is that they generally only work within the same LAN and cannot be routed across the Internet. Multicast UDP goes partway toward solving this problem. It is true that not everyone can send or receive multicasts to or from the Internet. Multicast data does have a tendency to flood networks, so not all service providers want to be bombarded with unsolicited data. To enable service providers who do accept multicast to communicate, the multicast backbone (MBONE) was developed. This links multicast-compatible providers together via point-to-point channels in non-multicast-compatible networks. It currently spans more than 24 countries, mostly in academic networks.

Multicast implies that data travels in all directions at once (floods), but in practice, it is not the UDP packets that flood, but multicast routing protocol packets that do this job for them. There are three multicast routing protocols: distance vector multicast routing (DVMRP), multicast open shortest path first (MOSPF), and protocol independent multicast (PIM).

A subscriber to a multicast will issue an Internet group management protocol (IGMP) packet to register its interest in receiving messages. This protocol is also used to leave groups.

There is no equivalent multicast TCP because of the constant one-to-one handshaking that is required. This causes some difficulties for application developers because data sent by UDP can be corrupted as a result of packet loss, duplication, and reordering. This problem can be counteracted by inserting headers in the data containing a sequence number, which the client can reorganize or request a once-off TCP/IP transfer of the missing packet from the server.

Similarly, it is difficult to implement public/private key security via multicast because every client would have a different public key. The IETF is scheduled to publish a standard security mechanism over multicast (MSEC) to address this issue.

11.3.3   Implementing multicast

Before you can implement a multicast-enabled application, you should ensure that your Internet connection supports multicast traffic and is connected to the MBONE network.

This example consists of two applications: a sender and a receiver. We start with the implementation of the sender. Open a new project in Visual Studio .NET and add three textboxes: `tbMulticastGroup`, `tbPort`, and `tbMessage`. You will also require a button named `btnSend`.

Click on the Send button, and add the following code:

C#

```
private void btnSend_Click(object sender, System.EventArgs e)
{
  send(tbMulticastGroup.Text , int.Parse(tbPort.Text),
  tbMessage.Text );
}
```

VB.NET

```
Private  Sub btnSend_Click(ByVal sender As Object, _
    ByVal e As System.EventArgs)
  send(tbMulticastGroup.Text,Integer.Parse(tbPort.Text), _
    tbMessage.Text)
End Sub
```

Multicast operation can be performed at both the socket level and Udp-Client level. To illustrate both techniques, the sender (client) will be implemented using sockets, whereas the receiver will be implemented using the UdpClient object. Before sending or receiving from a multicast group, it is necessary to join the group. This is done in the example below using the socket option AddMembership.

In the same way as if the socket was operating in point-to-point (unicast) mode, the remote endpoint must be specified with both a port and an IP address. The IP address in this case must be valid and within the multicast range (224.0.0.0 to 239.255.255.255). The TTL specifies how far the packet can travel; in this case, it is set to the maximum, 255.

The next step is to implement the Send function as follows:

C#

```
public void send(string mcastGroup, int port, string message)

{
  IPAddress ip=IPAddress.Parse(mcastGroup);
  Socket s=new Socket(AddressFamily.InterNetwork,
    SocketType.Dgram, ProtocolType.Udp);
  s.SetSocketOption(SocketOptionLevel.IP,
    SocketOptionName.AddMembership, new MulticastOption(ip));
  s.SetSocketOption(SocketOptionLevel.IP,
    SocketOptionName.MulticastTimeToLive, 255);
  byte[] b;
  b = Encoding.ASCII.GetBytes(message);
  IPEndPoint ipep=new IPEndPoint(
  IPAddress.Parse(mcastGroup), port);
  s.Connect(ipep);
  s.Send(b,b.Length,SocketFlags.None);
  s.Close();
}
```

VB.NET

```
Public  Sub send(ByVal mcastGroup As String, _
  ByVal port As Integer, ByVal message As String)
  Dim ip As IPAddress = IPAddress.Parse(mcastGroup)
  Dim s As Socket = New Socket(AddressFamily.InterNetwork, _
  SocketType.Dgram, ProtocolType.Udp)
  s.SetSocketOption(SocketOptionLevel.IP, _
```

```
            SocketOptionName.AddMembership, New MulticastOption(ip))
        s.SetSocketOption(SocketOptionLevel.IP, _
        SocketOptionName.MulticastTimeToLive, 255)
        Dim b As Byte()
        b = Encoding.ASCII.GetBytes(Message)
        Dim ipep As IPEndPoint = New _
        IPEndPoint(IPAddress.Parse(mcastGroup), port)
        s.Connect(ipep)
        s.Send(b, b.Length, SocketFlags.None)
        s.Close()
    End Sub
```

This code uses sockets rather than streams to send multicast data. Several parameters need to be applied to the newly created code in order for it to operate effectively in multicast mode. First, the protocol type is set to UDP with `ProtocolType.Udp` because this is the underlying protocol for all multicast broadcasts.

A socket option is then set such that the socket will request to join the specified group. The option `SocketOptionName.AddMembership` indicates that the socket is attaching to a multicast group. The final parameter is the TTL; in this case, the TTL is 255, which effectively means that the packet(s) can travel anywhere in the world.

The message, which is in string format, is converted to a byte array. The endpoint is set to the multicast address on the port specified. The socket then connects to the endpoint, sends the byte array, and then disconnects.

To complete the program, add the required namespaces at the top of the code:

C#

```
using System.Text;
using System.Net;
using System.Net.Sockets;
```

VB.NET

```
Imports System.Text
Imports System.Net
Imports System.Net.Sockets
```

The next step is to code the multicast receiver. Open a new project in Visual Studio .NET and draw a textbox named tbMessages with multi-line set to true on the form.

C#

```
private void Form1_Load(object sender, System.EventArgs e)
{
  Thread thdReceiver = new Thread(new
  ThreadStart(receiverThread));
  thdReceiver.Start();
}
```

VB.NET

```
Private  Sub Form1_Load(ByVal sender As Object, _
    ByVal e As System.EventArgs)
  Dim thdReceiver As Thread
  thdReceiver = New Thread(New ThreadStart _
    (AddressOf receiverThread))
  thdReceiver.Start()
End Sub
```

The receiving thread will remain in an infinite loop awaiting new data. It is therefore run in a separate thread named recieverThread().

In this case, the multicast functionality is implemented using the UdpClient object. Membership to the group is obtained by calling the JoinMulticastGroup. Again the TTL and port details must be specified.

Enter the following code to finish this application:

C#

```
public void receiverThread()
{
  UdpClient client = new UdpClient(5000);
  IPAddress group = IPAddress.Parse("224.5.4.6");
  int timeToLive = 255;
  int port = 5000;
  client.JoinMulticastGroup(group, timeToLive);
  IPEndPoint remoteEP = new IPEndPoint(group, port);
  while (true)
  {
    IPEndPoint ep = null;
```

```
        byte[] buffer = client.Receive(ref ep);
        string message = Encoding.ASCII.GetString(buffer);
        this.tbMessages.Text += message + "\n";
    }
}
```

VB.NET

```
Public  Sub receiverThread()
   Dim client As UdpClient =  New UdpClient(5000)
   Dim group As IPAddress =  IPAddress.Parse("224.5.4.6")
   Dim timeToLive As Integer =  255
   Dim port As Integer =  5000
   client.JoinMulticastGroup(group, timeToLive)
   Dim remoteEP As IPEndPoint =  New IPEndPoint(group,port)
   Do
      Dim ep As IPEndPoint =  Nothing
      Dim buffer() As Byte =  client.Receive( ep)
      Dim message as String = _
      System.Text.Encoding.ASCII.GetString(buffer)
      Me.tbMessages.Text += message + vbcrlf
   Loop
End Sub
```

This code uses a higher level of abstraction than the sender and implements a multicast receiver using UdpClient objects rather than bare sockets. In much the same way as you would receive standard UDP packets, the UdpClient is set to listen on a specified port (in this case, 5000) by passing the port number to the constructor. Where it differs is when JoinMulti-castGroup is called. This method is passed an IPAddress object that holds the multicast IP address and the TTL value for any packets sent. The program goes into an infinite loop at this point, receiving arrays of bytes from whomever happens also to be transmitting on that multicast IP address. These byte arrays are then converted into strings and displayed on-screen.

To finish this code, add the required namespaces as follows:

C#

```
using System.Threading;
using System.Net;
using System.Net.Sockets;
using System.Text;
```

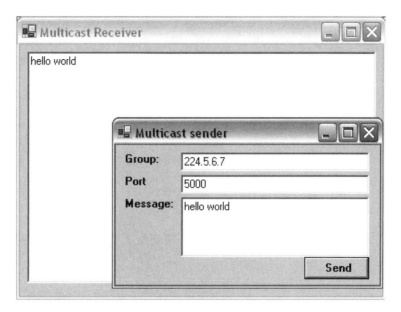

Figure 11.1
*Multicast UDP
client and server.*

VB.NET

```
Imports System.Threading
Imports System.Net
Imports System.Net.Sockets
Imports System.Text
```

To test this application, run both the sender and receiver from Visual Studio .NET. Set the group address on the sender to 224.5.6.7 and the port to 5000, type in a short message, and press send. You will see the text appearing in the receiver application (Figure 11.1). It should be possible to open multiple instances of the receiver application and have them all receive the same text simultaneously.

11.4 Data compression

The most effective way to send data between computers faster is to send less data. This does not mean that you send the recipient less information, just that it is packaged in a more compact way. The process of compressing data so that the decompressed data is identical to the original is known as *lossless compression* and is used in ZIP compression. The process of compressing data in a way that is not identical, but is not perceived as different from the original, is known as *lossy compression* and is used in JPEG and Mp3 compression.

11.5   Lossless compression

Lossless compression is used when the integrity of data is paramount. In the same way that it saves space to round the company's annual returns to the nearest million, there may be a risk that someone could run off with $499,999 without affecting the books.

There are two ways of compressing data without losing integrity: entropy encoding and source encoding. *Entropy encoding* is where the statistical similarity between bytes or byte sequences is recorded, rather than the bytes themselves. *Source encoding* is where the rate of change between bytes or byte sequences is recorded and not the bytes themselves. Entropy encoding is used in the ZIP format, whereas source encoding is used in adaptive delta pulse code modulation (ADPCM), an audio compression technique.

The most basic form of entropy encoding is run length encoding (RLE), where a byte sequence consisting entirely of the same byte is converted into a number followed by the byte. Therefore, the sequence (in hex) 00 00 00 00 00 could be shortened to 05 00. This approach achieves compression only on files with very high entropy, but it was used effectively in the rather outdated PCX format.

A more effective component of ZIP compression is Huffman compression, where the most common bytes are encoded into short bit sequences. The less common bytes are encoded into bit sequences longer than a byte, but because they are less common, the overall effect is a shorter file.

A table of bit-code-to-byte conversions is known as a *codebook*, which can be either static or dynamic. Because the codebook adds to the total length of the transmitted file, it is advantageous to have a short codebook or no codebook with a static codebook. There is no need to transmit the codebook with the data because the receiver will already have it.

Static codebooks have been around for years, in fact, since well before the time of computers. The first data compression scheme was Morse code. The designers of Morse code may not have had entropy reduction in mind, but they did happen to choose the shortest codes for the most common letters. E and T are encoded as a single dot and dash, whereas Z is encoded as a four "bit" sequence. Morse code is not applicable for computer data compression because it uses a pause as a delimiter, which cannot be represented in binary.

Dynamic codebooks are built up during compression, which is where the most common characters are ascertained and then assigned bit sequences. The codebook is then used to compress the data bytes into shorter bit sequences, which are joined together and padded to form a byte stream that should be smaller than the original data.

Codebooks cannot be built up arbitrarily. They must reflect the frequency of each character in the data and be easily delimitable. The simplest scheme is to assign a two-bit sequence to the most common character (i.e., 01). Each byte that follows this character frequencywise is represented by either an additional 1 or 00.

In English text, the most common character is a space, followed by e and then "t." Therefore, a space can be represented as 01, "e" as 011, and "t" as 0100. Using this method, the sequence "e   et" (6 bytes) can be represented as 01101010 10110100 (2 bytes). The process of building up a Huffman codebook (or "tree") is not processor intensive, and it is possible to implement in real time to provide higher effective bandwidth to clients.

11.5.1   Implementing ZIP compression

It is not necessary to reinvent the wheel when it comes to ZIP compression. Many third-party controls are available for download on the Internet. Some of these are under GPL and, thus, can be redistributed in binary (closed-source) form, once the license terms, as specified on the publisher's Web site, are adhered to. A good implementation of ZIP in .NET is the #ZipLib from *www.icsharpcode.net.* The following example demonstrates how to compress a file using #ZipLib, so it is worthwhile to download it from their Web site.

Where using third-party code is not an option, the official reference for the ZIP format is located in RFC 1950 through RFC 1952.

Create a new project in Visual Studio .NET, click Projects→Add References→Browse, and then select `SharpZipLib.dll` from the folder where #ZipLib was installed. Draw two textboxes named `tbInput` and `tbOutput` on the form with two corresponding buttons, `btnBrowseInput` and `btnBrowseOutput`. The two browse buttons should have corresponding File Open and File Save Dialog controls, OpenFileDialog and SaveFileDialog, respectively. Finally, a button named `btnCompress` is also required.

The first step is to tie the File Open and File Save dialog boxes to the buttons, to make it easier for users to select the relevant files. Click on the Browse button opposite the Input textbox and enter the following code:

C#

```
private void btnBrowseInput_Click(object sender,
System.EventArgs e)
{
  openFileDialog.ShowDialog();
  tbInput.Text = openFileDialog.FileName;
}
```

VB.NET

```
Private  Sub btnBrowseInput_Click(ByVal sender As Object, _
    ByVal e As System.EventArgs)
  openFileDialog.ShowDialog()
  tbInput.Text = openFileDialog.FileName
End Sub
```

Click on the Browse button opposite the Output textbox and enter the
following code:

C#

```
private void btnBrowseOutput_Click(object sender,
System.EventArgs e)
{
  saveFileDialog.ShowDialog();
  tbOutput.Text = saveFileDialog.FileName;
}
```

VB.NET

```
Private  Sub btnBrowseOutput_Click(ByVal sender As Object, _
    ByVal e As System.EventArgs)
  saveFileDialog.ShowDialog()
  tbOutput.Text = saveFileDialog.FileName
End Sub
```

The workhorse of the application is contained behind the Compress
button. ZIP files can contain more than one source file and retain CRC and
date information with each file to help maintain integrity. The ZipOutput-
Stream is appended to using ZipEntry objects. Each entry contains the
original file data, along with a CRC for that file and a date.

Note: Checksums (or CRCs) are similar to hash values, although they are used for integrity checks rather than security against data tampering.

The SetLevel method is used to define the strength of compression, where zero is no compression and nine is maximum compression. There is a small performance difference between the compression levels, but in most cases, it should be set to maximum.

Click on the Compress button and enter the following code:

C#

```csharp
private void btnCompress_Click(object sender,
System.EventArgs e)
{
  Crc32 crc = new Crc32();
  ZipOutputStream ZipStream =
    new ZipOutputStream(File.Create(tbOutput.Text));
  ZipStream.SetLevel(9);
  string file = tbInput.Text;
  FileStream fs = File.OpenRead(file);
  byte[] buffer = new byte[fs.Length];
  fs.Read(buffer, 0, buffer.Length);
  ZipEntry entry = new ZipEntry(file);
  entry.DateTime = DateTime.Now;
  entry.Size = fs.Length;
  fs.Close();
  crc.Reset();
  crc.Update(buffer);
  entry.Crc  = crc.Value;
  ZipStream.PutNextEntry(entry);
  ZipStream.Write(buffer, 0, buffer.Length);
  ZipStream.Finish();
  ZipStream.Close();
}
```

VB.NET

```vbnet
Private  Sub btnCompress_Click(ByVal sender As Object, _
  ByVal e As System.EventArgs)
      Dim crc As Crc32 = New Crc32
        Dim ZipStream As ZipOutputStream = _
```

```
            New ZipOutputStream( _
              System.IO.File.Create(tbOutput.Text))
        ZipStream.SetLevel(9)
        Dim file As String = tbInput.Text
        Dim fs As FileStream = System.IO.File.OpenRead(file)
        Dim buffer() As Byte = New Byte(fs.Length) {}
        fs.Read(buffer, 0, buffer.Length)
        Dim enTry As ZipEnTry = New ZipEnTry(file)
        enTry.DateTime = DateTime.Now
        enTry.Size = fs.Length + 1
        fs.Close()
        crc.Reset()
        crc.Update(buffer)
        enTry.Crc = crc.Value
        ZipStream.PutNextEnTry(enTry)
        ZipStream.Write(buffer, 0, buffer.Length)
        ZipStream.Finish()
        ZipStream.Close()
    End Sub
```

ZIP files consist of multiple entries, one entry for each file. Each entry has an associated CRC value, which is analogous to a hash value in proving integrity checks for files that could have been corrupted in transit. Creating a ZIP file takes three steps: (1) creating a zip stream, (2) defining the various entries, and (3) calculating the CRC values for each entry.

The zip stream is created with a constructor that is passed the final destination of the `.zip` file. The compression level is also set at this point: level 1 is fast, but offers little compression, whereas level 9 is slower, but offers better compression ratios.

The second step is to create an entry for the file that is to be compressed. Here a new `ZipEntry` object is instantiated. The constructor of this object is passed the filename and the path for the file to be compressed. The file's date and length are included in the entry. This entry is appended to the stream using the `PutNextEntry` method.

Every entry must have a corresponding CRC value. This value is calculated by first reading in the contents of the file and then passing the resultant byte array to the `Update` method of a `Crc32` object. The CRC value is stored in the `crc` property of the entry.

The ZIP file is written to disk, one entry at a time, by passing the contents of the uncompressed file to the Write method of the zip stream. Finally, the stream is flushed with the Finish command and then closed.

Add the following assemblies at the top of the code:

C#

```
using ICSharpCode.SharpZipLib.Checksums;
using ICSharpCode.SharpZipLib.Zip;
using ICSharpCode.SharpZipLib.GZip;
using System.IO;
```

VB.NET

```
Imports ICSharpCode.SharpZipLib.Checksums
Imports ICSharpCode.SharpZipLib.Zip
Imports ICSharpCode.SharpZipLib.GZip
Imports System.IO
```

To test the application, run it from Visual Studio .NET. Press the Browse button beside the Input textbox and select a text file from your computer. Press the second Browse button and enter a filename with the extension .zip. Press Compress, and then locate the newly created ZIP file. You should notice a reduction in file size (Figure 11.2).

Figure 11.2
ZIP data compression application.

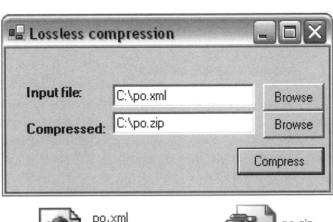

Examples of decompressing ZIP files and more advanced uses of this control may be found at the *www.icSharpcode.net* Web site. Interested readers should refer to this site for more information. In Chapter 4, a certain HTTP header may have particular relevance to developers working on Web-based applications that have browsers as clients. Specifically:

```
Accept-Encoding: gzip, deflate
```

As the name suggests, browsers can accept compressed data as well as plain text. Therefore, it is possible to improve the performance of a Web server by compressing its output, either on the fly or in cache compression.

The `gzip` and `deflate` compression algorithms are contained within the #ZipLib control, so furnishing this format to clients is easy. All that is required in addition to the compression aspect is that `Content-Encoding` is added to the header in the HTTP reply. An open-source implementation of this was developed by Ben Lowery and can be found at: *www.blowery.org/stories/2002/12/12/httpcompressionmodule.html.*

11.6 Lossy compression

In cases where data integrity is not as important, but good compression is imperative, lossy compression is a good option. This is particularly pertinent to audio and visual data, where users will put up with a little muffling or blurring, as long as they see or hear what they want without having to wait too long.

11.6.1 Audio compression

An audio file has very little byte-to-byte entropy, and compression schemes such as ZIP or Huffman will have little effect on the file size; however, if you open an audio file in a wave editor, such as Goldwave (*www.goldwave.com*), you will notice a definite pattern when you look closely at the data in Figure 11.3.

The screenshot is of a recording of a girl's voice. It contains only a fraction of a second (0.026 sec) of audio, but contains more than 2 Kb of data. To achieve CD-quality audio, a computer must output data at 44,100 (× 2) bytes per second.

Audio is made up of waves. Each sample in a wave is usually very similar to the preceding sample. The rate of change constantly increases and

Figure 11.3
*Typical speech
waveform.*

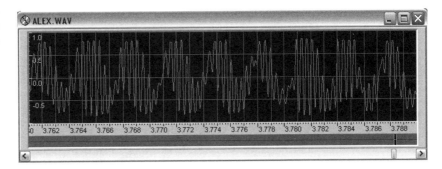

decreases in harmonic fashion. Therefore, instead of recoding the value of each sample, if the change between samples is recorded, then the amount of data is reduced.

In delta pulse code modulation (DPCM), an increase in sample value is represented by the bit 1 and a decrease is represented by the bit 0. During decompression, the sample value is incremented or decremented by 1, depending on the value of the current bit in the bitstream. This causes two detrimental effects: slope overload and granular noise. *Slope overload* is where the input signal changes substantially from sample to sample, resulting in a muffling effect in the decompressed signal. *Granular noise* is where the input signal does not change at all, in which case the output sound oscillates around the true value, which causes either a hiss or a high-pitched shrill in the audio.

To counteract the muffling effect, adaptive DPCM, or ADPCM, can be used. This is where, during the decompression process, a number that doubles with each contiguous sample increases the sample value. This process more closely mimics the harmonic action of the sine wave, but can produce a phase undershoot, which is a rasping, sharp noise.

You may never have heard of ADPCM (although it is used heavily in telecommunications and especially on international telephone lines), but Mp3 has become almost a household name. There is a good reason for this, in that Mp3 provides excellent compression ratios and acceptable sound quality and can be decompressed in real time by any PC and many portable digital music devices. Mp3 achieves this quality by recognizing how humans perceive sounds at an acoustic level. Our ears are designed to hear harmonic sounds, and standard lossy compression algorithms cause unnatural attenuations that are not pleasant to listen to. By filtering at the harmonic level, rather than at the byte level, a much more natural sound is produced.

Recognizing a pattern of cyclic values in a stream of data, which may be combined with thousands of other cyclic patterns, is not an easy task for a computer; however, a rather gifted mathematician developed a formula to produce a mathematical representation of the harmonics contained in a block of data.

In Figure 11.3, a pattern of waves can be seen in the audio; these are made primarily from a 300 Hz with a 2400 Hz harmonic. To extract this information from what appears to the computer as a block of ones and zeros, you need to use a mathematical formula known as the Discrete Cosine Transform (DCT):

$$S_8(u) = \frac{Cu}{2} \cdot \sum_{x=0}^{7} f(x) \cos \frac{(2x+1)\pi u}{16}$$

Cu is equal to 0.7071 (the reciprocal of root 2); when u is zero, Cu is one, for all u not equal to zero.

When the above formula is applied to an array of eight numbers (i.e., $f(1)$ to $f(7)$), the resultant array in S is a representation of the data in terms of frequencies. It is possible to represent any sequence of eight integers in terms of the values of the peaks and troughs of a wave composed of up to eight harmonics. When compressing audio data, most of the higher harmonics are zero or near zero and can be canceled out; thus the array in S can be compressed using traditional lossless encoding more efficiently.

The most famous audio compression format that uses DCT is the ubiquitous Mp3. This technology is not an easy implementation, and its exact format is a closely guarded secret. You can use third-party DLLs and applications such as Lame, BladeEnc, and L3enc to perform the compression. Alternately, you can license the technology from Fraunhoffer.

11.6.2 Image compression

Image compression is remarkably similar to audio compression, except that it works in two dimensions rather than one. There may not be the same obvious wave pattern in images, but in digital photographs the natural dithering in shades of color compresses very well when DCT/Huffman compression is applied.

During the JPEG compression process, the image is split into macroblocks, or 8×8 blocks of pixels. Each macroblock is then compressed using a two-dimensional DCT to isolate and reduce the number of color harmonics within each area of the picture. The idea of waves existing within an image may seem alien, but they exist everywhere in natural textures.

The two-dimensional DCT can be expressed mathematically as follows:

$$S(v,u) = \frac{Cv}{2}\frac{Cu}{2} \sum_{y=0}^{7} \sum_{x=0}^{7} f(y,x) \cos\frac{(2x+1)\pi u}{16} \cos\frac{(2y+1)\pi v}{16}$$

Cu is equal to 0.7071 (the reciprocal of root 2); when u is zero, Cu is one for all u not equal to zero. The same applies to Cv.

This formula produces a two-dimensional array, which can be compressed by rounding the near-zero values of the array to zero, then using RLE compression followed by Huffman compression.

Luckily, you will probably never have to implement JPEG compression from scratch. .NET has native support for JPEG, along with plenty of other image formats, including PNG, TIFF, and GIF. The following sample program shows you how to compress a bitmap image into a JPEG.

Start a new project in Visual Studio .NET. Draw a picture box, named `pictureBox` onto the form. Draw two textboxes named `tbInput` and `tbOutput` on the form, with two corresponding buttons, `btnBrowseInput` and `btnBrowseOutput`. The two browse buttons should have corresponding File Open and File Save Dialog controls, named `openFileDialog` and `saveFileDialog`, respectively. Finally, a button named `btnCompress` is also required.

The first step is to tie the File Open and File Save dialog boxes to the buttons to make it easier for users to select the relevant files. The open file procedure will also load the new image into the picture box.

Click on the Browse button opposite the Input textbox and enter the following code:

C#

```
private void btnBrowseInput_Click(object sender,
System.EventArgs e)
{
  openFileDialog.ShowDialog();
  tbInput.Text = openFileDialog.FileName;
  pictureBox.Image= Image.FromFile(openFileDialog.FileName);

}
```

VB.NET

```
Private  Sub btnBrowseInput_Click(ByVal sender As Object, _
  ByVal e As System.EventArgs)
  openFileDialog.ShowDialog()
  tbInput.Text = openFileDialog.FileName
  pictureBox.Image= Image.FromFile(openFileDialog.FileName)
End Sub
```

Click on the Browse button opposite the Output textbox and enter the
following code:

C#

```
private void btnBrowseOutput_Click(object sender,
System.EventArgs e)
{
  saveFileDialog.ShowDialog();
  tbOutput.Text = saveFileDialog.FileName;
}
```

VB.NET

```
Private  Sub btnBrowseOutput_Click(ByVal sender As Object, _
  ByVal e As System.EventArgs)
  saveFileDialog.ShowDialog()
  tbOutput.Text = saveFileDialog.FileName
End Sub
```

To save a JPEG from a loaded image, you may simply call the Save
method. The method requires the image format and a stream as input
parameters:

C#

```
private void btnCompress_Click(object sender,
System.EventArgs e)
{
  FileStream fs = new
  FileStream(tbOutput.Text,FileMode.CreateNew);
  PictureBox.Image.Save(fs,
  System.Drawing.Imaging.ImageFormat.Jpeg);
  fs.Close();
}
```

VB.NET

```
Private  Sub btnCompress_Click(ByVal sender As Object, _
  ByVal e As System.EventArgs)
  Dim fs As FileStream = New FileStream(tbOutput.Text, _
  FileMode.CreateNew)
  PictureBox.Image.Save(fs, _
  System.Drawing.Imaging.ImageFormat.Jpeg)
  fs.Close()
End Sub
```

To test this application, run it from Visual Studio .NET, press the Browse button next to the Input textbox, and choose a bitmap from your computer. Click the Browse button next to the Output textbox, and select a location to save the JPEG. Press Compress, and then locate the new saved JPEG on your computer; you should notice that it will have a smaller file size (Figure 11.4).

Figure 11.4
JPEG Compression application.

You may notice that it is possible to take a JPEG file as an input to this program. Although the application will allow you to do this, the end result will be a JPEG file of even lower quality than the original.

11.6.3   Video compression

With a healthy percentage of consumers using broadband technology in their homes, it will soon be possible to deliver video on demand to the average user. Without compression, the bandwidths required would be phenomenal. Various standards have been developed to compress video data into narrower channels, the most successful of which is Motion Pictures Expert Group (MPEG). MPEG encoders are not cheap, but they do provide the best compression of any other format.

A cheap alternative to MPEG is the audio-video interleaved (AVI) format. This is a technology built in to the Windows API. It has nowhere near the same compressing capabilities, but it saves time in developing a proprietary format. A good resource for creating AVI files programmatically is *www.shrinkwrapvb.com*. The code examples are in Visual Basic 6.0, but they can be ported to VB.NET from within Visual Studio .NET.

If a proprietary format is the only option, then examining the operation of MPEG or MJPEG may help. Video compression is similar to audio compression, except there are three data channels for imaging and one channel for audio. Every pixel is made from a combination of three colors: red, green, and blue (RGB format).

One important compression technique for motion pictures is subsampling. *Subsampling* is a technique employed by MPEG and JPEG, at the start of the encoding process. In this process, the first step is to convert the RGB format into the YUV format. The YUV format defines each color in terms of luminance and chrominance. *Chrominance* defines the color, from red to blue. *Luminance* defines the saturation, or greyness. Because luminance changes more often than chrominance, less color data can be sent. The rationalization for this is that a red car may turn dark red when traveling under a shadow, but it would rarely turn blue spontaneously.

When this phenomenon is applied to motion picture compression, chrominance levels are updated every frame, whereas the saturation levels are updated only every few frames. In the H.261 standard, the ratio of chrominance to luminance sampling is 4:1.

The most novel part of MPEG encoding is the motion-estimation algorithm. This is where the image is split into macroblocks, or 8×8 blocks of pixels. These blocks are compared for similarity with blocks in previous or future frames. Because most images do not change significantly between frames, this is an effective compression technique, albeit processor intensive on the encoder. Therefore, MPEG compression can rarely be done on-the-fly and must be pre-encoded before serving. MPEG decompression is on the order of 10 times faster than compression and can be performed as data is being received.

The final stage in MPEG compression is where each macroblock is compressed using JPEG image compression.

11.7 Conclusion

This chapter has dealt with the problem of furnishing clients with more data in less time. In many cases, this involves a trade-off in data integrity, timeliness, or quality; however, this trade-off is often entirely justified. A good percentage of people can tell the difference between CD-quality and Mp3 audio, but when given a choice to download a 20-Mb wave file or the equivalent 2-Mb Mp3, very few people will value the quality difference enough to wait 10 times longer to hear the music.

A trade-off is not always a necessary side effect of techniques to send more data faster across the phone networks. Lossless data compression guarantees the integrity of data, yet can compress high-entropy data, such as plain text or XML, to a mere fraction of its original size. As long as the server and client have the processing power to compress and decompress the data at a rate faster than the amount of time it would take to send the data over the wire, then compression is an excellent means of accelerating your applications' communications.

The next chapter deals with network protocols that are not ordinarily used to move data between computers, but that act as auxiliary protocols to help applications become more responsive and scalable. These protocols can be used to determine if computers are connected to the network or if there are alternative computers with which to communicate. An introduction to Windows Management Instrumentation (WMI) will demonstrate how to administer computers remotely over a network.

12

Ping, DNS, and WHOIS: Monitoring your Network

12.1 Introduction

Network protocols are not just used to move data from one point to another. Some protocols have specific purposes that help keep Internet traffic flowing and make using the network easier.

These utility protocols may not be required for every network application; however, because these are niche technologies, many developers may not know how to implement such features. By leveraging these technologies, it may be possible to add unique features to your products, which may provide that competitive advantage.

This chapter is divided into roughly equal sections describing three everyday utility protocols: DNS, WHOIS, and Ping. The chapter concludes with a discussion of an interesting utility protocol developed by Microsoft, named WMI.

12.2 DNS

DNS operates on UDP port 53 and is described in RFC 1010, RFC 1304, RFC 1035, and RFC 1183. As described in Chapter 1, the most common use for DNS is to convert domain names into IP addresses because people find it difficult to remember strings of numbers more than nine digits long. DNS was developed to provide a system that converts easily recognizable domain names into IP addresses.

No central computer stores a list of domain names against IP addresses. Instead, a worldwide network of DNS servers holds this information. Every Web site would typically be listed on two DNS servers; these machines are said to be authoritative in the domain. DNS servers routinely query each other for updated information, and in this way the information slowly propagates through the Internet. Therefore, if you change hosting providers on a Web site, it will take up to 48 hours for the new DNS information to propagate through the Internet.

You can use DNS.GetHostByName to convert a domain name (string) to an IP address (IPHostEntry). The reverse of this action, converting an IP address to a domain name, can be achieved using DNS.GetHostByAddress. There is more to DNS than converting IP addresses to domain names and vice versa, however. In fact, most DNS handling is behind the scenes, and most high-level network programming would rarely need to know the IP address of the servers or clients with which it was communicating.

An interesting facet of DNS is its role in sending and receiving emails. As mentioned in Chapter 5, SMTP servers discover the destination POP3 servers using DNS mail exchange (MX). This is where a specially formatted DNS query is sent to a (any) DNS server, which returns a list of mail servers associated with the specified domain in order of preference.

This technique can be used to provide email address validation, above and beyond the simple checks for the @ symbol followed by a period. It could also be used to simplify email software by skipping the need for end-users to enter SMTP server details. A final advantage of this technique is that it is much faster than relaying by SMTP, so it could improve the performance of email software.

12.2.1   Implementing DNS MX

Open a new project in Visual Studio .NET and draw three textboxes named tbDNSServer, tbDomain, and tbStatus, the latter having multiline set to true. You also require a button named btnFind.

Click on the Find button and enter the following code:

C#

```
private void btnFind_Click(object sender, System.EventArgs e)
{
  byte[] DNSQuery;
  byte[] DNSReply;
  UdpClient dnsClient = new UdpClient(tbDNSServer.Text , 53);
  DNSQuery = makeQuery(DateTime.Now.Millisecond *
  60,tbDomain.Text);
  dnsClient.Send(DNSQuery,DNSQuery.GetLength(0));
  IPEndPoint endpoint = null;
  DNSReply = dnsClient.Receive(ref endpoint);
```

```
    this.tbStatus.Text = makeResponse(DNSReply,tbDomain.Text);
}
```

VB.NET

```
Private  Sub btnFind_Click(ByVal sender As Object,_
 ByVal e As System.EventArgs)
  Dim DNSQuery() As Byte
  Dim DNSReply() As Byte
  Dim dnsClient As UdpClient = New _
    UdpClient(tbDNSServer.Text, 53)
  DNSQuery = makeQuery(DateTime.Now.Millisecond * 60, _
    tbDomain.Text)
  dnsClient.Send(DNSQuery, DNSQuery.GetLength(0))
  Dim endpoint As IPEndPoint = Nothing
  DNSReply = dnsClient.Receive(endpoint)
  Me.tbStatus.Text = makeResponse(DNSReply, tbDomain.Text)
End Sub
```

This opens a UDP connection on port 43 to the DNS server and sends an MX query to it. The response is then parsed and displayed by the make-Response function.

To prepare the MX query, we need to write a new function. It involves quite a bit of byte-by-byte writing, which we won't discussed in too much detail here. Interested readers should consult the RFCs quoted at the start of this section.

C#

```
public byte[] makeQuery(int id,string name)
{
  byte[] data = new byte[512];
  byte[] Query;
  data[0]  = (byte) (id >> 8);
  data[1]  = (byte) (id & 0xFF );
  data[2]  = (byte) 1; data[3] = (byte) 0;
  data[4]  = (byte) 0; data[5] = (byte) 1;
  data[6]  = (byte) 0; data[7] = (byte) 0;
  data[8]  = (byte) 0; data[9] = (byte) 0;
  data[10] = (byte) 0; data[11] = (byte) 0;
  string[] tokens = name.Split(new char[] {'.'});
  string label;
```

```
int position = 12;
for(int j=0; j<tokens.Length; j++)
{
  label = tokens[j];
  data[position++] = (byte) (label.Length & 0xFF);
  byte[] b = System.Text.Encoding.ASCII.GetBytes(label);
  for(int k=0; k < b.Length; k++)
  {
    data[position++] = b[k];
  }
}
data[position++] = (byte) 0 ; data[position++] = (byte) 0;
data[position++] = (byte) 15; data[position++] = (byte) 0 ;
data[position++] = (byte) 1 ;
Query = new byte[position+1];
for (int i=0;i<=position;i++)
{
  Query[i]= data[i];
}
return Query;
}
```

VB.NET

```
Public Function makeQuery(id as Integer,name as _
          String) as Byte()
    Dim data() As Byte = New Byte(512) {}
    Dim Query() As Byte
    data(0) = CType((id >> 8), Byte)
    data(1) = CType((id And &HFF), Byte)
    data(2) = 1 : data(3) = 0
    data(4) = 0 : data(5) = 1
    data(6) = 0 : data(7) = 0
    data(8) = 0 : data(9) = 0
    data(10) = 0 : data(11) = 0
    Dim tokens() As String = Name.Split(New Char() {"."})
    Dim label As String
    Dim position As Integer = 12
    Dim j As Integer
    For j = 0 To tokens.Length - 1
        label = tokens(j)
        data(position) = _
```

```
                    CType((label.Length And &HFF), Byte)
                    position = position + 1
                    Dim b() As Byte = _
                        System.Text.Encoding.ASCII.GetBytes(label)
                    Dim k As Integer
                    For k = 0 To b.Length - 1
                        data(position) = b(k)
                        position = position + 1
                    Next
                Next
                data(position) = 0
                position = position + 1
                data(position) = 0
                position = position + 1
                data(position) = 15
                position = position + 1
                data(position) = 0
                position = position + 1
                data(position) = 1
                Query = New Byte(position + 1) {}
                Dim i As Integer
                For i = 0 To position
                    Query(i) = data(i)
                Next
                Return Query
            End Function
```

Domain names in DNS queries appear in a rather unusual format. Instead of periods separating each level (word) in the domain, a byte value representing the next part of the domain is used. This would mean that www.google.com becomes 3www6google3com (the numbers represent the binary value and not the ASCII code for the number). For more information on this topic and the DNS format in general, please refer to the RFCs listed at the start of this chapter.

The next step is to analyze the response, so type in the makeResponse function as follows:

C#

```csharp
public string makeResponse(byte[] data,string name)
{
    int qCount = ((data[4] & 0xFF) << 8) | (data[5] & 0xFF);
```

```
int aCount = ((data[6] & 0xFF) << 8) | (data[7] & 0xFF);
int position=12;
for( int i=0;i<qCount; ++i)
{
  name = "";
  position = proc(position,data,ref name);
  position += 4;
}
string Response ="";
for (int i = 0; i < aCount; ++i)
{
  name = "";
  position = proc(position,data,ref name);
  position+=12;
  name="";
  position = proc(position,data,ref name);
  Response += name + "\r\n";
}
return Response;
}
```

VB.NET

```
Public Function makeResponse(ByVal data() As Byte, _
    ByVal DomainName As String) As String
  Dim qCount As Integer = ((data(4) And &HFF) << 8) Or _
    (data(5) And &HFF)
  Dim aCount As Integer = ((data(6) And &HFF) << 8) Or _
    (data(7) And &HFF)
  Dim position As Integer = 12
  Dim i As Integer
  For i = 0 To qCount - 1
    DomainName = ""
    position = proc(position, data, DomainName)
    position += 4
  Next
  Dim Response As String = ""
  For i = 0 To aCount - 1
    DomainName = ""
    position = proc(position, data, DomainName)
    position += 12
    DomainName = ""
```

```
      position = proc(position, data, DomainName)
      Response += DomainName + vbCrLf
    Next
    Return Response
  End Function
```

The preceding code extracts the MX servers from the DNS reply and displays them on-screen. It uses the proc function to convert between the native DNS format for domain names and the standard dot notation format.

The next step is to implement the proc function as follows:

C#

```csharp
private int proc(int position,byte[] data,ref string name)
{
  int len = (data[position++] & 0xFF);
  if(len == 0)
  {
    return position;
  }
  int offset;
  do
  {
    if ((len & 0xC0) == 0xC0)
    {
      if (position >= data.GetLength(0))
      {
        return -1;
      }
      offset = ((len & 0x3F) << 8) | (data[position++] &
        0xFF);
      proc(offset,data,ref name);
      return position;
    }
    else
    {
      if ((position + len) > data.GetLength(0))
      {
        return -1;
      }
      name += Encoding.ASCII.GetString(data, position, len);
      position += len;
```

```
    }
    if (position > data.GetLength(0))
    {
      return -1;
    }
    len = data[position++] & 0xFF;
    if (len != 0)
    {
      name += ".";
    }
  }
  while (len != 0);
  return position;
}
```

VB.NET

```
Private Function proc(ByVal position As Integer, ByVal data() _
  As Byte, ByRef DomainName As String) As Integer
  Dim len As Integer = data(position) And &HFF
  position = position + 1
  If len = 0 Then
    Return position
  End If
  Dim offset As Integer
  Do
    If (len And &HC0) = &HC0 Then
      If position >= data.GetLength(0) Then
        Return -1
      End If
      offset = ((len And &H3F) << 8) Or (data(position))
      position = position + 1
      proc(offset, data, DomainName)
      Return position
    Else
      If (position + len) > data.GetLength(0) Then
        Return -1
      End If
      DomainName+=Encoding.ASCII.GetString(data, _
      position, len)
      position += len
    End If
```

```
      If position > data.GetLength(0) Then
        Return -1
      End If
      len = data(position)
      position = position + 1
      If len <> 0 Then
        DomainName += "."
      End If
    Loop While len <> 0
    Return position
End Function
```

The proc function converts between the DNS native format for domain names and the standard notation. It stores the result in a private variable named name and advances the position pointer to the end of the domain name.

Finally, add the required namespaces:

C#

```
using System.Net;
using System.IO;
using System.Text;
using System.Net.Sockets;
```

VB.NET

```
Imports System.Net
Imports System.IO
Imports System.Text
Imports System.Net.Sockets
```

To run this application, first find the IP address of a DNS server. You can use 204.111.1.36 or your ISP's DNS server (type IPConfig /all in DOS to find it). Type the IP address of the DNS server into the box provided and a domain name (without the "www" prefix) into the second textbox. Press find, and you will see the associated MX server appear in the textbox.

Note: You will note that when you query hotmail.com, the MX servers cycle between 1 and 4. This is the effect of round-robin load balancing being used to handle the large volumes of mail handled by hotmail (Figure 12.1).

Figure 12.1
DNS MX client application.

12.3 Ping

Ping or, as it is more correctly known, Internet control message protocol (ICMP), is a protocol used to report broken network connections or other router-level problems that end hosts might need to know. When a router can't get its packet to the next hop, it discards the packet and sends an ICMP packet back to the sender. ICMP packets are not used to report lost routing problems for other ICMP packets in order to prevent network cascade effects.

Many developers are familiar with the *ping* utility, which can be used to determine if a computer is switched on or not and how much delay there is over the connection to it. This protocol can be implemented in .NET to provide applications with the ability to check quickly if a computer to which it needs to connect is turned on.

It is possible to send a ping by constructing it with a raw socket; an example of this can be seen at *www.eggheadcafe.com/articles/20020209.asp*. A simpler implementation is to use the ICMP DLL, which is standard to all Windows platforms.

Create a new project in Visual Studio .NET. Add a new module to the project, and enter the following code:

C#

```
public class PING
{
  public  struct IP_OPTION_INFORMATION
  {
    public byte TTL, Tos,Flags,OptionSize;
    [MarshalAs(UnmanagedType.ByValTStr,SizeConst=128)]
    public string OptionsData;
  }
  public struct ICMP_ECHO_REPLY
  {
    public uint Address, Status, RoundTripTime;
    public ushort DataSize,Reserved;
    public IP_OPTION_INFORMATION Options;
  }
  [DllImport("icmp.dll",SetLastError=true)]
  public static extern uint IcmpSendEcho (
    uint IcmpHandle,
    uint DestAddress,
    string RequestData,
    uint RequestSize,
    ref IP_OPTION_INFORMATION RequestOptns,
    ref ICMP_ECHO_REPLY ReplyBuffer,
    uint ReplySize,
    uint TimeOut);

  [DllImport("icmp.dll",SetLastError=true)]
  public static extern uint IcmpCreateFile ();

  public static IP_OPTION_INFORMATION pIPo;
  public static ICMP_ECHO_REPLY pIPe;
}
```

VB.NET

```
Option Strict Off
Option Explicit On
Module PING
    Structure IP_OPTION_INFORMATION
        Dim TTL As Byte
        Dim Tos As Byte
        Dim Flags As Byte
```

```
            Dim OptionsSize As Integer
            <VBFixedString(128), _
            System.Runtime.InteropServices.MarshalAs  _
        (System.Runtime.InteropServices.UnmanagedType.ByValTStr, _
            SizeConst:=128)> _
            Public OptionsData As String
        End Structure

        Structure IP_ECHO_REPLY
            Dim Address As Int32
            Dim Status As Integer
            Dim RoundTripTime As Integer
            Dim DataSize As Short
            Dim Reserved As Short
            Dim data As Integer
            Dim Options As IP_OPTION_INFORMATION
        End Structure

        Public pIPo As IP_OPTION_INFORMATION
        Public pIPe As IP_ECHO_REPLY

        Declare Function IcmpCreateFile Lib "icmp.dll" () As _
        Integer
        Declare Function IcmpSendEcho Lib "ICMP" (ByVal _
        IcmpHandle As Integer, ByVal DestAddress As UInt32, _
        ByVal RequestData As String, _
        ByVal RequestSize As Short, _
        ByRef RequestOptns As IP_OPTION_INFORMATION, _
        ByRef ReplyBuffer As IP_ECHO_REPLY, _
        ByVal ReplySize As Integer, _
        ByVal timeout As Integer) As Boolean

    End Module
```

With nearly all API code, it is rarely necessary to understand every parameter sent to each function.

`IcmpCreateFile` creates a handle to resources used when generating ping requests. Where a program may issue large numbers of ping requests, then `IcmpCloseHandle` should be used to reclaim memory.

IcmpSendEcho sends an ICMP echo request to a host as specified in the
DestAddress parameter. The format of the outgoing ping is set in the
RequestOptns parameter, and details of the reply (or lack thereof) are
stored in the ReplyBuffer.

Go to the form and draw a textbox named tbIP and a button named
btnPing. Click on the button and add the following code:

C#

```csharp
private void btnPing_Click(object sender, System.EventArgs e)
{
  uint LongIP;
  string buffer;
  UInt32 hIP;
  uint timeout;
  buffer = new StringBuilder().Append(' ',32).ToString();
  LongIP = convertIPtoLong(tbIP.Text);
  hIP = PING.IcmpCreateFile();
  PING.pIPo.TTL = 255;
  timeout = 2700;
  PING.IcmpSendEcho(hIP, LongIP, buffer,
            (uint)buffer.Length,
            ref PING.pIPo, ref PING.pIPe,
            (uint)Marshal.SizeOf(PING.pIPe) + 8,
            timeout);
  MessageBox.Show(describeResponse(PING.pIPe.Status));
}
```

VB.NET

```vbnet
Private Sub btnPing_Click(ByVal eventSender As _
System.Object, ByVal eventArgs As System.EventArgs) _
    Handles btnPing.Click
 Dim LongIP As UInt32
 Dim buffer As String
 Dim hIP As Integer
 Dim timeout As Short

 buffer = Space(32)
 LongIP = convertIPtoLong((tbIP.Text))
 hIP = IcmpCreateFile()
 pIPo.TTL = 255
 timeout = 2700
```

```
IcmpSendEcho(hIP, LongIP, buffer, Len(buffer), pIPo, _
   pIPe, Len(pIPe) + 8, timeout)
MsgBox(describeResponse(pIPe.Status))
End Sub
```

You may notice that the IP address is converted from a string to a Uint32 (unsigned 32-bit integer) by the ConvertIPtoLong function. This is required because the DestAddress parameter of IcmpSendEcho uses a binary representation of IP addresses.

So, add in the following function to implement convertIPtoLong:

C#

```
public UInt32 convertIPtoLong(string ip)
{
  string[] digits;
  digits = ip.Split(".".ToCharArray());
  return Convert.ToUInt32(
          Convert.ToUInt32(digits[3]) * Math.Pow(2,24) +
          Convert.ToUInt32(digits[2]) * Math.Pow(2,16) +
          Convert.ToUInt32(digits[1]) * Math.Pow(2,8) +
          Convert.ToUInt32(digits[0]));
}
```

VB.NET

```
Public Function convertIPtoLong(ByRef ip As String) As UInt32
        Dim digits() As String
        digits = Split(ip, ".")
        convertIPtoLong = Convert.ToUInt32(digits(3) * 2 ^ 24 _
          + digits(2) * 2 ^ 16 + _
          digits(1) * 2 ^ 8 + _
          digits(0))
End Function
```

This function splits an IP address into its four constituent bytes, multiplies each byte by a power of 2, and adds them together. In the case of the loop-back address 127.0.0.1, this is converted to $127 + 1 \times 2^{24}$, or 16,777,343.

You may also notice in the code above that a message box is displayed once IcmpSendEcho returns. This message could therefore describe to the user the result of the ping request. The function describeResponse performs the task of converting the rather cryptic response codes into meaningful phrases.

Enter the following code:

C#

```
public string describeResponse(uint code)
{
  string Rcode = "";
  switch(code)
  {
    case 0 : Rcode = "Success";break;
    case 11001 : Rcode = "Buffer too Small";break;
    case 11002 : Rcode = "Dest Network Not Reachable";break;
    case 11003 : Rcode = "Dest Host Not Reachable";break;
    case 11004 : Rcode = "Dest Protocol Not Reachable";break;
    case 11005 : Rcode = "Dest Port Not Reachable";break;
    case 11006 : Rcode = "No Resources Available";break;
    case 11007 : Rcode = "Bad Option";break;
    case 11008 : Rcode = "Hardware Error";break;
    case 11009 : Rcode = "Packet too Big";break;
    case 11010 : Rcode = "Rqst Timed Out";break;
    case 11011 : Rcode = "Bad Request";break;
    case 11012 : Rcode = "Bad Route";break;
    case 11013 : Rcode = "TTL Exprd in Transit";break;
    case 11014 : Rcode = "TTL Exprd Reassemb";break;
    case 11015 : Rcode = "Parameter Problem";break;
    case 11016 : Rcode = "Source Quench";break;
    case 11017 : Rcode = "Option too Big";break;
    case 11018 : Rcode = " Bad Destination";break;
    case 11019 : Rcode = "Address Deleted";break;
    case 11020 : Rcode = "Spec MTU Change";break;
    case 11021 : Rcode = "MTU Change";break;
    case 11022 : Rcode = "Unload";break;
    case 11050 : Rcode = "General Failure";break;
  }
  return Rcode;
}
```

VB.NET

```
Public Function describeResponse(ByRef code As Integer) _
    As String
```

```
Dim Rcode As String
Select Case code
  Case 0 : Rcode = "Success"
  Case 11001 : Rcode = "Buffer too Small"
  Case 11002 : Rcode = "Dest Network Not Reachable"
  Case 11003 : Rcode = "Dest Host Not Reachable"
  Case 11004 : Rcode = "Dest Protocol Not Reachable"
  Case 11005 : Rcode = "Dest Port Not Reachable"
  Case 11006 : Rcode = "No Resources Available"
  Case 11007 : Rcode = "Bad Option"
  Case 11008 : Rcode = "Hardware Error"
  Case 11009 : Rcode = "Packet too Big"
  Case 11010 : Rcode = "Rqst Timed Out"
  Case 11011 : Rcode = "Bad Request"
  Case 11012 : Rcode = "Bad Route"
  Case 11013 : Rcode = "TTL Exprd in Transit"
  Case 11014 : Rcode = "TTL Exprd Reassemb"
  Case 11015 : Rcode = "Parameter Problem"
  Case 11016 : Rcode = "Source Quench"
  Case 11017 : Rcode = "Option too Big"
  Case 11018 : Rcode = " Bad Destination"
  Case 11019 : Rcode = "Address Deleted"
  Case 11020 : Rcode = "Spec MTU Change"
  Case 11021 : Rcode = "MTU Change"
  Case 11022 : Rcode = "Unload"
  Case 11050 : Rcode = "General Failure"
End Select
describeResponse = Rcode
End Function
```

Many of the response codes listed would be rare and would probably indicate a programming error instead of a real network error. The most common are Success and Dest host not available.

C# programmers will also require the following namespaces in both the form and class file:

C#

```
using System.Text;
using System.Runtime.InteropServices;
```

Figure 12.2
ICMP (ping) client application.

To test the application, run it from Visual Studio .NET, type the IP address (not domain name!) of a well-known Web server into the box provided, and press Ping. It should respond with the message "Success" if the computer is accessible or "Dest Host Not Reachable" if it is not, as in Figure 12.2.

Ping can be used for more than simply checking whether a computer is switched on or not; it can also be used to trace the route of packets over the Internet. This is achieved by sending a ping request with a TTL of 1, followed by a ping with a TTL of 2, and so on. At each hop, a router will report a dead ping request and send a packet back to the original host, which will contain the IP address of the router. This technique is used by the *tracert* utility.

In .NET v2 (Whidbey), it is possible to retrieve statistics easily relating to the number and type of pings received and sent by your computer. Please refer to the `IcmpV4Statistics` class, as described in Chapter 13, for more information on this topic.

12.4 WHOIS

WHOIS ("who is") is a protocol that can be used to query the registrant of a domain name. It runs on TCP port 43 and is described definitively in RFC 954. This information includes the name and company of the person who bought the domain name, along with details of the DNS servers for that domain and the operator(s) of those servers.

Despite its usefulness, WHOIS is a poorly designed protocol. There are many WHOIS servers worldwide, each of which contains a subset of all the Internet domain names. There is no way to determine from a domain name which WHOIS server contains registrant information for that name. Furthermore, the content of WHOIS replies is not properly standardized, which makes it particularly difficult to parse replies properly.

Note: Operators of WHOIS servers generally limit the number of queries per day per IP address to 100 in order to prevent data mining.

Most countries have their own WHOIS server that covers the top-level domain for that country (such as .co.uk or .ie). International top-level domains such as .com, .net, and .org are stored in subsets in large WHOIS servers or allocated by central WHOIS servers on a continent-by-continent basis. A few well-known WHOIS servers are whois.networksolutions.com, whois.crsnic.net, and whois.ripe.net.

To perform a WHOIS query manually, run telnet from the command prompt, and type the following:

```
O whois.ripe.net 43
Google.de
```

The result will be as follows (abbreviated for clarity):

```
% This is the RIPE Whois server.
% The objects are in RPSL format.
% The object shown below is NOT in the RIPE database.
% It has been obtained by querying a remote server:
% (whois.denic.de) at port 43.
                                              %REFERRAL
START

    domain:      google.de
    descr:       Google Inc.
    descr:       Valentinskamp 24
    descr:       20354 Hamburg
    descr:       GERMANY
    nserver:     ns1.google.com
    nserver:     ns2.google.com
    nserver:     ns3.google.com
    nserver:     ns4.google.com

    status:      connect
```

```
changed:        20021125 170514
source:         DENIC
                                                          [admin-c]
                                                            Type:

PERSON
Name:           joel Fokke
Address:        Valentinskamp 24
City:           Hamburg
Pcode:          20354
Country:        DE
Changed:        20021023 150831
Source:         DENIC


[tech-c][zone-c]
Type:           ROLE
Name:           DENICoperations
Address:        DENIC eG
Address:        Wiesenhuettenplatz 26
City:           Frankfurt am Main
Pcode:          60329
Country:        DE
Phone:          +49 69 27235 272
Fax:            +49 69 27235 234
Email:          ops@denic.de
Changed:        20020621 194343
Source:         DENIC


%REFERRAL END
```

Unfortunately, as mentioned earlier, the WHOIS reply is not standardized, so expect different fields from different WHOIS servers. `Whois.NetworkSolutions.Com` will return fields in this format (abbreviated reply for hotmail.com):

```
Registrant: Microsoft Corporation (HOTMAIL-DOM)
    One Microsoft Way
    Redmond, CA 98052
    US



Domain Name: HOTMAIL.COM
```

```
Administrative Contact: Gudmundson, Carolyn
(PPUFRBYFWI)

                        domains@microsoft.com
                        One Microsoft Way
                        Redmond, WA 98052
                        US
                        (425) 882-8080
fax: (425) 936-7329

Technical Contact:      NOC, MSN   (RWJALTFZAI)
                        msnhst@microsoft.com
```

Note: For a bit of entertainment, look up the WHOIS entry for Microsoft.com with whois.crsnic.net. You'll find some interesting entries made by some Linux fans!

Performing a WHOIS query with .NET is easy. All that is required is to open a TCP connection on port 43, send the domain name followed by the new line character, and read back the response until the connection closes.

Create a new project in Visual Studio .NET. Draw three textboxes named tbServer, tbQuery, and tbStatus, the latter having multiline set to true. A button named btnSend is also required.

Click on the Send button, and add the following code:

C#

```csharp
private void btnSend_Click(object sender, System.EventArgs e)
{
  byte[] Query = Encoding.ASCII.GetBytes(
  tbQuery.Text + "\n");
  TcpClient clientSocket = new TcpClient(tbServer.Text,43);
  NetworkStream networkStream =  clientSocket.GetStream();
  networkStream.Write(Query,0,Query.GetLength(0));
  StreamReader Response = new StreamReader(networkStream);
  tbStatus.Text=Response.ReadToEnd();
  networkStream.Close();
}
```

VB.NET

```
Private  Sub btnSend_Click(ByVal sender As Object, _
        ByVal e As System.EventArgs)
  Dim Query() As Byte =  Encoding.ASCII.GetBytes _
        (tbQuery.Text + vbcrlf)
  Dim clientSocket As TcpClient =  New _
        TcpClient(tbServer.Text,43)
  Dim networkStream As NetworkStream = _
        clientSocket.GetStream()
  networkStream.Write(Query,0,Query.GetLength(0))
    Dim Response As StreamReader =  New _
        StreamReader(networkStream)
    tbStatus.Text=Response.ReadToEnd()
  networkStream.Close()
End Sub
```

You will also require a reference to some namespaces needed for the string handling and networking:

C#

```
using System.Text;
using System.Net;
using System.Net.Sockets;
using System.IO;
```

VB.NET

```
Imports System.Text
Imports System.Net
Imports System.Net.Sockets
Imports System.IO
```

To test the application, run it from Visual Studio .NET. Enter the name of a WHOIS server in the box provided, in this case whois.crsnic.net. Enter a domain name in the query box, omitting the "www" prefix. Press Send, and you should receive information about the registrant of that domain, similar to that shown in Figure 12.3.

Figure 12.3
*WHOIS client
application.*

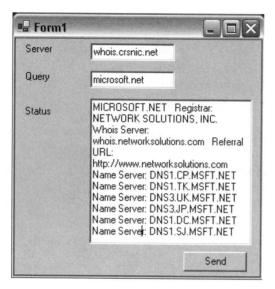

12.4.1 Telnet

In the days before GUIs, users of UNIX enjoyed the luxury of being able to control their server remotely via a command-line interface. Text-only interfaces may be passé, but many online services are still hosted on UNIX, and where configuration changes need to be made to the server, telnet is still the defacto standard for UNIX servers.

The protocol itself is straightforward: a TCP connection is opened on port 23, and this connection is persisted until one end closes the connection. Generally, any character typed on the keyboard is sent to the server and any returned data is displayed on-screen as text.

Telnet could be used as a back end to a remote configuration console for a UNIX product, but beyond that, it would rarely be used programmatically. It is, however, often used to debug servers and investigate new TCP-based protocols because all telnet clients provide the option to connect on ports other than 23.

A telnet client is included with Windows. In Windows 95 and 98, the telnet client has a GUI, but XP uses a DOS-based client. If you have a Web server on your computer, you can check that telnet is operational by typing the following code at the command prompt:

```
telnet localhost 80
GET /
```

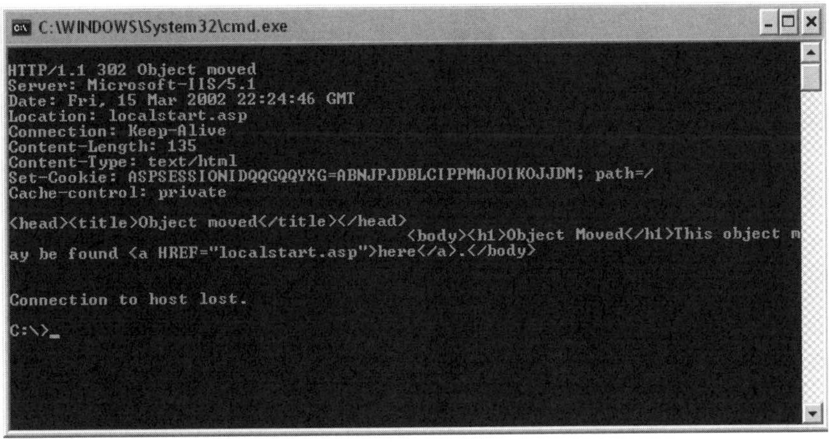

Figure 12.4
Telnet MS-DOS
utility.

If the server is online, an HTTP reply will be displayed on-screen similar to Figure 12.4. Otherwise, a "Could not open connection to the host" message will be displayed.

A secure version of telnet named SSH is now widely used to communicate with Linux and UNIX boxes.

12.5   Other members of the TCP/IP suite

Many protocols work behind the scenes in IP networks to provide the service. These would generally not be used programmatically, but they are worth being aware of.

12.5.1   ARP

Address resolution protocol (ARP) resolves IP addresses into their equivalent MAC addresses. Reverse ARP (RARP) performs the reverse of this function.

To view the ARP entries stored on your system, try the following:

```
DOS
C:\>arp -a
```

12.5.2   RIP

Routing information protocol (RIP) works by counting the number of times a packet moves toward its destination. Each new routing is called a *hop*, and the maximum hop count is usually set to 16. RIP will discard packets that are routed more than 16 times.

12.5.3 OSPF

Open shortest path first (OSPF) is a routing protocol that uses a link-state algorithm. This type of algorithm looks at the available routes a data packet can take to its destination and decides the fastest route. OSPF does not have a maximum hop count.

12.5.4 BGP/EGP

Border gateway protocol (BGP) supersedes exterior gateway protocol (EGP) and is used to route packets outside of a network to other people's networks. It differs from OSPF, which is used in internal networks.

Note: You should never have two BGP routers on the same network without support for OSPF or RIP.

12.5.5 SNMP

Simple network management protocol (SNMP) enables network administrators to connect and manage network devices. It is being superseded with RMON, but is still widely used by network devices. It operates over UDP port 161 and is generally accessed using a managed information base (MIB) browser (downloadable from *www.mg-soft.com*). An MIB is a collection of resource variables, providing information about the status of the device. SNMP can issue traps (events) when something goes wrong with a network device.

12.5.6 PPP

Point-to-point protocol (PPP) can be used to transport IP, IPX, and Net-BEUI over serial links such as modem connections. PPP is commonly used by ISPs to provide subscribers with modem or ISDN Internet access. PPP requires a phone number and, usually, a DNS server address, with username and password. PPP supersedes Serial Line Internet Protocol (SLIP) because of its speed, simplicity, and flexibility.

12.6 WMI

WMI, or Windows Management Instrumentation, is used within a Windows intranet to provide a facility to perform simple administrative tasks remotely. The main advantage this provides is that the WMI client is built into Windows, so there is no need to write or install a proprietary client, as long as the Windows Management Instrumentation service is running on the remote machine.

One of the main uses of WMI is to extract technical information about remote Windows systems. Whether you want to tell how much free disk space is on a remote computer or discover its CPU clock speed, WMI can do the job.

WMI is structured somewhat like a database. The CIM (Common Information Model) repository holds multiple namespaces. These in turn hold many classes, which have properties which correspond to either devices such as a CD-ROM drive or intangiable processes or data such as the NT event log.

To view the CIM namespaces installed on your system, run WBEMTEST from the command line. Press Connect→type Root→Connect→ Enum Instances→type __NAMESPACE→ok. A few namespaces of interest are:

- `root\directory\ldap`: provides access to active directory services

- `root\snmp`: provides access to SNMP MIB data

- `root\default`: provides access to the windows registry

- `root\WMI`: provides access to Windows Device Model (WDM) devices.

The `root\cimv2` namespace is the largest of all the CIM namespaces, and forms the basis of the following examples. To view a list of all the classes contained within the `root\cimv2` namespace, load WBEMTEST, press Connect→Type root\cimv2→Connect→Enum Classes→Check Recursive→click Ok. The data contained in these classes can be queried using a language known as WQL (WMI Query Language), as the example in section 12.6.1 demonstrates.

12.6.1   Reading WMI data

WMI data may resemble a database conceptually, but the `System.Management` namespace, which encapsulates WMI, is dissimilar to the data access namespaces. In the same way as a database connection is required before SQL can be executed, a scope must be defined before WQL can be used. WMI uses a `ManagementScope` that is passed the location of the remote computer in the format \\<host name>\root\namespace and a `ConnectionOptions` object that contains the logon credentials (username and password).

A `ManagementObjectSearcher` processes the WQL. This object returns a `ManagementObjectCollection` when the `Get()` method is called. This collection is similar to a table, where every element represents a row in the table. This row is represented as a `ManagementBaseObject`. Every row has a variable number of columns, which are represented by a collection of `PropertyData` objects held within the `Properties` collection contained in each `ManagementBaseObject` object.

Start a new project in Visual Studio .NET. Under Project→Add References, add a reference to `System.Management`. Draw four textboxes onto the form named `tbHost`, `tbUsername`, `tbPassword`, and `tbExecute`. You will also require a list view named `lvWMI` and a button named `btnExecute`.

Click on the Execute button and add the following code:

C#

```
private void btnExecute_Click(object sender, System.EventArgs
e)
{
 ConnectionOptions Options = new ConnectionOptions();
 if(tbPassword.Text != "" && tbUsername.Text != "")
 {
  Options.Username = tbHost.Text + "\\" + tbUsername.Text;
  Options.Password = tbPassword.Text;
 }
 ManagementScope Scope = new ManagementScope("\\\\" +
 tbHost.Text "\\root\\cimv2", Options);
 Scope.Connect();
 ObjectQuery Query = new ObjectQuery(tbExecute.Text);
 ManagementObjectSearcher Searcher = new
 ManagementObjectSearcher(Scope, Query);
 ManagementObjectCollection ItemCollection;
```

```
         ItemCollection = Searcher.Get();
         lvWMI.Clear();
         lvWMI.Columns.Clear();
         lvWMI.View = View.Details;
         foreach(ManagementBaseObject Item in ItemCollection)
         {
          if (lvWMI.Columns.Count==0)
          {
           foreach (PropertyData prop in Item.Properties)
           {
            lvWMI.Columns.Add(prop.Name,
                              lvWMI.Width/4,
                              HorizontalAlignment.Left);
           }
          }
          ListViewItem lvItem = new ListViewItem();
          bool firstColumn = true;
          foreach (PropertyData prop in Item.Properties)
          {
           if (firstColumn)
           {
            lvItem.SubItems[0].Text = prop.Value+"";
            firstColumn=false;
           }
           else
           {
            lvItem.SubItems.Add(prop.Value+"");
           }
          }
          lvWMI.Items.Add(lvItem);
         }
        }
```

VB.NET

```
    Private  Sub btnExecute_Click(ByVal sender As Object, _
           ByVal e As System.EventArgs)
    Dim Options As ConnectionOptions
    If tbPassword.Text <> "" And tbUsername.Text <> "" Then
           Options.Username = tbHost.Text + "\\" + _
                  tbUsername.Text
           Options.Password = tbPassword.Text
```

```
      End If
      Dim Scope As ManagementScope = New ManagementScope _
            ("\\" + tbHost.Text + "\root\cimv2", Options)
      Scope.Connect()
      Dim Query As ObjectQuery = New ObjectQuery(tbExecute.Text)
      Dim Searcher As ManagementObjectSearcher = New _
            ManagementObjectSearcher(Scope, Query)
      Dim ItemCollection As ManagementObjectCollection
      ItemCollection = Searcher.Get()
      lvWMI.Clear()
      lvWMI.Columns.Clear()
      lvWMI.View = View.Details
      Dim Item As ManagementBaseObject
      For Each Item In ItemCollection
       Dim prop As PropertyData
       If lvWMI.Columns.Count = 0 Then
         For Each prop In Item.Properties
          lvWMI.Columns.Add(prop.Name, _
                lvWMI.Width / 4, _
                HorizontalAlignment.Left)
         Next
       End If
       Dim lvItem As ListViewItem = New ListViewItem
       Dim firstColumn As Boolean = True
       For Each prop In Item.Properties
         If firstColumn = True Then
           lvItem.SubItems(0).Text = Convert.ToString(prop.Value)
           firstColumn = False
         Else
           lvItem.SubItems.Add(Convert.ToString(prop.Value))
         End If
       Next
       lvWMI.Items.Add(lvItem)
      Next
    End Sub
```

You will also require a reference to the relevant namespaces, so add this code to the top of the application:

C#

```
using System.Management;
```

VB.NET

```
Imports System.Management
```

To test the application, run it from Visual Studio .NET, and type `localhost` into the host box provided, entering a username and password if one is required on your machine. Type a WQL query such as `Select * from Win32_NetworkAdapterConfiguration` and press Execute. The list view should fill with information about your system (Figure 12.5).

To run WMI queries against remote machines, you must have administrator privileges on those computers.

12.6.2 Leveraging WMI

You are not restricted to reading data when using WMI; you can also perform actions on remote computers using this technology. Functions such as starting and stopping services, rebooting, and starting and terminating processes can all be performed directly from WMI. In order to view which methods may be called on any given WMI class, load WBEMTEST, connect to the container namespace (i.e. `root\cimv2`), click Create Class, then type the name of the WMI Class (i.e. WIN32_PROCESS), and press continue. The supported methods will be listed on-screen. The most generic task that can be performed with WMI is to start a process. This process (application) could then carry out any function that is required.

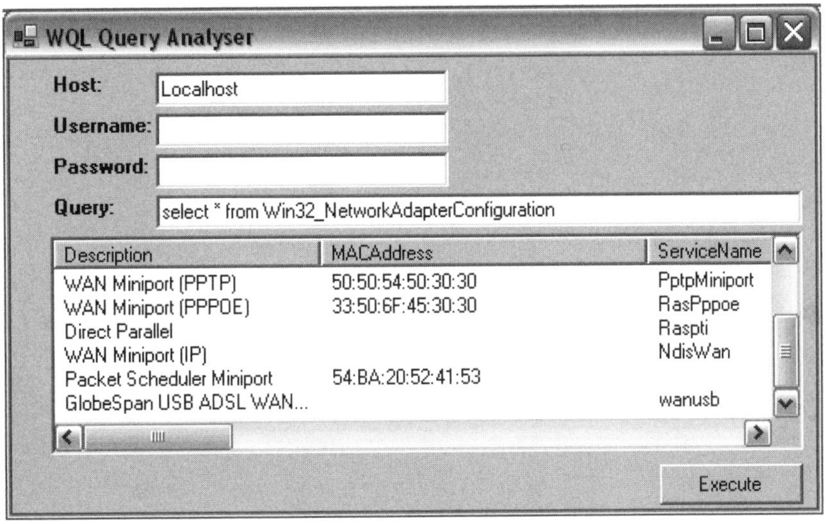

Figure 12.5
WMI query language analyzer application.

Like the previous WMI example, a connection, or scope, is required to the remote computer. This is created in exactly the same way. Instead of executing a WQL query, a `ManagementClass` is obtained for the Win32_Process class. This WMI class holds a method named `Create` that can spawn new processes. This method is passed parameters via a `ManagementBaseObject` object.

Create a new project in Visual Studio .NET. Under Project→Add References, add a reference to `System.Management`. Draw four textboxes onto the form named `tbHost`, `tbUsername`, `tbPassword`, and `tbExecute`. Add a button named `btnExecute`. Click on it and enter the following code:

C#

```
private void btnExecute_Click(object sender, System.EventArgs
e)
{
 ConnectionOptions Options = new ConnectionOptions();
 if(tbPassword.Text != "" && tbUsername.Text != "")
 {
  Options.Username = tbHost.Text + "\\" + tbUsername.Text;
  Options.Password = tbPassword.Text;
 }
 ManagementScope Scope = new ManagementScope("\\\\" +
 tbHost.Text + "\\root\\cimv2", Options);
 Scope.Connect();
 ManagementClass ProcessClass = new
 ManagementClass("Win32_Process");
 ManagementBaseObject inParams =
 ProcessClass.GetMethodParameters("Create");
 ProcessClass.Scope = Scope;
 inParams["CommandLine"] = tbExecute.Text;
 ProcessClass.InvokeMethod("Create", inParams, null);
}
```

VB.NET

```
Private  Sub btnExecute_Click(ByVal sender As Object, _
    ByVal e As System.EventArgs)
 Dim Options As ConnectionOptions =  New ConnectionOptions()
 If tbPassword.Text <> "" and tbUsername.Text <> ""
  Options.Username = tbHost.Text + "\\" + tbUsername.Text
  Options.Password = tbPassword.Text
 End if
 Dim Scope as ManagementScope = New ManagementScope _
```

```
                    ("\\" + tbHost.Text + "\root\cimv2" ,Options)
       Scope.Connect()
       Dim ProcessClass As ManagementClass =  New _
               ManagementClass("Win32_Process")
       Dim inParams As ManagementBaseObject = _
                ProcessClass.GetMethodParameters("Create")
       ProcessClass.Scope = Scope
       inParams("CommandLine") = tbExecute.Text
       ProcessClass.InvokeMethod("Create", inParams, Nothing)
       End Sub
```

You will also require a reference to the relevant namespaces, so add this code to the top of the application:

C#

```
using System.Management;
```

VB.NET

```
Imports System.Management
```

To test the application, run it from Visual Studio .NET, type in local-host for the host, and provide the username and password if required. Type notepad.exe into the command-line box as shown in Figure 12.6, and press Execute. You should see Notepad opening on-screen.

Again, this can be run remotely, as long as you have administrator privileges on a remote computer on the network.

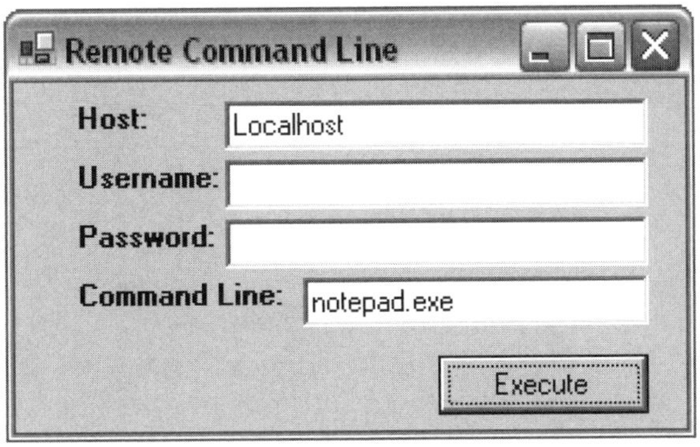

Figure 12.6
WMI remote process manager application.

12.7 Conclusion

This chapter has dealt with a set of network protocols that are not suited to moving bulk data among machines, but are particularly valuable in adding features and improving the performance of distributed applications. These utility protocols can be used to test quickly if machines are online, what domain names or hosts are associated with them, and who is the registrant of the domain name. This provides vital extra information that ultimately adds value to your final product.

The chapter concluded with a look at a surprisingly versatile Microsoft technology, WMI, which can pull virtually every conceivable piece of technical information from a remote computer over. WMI is an absolutely essential technology for internal IT support.

The next chapter takes a microscope to the network and looks at exactly what gets sent down the phone line when you use the Internet. If you're on a LAN, you might be surprised to see what passes through your computer without your knowledge. Be warned: Read the following chapter, and you'll never play multiplayer games on your company network again!

13

Analyzing Network Packets

13.1 Introduction

Network programming is very much concerned with moving data from client to server, but when you need to look at what is moving between the client and server, you encounter a problem.

In most cases, there is no need for a program to know what data is being received by other applications. Furthermore, it is a security risk to have one program that could scan third-party applications, such as FTP software, and retrieve the username and password for your Web site; however, if you are building a value-added package to a third-party application, such as a content filter for a proprietary or legacy application, tapping into what is being sent between client and server is a good start.

Packet capture isn't something new. It has been around for many years. But very few applications actually leverage the technology to provide tools that can be used in conjunction with other software to provide virus or computer-misuse detection. What is available, though, are extensive tools that can tell you what each byte in every packet means, down to even the computer manufacturer that sent the packet. Figure 13.1 shows the demo version of TracePlus from *www.sstinc.com*.

Note: In order to determine the manufacturer of a particular piece of equipment from its MAC address, access the listing at *http://standards.ieee.org/regauth/oui/oui.txt*, which contains most, if not all, network equipment manufacturers with their allocated MAC address space.

Software that can leverage packet-level data can be useful for businesses. We have all heard of the scenario where a few employees decide to download their favorite band's latest album on Mp3 the day of a big presentation,

Figure 13.1
TracePlus utility.

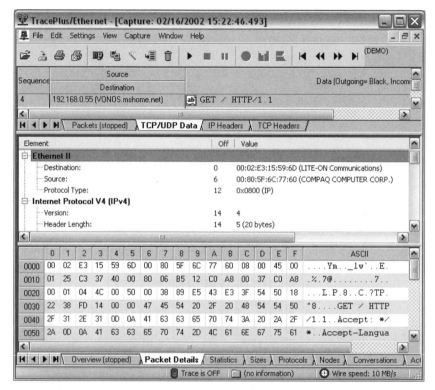

causing a total misallocation of bandwidth within a company. This is where traffic-detection software comes into its own, providing an early warning system for bandwidth misuse.

Traffic-detection software can be used to detect packets on a network that could uncover viruses, use of unauthorized software, and email forgery. Let's look briefly at how the applications mentioned above could be implemented using packet-level monitoring.

You can use traffic detection to discover the presence of viruses and attacks in progress, but unfortunately not to prevent them. It could, however, be used to provide companywide detection of infected computers and denial-of-service attacks. The telltale signs of virus propagation could be rapid sequential accesses to computers within the subnet on port 80 (scanning for servers to infect) or heartbeat signals coming from a nonstandard port to an external server (firewall tunneling).

Denial-of-service attacks could be detected from the presence of a large number of corrupted packets sent to a particular server. A fragmented ping request would indicate a ping-of-death attack. Large numbers of incomplete TCP connections would indicate a SYN flood attack, in which the first packet of a TCP handshake is sent repetitively and rapidly. The victim attempts to establish TCP sessions for each of the packets by sending ACK (acknowledge) packets to the attacker, which are not responded to. The victim eventually becomes overwhelmed with pending TCP sessions and denies all network traffic.

Detection of unauthorized software usage could be useful in a company where employees may be partial to spending time playing computer games during work hours. Multiplayer computer games generally operate on a high port over TCP/IP or IPX. Games produce a lot of network traffic and, thus, can be spotted easily in a TCP/IP trace. The IP addresses of the offending employee's computers could be logged, and the employee could be suitably warned.

Email traffic could also be monitored remotely using these techniques. This could be used to detect company secrets being sent to a competitor. Furthermore, a system to prevent email spoofing and forgery could be implemented if SMTP traffic were monitored. An application could keep a record of each employee's computer's IP address and email address. In the event of a mismatch between the IP and email address, an alarm could be raised, possibly sending an email to the recipient warning of the possibility of email forgery.

This chapter begins with information about how to read and interpret IP-level traffic on your network. It then progresses to more complex examples about how to drill down further into the network stack and extract lower-level data at the frame level. The chapter concludes with information about how to use new classes introduced in .NET 2.0 Whidbey to gather systemwide network information.

13.2 IP-level network tapping

Network tapping anything that runs at the IP level includes TCP/IP and UDP and everything above that, such as DNS, HTTP, FTP, and so forth. At this level, you don't need to use any special software. Everything can be done natively in .NET.

To implement a layer 3 network tap in .NET, open a new project in Visual Studio .NET and add a list box named lbPackets and two buttons, btnStart and btnStop. It may be worthwhile to set the font for the list box to Courier for easier reading.

After designing the user interface, you should add the following public variable, a reference to the main listener thread:

C#

```
public Thread Listener;
```

VB.NET

```
Public Listener as Thread
```

Click on the Start button and enter the following code:

C#

```
private void btnStart_Click(object sender, System.EventArgs e)
{
  btnStart.Enabled = false;
  btnStop.Enabled = true;
  Listener = new Thread(new ThreadStart(Run));
  Listener.Start();
}
```

VB.NET

```
Private Sub btnStart_Click(ByVal sender As Object, _
        ByVal e As System.EventArgs)
  btnStart.Enabled = False
  btnStop.Enabled = True
  Listener = New Thread(New ThreadStart(AddressOf Run))
  Listener.Start()
End Sub
```

The Run method is where the network tap takes place. It is a processor-intensive task, so it is executed in its own thread, as can be seen from the code. Click on the Stop button and enter the following code:

C#

```
private void btnStop_Click(object sender, System.EventArgs e)
{
  btnStart.Enabled = true;
  btnStop.Enabled = false;
  if(Listener != null)
```

```
    {
      Listener.Abort();
      Listener.Join();
      Listener = null;
    }
  }
```

VB.NET

```
Private Sub btnStop_Click(ByVal sender As Object, _
        ByVal e As System.EventArgs)
  btnStart.Enabled = True
  btnStop.Enabled = False
  If Not Listener Is Nothing Then
    Listener.Abort()
    Listener.Join()
    Listener = Nothing
  End If
End Sub
```

This code simply kills the thread containing the network tap, which effectively stops reporting the arrival of new packets.

C#

```
public void Run()
{
  int len_receive_buf = 4096;
  int len_send_buf = 4096;
  byte[] receive_buf = new byte[len_receive_buf];
  byte[] send_buf = new byte[len_send_buf];
  int cout_receive_bytes;
  Socket socket = new Socket(AddressFamily.InterNetwork,
  SocketType.Raw, ProtocolType.IP);
  socket.Blocking = false;
  IPHostEntry IPHost = Dns.GetHostByName(Dns.GetHostName());
  socket.Bind(new
  IPEndPoint(IPAddress.Parse
  (IPHost.AddressList[0].ToString()), 0));
  socket.SetSocketOption(SocketOptionLevel.IP,
     SocketOptionName.HeaderIncluded, 1);
  byte []IN = new byte[4]{1, 0, 0, 0};
  byte []OUT = new byte[4];
```

```csharp
    int SIO_RCVALL = unchecked((int)0x98000001);
    int ret_code = socket.IOControl(SIO_RCVALL, IN, OUT);
    while(true)
    {
      IAsyncResult ar = socket.BeginReceive(receive_buf, 0,
      len_receive_buf, SocketFlags.None, null, this);
      cout_receive_bytes = socket.EndReceive(ar);
      Receive(receive_buf, cout_receive_bytes);
    }
  }
```

VB.NET

```vbnet
Public Sub Run()
 Dim len_receive_buf As Integer = 4096
 Dim len_send_buf As Integer = 4096
 Dim receive_buf() As Byte = New Byte(len_receive_buf) {}
 Dim send_buf() As Byte = New Byte(len_send_buf) {}
 Dim cout_receive_bytes As Integer
 Dim socket As Socket = New _
   Socket(AddressFamily.InterNetwork, _
   SocketType.Raw, ProtocolType.IP)
 socket.Blocking = False
 Dim IPHost As IPHostEnTry = _
 Dns.GetHostByName(Dns.GetHostName())
 socket.Bind(New _
   IPEndPoint(IPAddress.Parse _
   (IPHost.AddressList(0).ToString()), 0))
 socket.SetSocketOption(SocketOptionLevel.IP, _
   SocketOptionName.HeaderIncluded, 1)
 Dim bIN As Byte() = New Byte() {1, 0, 0, 0}
 Dim bOUT As Byte() = New Byte() {0, 0, 0, 0}
 Dim SIO_RCVALL As Integer = &H98000001
 Dim ret_code As Integer = socket.IOControl _
       (SIO_RCVALL, bIN, bOUT)
 Do
   Dim ar As IAsyncResult = socket.BeginReceive _
     (receive_buf, 0, _
     len_receive_buf, SocketFlags.None, Nothing, Me)
   cout_receive_bytes = socket.EndReceive(ar)
   Receive(receive_buf, cout_receive_bytes)
 Loop
End Sub
```

The Run method is the core thread of the application. It creates a raw socket bound to the local machine on the default adapter. The socket's normal operating parameters are then modified using the IOControl method, which accesses the underlying socket API function WSAIoctl. This function is passed a parameter SIO_RCVALL (98000001 Hex). Use of this parameter enables a socket to receive all IP packets on the network. The socket must be in RAW mode, using the IP protocol, and bound to a specific local adapter. This feature requires administrator privilege on the local machine. The packet parsing and display has been separated from the tapping thread to make the program more legible. This method is called Receive and should be implemented thus:

C#

```
public void Receive(byte []buf, int len)
{
 if (buf[9]==6)
 {
   lbPackets.Items.Add
   (Encoding.ASCII.GetString(buf).Replace("\0"," "));
 }
}
```

VB.NET

```
Public Sub Receive(ByVal buf as byte(), ByVal len As Integer)
 If buf(9)=6 then
  lbPackets.Items.Add(Encoding.ASCII.GetString _
    (buf).Replace(chr(0)," "))
 end if
End Sub
```

In this example, traffic is filtered so that only TCP/IP packets are shown. This means that the screen is not cluttered with DNS queries, pings, and UDP data. TCP/IP packets will always have the ninth byte in the header set to 6. All null (ASCII code 0) characters are displayed as spaces so that the list box does not crop the string at the first null character.

Finally, you need to add some standard namespaces to the code:

C#

```
using System;
using System.Windows.Forms;
```

```
using System.Net.Sockets;
using System.Net;
using System.Threading;
using System.Text;
```

VB.NET

```
Imports System
Imports System.Windows.Forms
Imports System.Net.Sockets
Imports System.Net
Imports System.Threading
Imports System.Text
```

To test the application, run it from Visual Studio .NET, and visit a Web site using your browser. You should see the raw TCP data flowing between your browser and the Web server appear in the list box, as shown in Figure 13.2.

13.2.1 Interpreting raw network data

Capturing and interpreting raw network data are totally separate things. Being able to recognize anomalies in the network data is the key to providing a useful tool that could be of real benefit to network managers and administrators.

Figure 13.2
IP-layer packet sniffer application.

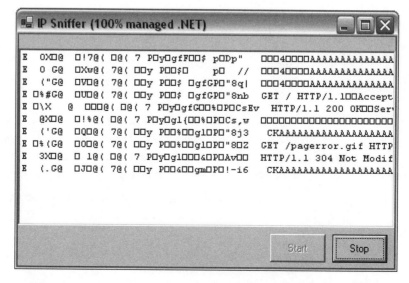

Raw network data can appear totally unordered, with HTTP packets mixed in with NETBIOS (Microsoft file sharing) and ARP, each performing different tasks, but working simultaneously. Some of these packets can be recognized immediately: familiar snippets of HTML generally indicate HTTP (although it could be a rich-text email or a Web page being uploaded). Most networks will primarily ferry IP traffic, but will also carry non-IP traffic such as NETBIOS and ARP.

Every packet carries a header that is in a strictly defined binary format. To define the standards involved most concisely, the tables in this chapter list the name and starting point of each field in the relevant header. Every field runs contiguously with the next; thus, the length of any field can be calculated by subtracting its starting point from the following field's starting point.

Because fields do not need to start at a byte boundary, the bit number is also provided in the second column. Where a field is commonly known as being part of a collective field, it is separated in the description column from the parent field by a colon.

The frame header (Table 13.1) is the only part that the hardware within the network card will actually read or process. It is 14 bytes long, containing the hardware address of the source and destination computers. In the case where the hardware address of the destination computer is unknown, this address is set to FF–FF–FF–FF–FF–FF (hex). Over PPP connections, the source and destination MAC address may be omitted and replaced by SRC and DEST.

Table 13.1   *Ethernet frame header.*

Byte Offset	Bit Offset	Description
1	1	Destination MAC address
6	1	Source MAC address
12	1	Ethernet type code (2 bytes)

The Ethernet type code is a two-digit hex number that specifies the packet protocol (Table 13.2). A fairly comprehensive list of Ethernet type codes can be seen at *www.cavebear.com/CaveBear/Ethernet.*

Table 13.2   *Ethernet type codes.*

Type Code (Hex)	Meaning
0800	IP version 4
0805	X.25
0806	ARP
8035	RARP
8037	IPX
809B	AppleTalk
80F3	AppleTalk ARP
814C	SNMP
86DD	IP version 6

13.2.2   IP packets in detail

In IP packets, the IP header (Table 13.3) immediately follows the frame header at byte 14. IP is definitively described in RFC 791.

Table 13.3   *IP header .*

Byte Offset	Bit Offset	Description
1	1	Version
1	5	Header length
2	1	Type of service: Precedence
2	4	Type of service: Delay
2	5	Type of service: Throughput
2	6	Type of service: Reliability
2	7	Type of service: (Reserved)
3	1	Data length
5	1	Identification
7	1	Flags
7	4	Fragment offset

Table 13.3 *IP header (continued).*

9	1	TTL
10	1	Protocol
11	1	Header checksum
13	1	Source address
17	1	Destination address
21	1	Option: code: Flag
21	2	Option: code: Class
21	4	Option: code: Number
22	1	Option: Length
23	1	Option: Data (variable length)
		Data (variable length)

- *Version:* Set to 0100 for IPv4 and 0110 for IPv6.

- *Header length:* The length of the header divided by 4. Max length is 60.

- *Type of service:* May be used to increase quality of service on some networks.

- *Data length:* The combined length of the header and data.

- *Identification:* A random number used to identify duplicate packets.

- *Flags:* Indicates the fragmentation status of the packet. Bit 2 is set to 1 when the datagram cannot be fragmented (0 when it can). Bit 3 is set to 1 when there are more fragments in the datagram, and 0 when this packet is the last fragment.

- *Fragment offset:* Indicates the position a packet should occupy within a fragmented datagram.

- *TTL:* Indicates the number of nodes through which the datagram can pass before being discarded. Used to avoid infinite routing loops.

- *Protocol:* Set to 6 for TCP, 17 for UDP, 1 for ICMP, and 2 for IGMP.

- *Checksum:* A checksum of the IP header calculated using a 16-bit ones complement sum.

- *Source:* The IP address of the sending computer.

- *Destination:* The IP address of the receiving computer.

- *Option:* An optional field that may contain security options, routing records, timestamps, and so forth.

13.2.3   ICMP packets in detail

In ICMP (ping) packets immediately following the IP header make up a 4-byte header (Table 13.4) followed by a body of variable length. A definitive description of ICMP can be found in RFC 792.

Table 13.4   *ICMP header.*

Byte Offset	Bit Offset	Description
1	1	Type
2	1	Code
3	1	Checksum

Type: Defines the purpose or function of the packet. See Table 13.5.

Code: A type code–specific identifier that more accurately describes the function of the packet. In a destination unreachable (3) packet, 0 indicates the subnet is down, whereas 1 indicates that only the host is down.

Checksum: The checksum is the 16-bit ones complement of the ones complement sum of the ICMP message starting with the ICMP type.

Table 13.5   *ICMP type codes .*

Type Code	Meaning
0	Echo reply
3	Destination unreachable
4	Source quench
5	Redirect
8	Echo request
11	Timeout
12	Parameter unintelligible
13	Timestamp request

Table 13.5 *ICMP type codes (continued).*

Type Code	Meaning
14	Timestamp reply
15	Info request
16	Info reply
17	Address request
18	Address reply

13.2.4 TCP/IP packets in detail

In TCP/IP packets, immediately following the IP header is a 24-byte TCP header (Table 13.6). A definitive description of TCP can be found in RFC 793.

Table 13.6 *TCP header.*

Byte Offset	Bit Offset	Description
1	1	Source port
3	1	Destination port
5	1	Sequence number
9	1	Acknowledgment number
13	1	Data offset
13	4	Reserved
14	3	Urgent (URG)
14	4	Acknowledge (ACK)
14	5	Push (PSH)
14	6	Reset (RST)
14	7	Synchronize (SYN)
14	8	Finish (FIN)
15	1	Window
17	1	Checksum
19	1	Urgent pointer

Table 13.6   *TCP header. (continued)*

Byte Offset	Bit Offset	Description
21	1	Options
24	1	Padding

- *Source port:* The port the TCP connection is made from, usually a high port.

- *Destination port:* The destination port, 80 for HTTP and 25 for SMTP, etc.

- *Sequence number:* The sequence number of the first data octet in this segment (except when SYN is present). If SYN is present, the sequence number is the initial sequence number (ISN), and the first data octet is ISN + 1.

- *Acknowledgment number:* If the ACK control bit is set, this field contains the value of the next sequence number the segment sender is expecting to receive. Once a connection is established, this is always sent.

- *Data offset:* The number of 32-bit words in the TCP header. This indicates where the data begins. The TCP header (even one including options) is an integral number 32 bits long.

- *Urgent (URG):* When set to 1, the urgent pointer field is significant.

- *Acknowledge (ACK):* When set to 1, the acknowledgment field is significant.

- *Push (PSH):* Implements a push function.

- *Reset (RST):* When set to 1, it will reset the connection.

- *Synchronize (SYN):* Synchronizes sequence numbers.

- *Finish (FIN):* Indicates that there is no more data from the sender.

- *Window:* The number of data octets indicated in the acknowledgment field that the sender of this segment is willing to accept.

- *Checksum:* The checksum field is the 16-bit ones complement of the ones complement sum of all 16-bit words in the header and text, if segments are zero-padded to form a multiple of 16-bit words for checksum purposes. The pad is not transmitted as part of the segment. While computing the checksum, the checksum field is replaced with zeros. The checksum also covers a pseudoheader that is prefixed to the TCP header while computing the checksum only. This pseudoheader contains the source address, the destination address, the protocol, and TCP length.

- *Urgent pointer:* Indicates the current value of the urgent pointer as an offset from the sequence number in this segment. The urgent pointer points to the sequence number of the byte following the urgent data. This field is only to be interpreted in segments with the URG control bit set.

- *Options:* This contains vendor-specific IP options that may not be implemented on all systems. It is guaranteed to end on a 32-bit boundary with zero padding.

TCP is a connection-oriented protocol with built-in protection from duplicated, dropped, and out-of order packets. This is done by explicitly opening a connection between client and server and assigning each packet a sequence number. The client will reply to the server with an acknowledgment for every packet sent; if sequence numbers go missing, appear twice, or appear out of order to the client, the acknowledgment will not be sent, and the server can take appropriate action.

A TCP connection is established with a three-way handshake. Initially, the client sends a SYN request to the server, and the server replies with an ACK response, to which the client replies with an ACK reply. Similarly, a TCP connection is closed with a two-way handshake, where one party sends a FIN request to the other, which then replies with an ACK response.

13.2.5 UDP packets in detail

In UDP packets, immediately following the IP header is an 8-byte UDP header (Table 13.7). A definitive description of UDP can be found in RFC 768.

Table 13.7 *UDP header.*

Byte Offset	Bit Offset	Description
1	1	Source port
3	1	Destination port
5	1	Length
7	1	Checksum

UDP is the most basic data-carrying protocol that is valid for the Internet. It contains no protection against lost or duplicated packets, and therefore is not applicable to media that require high integrity. It is acceptable for live streaming audio and video formats.

- *Source port:* The port the UDP connection is made from, usually a high port.

- *Destination port:* The destination port, 161 for SNMP and 53 for DNS, etc.

- *Length:* The number of bytes following the header, plus the header itself.

- *Checksum:* Computed as the 16-bit ones complement of the ones complement sum of a pseudoheader of information from the IP header, the UDP header, and the data, padded as needed with zero bytes at the end to make a multiple of 2 bytes. If the checksum is set to 0, then check summing is disabled. If the computed checksum is 0, then this field must be set to 0xFFFF.

13.2.6 DNS packets in detail

In DNS packets, immediately following the UDP header (port 53) is a 12-byte DNS header (Table 13.8). A definitive description of DNS can be found in RFC 1035.

Table 13.8   *DNS header .*

Byte Offset	Bit Offset	Description
1	1	ID
3	1	Query or response
3	2	Query
3	6	Authoritative answer
3	7	Truncation
3	8	Recursive
3	1	Availability
4	2	Set to 0 for future use
4	5	Result code

Table 13.8   *DNS header (continued).*

Byte Offset	Bit Offset	Description
5	1	Question count
7	1	Answer count
9	1	Authority count
11	1	Additional count

- *ID:* Used to correlate queries and responses.

- *Query or response:* Identifies the message as a query or response.

- *Query:* Field that describes the type of message: 0 for standard query (name to address), 1 for inverse query (address to name), and 2 for server status request.

- *Authoritative answer:* Identifies the response as one made by an authoritative name server when set to 1.

- *Truncation:* Indicates the message has been truncated when set to 1.

- *Recursive:* Set to 1 to request the name server to perform recursive searches.

- *Availability:* Indicates if the name server can provide recursive service.

- *Result code (RCODE):* Used to indicate errors in processing the DNS query.

- *Question count:* Indicates the number of entries in the question section.

- *Answer count:* Indicates the number of resource records in the answer section.

- *Authority count:* Indicates the number of name server resource records in the authority section.

- *Additional count:* Indicates the number of resource records in the additional records section.

  DNS is used primarily to resolve IP addresses from domain names; however, it can also be used to locate mail exchanges and so forth.

13.3 **Layer 2 network tapping**

When you tap into (sniff) network traffic at level 2, you receive not only data from other applications on your computer, but also from other applications on different computers that are on the same network. Furthermore, you get more than just IP traffic: you start to see ARP requests, NETBIOS packets, and many other weird and wonderful inhabitants of the network, and they all come complete with frame headers.

WinPCap is, in essence, a driver that enables you to read packets directly from a network adapter. It was developed by the Politecnico di Torino (Italy) and can be distributed in binary format with the addition of a copyright notice and disclaimer to your application. WinPCap can be downloaded from *http://winpcap.mirror.ethereal.com*.

The WinPCap DLL is designed for use with Visual C++ and is difficult to use directly from C# or VB.NET. A wrapper of some description is required to import this library into your .NET application. One of the well-known wrappers is an ActiveX control named PacketX, which is available from *www.beesync.com*. This software is shareware and, therefore, may not be applicable for inclusion in freeware packages.

Alternatively, I have prepared a wrapper (a C++ DLL) named rvpacket.dll that is available for download at *http://network.programming-in.net/downloads/rvPacket.zip*. This DLL is open source and can be redistributed as required. The DLL is only a basic implementation of WinPCap, but the source code is available for those who are savvy in C++ to extend the functionality.

Developers should be aware of the following known limitations to WinPCap:

- It will not operate correctly on Windows NT, 2000, or XP dial-up connections.
- It may reset dial-up connections on Windows 95.
- Wireless network cards are not fully supported.
- Some implementations of VPN are not supported.

13.3.1 **Using rvPacket and WinPCap**

This first example uses WinPCap with the rvPacket wrapper to display all network traffic on a textbox. It is normal for network data to pass through the adapter faster than it can appear on-screen, so there may be some time lag between data passing through the network and what is displayed on-screen. The first step in developing this application is to download and install WinPCap from *http://winpcap.mirror.ethereal.com*, then to download rvPacket from *http://network.programming-in.net/downloads/rvPacket.zip*, and copy the DLL into your Windows system folder.

Create a new project in Visual Studio .NET, and draw a textbox named tbPackets with multiline set to true. Two buttons named btnStart and btnStop are required. VB.NET developers will need to add a reference to Microsoft.VisualBasic.Compatibility using Project→Add References.

Click on the Start button and add the following code:

C#

```csharp
private void btnStart_Click(object sender, System.EventArgs
e)
{
  short Qid;
  string packetBuffer;
  short openSuccess;
  short packetQueue;
  short packetLen;
  string rawAdapterDetails = "";
  int posDefaultAdapter;
  getAdapterNames(rawAdapterDetails);
  Adapter="\\"; // default adapter
  openSuccess = openAdapter("\\");
  if (openSuccess != ERR_SUCCESS)
  {
    MessageBox.Show(
    "Unable to start. Check WinPCap is installed");
    return;
  }
  while(true)
  {
    packetQueue = checkPacketQueue(Adapter);
    for (Qid = 1; Qid<packetQueue;Qid++)
    {
      packetBuffer = new
      StringBuilder().Append
      (' ',MAX_PACKET_SIZE).ToString();
      packetLen = getQueuedPacket(packetBuffer);
```

```
          packetBuffer = packetBuffer.Substring(0, packetLen);
          tbPackets.Text = tbPackets.Text +
                packetBuffer.Replace("\0"," ");
          tbPackets.SelectionStart = tbPackets.Text.Length;
          Application.DoEvents();
        }
        Application.DoEvents();
      }
    }
```

VB.NET

```
  Private Sub cmdStart_Click(ByVal eventSender As _
      System.Object, ByVal eventArgs As _
      System.EventArgs) Handles cmdStart.Click
   Dim Qid As Short
   Dim packetBuffer As String
   Dim adapters() As String
   Dim openSuccess As Short
   Dim packetQueue As Short
   Dim packetLen As Short
   Dim rawAdapterDetails As String
   Dim posDefaultAdapter As Short
   rawAdapterDetails = Space(MAX_ADAPTER_LEN)
   getAdapterNames(rawAdapterDetails)
   posDefaultAdapter = _
   rawAdapterDetails.IndexOf(ADAPTER_DELIMITER)
   Adapter = rawAdapterDetails.Substring(0, posDefaultAdapter)
   openSuccess = openAdapter(Adapter)
   If openSuccess <> ERR_SUCCESS Then
    MsgBox("Unable to start. Check WinPCap is installed")
    Exit Sub
   End If
   Do
    packetQueue = checkPacketQueue(Adapter)
    For Qid = 1 To packetQueue
     packetBuffer = Space(MAX_PACKET_SIZE)
     packetLen = getQueuedPacket(packetBuffer)
     packetBuffer = packetBuffer.Substring(0, packetLen)
     tbPackets.Text = tbPackets.Text & Replace _
          (packetBuffer, Chr(0), " ")
     tbPackets.SelectionStart = Len(tbPackets.Text)
```

```
        System.Windows.Forms.Application.DoEvents()
    Next
    System.Windows.Forms.Application.DoEvents()
  Loop
End Sub
```

The code listed above performs two functions; first, detects all of the network adapters on the system, bearing in mind that computers can have more than one means of connecting to a network, either by modem, Ethernet, or some other system. The `getAdapterNames` returns a list of adapter names separated by a pipe character ("|"). Here the first default adapter is used.

Network traffic regularly arrives faster than it can be read and handled by an application; thus, the data is buffered internally in a linked-list structure. The `rvPacket` library has two functions for reading this buffer, `checkPacketQueue` and `getQueuedPacket`. As the names suggest, the former is a nonblocking function that retrieves the number of packets in the queue, and the latter will then read each packet in the queue sequentially. The queue is guaranteed not to grow in size between calls to `checkPacketQueue`, and no data on this buffer will be altered.

The threading model is primitive, using nothing more than a `DoEvents` call to maintain responsiveness for the user interface. This has the side effect of pushing CPU usage to 100%, which looks unprofessional in a consumer product. In a more polished version, proper threading should be used.

Note: All bytes of value 0 are replaced with a space character in the code above to help display the text on-screen; this serves no other purpose.

Although not strictly necessary, the adapter should be closed after use. If it is not closed before the application is destroyed, then a memory leak will result. More importantly, if two separate processes open the adapter at once, Windows will crash.

Click on the Stop button, and enter the following code:

C#

```
private void btnStop_Click(object sender, System.EventArgs e)
{
    closeAdapter(Adapter);
}
```

VB.NET

```
Private Sub btnStop_Click(ByVal sender As _
    System.Object, ByVal e As System.EventArgs) _
    Handles btnStop.Click
        closeAdapter(Adapter)
  End Sub
```

Several API declarations have to be made to make the rvPacket library accessible. Insert this code directly after the form constructor:

C#

```
[DllImport("rvPacket.dll")]
public static extern short getAdapterNames (string s);

[DllImport("rvPacket.dll")]
public static extern short openAdapter (string Adapter);

[DllImport("rvPacket.dll")] public static extern short
checkPacketQueue(string Adapter);

[DllImport("rvPacket.dll")] public static extern short
getQueuedPacket(string s);

[DllImport("rvPacket.dll")] public static extern void
closeAdapter(string Adapter);

const short SIMULTANEOUS_READS = 10;
const short MAX_ADAPTER_LEN = 512;
const string ADAPTER_DELIMITER = "|";
const short MAX_PACKET_SIZE = 10000;
const short ERR_SUCCESS = 1;
const short ERR_ADAPTER_ID= 2;
const short ERR_INVALID_HANDLE= 3;
const short ERR_INVALID_ADAPTER= 4;
const short ERR_ALLOCATE_PACKET= 5;
string Adapter = "";
```

VB.NET

```
Private Declare Function getAdapterNames Lib _
        "rvPacket.dll" (ByVal s As String) As Short
Private Declare Function openAdapter Lib _
```

```
                    "rvPacket.dll" (ByVal Adapter As String) As Short
           Private Declare Function checkPacketQueue Lib _
                    "rvPacket.dll" (ByVal Adapter As String) As Short
           Private Declare Function getQueuedPacket Lib _
                    "rvPacket.dll" (ByVal s As String) As Short
           Private Declare Sub closeAdapter Lib _
                    "rvPacket.dll" (ByVal Adapter As String)


           Private Const SIMULTANEOUS_READS As Short = 10
           Private Const MAX_ADAPTER_LEN As Short = 512
           Private Const ADAPTER_DELIMITER As String = "|"
           Private Const MAX_PACKET_SIZE As Short = 10000
           Private Const ERR_SUCCESS As Short = 1
           Private Const ERR_ADAPTER_ID As Short = 2
           Private Const ERR_INVALID_HANDLE As Short = 3
           Private Const ERR_INVALID_ADAPTER As Short = 4
           Private Const ERR_ALLOCATE_PACKET As Short = 5
           Public Adapter As String
```

The rvPacket library is developed in unmanaged C++; therefore, these rather cryptic function declarations must be used, in the same way as they were required to access the Windows API. The calling conventions for each of the functions are identical: they all accept a string and return a number.

GetAdapterNames is used to retrieve a list of network adapters present on the system. One of these adapter names would be passed to openAdapter, which effectively begins the sniffing process on that network adapter.

CheckPacketQueue returns the number of packets that are currently held in the network card buffer. The GetQueued packet can then retrieve each of these packets one at a time.

CloseAdapter stops the sniffing process and frees up the adapter for any other process to use it. Immediately following the declarations are several constants that can be used within the code to better explain errors to users, and so forth.

Finally, C# programmers require the following namespaces:

C#

```
using System.Text;
using System.Runtime.InteropServices;
```

Figure 13.3
Frame-layer packet sniffer with
`rvPacket`.

To test the application, make sure you are connected to an active network and that `WinPCap` and `rvPacket` have been installed. Run the program from Visual Studio .NET and press Start. If you open a browser and start using the Web, you will see the HTTP sent and received in the textbox (Figure 13.3).

Note: Data sent to the loop-back address 127.0.0.1 (localhost) does not actually register with `WinPCap` because it never actually moves through the network card.

13.3.2 Using PacketX and WinPCap

The following example uses BeeSync's `packetX` control (*www.beesync.com*) to illustrate the concept. There would be no problem in using `rvPacket` for this example, but `packetX` is a useful alternative to know how to use. The object of the example is to log packets that match a certain criterion. In this case, only TCP/IP traffic will be logged.

TCP/IP traffic can be isolated from raw network traffic by checking two bytes in the packet. In an IP packet, the IP header follows the frame header and, thus, will appear at the 14th byte in the packet. The first byte in the IP header will always be 69 when IPv4 is used with standard priority. The sec-

ond byte to check is the protocol byte, the 10th byte in the IP header. This
byte will always be 6 when TCP/IP is used.

You will need to have downloaded and installed both `WinPCap` and
`PacketX` before starting to code this program. Start a new project in Visual
Studio .NET, right-click on the toolbox on the left, and click Customize
Toolbox (or Add/Remove Items in Visual Studio .NET 2003), click the
COM tab, check `PacketXCtrl Class`, and press OK. Drag the new icon
onto the form. Draw a List View control named `lvPackets` onto the form
as well as a Start button named `btnStart`.

To start with, add a few column headers into the list view so that the
results it displays will be evenly tabulated. Add the following lines of code
to the `load` event:

C#

```csharp
private void Form1_Load(object sender, System.EventArgs e)
{
  lvPackets.Columns.Add("From", lvPackets.Width / 3,
                        HorizontalAlignment.Left);
  lvPackets.Columns.Add("To", lvPackets.Width / 3,
                        HorizontalAlignment.Left);
  lvPackets.Columns.Add("Size", lvPackets.Width / 3,
                        HorizontalAlignment.Left);
  lvPackets.View = View.Details;
}
```

VB.NET

```vbnet
Private Sub Form1_Load(ByVal sender As System.Object, _
 ByVal e As System.EventArgs) Handles MyBase.Load
 With lvPackets
  .Columns.Add("From", .Width / 3, HorizontalAlignment.Left)
  .Columns.Add("To", .Width / 3, HorizontalAlignment.Left)
  .Columns.Add("Size", .Width / 3, HorizontalAlignment.Left)
  .View = View.Details
 End With
End Sub
```

The `PacketX` control will not start detecting packets until the Start
method is called. This is to facilitate choosing nondefault adapters:

C#

```csharp
private void btnStart_Click(object sender, System.EventArgs
e)
```

```
{
  axPacketXCtrl1.Start( );
}
```

VB.NET

```
Private Sub btnStart_Click(ByVal eventSender As _
    System.Object, ByVal eventArgs As System.EventArgs) _
    Handles Command1.Click
  axPacketXCtrl1.Start()
End Sub
```

Unlike the polling mechanism of the `rvPacket` library, `PacketX` uses an event to notify the host application of the arrival of packets. The event delivers an object that effectively derives from `System.EventArgs`, yet contains a `PacketClass` object that contains information on the packet contents and the exact time (with microsecond accuracy) the packet was received.

The packet contents are stored in a byte array named `Data`. This byte array appears to .NET as a generic object; thus, to handle it without causing type cast errors, `Option Strict Off` must be added as the first line of the VB.NET code:

C#

```
private void axPacketXCtrl1_OnPacket(object sender,
AxPACKETXLib._IPktXPacketXCtrlEvents_OnPacketEvent e)
{
  short I;
  string thisPacket;
  string SourceIP;
  string DestIP;
  ListViewItem item = new ListViewItem( );
    thisPacket = "";
  byte[] packetData = (byte[])e.pPacket.Data;
  for (I = 0;I<e.pPacket.DataSize - 1;I++)
  {
    thisPacket = thisPacket + Convert.ToChar(packetData[I]);
  }
  if (packetData[14] == 69 && packetData[23] == 6)
  {
    SourceIP = packetData[26] + "." +
      packetData[27] + "." +
```

```
        packetData[28] + "." +
        packetData[29];

      DestIP = packetData[30] + "." +
        packetData[31] + "." +
        packetData[32] + "." +
        packetData[33] + ".";

      item.SubItems[0].Text = SourceIP;
      item.SubItems.Add(DestIP);
      item.SubItems.Add(e.pPacket.DataSize.ToString());
      lvPackets.Items.Add(item);
    }
  }
```

VB.NET

```
Private Sub axPacketXCtrl1_OnPacket(ByVal eventSender _
      As System.Object, ByVal e As _
      AxPACKETXLib.IPktXPacketXCtrlEvents_OnPacketEvent) _
    Handles axPacketXCtrl1.OnPacket
  Dim I As Short
  Dim thisPacket As String
  Dim SourceIP As String
  Dim DestIP As String
  Dim item As New ListViewItem()

  thisPacket = ""
  For I = 0 To e.pPacket.DataSize - 1
    thisPacket = thisPacket & Chr(eventArgs.pPacket.Data(I))
  Next
  If e.pPacket.Data(14) = 69 And e.pPacket.Data(23) = 6 Then
    SourceIP = e.pPacket.Data(26) & "." & _
               e.pPacket.Data(27) & "." & + _
               e.pPacket.Data(28) & "." & + _
               e.pPacket.Data(29)
    DestIP = e.pPacket.Data(30) & "." & _
               e.pPacket.Data(31) & "." & + _
               e.pPacket.Data(32) & "." & + _
               e.pPacket.Data(33)
    item.SubItems(0).Text = SourceIP
    item.SubItems.Add(DestIP)
```

```
      item.SubItems.Add(e.pPacket.DataSize)
      lvPackets.Items.Add(item)
    End If
  End Sub
```

The actual network packet that is passed within the eventArgs or e parameter of the event takes the form of an object stored in e.pPacket.Data, which can be cast to a byte array (implicitly so, in the case of VB.NET). This array is examined for key bytes, first to filter out non-TCP/IP data and then to extract the Local and Remote IP addresses from the header. The extracted data is displayed on-screen in a list box.

To test this application, run it from Visual Studio .NET and wait for a TCP/IP connection to take place on the network. Alternately, simply opening a browser should generate a TCP/IP connection to the server hosting your browser's home page.

The example shown in Figure 13.4 is one single HTTP request between two computers on a LAN. Note that it does not involve simply one packet for the request and one for the response, but a fair amount of handshaking takes place between client and server, before a connection is made. This may be worth knowing if, for instance, you were using a TCP trace to build up statistics on user browsing habits. You cannot equate the number of packets to the amount of Web pages or emails sent. It might be better to count occurrences of the string HTTP/1.1 or HELLO in outgoing packets on ports 80 and 25, respectively, in this instance.

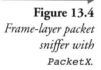

Figure 13.4
Frame-layer packet sniffer with PacketX.

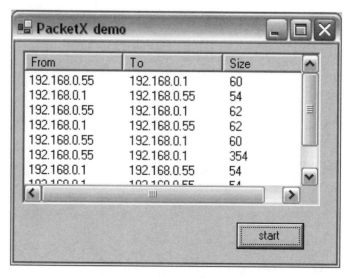

A busy network may produce an overwhelming number of packets, and it is likely that .NET will not be able to process 10 Mb of packets per second, as is commonplace on LANs. In this case, we can use hardware filters that are built into network cards to cope with high-volume traffic.

To detect only packets destined for the local machine, we can apply the directed packet hardware filter to the `WinPCap` driver by setting a parameter in the `PacketX` object with:

```
PacketXCtrl1.Adapter.HWFilter = 1
```

The default hardware filter is promiscuous mode, which will pass up every packet seen by the network adapter. The `rvPacket` library only operates in promiscuous mode. Wireless network cards cannot operate in promiscuous mode; therefore, a nonpromiscuous hardware filter (Table 13.9) must be applied for wireless devices.

Table 13.9   `WinPCap` *hardware filters* .

Filter ID	Purpose
1	Directed packets that contain a destination address equal to the station address of the NIC
2	Multicast address packets sent to addresses in the multicast address list
4	All multicast address packets, not just the ones enumerated in the multicast address list
8	Broadcast packets
16	All source routing packets
32	Default, promiscuous mode; specifies all packets
64	SMT packets that an FDDI NIC receives
128	All packets sent by installed protocols
4096	Packets sent to the current group address
8192	All functional address packets, not just the ones in the current functional address
16384	Functional address packets sent to addresses included in the current functional address
32768	NIC driver frames that a Token Ring NIC receives

`WinPCap` also has the capability to send and receive packets. This functionality can be accessed through `Adapter.SendPacket`, which could be useful for generating non-IP-based packets, such as ARP requests or raw server message block (SMB) data. These packets would not be routable over the Internet, but they may have applications within company networks.

13.4 Physical network tapping

Although there would be no conceivable reason for software to read data at this low level, it might be important to know whether the phone line is connected to the computer or not.

A program might also want to determine the type of connection the computer has to the Internet. To cite an example, when developing a peer-to-peer network, clients that have a fast connection via a LAN should be given higher weighting in the index server(s) than 56K dial-up connections. This would ensure that new clients do not waste time attempting to connect to dial-up connections, which would be more than likely disconnected, but instead run queries against more reliable, faster connections.

The `Adapter.LinkType` and `Adapter.LinkSpeed` properties of `PacketX` provide information on the network type (Table 13.10) and link speed in bits per second, respectively.

Using `WinPCap` and `PacketX` may seem like overkill to determine whether a computer is connected to the Internet, but you could, of course, always ping a well-known Web site address or use the `getInternetConnectedState` API function call.

In .NET version 2 (Whidbey), the `NetworkInformation` class provides a simple mechanism to determine whether a computer is connected to the network as follows:

Table 13.10   *Link types.*

Link Type Code	Meaning
0	None
1	Ethernet (802.3)
2	Token Ring (802.5)
3	FDDI (Fiber Distributed Data Interface)
4	WAN (Wide Area Network)
5	LocalTalk

Table 13.10 *Link types. (continued)*

Link Type Code	Meaning
6	DIX (DEC- Intel - Xerox)
7	ARCNET (raw)
8	ARCNET (878.2)
9	ATM (Asynchronous Transfer Mode)
10	Wireless

C#

```
NetworkInformation netInfo = new NetworkInformation();
If (netInfo.GetIsConnected() == true)
{
 // connected to network
}
```

VB.NET

```
Dim netInfo as new NetworkInformation()
If  (netInfo.GetIsConnected()= True)
 ' connected to network
end if
```

The `NetworkInformation` class (Table 13.11) inherits from `System.Net.NetworkInformation`. It contains a host of useful properties, which describe low-level network activities. The last five methods listed in table 13.11 may be alternatively retrieved from the `GetNetworkParams` Windows API function.

The `ActiveUdpListener` class, as returned by `GetActiveUdpListeners`, is descried in Table 13.12. This is equivalent to calling the `GetUdpTable` Windows API, or running `NETSTAT -p udp -a` from the command line.

Table 13.11 *Significant members of the `NetworkInformation` class.*

Method or Property	Purpose
`AddressChanged`	Sets `AddressChangedEventHandler` `(Object,EventArgs)` delegate.
`GetActiveUdpListeners`	Lists all active UDP ports. Returns `ActiveUdpListener[]`.

Table 13.11 *Significant members of the* NetworkInformation *class (continued).*

Method or Property	Purpose
GetIcmpV4Statistics	Retrieves statistics of ping (ICMP) activity. Returns IcmpV4Statistics.
GetIPStatistics	Retrieves statistics of IP activity. Returns IPStatistics.
GetIsConnected	Determines if the computer is connected to the network. Returns Boolean.
GetNetworkInterfaces	Retrieves information about connected network hardware. Returns NetworkInterface[].
GetTcpConnections	Retrieves statistics of TCP/IP activity. Returns TcpStatistics.
GetUdpStatistics	Retrieves statistics of UDP/IP activity. Returns UdpStatistics.
DhcpScopeName	Gets the DHCP scope name. Returns String.
DomainName	Gets the locally registered domain name. Returns String.
HostName	Gets the host name for the local computer. Returns String.
IsWinsProxy	Specifies if the computer is acting as a WINS proxy. Returns Boolean.
NodeType	Gets the NetBIOS node type of the computer. Returns NodeType (e.g., broadcast, P2P, mixed, hybrid).

Table 13.12 *Significant members of the* ActiveUdpListener *class.*

Method or Property	Purpose
LocalEndPoint	The logical location of the port holding the active UDP connection. Returns IPEndPoint

The IcmpV4Statistics class, as returned by GetIcmpV4Statistics, is described in Table 13.13 (all properties return int64 unless otherwise specified). This class is equivalent to the GetIcmpStatistics Windows IP Helper API.

Table 13.13   *Significant members of the* `IcmpV4Statistics` *class.*

Method or Property	Purpose
`AddressMaskRepliesReceived`	Gets the number of address mask replies received
`AddressMaskRepliesSent`	Gets the number of address mask replies sent
`AddressMaskRequestsReceived`	Gets the number of address mask requests received
`AddressMaskRequestsSent`	Gets the number of address mask requests sent
`DestinationUnreachableMessagesReceived`	Gets the number of destination unreachable messages received
`DestinationUnreachableMessagesSent`	Gets the number of destination unreachable messages sent
`EchoRepliesReceived`	Gets the number of echo replies received
`EchoRepliesSent`	Gets the number of echo replies sent
`EchoRequestsReceived`	Gets the number of echo requests received
`EchoRequestsSent`	Gets the number of echo requests sent
`ErrorsReceived`	Gets the number of errors received
`ErrorsSent`	Gets the number of errors sent
`MessagesReceived`	Gets the number of messages received
`MessagesSent`	Gets the number of messages sent
`ParameterProblemsReceived`	Gets the number of parameter problems received
`ParameterProblemsSent`	Gets the number of parameter problems sent

Table 13.13   *Significant members of the* `IcmpV4Statistics` *class (continued).*

Method or Property	Purpose
RedirectsReceived	Gets the number of redirects received
RedirectsSent	Gets the number of redirects sent
SourceQuenchesReceived	Gets the number of source quenches received
SourceQuenchesSent	Gets the number of source quenches sent
TimeExceededMessagesReceived	Gets the number of time exceeded messages received
TimeExceededMessagesSent	Gets the number of time exceeded messages sent
TimestampRepliesReceived	Gets the number of timestamp replies received
TimestampRepliesSent	Gets the number of timestamp replies sent
TimestampRequestsReceived	Gets the number of timestamp requests received
TimestampRequestsSent	Gets the number of timestamp requests sent

The `IPStatistics` class, as returned by `GetIPStatistics`, is described in Table 13.14 (all properties return `int64` unless otherwise specified). This is equivalent to calling the `GetIpStatistics` Windows IP Helper API, or running NETSTAT -s from the command line.

Table 13.14   *Significant members of the* `IPStatistics` *class .*

Method or Property	Purpose
DefaultTtl	Gets the default TTL
ForwardingEnabled	Determines if forwarding is enabled; returns `Boolean`
Interfaces	Gets the number of interfaces

Table 13.14   *Significant members of the IPStatistics class (continued).*

Method or Property	Purpose
IPAddresses	Gets the number of IP addresses
OutputPacketRequests	Gets the number of output packet requests
OutputPacketRoutingDiscards	Gets the number of output packet routing discards
OutputPacketsDiscarded	Gets the number of output packets discarded
OutputPacketsWithNoRoute	Gets the number of output packets with no route
PacketFragmentFailures	Gets the number of packet fragment failures
PacketReassembliesRequired	Gets the number of packet reassemblies required
PacketReassemblyFailures	Gets the number of packet reassembly failures
PacketReassemblyTimeout	Retrieves the packet reassembly timeout
PacketsFragmented	Gets the number of packets fragmented
PacketsReassembled	Gets the number of packets reassembled
ReceivedPackets	Gets the number of received packets
ReceivedPacketsDelivered	Gets the number of received packets delivered
ReceivedPacketsDiscarded	Gets the number of received packets discarded
ReceivedPacketsForwarded	Gets the number of received packets forwarded
ReceivedPacketsWithAddressErrors	Gets the number of received packets with address errors
ReceivedPacketsWithHeadersErrors	Gets the number of received packets with headers errors

Table 13.14   *Significant members of the* IPStatistics *class (continued).*

Method or Property	Purpose
ReceivedPacketsWithUnknownProtocol	Gets the number of received packets with unknown protocol
Routes	Gets the number of routes used

The NetworkInterface class, as returned by GetNetworkInterfaces, is described in Table 13.15.

Table 13.15   *Significant members of the* NetworkInterface *class .*

Method or Property	Purpose
GetInterfaceStatistics	Retrieves information on network activity on the interface. Returns InterfaceStatistics.
GetIPAddressInformation	Returns information on the IP address assigned to the interface. Returns IPAddressInformation.
GetIPv4Properties	Gets information concerning local IP routing, etc. Returns IPv4Properties.
GetPhysicalAddress	Retrieves the interface's MAC address. Returns byte[ ].
Description	A friendly name for the interface. Returns String.
DnsEnabled	Determines if DNS is enabled on the interface. Returns Boolean.
DynamicDnsEnabled	Determines if Dynamic DNS is enabled on the interface. Returns Boolean.
Ipv4Index	Determines the IP version 4 index on the interface. Returns int64.
Ipv6Index	Determines the IP version 6 index on the interface. Returns int64.
IPVersionSupported	Determines the IP version(s) supported by the interface. Returns IPVersionSupportedFlags.
IsConnected	Determines if the interface is connected to an active network. Returns Boolean.

Table 13.15 *Significant members of the* NetworkInterface *class (continued).*

Method or Property	Purpose
Mtu	Determines the maximum transmission unit of the interface. Returns int64.
Name	Gets a name for the interface. Returns string.
OperationalStatus	Gets the operational status of the interface. Returns OperationalStatus.
Type	Determines the interface hardware. Returns InterfaceType (e.g., modem, ISDN, ADSL, Ethernet, etc.).

The InterfaceStatistics class, as returned by GetInterfaceStatistics, is described in Table 13.16 (all properties return int64 unless otherwise specified).

Table 13.16 *Significant members of the* InterfaceStatistics *class .*

Method or Property	Purpose
BytesReceived	Gets the number of bytes received
BytesSent	Gets the number of bytes sent
IncomingPacketsDiscarded	Gets the number of incoming packets discarded
IncomingPacketsWithErrors	Gets the number of incoming packets with errors
IncomingUnknownProtocolPackets	Gets the number of incoming unknown protocol packets
NonUnicastPacketsReceived	Gets the number of non-Unicast packets received
NonUnicastPacketsSent	Gets the number of non-Unicast packets sent
OutgoingPacketsDiscarded	Gets the number of outgoing packets discarded
OutgoingPacketsWithErrors	Gets the number of outgoing packets with errors
OutputQueueLength	Gets the number of output queue length

Table 13.16   *Significant members of the* `InterfaceStatistics` *class (continued).*

Method or Property	Purpose
`Speed`	Gets the speed of the interface
`UnicastPacketsReceived`	Gets the number of Unicast packets received
`UnicastPacketsSent`	Gets the number of Unicast packets sent

The `IPAddressInformation` class, as returned by `GetIPAddressInfor-`
mation, is described in Table 13.17.

Table 13.17   *Significant members of the IPAddressInformation class.*

Method or Property	Purpose
`Address`	Gets the IP address
`DnsEligible`	Determines if the address is eligible for DNS
`Transient`	Determines if the address is transient

The `IPv4Properties` class, as returned by `GetIPv4Properties`, is
described in Table 13.18. These properties may be alternatively ascertained
on an adapter-by-adapter basis through the `GetAdaptersInfo` Windows IP
Helper API function.

Table 13.18   *Significant members of the* `IPv4Properties` *class .*

Method or Property	Purpose
`GetDhcpServerAddresses`	Retrieves the local DHCP server addresses. Returns `IPAddress[]`.
`GetGatewayAddresses`	Retrieves the local gateway addresses. Returns `IPAddress[]`.
`GetWinsServersAddresses`	Retrieves the local WINS servers addresses. Returns `IPAddress[]`.
`AutomaticPrivateAddressingActive`	Determines if automatic private addressing is active. Returns `Boolean`.

Table 13.18   *Significant members of the* `IPv4Properties` *class (continued).*

Method or Property	Purpose
`AutomaticPrivateAddressingEnabled`	Determines if automatic private addressing is enabled. Returns `Boolean`.
`DhcpEnabled`	Determines if DHCP is enabled. Returns `Boolean`.
`RoutingEnabled`	Determines if routing is enabled. Returns `Boolean`.
`UsesWins`	Determines if the computer uses WINS. Returns `Boolean`.

The `TcpStatistics` class, as returned by `GetTcpStatistics`, is described in Table 13.19 (all properties return `int64` unless otherwise stated). This is equivalent to calling the `GetTcpTable` Windows IP Helper API, or running `NETSTAT -p tcp -a` from the command line.

Table 13.19   *Significant members of the* `TcpStatistics` *class.*

Method or Property	Purpose
`ConnectionsAccepted`	Determines the number of connections accepted
`ConnectionsInitiated`	Determines the number of connections initiated
`CumulativeConnections`	Determines the number of cumulative connections
`CurrentConnections`	Determines the number of current connections
`ErrorsReceived`	Determines the number of errors received
`FailedConnectionAttempts`	Determines the number of failed connection attempts
`MaximumConnections`	Determines the maximum number of connections
`MaximumTransmissionTimeOut`	Determines the maximum transmission time out

Table 13.19 *Significant members of the* `TcpStatistics` *class (continued).*

Method or Property	Purpose
`MinimumTransmissionTimeOut`	Determines the minimum transmission time out
`ResetConnections`	Determines the number of reset connections
`SegmentsReceived`	Determines the number of segments received
`SegmentsResent`	Determines the number of segments resent
`SegmentsSent`	Determines the number of segments sent
`SegmentsSentWithReset`	Determines the number of segments sent with reset

The `UdpStatistics` class, as returned by `GetUdpStatistics`, is described in Table 13.20 (all properties return `int64` unless otherwise stated). This is equivalent to the `GetUdpStatistics` Windows IP Helper API function.

Table 13.20 *Significant members of the* `UdpStatistics` *class.*

Method or Property	Purpose
`DatagramsReceived`	Determines the number of datagrams received
`DatagramsSent`	Determines the number of datagrams sent
`IncomingDatagramsDiscarded`	Determines the number of incoming datagrams discarded
`IncomingDatagramsWithErrors`	Determines the number of incoming datagrams with errors
`UdpListeners`	Determines the number of active UDP listeners

13.5 Conclusion

This chapter has shown three different means to tap nonintrusively into the data that flows between computers. When local system traffic monitoring is all that is required, then use of the pure .NET implementation is highly recommended, but for an enterprisewide implementation, then `PacketX` combined with `WinPCap` is possibly the best option. Where financial constraints prevent the use of a third-party commercial component, then `rvPacket` will probably point you in the right direction.

It would be impossible to document the format of every protocol that could exist on a network, so only IP and TCP have been described in this chapter. Interested readers are advised to consult the relevant RFC for information on any specific protocol.

The next chapter deals with a form of telecommunication that has been with us since the 1880s (i.e., the ubiquitous phone call); however, the chapter is taken from a Computer Telephony Integration (CTI) developer's perspective. Prepare to be introduced to the telephony API.

14

Adding Digital Telephony

14.1 Introduction

If you call any large cinema looking for times for films, you will undoubtedly be forwarded to an automated system that tells you when each film is on. This system is made possible by digital telephony.

Computer Telephony Integration, or CTI, systems routinely cost $10,000 and upward for enterprise-scale systems. The high cost is largely a result of the misconceived idea that any telephony system requires loads of specialized hardware and, thus, is out of reach for the humble developer. In fact, you can put a simple system together using no more than a cheap modem.

Any company that employs staff to answer phone calls can save money by implementing a CTI system. Such a system can be used to route calls to different departments automatically or to match a caller with customer ID and associated purchase history.

This chapter is mainly devoted to one rather large code example built up in three sections. The first section explains how to pick up and drop a call. The following section explains how to detect key presses on the remote handset, and the chapter concludes with a demonstration of how to play back audio to the caller.

Note: You will need a voice modem and phone line to test the following examples. Access to a second phone (such as a mobile phone) is beneficial. Calls made from any phone line may incur charges if the line is opened.

14.2   Basic telephony

This chapter is focused on using the telephony API, but it is possible to control a modem by issuing COM port commands. These will provide the ability to dial telephone numbers and control the physical connection to the phone line.

Even if your modem is internal or connected via USB, it will always be mapped to a COM port. To discover the number of this COM port, you can look at Start→Control Panel→phone and Modem options→Modems. Under the Attached To tab will be the number of the COM port to which the modem is attached.

Any command that is sent to this COM port will be interpreted by the modem. A list of common AT commands shown in Table 14.1.

Table 14.1   *AT commands.*

AT Command	Purpose
ATDT<*phone number*><enter>	Dials the specified phone number using touch-tone dialing. A comma in the number represents a pause, a W waits for a second dial tone, and an @ waits for a five-second silence.
ATPT<*phone number*><enter>	Dials the specified number using pulse dialing.
AT S0=<*number*>	Picks up the line after the specified number of rings.
+++	Drop line.

The responses the modem will send back shown in Table 14.2.

Table 14.2   *Modem responses .*

Response	Meaning
OK	The command has executed without errors.
CONNECT	A connection to the remote phone has been made.
RING	An incoming call is detected.
NO CARRIER	No carrier signal has been detected (in GSM modems, this can mean that there is no network).
ERROR	The command is not understood.

Table 14.2 *Modem responses (continued).*

Response	Meaning
NO DIAL TONE	There is no dial tone on the phone line.
BUSY	The remote end is too busy to take the call.
NO ANSWER	The remote end did not take the call.

To implement a simple phone dialer in .NET, open Visual Studio .NET and start a new Windows forms project. Right-click on the toolbox and click Customize Toolbox (or Add/Remove Items in Visual Studio .NET 2003). Click on the COM Controls tab, and then add the Microsoft Communications control (MSCOMM.OCX). Drag this onto the form, and set the comport property to the COM port number to which your modem is connected. Add a button to the form, named btnPhone, click it, and add this code:

C#

```
private void btnPhone_Click(object sender, System.EventArgs e)
{
  axMSComm1.PortOpen=true;
  axMSComm1.Output="ATDT00353877519575\r\n";
}
```

VB.NET

```
Private Sub btnPhone_Click(ByVal sender As Object, _
     ByVal e As System.EventArgs)
  axMSComm1.PortOpen=True
  axMSComm1.Output="ATDT00353877519575" + vbcrlf
End Sub
```

Note: Running the code listed above may incur phone charges. It is advisable to change the phone number listed (00353877519575) to some other, less expensive number.

Only one program can control each COM port at a time. This code will fail if you are using the modem at the time. Several settings are associated with a COM port; in this case, however, the default parameters (9600 baud, no parity, 8 data bits, 1 stop bit—or "9600,n,8,1") are suitable for communication with a modem. When the modem begins communication at full speed, it will use a baud rate of 56 Kbps. This can be set using the settings property of the Microsoft communications control.

14.3   Listening for incoming phone calls

You can only do a certain number of things with a modem by sending commands back and forth via a COM port. In order to develop serious applications, you have to use the Telephony Application Programming Interface (TAPI). The TAPI libraries were designed with C++ in mind, not .NET, so there is a steep learning curve. It is worthwhile to evaluate the various commercial components available before tinkering with low-level TAPI code. A few interesting Web sites, such as *www.shrinkwrapvb.com and www.pron-exus.com,* contain a wealth of information on TAPI.

The overall architecture of TAPI is modeled on a collection of phone lines that are connected to the computer. Not all of these phone lines are physical connections. Some of them are software representations of phone lines used for various internal processes. Each phone line may be opened or closed, which is analogous to a phone being on or off hook. An open phone line does not necessarily incur charges, unless a call is active.

When a phone line is open (off hook), it generates callbacks detailing any event that has happened on the line, such as an incoming call. A callback is simply a function that is called asynchronously by an underlying process.

When an incoming call is detected, the callback will contain a handle that can be passed to a function that accepts the call. At this point, call charges are applied to the line by the phone operator. Once the call is open, the modem behaves like a rudimentary audio device, which can play and receive basic audio. The line can still generate callbacks, such as a line dropping or the detection of the remote user pressing digits on the phone's keypad.

When the call is dropped, the line remains open, but the modem can no longer function as an audio device. Phone charges will no longer be applied when the call is dropped. Callbacks will be generated until the line is closed.

Note: Warning: If a line is not closed before the application exits, the computer may need to be restarted before the line can be reopened.

Without further ado, here is the first example of TAPI. This sample application will enable you to open and close a phone line, as well as detect and accept incoming calls.

Open a new project in Visual Studio .NET. Name the form `frmTapi`, and add to it three buttons: `btnStart`, `btnStop`, and `btnAccept`. You should also include a textbox named `tbStatus` with `multiline` set to `true`.

Add a module named `TAPI`, and add the following code. In C#, you add a class file instead of a module. Note that in C#, the class namespace is assumed to be `tapi1_cs`, so substitute this for the name of your project.

C#

```csharp
using System;
using System.Runtime.InteropServices;

namespace tapi1_cs
{

  public class TAPI
  {

    public static int hCall;
    public static int hTAPI;
    public static int lNumLines;
    public static int hLine;
    public static linedevcaps lpLineDevCaps;
    public static frmTAPI userInterface;
    public const int TAPIVERSION = 0x10004;
    public const short LINECALLPRIVILEGE_OWNER = 0x4;
    public const short LINECALLPRIVILEGE_MONITOR = 0x2;
    public const short LINEMEDIAMODE_AUTOMATEDVOICE = 0x8;
    public const int LINE_LINEDEVSTATE = 8;
    public const int LINE_CALLSTATE = 2;
    public const int LINECALLSTATE_OFFERING = 0x2;
    public const int LINECALLSTATE_ACCEPTED = 0x4;
    public const int LINECALLSTATE_DISCONNECTED = 0x4000;

    public struct linedialparams
    {
      int dwDialPause;
      int dwDialSpeed;
```

```
    int dwDigitDuration;
    int dwWaitForDialtone;
}


public struct lineextensionid
{
    int dwExtensionID0;
    int dwExtensionID1;
    int dwExtensionID2;
    int dwExtensionID3;
}
public struct linedevcaps
{
    public int dwTotalSize;
    public int dwNeededSize;
    public int dwUsedSize;
    public int dwProviderInfoSize;
    public int dwProviderInfoOffset;
    public int dwSwitchInfoSize;
    public int dwSwitchInfoOffset;
    public int dwPermanentLineID;
    public int dwLineNameSize;
    public int dwLineNameOffset;
    public int dwStringFormat;
    public int dwAddressModes;
    public int dwNumAddresses;
    public int dwBearerModes;
    public int dwMaxRate;
    public int dwMediaModes;
    public int dwGenerateToneModes;
    public int dwGenerateToneMaxNumFreq;
    public int dwGenerateDigitModes;
    public int dwMonitorToneMaxNumFreq;
    public int dwMonitorToneMaxNumEntries;
    public int dwMonitorDigitModes;
    public int dwGatherDigitsMinTimeout;
    public int dwGatherDigitsMaxTimeout;
    public int dwMedCtlDigitMaxListSize;
    public int dwMedCtlMediaMaxListSize;
    public int dwMedCtlToneMaxListSize;
    public int dwMedCtlCallStateMaxListSize;
```

```
            public int dwDevCapFlags;
            public int dwMaxNumActiveCalls;
            public int dwAnswerMode;
            public int dwRingModes;
            public int dwLineStates;
            public int dwUUIAcceptSize;
            public int dwUUIAnswerSize;
            public int dwUUIMakeCallSize;
            public int dwUUIDropSize;
            public int dwUUISendUserUserInfoSize;
            public int dwUUICallInfoSize;
            public linedialparams MinDialParams;
            public linedialparams MaxDialParams;
            public linedialparams DefaultDialParams;
            public int dwNumTerminals;
            public int dwTerminalCapsSize;
            public int dwTerminalCapsOffset;
            public int dwTerminalTextEntrySize;
            public int dwTerminalTextSize;
            public int dwTerminalTextOffset;
            public int dwDevSpecificSize;
            public int dwDevSpecificOffset;
            public int dwLineFeatures; // TAPI v1.4
            public string bBytes;
        }

[DllImport("Tapi32.dll",SetLastError=true)]
public static extern int lineAnswer (int hCall, ref string
lpsUserUserInfo, int dwSize);

[DllImport("Tapi32.dll",SetLastError=true)]
public static extern int lineInitialize (ref int hTAPI,int
    hInst, LineCallBackDelegate fnPtr ,
    ref int szAppName, ref int dwNumLines);

[DllImport("Tapi32.dll",SetLastError=true)]
public static extern int lineNegotiateAPIVersion(int hTAPI,
    int dwDeviceID,  int dwAPILowVersion,
    int dwAPIHighVersion,
    ref int lpdwAPIVersion,
    ref lineextensionid lpExtensionID);
```

```
[DllImport("Tapi32.dll",SetLastError=true)]
public static extern int lineOpen (int hLineApp, int
    dwDeviceID, ref int lphLine, int dwAPIVersion,
    int dwExtVersion, ref int dwCallbackInstance,
    int dwPrivileges, int dwMediaModes,
    ref int lpCallParams);

[DllImport("Tapi32.dll",SetLastError=true)]
public static extern int lineGetDevCaps (int hLineApp, int
    dwDeviceID, int dwAPIVersion, int dwExtVersion,
    ref linedevcaps lpLineDevCaps);
[DllImport("Tapi32.dll",SetLastError=true)]
public static extern int lineSetStatusMessages (int hLine,
        int dwLineStates, int dwAddressStates);

[DllImport("Tapi32.dll",SetLastError=true)]
public static extern int lineDrop (int hCall, string
lpsUserUserInfo, int dwSize);

[DllImport("Tapi32.dll",SetLastError=true)]
public static extern int lineShutdown(int hLineApp);
}

}
```

VB.NET

```
Option Strict Off
Option Explicit On
Module VB_TAPI
    Public LastTAPIEvent As Object
    Public aditionalTAPIEventInfo As Object
    Public hCall As Integer
    Public hTAPI As Integer
    Public lNumLines As Integer
    Public hLine As Integer
    Public lpLineDevCaps As linedevcaps
    Public userInterface As frmTAPI

    Public Const TAPIVERSION As Integer = &H10004
    Public Const LINECALLPRIVILEGE_OWNER As Short = &H4S
    Public Const LINECALLPRIVILEGE_MONITOR As Short = &H2S
```

```
Public Const LINEMEDIAMODE_AUTOMATEDVOICE As Short = &H8S
Public Const LINE_LINEDEVSTATE = 8
Public Const LINE_CALLSTATE = 2
Public Const LINECALLSTATE_OFFERING = &H2
Public Const LINECALLSTATE_ACCEPTED = &H4
Public Const LINECALLSTATE_DISCONNECTED = &H4000

Structure linedialparams
    Dim dwDialPause As Integer
    Dim dwDialSpeed As Integer
    Dim dwDigitDuration As Integer
    Dim dwWaitForDialtone As Integer
End Structure

Structure lineextensionid
    Dim dwExtensionID0 As Integer
    Dim dwExtensionID1 As Integer
    Dim dwExtensionID2 As Integer
    Dim dwExtensionID3 As Integer
End Structure

Structure linedevcaps
    Dim dwTotalSize As Integer
    Dim dwNeededSize As Integer
    Dim dwUsedSize As Integer
    Dim dwProviderInfoSize As Integer
    Dim dwProviderInfoOffset As Integer
    Dim dwSwitchInfoSize As Integer
    Dim dwSwitchInfoOffset As Integer
    Dim dwPermanentLineID As Integer
    Dim dwLineNameSize As Integer
    Dim dwLineNameOffset As Integer
    Dim dwStringFormat As Integer
    Dim dwAddressModes As Integer
    Dim dwNumAddresses As Integer
    Dim dwBearerModes As Integer
    Dim dwMaxRate As Integer
    Dim dwMediaModes As Integer
    Dim dwGenerateToneModes As Integer
    Dim dwGenerateToneMaxNumFreq As Integer
    Dim dwGenerateDigitModes As Integer
```

```
            Dim dwMonitorToneMaxNumFreq As Integer
            Dim dwMonitorToneMaxNumEntries As Integer
            Dim dwMonitorDigitModes As Integer
            Dim dwGatherDigitsMinTimeout As Integer
            Dim dwGatherDigitsMaxTimeout As Integer
            Dim dwMedCtlDigitMaxListSize As Integer
            Dim dwMedCtlMediaMaxListSize As Integer
            Dim dwMedCtlToneMaxListSize As Integer
            Dim dwMedCtlCallStateMaxListSize As Integer
            Dim dwDevCapFlags As Integer
            Dim dwMaxNumActiveCalls As Integer
            Dim dwAnswerMode As Integer
            Dim dwRingModes As Integer
            Dim dwLineStates As Integer
            Dim dwUUIAcceptSize As Integer
            Dim dwUUIAnswerSize As Integer
            Dim dwUUIMakeCallSize As Integer
            Dim dwUUIDropSize As Integer
            Dim dwUUISendUserUserInfoSize As Integer
            Dim dwUUICallInfoSize As Integer
            Dim MinDialParams As linedialparams
            Dim MaxDialParams As linedialparams
            Dim DefaultDialParams As linedialparams
            Dim dwNumTerminals As Integer
            Dim dwTerminalCapsSize As Integer
            Dim dwTerminalCapsOffset As Integer
            Dim dwTerminalTextEntrySize As Integer
            Dim dwTerminalTextSize As Integer
            Dim dwTerminalTextOffset As Integer
            Dim dwDevSpecificSize As Integer
            Dim dwDevSpecificOffset As Integer
            Dim dwLineFeatures As Integer ' TAPI v1.4
            Dim bBytes As String
        End Structure

    Public Declare Function lineAnswer Lib "Tapi32" _
        (ByVal hCall As Integer, ByRef lpsUserUserInfo _
        As String, ByVal dwSize As Integer) As Integer

    Public Declare Function lineInitialize Lib "Tapi32" _
        (ByRef hTAPI As Integer, ByVal hInst As Integer, _
```

```
            ByVal fnPtr As LineCallBackDelegate, ByRef _
            szAppName As Integer, ByRef dwNumLines As _
        Integer) As Integer

        Public Declare Function lineNegotiateAPIVersion Lib _
            "Tapi32" (ByVal hTAPI As Integer, ByVal _
            dwDeviceID As Integer, ByVal dwAPILowVersion _
            As Integer, ByVal dwAPIHighVersion As Integer, _
            ByRef lpdwAPIVersion As Integer, ByRef _
            lpExtensionID As lineextensionid) _
            As Integer
        Public Declare Function lineOpen Lib "Tapi32" _
            (ByVal hLineApp As Integer, ByVal dwDeviceID _
            As Integer, ByRef lphLine As Integer, ByVal _
            dwAPIVersion As Integer, ByVal dwExtVersion _
            As Integer, ByRef dwCallbackInstance _
            As Integer, ByVal dwPrivileges As Integer, _
            ByVal dwMediaModes As Integer, ByRef _
            lpCallParams As Integer) As Integer

        Public Declare Function lineGetDevCaps Lib "Tapi32" _
            (ByVal hLineApp As Integer, ByVal dwDeviceID _
            As Integer, ByVal dwAPIVersion As Integer, _
            ByVal dwExtVersion As Integer, ByRef _
            lpLineDevCaps As linedevcaps) As Integer

        Public Declare Function lineSetStatusMessages Lib _
            "Tapi32" (ByVal hLine As Integer, ByVal _
            dwLineStates As Integer, ByVal _
            dwAddressStates As Integer) As Integer

        Public Declare Function lineDrop Lib "Tapi32" _
            (ByVal hCall As Integer, ByVal lpsUserUserInfo _
            As String, ByVal dwSize As _
            Integer) As Integer

        Public Declare Function lineShutdown Lib "Tapi32" _
            (ByVal hLineApp As Integer) As Integer

    End Module
```

The code for the module may look daunting because these function definitions are ported directly from the `TAPI.H` C++ code from the Windows platform SDK. It is not important to understand every parameter sent to these API calls, but for the moment, Table 14.3 gives an overview of all the API calls involved.

The core element of every TAPI application is the callback function `LineCallBack`. This is used to detect changes in the phone line, such as incoming calls, dropped calls, or key presses on the remote telephone keypad.

Add the following code to the TAPI module:

Table 14.3   *Telephony API functions.*

API Function	Purpose
`lineAnswer`	Picks up the phone when an incoming call is detected. This may incur phone charges.
`lineInitialize`	Indicates the name of the callback function to TAPI, and retrieves the number of modems (virtual and physical) installed on the system.
`lineNegotiateAPIVersion`	Determines whether a modem can support a specified version of TAPI (i.e., 1.4 in this case).
`lineOpen`	Indicates to TAPI that the callback should now start receiving events for a specified modem.
`lineGetDevCaps`	Retrieves a host of technical information about a specified modem (see the `lineDevCaps` structure listed above).
`lineSetStatusMessages`	Indicates which, if any, events should be passed to the callback.
`lineDrop`	Shuts down a modem temporarily, dropping any active call.
`lineShutdown`	Shuts down a modem permanently, cleaning up any resources.

Note: The purpose of the `LineCallBackDelegate` delegate is to ensure that the underlying telephony processes have something to call back to even after the program closes. This prevents Windows from crashing if your application does not shut down cleanly.

C#

```csharp
public delegate int LineCallBackDelegate(int dwDevice, int
    dwMessage, int dwInstance, int dwParam1, int dwParam2,
    int dwParam3);

public static int LineCallBack(int dwDevice, int dwMessage,
int dwInstance, int dwParam1, int dwParam2, int dwParam3)
{
 string msgEvent="";
 msgEvent = Convert.ToString(dwMessage);
 switch (dwMessage)
 {
  case LINE_CALLSTATE:
  switch(dwParam1)
    {
      case LINECALLSTATE_OFFERING:
        msgEvent = "Incomming call";
        hCall = dwDevice;
        break;
      case LINECALLSTATE_ACCEPTED:
        msgEvent = "Call accepted";
        break;
      case LINECALLSTATE_DISCONNECTED:
        msgEvent = "Call disconnected";
        break;
    }
    break;
  case LINE_LINEDEVSTATE:
    msgEvent = "Ringing";
    break;
 }
 userInterface.showMessage("Event: " + msgEvent + " Data:"
                        + dwParam1 + "\r\n");

 return 1;
}
```

VB.NET

```vbnet
Delegate Function LineCallBackDelegate(ByVal dwDevice _
As Integer, ByVal dwMessage As Integer, ByVal _
dwInstance As Integer, ByVal dwParam1 As _
Integer, ByVal dwParam2 As Integer, ByVal dwParam3 _
```

```
As Integer) As Integer

Public Function LineCallBack(ByVal dwDevice As _
Integer, ByVal dwMessage As Integer, ByVal dwInstance _
As Integer, ByVal dwParam1 As Integer, ByVal dwParam2 _
As Integer, ByVal dwParam3 As Integer) As Integer
        Dim msgEvent As String
        msgEvent = CStr(dwMessage)
        Select Case dwMessage
            Case LINE_CALLSTATE
                Select Case dwParam1
                    Case LINECALLSTATE_OFFERING
                        msgEvent = "Incomming call"
                        hCall = dwDevice
                    Case LINECALLSTATE_ACCEPTED
                        msgEvent = "Call accepted"
                    Case LINECALLSTATE_DISCONNECTED
                        msgEvent = "Call disconnected"
                End Select
            Case LINE_LINEDEVSTATE
                msgEvent = "Ringing"
            Case Else
                msgEvent = dwMessage.ToString()
        End Select
        userInterface.tbStatus.Text += "Event: " & _
            msgEvent & " Data:" & dwParam1 & vbCrLf
    End Function
```

To explain the above code briefly: Once a line has been opened, every event on that line will cause TAPI to make a call to this function. The parameter dwMessage indicates broadly what has happened on the line, and dwParam1 defines the event more concisely.

The most important message type is LINE_CALLSTATE. This indicates significant state changes on the line. To determine the exact nature of the event, it is necessary to drill-down and look at dwParam1. When this parameter is set to LINECALLSTATE_OFFERING (0x2), a call has just been detected, and the handle to that call has been passed in dwDevice. This handle can be later passed to lineAnswer to pick up the phone. Other events such as LINECALLSTATE_ACCEPTED (0x4) and LINECALLSTATE_DISCONNECTED (0x4000) determine when a call becomes active and when the call is terminated.

In some cases, the event can be assumed by looking at the dwMessage parameter only. A LINE_LINEDEVSTATE (0x8) event is most likely to be the ringing sound from an incoming call, but it could also be that the phone line is out of service, indicated by a dwParam1 of LINEDEVSTATE_OUTOFSERVICE (0x80), or that the phone line is under maintenance, indicated by LINEDEVSTATE_MAINTENANCE (0x100). Because this type of occurrence is rare, and a computer program can hardly resolve the problem, the event can be ignored.

At this point, the user interface should have already been prepared with three buttons named btnStart, btnStop, and btnAccept on the form. A large textbox named tbStatus is required. The multiline property should be set to true.

Click the Start button and enter the following code:

C#

```csharp
private void btnStart_Click(object sender, System.EventArgs e)
{
    startModem();
}
```

VB.NET

```vbnet
Private Sub btnStart_Click(ByVal eventSender As _
System.Object, ByVal eventArgs As System.EventArgs) _
Handles btnStart.Click
        startModem()
End Sub
```

Click the Stop button and enter the following code:

C#

```csharp
private void btnStop_Click(object sender, System.EventArgs e)
{
    stopModem();
}
```

VB.NET

```vbnet
Private Sub btnStop_Click(ByVal eventSender As _
System.Object, ByVal eventArgs As System.EventArgs) _
Handles btnStop.Click
```

```
        stopModem()
    End Sub
```

Click the Accept button and enter the following code:

C#

```
private void btnAcceptCall_Click(object sender,
System.EventArgs e)
{
   acceptCall();
}
```

VB.NET

```
    Private Sub btnAccept_Click(ByVal eventSender As _
    System.Object, ByVal eventArgs As System.EventArgs) _
    Handles btnAccept.Click
         acceptCall()
    End Sub
```

C# developers will also require the following function:

C#

```
public void showMessage(string message)
{
   tbStatus.Text += message;
}
```

The reason for the extra function is that in VB.NET the TAPI module exposes functions and types contained within it globally. In C#, a class is used to hold the functions and types; therefore, any calls to these functions must be through a reference to the class. Because the functions are static, the only programmatic difference is the TAPI prefix; however, the class needs to have a reference to the form so that it can display text on the screen when the TAPI callback occurs.

A computer may have more than one modem attached and will almost certainly have a few virtual modems, which are used for various other internal purposes. Voice modems are much more useful when it comes to telephony applications, but a data modem can still pick up and drop calls, even if it cannot communicate with a human user once the line is active. This limited functionality may be all that is required, however, if, for instance, the computer needs to do only one task in response to an incoming phone call, such as connecting to the Internet or rebooting.

This code is designed to open the first line it can find that is capable of detecting incoming calls. A more advanced system would select a voice modem over a data modem by selecting a modem with the lowest acceptable lMediaMode. A voice modem can work with a media mode set to LINEMEDIAMODE_INTERACTIVEVOICE (4 hex), whereas a data modem will generally only use LINEMEDIAMODE_DATAMODEM (10 hex). Hybrid modems do exist, so the code below will scan all media modes from 1 to 100.

C#

```
public void startModem()
{
  int nError=0;
  TAPI.lineextensionid lpExtensionID = new
  TAPI.lineextensionid();
  int lUnused=0;
  int lLineID=0;
  int lNegVer=0;
  long lPrivilege=0;
  long lMediaMode=0;
  IntPtr HInstance=(IntPtr)0;

  lPrivilege = TAPI.LINECALLPRIVILEGE_OWNER +
               TAPI.LINECALLPRIVILEGE_MONITOR;
  lMediaMode = 4;

  Module thisModule;
  thisModule =
  Assembly.GetExecutingAssembly().GetModules()[0];
  HInstance = Marshal.GetHINSTANCE(thisModule);
  TAPI.LineCallBackDelegate callback = new
  TAPI.LineCallBackDelegate(TAPI.LineCallBack);
  int Unused = 0;
  nError = TAPI.lineInitialize(ref TAPI.hTAPI,
  HInstance.ToInt32(),
    callback, ref Unused, ref TAPI.lNumLines);

  for (lLineID = 0;lLineID<TAPI.lNumLines;lLineID++)
  {
    nError = TAPI.lineNegotiateAPIVersion(TAPI.hTAPI,
```

```
lLineID,
    TAPI.TAPIVERSION,TAPI.TAPIVERSION,
    ref lNegVer, ref lpExtensionID);
do
{
  nError = TAPI.lineOpen(TAPI.hTAPI, lLineID,
  ref TAPI.hLine,
    lNegVer, lUnused, ref lUnused,
    (int)lPrivilege, (int)lMediaMode, ref lUnused);
    lMediaMode ++;
} while (nError < 0 && lMediaMode < 100);
  if (nError == 0) break;
}
TAPI.lpLineDevCaps.dwTotalSize =
Marshal.SizeOf(TAPI.lpLineDevCaps);
TAPI.lpLineDevCaps.bBytes = new
    StringBuilder().Append(' ',2000).ToString();
TAPI.lineGetDevCaps(TAPI.hTAPI, lLineID, lNegVer, lUnused,
    ref TAPI.lpLineDevCaps);
TAPI.lineSetStatusMessages(TAPI.hLine,
    TAPI.lpLineDevCaps.dwLineStates, 0);
}
```

VB.NET

```
Public Sub startModem()
 Dim nError As Integer
 Dim lpExtensionID As lineextensionid
 Dim lUnused As Integer
 Dim lLineID As Integer
 Dim i As Short
 Dim lNegVer As Integer
 Dim lPrivilege As Long
 Dim lMediaMode As Long
 lPrivilege = LINECALLPRIVILEGE_OWNER + _
   LINECALLPRIVILEGE_MONITOR
 lMediaMode = 4

 nError = lineInitialize(hTAPI, _
 Microsoft.VisualBasic.Compatibility.VB6.GetHInstance.ToInt32, _
 AddressOf LineCallBack, 0, lNumLines)
```

```
For lLineID = 0 To lNumLines
  nError = lineNegotiateAPIVersion(hTAPI, _
  lLineID,TAPIVERSION,TAPIVERSION, _
        lNegVer, lpExtensionID)
   Do
    nError = lineOpen(hTAPI, lLineID, hLine, lNegVer, _
          lUnused, lUnused, lPrivilege, lMediaMode, 0)
   lMediaMode = lMediaMode + 1
   Loop Until nError >= 0 Or lMediaMode = 100
   If nError = 0 Then Exit For
  Next

  lpLineDevCaps.dwTotalSize = Len(lpLineDevCaps)
  lpLineDevCaps.bBytes = Space(2000)
  lineGetDevCaps(hTAPI, lLineID, lNegVer, lUnused, _
     lpLineDevCaps)
  lineSetStatusMessages(hLine, lpLineDevCaps.dwLineStates, 0)
End Sub
```

It is important to shut down the line after use because no other program can use the modem until the line has been closed. If you close your program before the line is closed, there may be problems reopening the line, and you may have to restart your computer.

C#

```
public void stopModem()
{
  int nError;
  nError = TAPI.lineShutdown(TAPI.hTAPI);
}
```

VB.NET

```
Public Sub stopModem()
  Dim nError As Integer
  nError = lineShutdown(hTAPI)
End Sub
```

Whenever an incoming call is detected, the callback function will set a public variable named hCall to a reference number (a handle) that TAPI recognizes. When this handle is passed to lineAnswer, the phone line is opened. The modem is then in a position to send and receive audio data from the remote user, provided the modem supports that functionality.

C#

```csharp
public void acceptCall()
{
    int nError;
    string szUnused="";
    nError = TAPI.lineAnswer(TAPI.hCall, ref szUnused, 0);
}
```

VB.NET

```vbnet
Public Sub acceptCall()
    Dim nError As Integer
    nError = lineAnswer(hCall, "", 0)
End Sub
```

Because this is a demonstration program, it is worthwhile to display in real time what is happening to the callback function. A reference to the form is stored in a public variable so that the callback function can use that reference to display status messages in tbStatus.

C#

```csharp
private void frmTAPI_Load(object sender, System.EventArgs e)
{
    TAPI.userInterface = this;
}
```

VB.NET

```vbnet
Private Sub frmTAPI_Load(ByVal sender As System.Object, _
ByVal e As System.EventArgs) Handles MyBase.Load
        userInterface = Me
End Sub
```

VB.NET developers will need to set option strict off at the top of their code and include a reference to Microsoft Visual Basic .NET Compatibility Runtime.

C# developers will require the following namespaces, whereas VB.NET developers will need to add a reference to the Microsoft.VisualBasic.Compatibility assembly in Project→Add References.

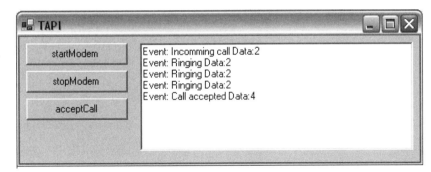

Figure 14.1
Basic TAPI call-receiver application.

C#

```
using System.Runtime.InteropServices;
using System.Text;
using System.Reflection;
```

To test this program, run it from Visual Studio .NET and press startModem (see Figure 14.1). Connect your modem to a phone line. With a second phone, dial the number of the phone line that is connected to your modem. When an incoming call is detected and displayed –on-screen, you can press acceptCall. You will hear the ringing stop once the line is open. Hang up, or press stopModem to disconnect the call.

14.4   DTMF tones

Dual-tone modulated frequency (DTMF) is a way of encoding a number into an audible sound composed of two sine waves played simultaneously. These sounds are generated when someone presses a digit on a phone's keypad. This is particularly useful for automated phone conversations, such as "Press 1 if you have a billing inquiry. Press 2 if you require technical support," and so on.

These sounds are decoded by the modem hardware and passed up to the TAPI callback as an event with dwMessage set to LINE_MONITORDIGITS (9 hex). The digit pressed is being held in dwParam1.

To use DTMF within a TAPI application, a few small changes need to be made. First, add a new API definition and two new constants to the TAPI module thus:

C#

```
public const short LINEDIGITMODE_DTMF = 0x2;
```

```
public const short LINE_MONITORDIGITS = 9;

[DllImport("Tapi32.dll",SetLastError=true)]
public static extern int lineMonitorDigits(int hCall,int
dwDigitModes);
```

VB.NET

```
Public Const LINEDIGITMODE_DTMF As Short = &H2S
Public Const LINE_MONITORDIGITS = 9

Public Declare Function lineMonitorDigits Lib "Tapi32" _
(ByVal hCall As Integer, ByVal dwDigitModes As _
Integer) As Integer
```

Then add a new case to the callback function:

C#

```
public static int LineCallBack(...)
{
 ...
 switch (dwMessage)
 {
  ...
    case LINE_MONITORDIGITS:
   msgEvent = "DTMF";
   break;
 }
 ...
}
```

VB.NET

```
Public Function LineCallBack(...) As Integer
 ...
 Select Case dwMessage
 ...
  Case LINE_MONITORDIGITS
   MsgEvent = "DTMF"
 End Select
```

Then add a call to lineMonitorDigits to acceptCall:

C#
```
public void acceptCall()
{
    int nError;
    string szUnused="";
    nError = TAPI.lineAnswer(TAPI.hCall, ref szUnused, 0);
    TAPI.lineMonitorDigits(TAPI.hCall,
    TAPI.LINEDIGITMODE_DTMF);
}
```

VB.NET
```
Public Sub acceptCall()
    Dim nError As Integer
    nError = lineAnswer(hCall, "", 0)
    lineMonitorDigits(hCall, LINEDIGITMODE_DTMF)
End Sub
```

14.5   Audio playback

Playing audio back through a voice modem is the core feature of any CTI system. The following example demonstrates how to send a prerecorded wave file as audio to a standard telephone handset. Using prerecorded messages should be adequate in most situations, where even dynamic data such as times, dates, and prices can be composed of snippets of audio like "one," "two," "three," "four," … "thirteen," "teen", "twenty," "thirty," "fourty," etc.

When recordings are so varied that it would be impossible to prerecord audio snippets, a speech synthesizer such as such as the text-to-speech application contained in the `Samples\CSharp\SimpleTTS` folder of Microsoft SAPI 5.1 (Speech Application Programming Interface) could be used. This, however, is beyond the scope of this book.

To illustrate the principle of audio playback, the first example demonstrates how to play a wave (`.wav`) file through your sound card. The same technique is then applied to playing audio over an active phone call. The code required to play a simple wave file may seem like overkill. It is true that if all you require is to play a sound through the sound card, you should look at API calls like `sndPlaySound`, or if sound recording is required, then the `mciSendString` API should be of interest. The reason behind using low-level code to play a wave file though a sound card is that this method can be easily adapted to play audio directly through the phone line, albeit at lesser quality.

Open a new project in Visual Studio .NET, and add a new module. Type the following code into it. In C#, you will create a new class. Ensure that the namespace is the same as that used in your form; here it is assumed to be audio. You may replace this as necessary.

C#

```
namespace audio
{
  public class audio
  {
    public static WAVEHDR whdr;
    public static WAVEFORMAT format_wave;
    public static WAVEHDR outHdr;
    public static int bufferIn;
    public static int numSamples;
    public static int hWaveOut;

    public const short MMIO_READ = 0x0;
    public const int CALLBACK_FUNCTION  = 0x30000;
    public const short WAVE_MAPPED  = 0x4;
    public const short MMIO_FINDCHUNK  = 0x10;
    public const short MMIO_FINDRIFF  = 0x20;

    public struct MMCKINFO
    {
      public int ckid;
      public int ckSize;
      public int fccType;
      public int dwDataOffset;
      public int dwFlags;
    }

    public struct mmioinfo
    {
      public int dwFlags;
      public int fccIOProc;
      public int pIOProc;
      public int wErrorRet;
      public int htask;
      public int cchBuffer;
      public string pchBuffer;
```

```
         public string pchNext;
         public string pchEndRead;
         public string pchEndWrite;
         public int lBufOffset;
         public int lDiskOffset;
         public string adwInfo;
         public int dwReserved1;
         public int dwReserved2;
         public int hmmio;
       }

     public struct WAVEFORMAT
     {
       public short wFormatTag;
       public short nChannels;
       public int nSamplesPerSec;
       public int nAvgBytesPerSec;
       public short nBlockAlign;
       public short wBitsPerSample;
       public short cbSize;
     }
     public struct WAVEHDR
     {
       public int lpData;
       public int dwBufferLength;
       public int dwBytesRecorded;
       public int dwUser;
       public int dwFlags;
       public int dwLoops;
       public int lpNext;
       public int Reserved;
     }
[DllImport("winmm.dll",SetLastError=true)]
public static extern int waveOutWrite(int hWaveOut,
   ref WAVEHDR lpWaveOutHdr, int uSize);

[DllImport("winmm.dll",SetLastError=true)]
public static extern int waveOutPrepareHeader(int hWaveIn,
   ref WAVEHDR lpWaveInHdr, int uSize);

[DllImport("winmm.dll",SetLastError=true)]
```

```
public static extern int mmioRead (int hmmio,
    int pch, int cch);

[DllImport("winmm.dll",SetLastError=true)]
public static extern int waveOutOpen(ref int lphWaveIn, int
    uDeviceID, ref WAVEFORMAT lpFormat, int dwCallback,
    int dwInstance,int dwFlags);

[DllImport("kernel32.dll",SetLastError=true)]
public static extern int GlobalAlloc (int wFlags, int
dwBytes);

[DllImport("kernel32.dll",SetLastError=true)]
public static extern int GlobalLock (int hmem);

[DllImport("winmm.dll",SetLastError=true)]
public static extern int mmioAscend (int hmmio, ref MMCKINFO
lpck, int uFlags);

[DllImport("kernel32.dll",SetLastError=true)]
public static extern int GlobalFree (int hmem);

[DllImport("winmm.dll",SetLastError=true)]
public static extern int mmioOpenA (string szFileName, ref
mmioinfo lpmmioinfo, int dwOpenFlags);

[DllImport("winmm.dll",SetLastError=true)]
public static extern int mmioDescend (int hmmio, ref MMCKINFO
lpck, int x, int uFlags);

[DllImport("winmm.dll",SetLastError=true)]
public static extern int mmioRead(int hmmio, ref WAVEFORMAT
pch, int cch);

[DllImport("winmm.dll",SetLastError=true)]
public static extern int mmioClose(int hmmio, int uFlags);

[DllImport("winmm.dll",SetLastError=true)]
public static extern int mmioStringToFOURCCA (string sz, int
uFlags);

[DllImport("winmm.dll",SetLastError=true)]
```

```
public static extern int mmioDescend (int hmmio, ref MMCKINFO
lpck, ref MMCKINFO lpckParent, int uFlags);
}
}
```

VB.NET

```
Option Strict Off
Option Explicit On
Module modAudio
 Public whdr As WAVEHDR
 Public format_wave As WAVEFORMAT
 Public outHdr As WAVEHDR
 Public bufferIn As Integer
 Public numSamples As Integer
 Public hWaveOut As Integer

 Public Const MMIO_READ As Short = &H0s
 Public Const CALLBACK_FUNCTION As Integer = &H30000
 Public Const WAVE_MAPPED As Short = &H4s
 Public Const MMIO_FINDCHUNK As Short = &H10s
 Public Const MMIO_FINDRIFF As Short = &H20s

 Structure MMCKINFO
   Dim ckid As Integer
   Dim ckSize As Integer
   Dim fccType As Integer
   Dim dwDataOffset As Integer
   Dim dwFlags As Integer
 End Structure

 Structure mmioinfo
   Dim dwFlags As Integer
   Dim fccIOProc As Integer
   Dim pIOProc As Integer
   Dim wErrorRet As Integer
   Dim htask As Integer
   Dim cchBuffer As Integer
   Dim pchBuffer As String
   Dim pchNext As String
   Dim pchEndRead As String
   Dim pchEndWrite As String
```

```
        Dim lBufOffset As Integer
        Dim lDiskOffset As Integer
        Dim adwInfo As String
        Dim dwReserved1 As Integer
        Dim dwReserved2 As Integer
        Dim hmmio As Integer
    End Structure


    Structure WAVEFORMAT
        Dim wFormatTag As Short
        Dim nChannels As Short
        Dim nSamplesPerSec As Integer
        Dim nAvgBytesPerSec As Integer
        Dim nBlockAlign As Short
        Dim wBitsPerSample As Short
        Dim cbSize As Short
    End Structure


    Structure WAVEHDR
        Dim lpData As Integer
        Dim dwBufferLength As Integer
        Dim dwBytesRecorded As Integer
        Dim dwUser As Integer
        Dim dwFlags As Integer
        Dim dwLoops As Integer
        Dim lpNext As Integer
        Dim Reserved As Integer
    End Structure


    Declare Function waveOutWrite Lib "winmm.dll" (ByVal _
    hWaveOut As Integer, ByRef lpWaveOutHdr As WAVEHDR, _
    ByVal uSize As Integer) As Integer

    Declare Function waveOutPrepareHeader Lib "winmm.dll" _
    (ByVal hWaveIn As Integer, ByRef lpWaveInHdr As _
    WAVEHDR, ByVal uSize As Integer) As Integer

    Declare Function mmioRead Lib "winmm.dll" (ByVal hmmio _
    As Integer, ByVal pch As Integer, ByVal cch As _
    Integer) As Integer
```

```
Declare Function waveOutOpen Lib "winmm.dll" (ByRef _
lphWaveIn As Integer, ByVal uDeviceID As Integer, _
ByRef lpFormat As WAVEFORMAT, ByVal dwCallback As _
Integer, ByVal dwInstance As Integer, ByVal dwFlags _
As Integer) As Integer

Declare Function GlobalAlloc Lib "kernel32" (ByVal _
wFlags As Integer, ByVal dwBytes As Integer) As Integer

Declare Function GlobalLock Lib "kernel32" (ByVal hmem _
As Integer) As Integer

Declare Function mmioAscend Lib "winmm.dll" (ByVal _
hmmio As Integer, ByRef lpck As MMCKINFO, ByVal uFlags _
As Integer) As Integer

Declare Function GlobalFree Lib "kernel32" (ByVal hmem _
As Integer) As Integer

Declare Function mmioOpen Lib "winmm.dll"  Alias _
"mmioOpenA"(ByVal szFileName As String, ByRef _
lpmmioinfo As mmioinfo, ByVal dwOpenFlags As _
Integer) As Integer
Declare Function mmioDescendParent Lib "winmm.dll" _
Alias "mmioDescend"(ByVal hmmio As Integer, ByRef lpck _
As MMCKINFO, ByVal x As Integer, ByVal uFlags As _
Integer) As Integer

Declare Function mmioReadFormat Lib "winmm.dll"  Alias _
"mmioRead"(ByVal hmmio As Integer, ByRef pch As _
WAVEFORMAT, ByVal cch As Integer) As Integer

Declare Function mmioClose Lib "winmm.dll" (ByVal _
hmmio As Integer, ByVal uFlags As Integer) As Integer

Declare Function mmioStringToFOURCC Lib "winmm.dll" _
Alias "mmioStringToFOURCCA"(ByVal sz As String, ByVal _
uFlags As Integer) As Integer

Declare Function mmioDescend Lib "winmm.dll" (ByVal _
hmmio As Integer, ByRef lpck As MMCKINFO, ByRef _
```

```
lpckParent As MMCKINFO, ByVal uFlags As Integer) As Integer

End Module
```

This code is ported from the C++ prototypes, so it may appear to be complex. Again, it is not necessary to know every parameter passed to each

Table 14.4   *Windows Multimedia API functions .*

waveOutPrepareHeader	Indicates the format of the raw audio data to the wave-out device, so that it can play the sound at the correct speed and knows its format
mmioRead	Reads data from an audio source into memory
GlobalAlloc	Allocates a block of memory of a specified size
GlobalLock	Prevents other processes from using a specified block of memory
GlobalFree	Releases a block of memory
mmioOpen	Opens an audio source (e.g., a wave file)
mmioReadFormat	Retrieves the format of an audio source and details including bit rate, stereo/mono, quality, etc.
mioStringToFOURCC	Converts a null-terminated string to a four-character code
mmioDescend	Descends into a chunk of a RIFF file that was opened by using the mmioOpen function; can also search for a given chunk
waveOutOpen	Opens an audio output device
mmioAscend	Ascends out of a chunk in a RIFF file descended into with the mmioDescend function or created with the mmioCreateChunk function
mmioDescendParent	Descends into a chunk of a RIFF file that was opened by using the mmioOpen function; can also search for a given chunk
mmioClose	Closes an audio input or output device
waveOutWrite	Tells the audio output device to begin playing the sound

of these API calls, but Table 14.4 provides a synopsis of the functions involved.

This application will load a wave file from disk into memory and then play it through the sound card on request. Loading a wave file into memory is done in two stages. The first is where the format of the audio is extracted from the wave file. The audio format includes details about the quality (16-bit or 8-bit), bit rate (44 kbps for CD quality), and whether the audio is mono or stereo. The audio format is stored in a public variable named `format_wave`.

The next step is to pull the data segment of the wave file into memory. A wave file can be several megabytes in size, so for better performance, the memory is allocated directly from the heap using `GlobalAlloc`. The wave file is then read into this memory using `mmioRead`. Once the operation is complete, the file is closed.

Add the following code to the module:

C#

```
public static void LoadFile(ref string inFile)
{
  int hmem = 0;
  MMCKINFO mmckinfoParentIn = new MMCKINFO();
  MMCKINFO mmckinfoSubchunkIn = new MMCKINFO();
  int hmmioIn = 0;
  mmioinfo mmioinf = new mmioinfo();
  mmioinf.adwInfo =
  (new StringBuilder()).Append(' ',4).ToString();
  hmmioIn = mmioOpenA(inFile, ref mmioinf, MMIO_READ);
  if (hmmioIn == 0) return;
  mmioDescend(hmmioIn, ref mmckinfoParentIn, 0,
  MMIO_FINDRIFF);
  mmckinfoSubchunkIn.ckid = mmioStringToFOURCCA("fmt", 0);
  mmioDescend(hmmioIn, ref mmckinfoSubchunkIn,
      ref mmckinfoParentIn, MMIO_FINDCHUNK);
  mmioRead(hmmioIn, ref format_wave,
      Marshal.SizeOf(format_wave));
  mmioAscend(hmmioIn, ref mmckinfoSubchunkIn, 0);
  mmckinfoSubchunkIn.ckid = mmioStringToFOURCCA("data", 0);
  mmioDescend(hmmioIn, ref mmckinfoSubchunkIn,
      ref mmckinfoParentIn,
      MMIO_FINDCHUNK);
```

```
    GlobalFree(hmem);
    hmem = GlobalAlloc(0x40, mmckinfoSubchunkIn.ckSize);
    bufferIn = GlobalLock(hmem);
    mmioRead(hmmioIn, bufferIn, mmckinfoSubchunkIn.ckSize);
    numSamples =
        mmckinfoSubchunkIn.ckSize / format_wave.nBlockAlign;
    mmioClose(hmmioIn, 0);
}
```

VB.NET

```
Sub LoadFile(ByRef inFile As String)
 Dim hmem As Integer
 Dim mmckinfoParentIn As MMCKINFO
 Dim mmckinfoSubchunkIn As MMCKINFO
 Dim hmmioIn As Integer
 Dim mmioinf As mmioinfo

 mmioinf.adwInfo = Space(4)
 hmmioIn = mmioOpen(inFile, mmioinf, MMIO_READ)
 If hmmioIn = 0 Then Exit Sub
 mmioDescendParent(hmmioIn, mmckinfoParentIn, 0, _
 MMIO_FINDRIFF)
 mmckinfoSubchunkIn.ckid = mmioStringToFOURCC("fmt", 0)
 mmioDescend(hmmioIn, mmckinfoSubchunkIn, _
 mmckinfoParentIn, MMIO_FINDCHUNK)
 mmioReadFormat(hmmioIn, format_wave, Len(format_wave))
 mmioAscend(hmmioIn, mmckinfoSubchunkIn, 0)
 mmckinfoSubchunkIn.ckid = mmioStringToFOURCC("data", 0)
 mmioDescend(hmmioIn, mmckinfoSubchunkIn, _
 mmckinfoParentIn, MMIO_FINDCHUNK)
 GlobalFree(hmem)
 hmem = GlobalAlloc(&H40S, mmckinfoSubchunkIn.ckSize)
 bufferIn = GlobalLock(hmem)
 mmioRead(hmmioIn, bufferIn, mmckinfoSubchunkIn.ckSize)
 numSamples = mmckinfoSubchunkIn.ckSize / _
 format_wave.nBlockAlign
 mmioClose(hmmioIn, 0)
End Sub
```

Once the wave file is in memory, the sound card can be instructed to play the audio with a call to this next function, named Play. This function is asynchronous and can be called more than once during the playing of a sound clip, provided the hardware supports it. The sound card will fetch the audio from memory as required using a process known as direct memory access (DMA).

Because the audio format is stored in public variables, that data needs to be transferred to the sound card such that it can correctly play back the sounds at the right speed and quality. Once `waveOutPrepareHeader` has set the sound card up, `waveOutWrite` then starts the sound playing.

C#

```
public static void Play(short soundcard)
{
  int rc = 0;
  int lFlags = 0;
  lFlags = CALLBACK_FUNCTION;
  if (soundcard != -1) lFlags = lFlags | WAVE_MAPPED;
  rc = waveOutOpen(ref hWaveOut, soundcard,
      ref format_wave, 0, 0, lFlags);
  if (rc != 0) return;
  outHdr.lpData = bufferIn;
  outHdr.dwBufferLength =
      numSamples * format_wave.nBlockAlign;
  outHdr.dwFlags = 0;
  outHdr.dwLoops = 0;
  waveOutPrepareHeader(hWaveOut, ref outHdr,
      Marshal.SizeOf(outHdr));
  waveOutWrite(hWaveOut, ref outHdr, Marshal.SizeOf(outHdr));
}
```

VB.NET

```
Sub Play(ByVal soundcard As Short)
 Dim rc As Integer
 Dim lFlags As Integer
 lFlags = CALLBACK_FUNCTION
 If soundcard <> -1 Then lFlags = lFlags Or WAVE_MAPPED
 rc = waveOutOpen(hWaveOut, soundcard, format_wave, 0, _
 0, lFlags)
 If (rc <> 0) Then Exit Sub
 outHdr.lpData = bufferIn
 outHdr.dwBufferLength = numSamples * format_wave.nBlockAlign
 outHdr.dwFlags = 0
```

```
outHdr.dwLoops = 0
waveOutPrepareHeader(hWaveOut, outHdr, Len(outHdr))
waveOutWrite(hWaveOut, outHdr, Len(outHdr))
End Sub
```

C# developers will also require the following namespaces:

C#

```
using System.Runtime.InteropServices;
using System.Text;
```

The next step is to design the user interface. Open the form and drag on two buttons named btnBrowse and btnPlaySound. Add a textbox name tbWave and a File Open Dialog control named OpenFileDialog.

Click on the Browse button and add the following code:

C#

```
private void btnBrowse_Click(object sender, System.EventArgs
e)
{
  openFileDialog.ShowDialog();
  tbWave.Text = openFileDialog.FileName;
}
```

VB.NET

```
Private Sub btnBrowse_Click(ByVal sender As System.Object, _
ByVal e As System.EventArgs) Handles btnBrowse.Click
    OpenFileDialog.ShowDialog()
    tbWave.Text = OpenFileDialog.FileName
End Sub
```

The –1 in the code below signifies that we are using the default output device and not a modem.

Click on the Play sound button, and add the following code:

C#

```
private void btnPlaySound_CSlick(object sender,
System.EventArgs e)
{
    string filename = tbWave.Text;
    audio.LoadFile(ref filename);
    audio.Play(-1);
}
```

Figure 14.2
*Wave sound player
application.*

VB.NET

```
Private Sub btnPlaySound_Click(ByVal eventSender As _
System.Object, ByVal eventArgs As System.EventArgs) _
Handles btnPlaySound.Click
LoadFile(tbWave.Text)
  Play(-1)
End Sub
```

You will need to set option strict off at the top of your code and include a reference to Microsoft Visual Basic .NET Compatibility Runtime.

To test the application, run it from Visual Studio .NET, press Browse, and locate a wave file on your hard disk. Press Play sound, and you should hear the audio being played (Figure 14.2).

14.5.1   Audio playback over TAPI

By combining the previous two example programs, and with the addition of a few extra lines of code, we can now send audio down the phone line, completing this introduction to CTI in .NET.

Open the first example program and include the module from the second example program. Copy the user interface from the second example program (including openFileDialog) and place the buttons and textbox on the form.

The only hurdle in combining these two programs is to find a way to map a handle to a line to a handle to an output device. Luckily, an API call does that for us: lineGetID. Open the TAPI module and enter the following code:

C#

```
public const short LINECALLSELECT_CALL = 0x4;
```

```
public struct varString
{
  public long dwTotalSize;
  public long dwNeededSize;
  public long dwUsedSize;
  public long dwStringFormat;
  public long dwStringSize;
  public long dwStringOffset;
  public string bBytes;
}

[DllImport("Tapi32.dll",SetLastError=true)]
public static extern long lineGetID (long hLine, long
   dwAddressID, long hCall, long dwSelect,
   varString lpDevice, string lpszDeviceClass);
```

VB.NET

```
Public Const LINECALLSELECT_CALL = &H4

Structure varString
 Dim dwTotalSize As Long
 Dim dwNeededSize As Long
 Dim dwUsedSize As Long
 Dim dwStringFormat As Long
 Dim dwStringSize As Long
 Dim dwStringOffset As Long
 Dim bBytes As String
End Structure

Public Declare Function lineGetID Lib "Tapi32" _
(ByVal hLine As Long, ByVal dwAddressID As _
Long, ByVal hCall As Long, ByVal dwSelect As Long, _
ByRef lpDevice As varString, ByVal lpszDeviceClass As _
String) As Long
```

Go to the user interface, click on the Browse button, and add the following code:

C#

```
private void btnBrowse_Click(object sender, System.EventArgs
e)
```

```
{
  openFileDialog.ShowDialog();
  tbWave.Text = openFileDialog.FileName;
}
```

VB.NET

```
Private Sub btnBrowse_Click(ByVal sender As System.Object, _
 ByVal e As System.EventArgs) Handles btnBrowse.Click
  OpenFileDialog.ShowDialog()
  tbWave.Text = OpenFileDialog.FileName
End Sub
```

Because we are not playing through the default audio output device, we can no longer specify −1 for the sound card parameter in Play; we have to use GetLineID.

C#

```
private void btnPlaySound_Click(object sender,
System.EventArgs e)
{
  string filename = tbWave.Text;
  audio.LoadFile(ref filename);
  audio.Play((short)Convert.ToInt32
     (TAPI.GetLineID("wave/out")));
}
```

VB.NET

```
Private Sub btnPlaySound_Click(ByVal sender As _
System.Object, ByVal e As System.EventArgs) Handles _
btnPlaySound.Click
  LoadFile(tbWave.Text)
  Play(GetLineID("wave/out"))
End Sub
```

The final step is to implement the GetLineID function. This retrieves the audio output device from the current call handle. As the parameters imply, this function is only valid when an active call is in progress (i.e., you can't send audio down a phone line if no one is listening).

The string manipulation is used to convert a C++ representation of a variable-length string to the .NET string type.

C#

```csharp
public static string GetLineID(string sWave)
{
  long nError = 0;
  string sTemp = "";
  TAPI.varString oVar = new TAPI.varString();
  System.Text.StringBuilder sb = new
    System.Text.StringBuilder();
  oVar.bBytes = sb.Append(' ',2000).ToString();
  oVar.dwTotalSize = Marshal.SizeOf(oVar);
  nError = lineGetID(hLine, 0, hCall,
      LINECALLSELECT_CALL, oVar, sWave);
  if (oVar.dwStringOffset == 0) return "-1";
  sTemp = oVar.bBytes.Substring(0,
    (int)oVar.dwStringSize).Trim();
  return sTemp;
}
```

VB.NET

```vbnet
Public Function GetLineID(ByVal sWave As String) as String
 Dim nError As Long
 Dim sTemp As String
 Dim oVar As varString

 oVar.bBytes = Space(2000)
 oVar.dwTotalSize = Len(oVar)

 nError = lineGetID(hLine, 0, hCall, _
 LINECALLSELECT_CALL, oVar, sWave)
 If oVar.dwStringOffset = 0 Then Return -1
 sTemp = Trim(oVar.bBytes.Substring(0, oVar.dwStringSize))
 Return sTemp
End Function
```

To test this program, run it from Visual Studio .NET and press startModem (Figure 14.3). Connect your modem to a phone line. With a second phone, dial the number of the phone line that is connected to your modem. When an incoming call is detected and displayed on-screen, you can press acceptCall. You will hear the ringing stop once the line is open. Press Browse, and locate a file on your hard drive, press Play Sound, and you should hear it through your phone.

Figure 14.3
*TAPI call receiver
with DTMF and
playback.*

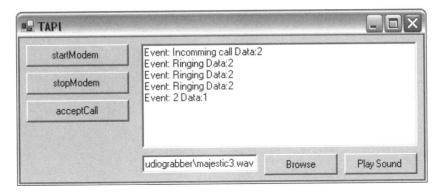

You may notice a distinct loss in sound quality when audio is sent over the phone line. Choosing different file types can lessen this effect. The official format for TAPI is u-Law 56 Kbps (7 KHz, 8-bit mono) in the United States and a-law 64 Kbps (8 KHz, 8-bit mono) in Europe; however, from personal experience, I have found that 22,050 Hz is clearer, even over TAPI connections.

14.6 Conclusion

This chapter detailed the technology involved in making a computer perform a task that most of us do every day—answering the phone. Systems like these can be used to assist any organization's customer service activities, providing scalable call routing, and can answer simple queries without requiring full-time phone operators.

The applications of such a system are virtually unlimited because it can be used to provide information and services to people who can't or don't have time to log into the Internet. They are used in cinemas, ticket booking agencies, and mobile phone top-up centers.

The next chapter deals with an interesting technology that solves the problem of reliably sending data between a client and server that are not always connected to each other. Say hello to MSMQ!

15

Message Queues

15.1 Introduction

In all of the networking examples so far, it is necessary for the client and server to be running at the same time in order for communication to be sent between them. Message queuing software facilitates the construction of queues between client and server over an impermanent connection, such that messages are stored until a connection is present. Microsoft Message Queue (MSMQ) is the most applicable system for .NET, but other products such as IBM WebSphere MQ (*www.ibm.com/software/ts/mqseries*) or TIBCO *RendezVous (http://www.tibco.com/software/enterprise_backbone/ rendezvous.jsp)* are alternatives.

Message queuing is often used as a backup system for whenever a communication link fails between two servers. This improves overall system stability in the event of catastrophic failure. This type of fallback mechanism is vital in systems where out-of-sync data between sites could cause opportunities for malicious users to defraud the system. One could imagine if a person were to withdraw funds from two ATMs simultaneously, during a temporary interbank communications link failure. If the ATMs did not propagate the transactions back to the bank once the link was restored, then the person could run away with double the available balance.

This chapter begins by describing the basics of MSMQ and providing examples of how to send and receive objects via a message queue. This topic is then developed toward the end of the chapter by detailing other features of MSMQ, which help manage how messages are sent through the system.

15.2 MSMQ

A common application for MSMQ is where a business may have many different regional outlets and one head office, where stock replacement and

Figure 15.1
*Computer
Management
dialog, MSMQ
console.*

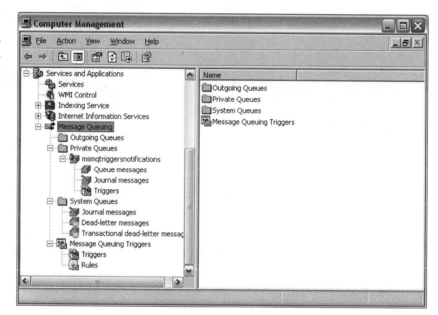

auditing takes place. Each outlet may have only a dial-up Internet connection, but a system still needs to be in place to provide good, reliable data consolidation whenever the satellite offices are connected to the head office. The amount of work involved in implementing a custom solution is substantial, especially if the system is expected to scale upward.

MSMQ is included with Windows XP Professional and available as part of the Windows NT4 Option Pack. To install it, click Start→Control Panel→Add or Remove Programs→Windows components, and check Message Queuing, and then Next.

You can administer MSMQ by clicking Start→Control Panel→ Administrative Tools→Computer Management→Services and Applications→ Message Queuing (Figure 15.1).

15.3 Implementing a message queue

To run this example, you will need MSMQ running on your computer. In this example, a message will be passed between two computers with an impermanent link between them. If you are on a LAN, you can simulate the dropout in connectivity by unplugging the Ethernet cable; for readers with only one computer, the effect can be simulated by running the client and server one after the other (not simultaneously).

An application not too dissimilar from this example could be used to perform database replication, where the string being sent via MSMQ could be an SQL statement, and the receiver could execute the statement, rather than simply displaying it. In this way, each action performed on the local database could be mirrored on a remote database whenever they are connected.

The types of data that can be placed on queues are not limited to strings. All objects that can be serialized can be placed on the message queue as XML.

Create a new Visual Studio .NET application as per usual. Add a reference to `System.Messaging.dll` with Projects→Add Reference.

This code will first check if a queue is available, and then create it if it is not available. Once that is done, the contents of a textbox will be sent to the queue. Draw a textbox named `tbMessage` and a button named `btnSend`, and then click on the button.

C#

```csharp
private void btnSend_Click(object sender, System.EventArgs e)
{
    string queueName = ".\\private$\\test";
    MessageQueue mq;
    if (MessageQueue.Exists(queueName))
    {
        mq=new MessageQueue(queueName);
    }
    else
    {
        mq = MessageQueue.Create(queueName);
    }
    mq.Send(tbMessage.Text);
}
```

VB.NET

```vbnet
Private  Sub btnSend_Click(ByVal sender As Object, _
ByVal e As System.EventArgs)
    Dim queueName As String =  ".\private$\test"
    Dim mq As MessageQueue
    If MessageQueue.Exists(queueName) Then
        mq=New MessageQueue(queueName)
```

```
        Else
            mq = MessageQueue.Create(queueName)
        End If
        mq.Send(tbMessage.Text)
    End Sub
```

Table 15.1   *Significant members of the MessageQueue class .*

Formatter	Specifies the formatter used to serialize or deserialize the message body; can be either XmlMessageFormatter, ActiveXMessageFormatter, or BinaryMessageFormatter
Label	Specifies a human-readable queue description
Path	Specifies the location of the queue
Transactional	Specifies whether the queue can accept nontransactional messages
Authenticate	Specifies whether the queue can accept unauthenticated messages
EncryptionRequired	Specifies whether the queue can accept unencrypted messages
Close	Frees all resources used by the handle to the queue
Create	Creates a new queue at the specified path
Delete	Removes a queue from MSMQ, deleting all messages contained therein
GetAllMessages	Returns an array of messages from the specified queue
GetPrivateQueuesByMachine	Returns an array of private message queues from the specified machine
GetPublicQueues	Returns an array of queues on the local network
Receive	Returns a message from the top of the specified queue
Send	Sends a message to the tail of the specified queue
Purge	Deletes all messages from a queue, but does not delete the queue itself

This code first looks at MSMQ to see if a queue of the name \private$\ test has been created on the local machine. If it has not, then a Message-Queue object (Table 15.1) points to the existing one. The contents of the text-box (tbMessage) are then sent as a message to this queue.

More than one queue can be held on one MSMQ server. They are named < *Server name* >\private$\< *Queue name* >, where < *Server name* > can be either the computer name of the MSMQ server or "." for the local server. When the MSMQ server is not on the local intranet, then MSMQ over HTTP may be used. In this case, the server name can be an IP address or domain name. MSMQ HTTP support must be installed from Add/Remove Windows components in the Control Panel (Figure 15.2).

HTTP message queues are hosted by IIS and reside in the msmq virtual folder. In this way, queues over HTTP take the form:

```
http://<domain name>/msmq/<queue name>
```

You will also require the following namespace:

C#

```
using System.Messaging;
```

VB.NET

```
Imports System.Messaging
```

To test this application, ensure that you have MSMQ installed on your system, and then run this program from Visual Studio .NET. You should then type some text into the box provided and press Send, as shown in Figure 15.3.

Go to Message Queuing in Computer Management, and click on Private Queues→Test→Queue Messages. Double-click on the envelope icon on the right-hand side, and click on the Body tab in the new window. You should see an XML representation of the text that was sent (Figure 15.4).

To complete the example, it is also necessary to know how to read in a message from a message queue, as well as how to write to it.

Draw a textbox, tbStatus, and a button, btnListen. Ensure that Mul-tiLine is set to true for the textbox. Click on btnListen and enter the fol-lowing code:

Figure 15.2
*MSMQ HTTP
support.*

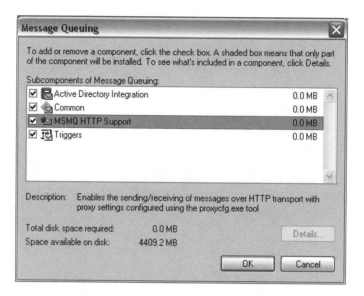

Figure 15.3
*Basic MSMQ
application.*

C#

```csharp
private void btnListen_Click(object sender, System.EventArgs
e)
{
  Thread thdListener = new Thread(new ThreadStart(QThread));
  thdListener.Start();
}
```

VB.NET

```vbnet
Private  Sub btnListen_Click(ByVal sender As Object, _
ByVal e As System.EventArgs)
  Dim thdListener As Thread =  New Thread(New _
  ThreadStart(AddressOf QThread))
  thdListener.Start()
End Sub
```

Because it is possible that there are no messages on the queue, the server will block (hang) at the point of calling the Receive method; therefore, QThread is invoked as a new thread.

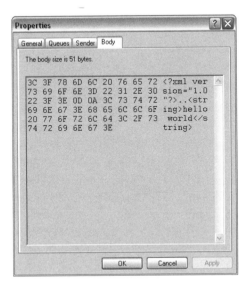

Figure 15.4
*Native XML
format of a message
in MSMQ.*

C#

```
public void QThread()
{
  string queuePath = ".\\private$\\test";
  MessageQueue queue = new MessageQueue(queuePath);
  System.Messaging.Message msg;
  ((XmlMessageFormatter)queue.Formatter).TargetTypes =
      new Type[1];
  ((XmlMessageFormatter)queue.Formatter).TargetTypes[0] =
    "".GetType();
  while(true)
  {
    msg= queue.Receive();
    tbStatus.Text += msg.Body + "\n";
  }
}
```

VB.NET

```
Public  Sub QThread()
  Dim queuePath As String =  ".\private$\test"
  Dim queue As MessageQueue =  New MessageQueue(queuePath)
```

```
Dim msg As System.Messaging.Message
CType(queue.Formatter, XmlMessageFormatter).TargetTypes _
= New Type(0){}
CType(queue.Formatter, XmlMessageFormatter).TargetTypes(0) _
= "".GetType()
Do
  msg= queue.Receive()
  tbStatus.Text += msg.Body + VbCrLf
Loop
End Sub
```

In Figure 15.4, it is clear that messages are stored internally in XML format. This permits the storage of complex types as well as simple strings, but it is necessary to indicate to MSMQ the target type of the object that you want to read back into. In this case, we are reading a string, so the `TargetType` is set to `string` (obtained by the `"".GetType()` construct). It is not necessary to specify the object type when sending to a message queue because .NET can determine this from reflection. The deserialized version of the object is then held in the `Message` object (Table 15.2).

Table 15.2 *Significant members of the `Message` class.*

AcknowledgeType	Specifies the events that require acknowledgment from MSMQ
Acknowledgment	Determines the type of acknowledgment that is flagged by the message
AdministrationQueue	Specifies the queue to which acknowledgment messages are to be sent
AttachSenderId	Includes the ID of the sending machine in the message
Body	Specifies the message payload, which can be any type of object
Label	Includes a human-readable description of the message
MessageType	Indicates that the message is normal, an acknowledgment, or a report
Priority	Determines where in the queue the message is to be placed

Table 15.2 *Significant members of the* **Message** *class (continued).*

Recoverable	Specifies whether the message is stored in memory or disk
SenderId	Indicates the sending machine
TimeToReachQueue	Specifies the maximum length of time it should take for a message to reach a queue
UseDeadLetterQueue	Determines if the time-expired messages should go to the dead-letter queue
UseJournalQueue	Determines if received messages should be archived in the journal

You will need a reference to **System.Messaging.dll** and the following namespaces:

C#

```
using System.Threading;
using System.Messaging;
```

VB.NET

```
imports System.Threading
imports System.Messaging
```

To test this application, run them both from their .exe files. Type "hello world" into the client, and press Send. The message will not appear on the server because it is not listening yet. Press the Listen button on the server, and the message will appear in the status box, as shown in Figure 15.5.

15.3.1 Queuing complex objects

It is perfectly valid to use the serialization and deserialization techniques described in Chapter 2 to send complex objects as strings through MSMQ. In the interest of efficiency and simplicity, it is better to use the built-in functionality in MSMQ to perform this task.

In the following example, imagine a situation where a chain of hotels has a central booking agency. This agency takes phone reservations from overseas customers and places each booking in a queue destined for a particular hotel. This hotel would periodically dial in to collect the latest bookings from this queue.

Figure 15.5
Basic MSMQ
receiver
application.

A hotel needs to know the names of the tourists, when they are coming and leaving, and what type of room they are looking for. Furthermore, the reservation system at the hotel is automated, so the message has to be in a well-defined format.

Building on the previous example to send strings to a message queue, include a class that represents a hotel reservation. Add the following code directly at the start of the namespace:

C#

```
public class booking
{
  public enum RoomType
  {
    BASIC,
    EN_SUITE,
    DELUXE
  }
  public class Room
  {
    public Int16 occupants;
    public RoomType roomType;
  }
  public string name;
  public Room room;
  public DateTime arrival;
  public DateTime departure;
```

```
    }
```

VB.NET

```
Public Class booking
    Public Enum RoomType
      BASIC
      EN_SUITE
      DELUXE
    End Enum

    Public Class Room
      Public occupants As Int16
      Public roomType As RoomType
    End Class
    Public name As String
    Public myRoom As Room
    Public arrival As DateTime
    Public departure As DateTime
End Class
```

Select the Form Design tab, and remove the textbox (tbMessage) from the form. Now drag on two textboxes named tbName and tbOccupants. If you wish, you can use labels to indicate what each textbox is used for, although this is not essential. Draw on two Date-Picker controls named dtArrival and dtDeparture. A combo box named cbType is also required. You must click on the Items property for the combo box and add three strings: basic, en suite, and deluxe.

Click on the Send button and add the following code:

C#

```
private void btnSend_Click(object sender, System.EventArgs e)
{
  string queueName = ".\\private$\\test";
  MessageQueue mq;
  if (MessageQueue.Exists(queueName))
  {
    mq=new MessageQueue(queueName);
  }
  else
  {
```

```
      mq = MessageQueue.Create(queueName);
    }
    booking hotelBooking = new booking();
    hotelBooking.name = tbName.Text;
    hotelBooking.departure = DateTime.Parse(dtDeparture.Text);
    hotelBooking.arrival = DateTime.Parse(dtArrival.Text);
    hotelBooking.room = new booking.Room();
    hotelBooking.room.occupants =
    Convert.ToInt16(tbOccupants.Text);
    switch(cbType.SelectedIndex.ToString())
    {
      case "basic":
        hotelBooking.room.roomType = booking.RoomType.BASIC;
        break;
      case "en suite":
        hotelBooking.room.roomType = booking.RoomType.EN_SUITE;
        break;
      case "deluxe":
        hotelBooking.room.roomType = booking.RoomType.DELUXE;
        break;
    }
    mq.Send(hotelBooking);
  }
```

VB.NET

```
Private  Sub btnSend_Click(ByVal sender As Object, _
ByVal e As System.EventArgs)
  Dim queueName As String =  ".\private$\test"
  Dim mq As MessageQueue
  If MessageQueue.Exists(queueName) Then
    mq=New MessageQueue(queueName)
  Else
    mq = MessageQueue.Create(queueName)
  End If
  Dim hotelBooking As booking =  New booking()
  hotelBooking.name = tbName.Text
  hotelBooking.departure = DateTime.Parse(dtDeparture.Text)
  hotelBooking.arrival = DateTime.Parse(dtArrival.Text)
  hotelBooking.myroom = New booking.Room()
  hotelBooking.myroom.occupants = _
    Convert.ToInt16(tbOccupants.Text)
```

```
Select Case cbType.SelectedIndex.ToString()
  Case "basic"
    hotelBooking.myroom.roomType = booking.RoomType.BASIC
    Exit Sub
  Case "en suite"
    hotelBooking.myroom.roomType = _
      booking.RoomType.EN_SUITE
    Exit Sub
  Case "deluxe"
    hotelBooking.myroom.roomType = booking.RoomType.DELUXE
    Exit Sub
  End Select
  mq.Send(hotelBooking)
End Sub
```

You will need a reference to `System.Messaging.dll` and the following namespaces:

C#

```
using System.Threading;
using System.Messaging;
```

VB.NET

```
imports System.Threading
imports System.Messaging
```

To test the application at this stage, you can run it from Visual Studio .NET. Type some reservation details into the boxes provided, and press send (Figure 15.6).

If you open the test queue in Computer Management and right-click on Properties→Body for the new message, you will notice a more verbose XML representation of the booking object:

```
<?xml version="1.0"?>
<booking xmlns:xsd="http://www.w3.org/2001/XMLSchema"
 xmlns:xsi="http://www.w3.org/2001/XMLSchema-instance">
 <name>Fiach Reid</name>
 <room>
  <occupants>
   1
  </occupants>
  <roomType>
```

Figure 15.6
*Complex object
MSMQ transfer
example.*

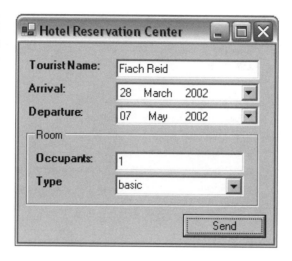

```
    BASIC
   </roomType>
  </room>
  <arrival>
   2002-04-28T00:00:00.0000000-00:00
  </arrival>
  <departure>
   2002-05-07T00:00:00.0000000-00:00
  </departure>
 </booking>
```

Now, to deserialize the object at the receiving end, it is just a matter of altering the TargetType in the queue formatter from string to booking. You will also need to display the new booking, and of course, you still need to include the booking class after the namespace.

Replace the code in the QThread function with the following:

C#

```csharp
public void QThread()
{
  string queuePath = ".\\private$\\test";
  MessageQueue queue = new MessageQueue(queuePath);
  System.Messaging.Message msg;
  ((XmlMessageFormatter)queue.Formatter).TargetTypes =
    new Type[1];
  ((XmlMessageFormatter)queue.Formatter).TargetTypes[0] =
```

```
            (new booking()).GetType();
        while(true)
        {
            msg= queue.Receive();
            booking hotelBooking = (booking)msg.Body;
            tbStatus.Text += "tourist name:" +
            hotelBooking.name + "\n";
            tbStatus.Text += "arrival:" +
            hotelBooking.arrival + "\n";
            tbStatus.Text += "departure:" +
            hotelBooking.departure + "\n";
            if (hotelBooking.room!=null)
            {
                tbStatus.Text += "room occupants:" +
                hotelBooking.room.occupants + "\n";
                tbStatus.Text += "room type:" +
                hotelBooking.room.roomType.ToString() + "\n";        }
        }
    }
```

VB.NET

```
Public  Sub QThread()
    Dim queuePath As String =  ".\private$\test"
    Dim queue As MessageQueue =  New MessageQueue(queuePath)
    Dim msg As System.Messaging.Message
    CType(queue.Formatter, XmlMessageFormatter).TargetTypes = _
        New Type(0) {}
    CType(queue.Formatter, _
        XmlMessageFormatter).TargetTypes(0) = _
        (New booking()).GetType()
    Do
        msg= queue.Receive()
        Dim hotelBooking As booking = CType(msg.Body, booking)
        tbStatus.Text += "tourist name:" + _
        hotelBooking.name + vbcrlf
        tbStatus.Text += "arrival:" + _
        hotelBooking.arrival + vbcrlf
        tbStatus.Text += "departure:" + _
        hotelBooking.departure + vbcrlf
        if not hotelBooking.room is nothing then
            tbStatus.Text += "room occupants:" & _
```

```
                    hotelBooking.myroom.occupants & vbcrlf _
                    tbStatus.Text += "room type:" & _
                    hotelBooking.myroom.roomType.ToString() & vbcrlf
            end if
        Loop
    End Sub
```

This code locates an existing queue named `\private$\test` on the local machine. Because the message contains only one type of object, the `TargetTypes` property is set to an array of one type. The first and only object passed is a `booking`, and therefore element 0 in the array of target types is set to the `booking` type.

The thread now enters an infinite loop. Where it encounters the `Receive` method, the execution blocks until a new message appears in the queue. This message is converted into a `booking` and then displayed on-screen.

To test this, first check that the top message in the test queue is one that represents a hotel booking. If you are unsure, delete the queue, and then run the preceding program to post a new reservation to the queue. Now run this program from Visual Studio .NET and press Listen. You should see the details of a new booking in the textbox, as shown in Figure 15.7.

Figure 15.7
Complex object MSMQ receiver example.

15.3.2 **Transactions**

Like databases, MSMQ supports transactions. A *transaction* is an atomic unit of work that either succeeds or fails as a whole. In a banking system, a transaction might involve debiting a checking account via one message queue and crediting a savings account via another queue. If a system failure were to occurr in the middle of the transaction, the bank would be liable for theft, unless the transaction were rolled back. After the system restarted, the transaction could be carried out again.

The following code attempts to add two messages to a queue. The code has a deliberate division by zero error between the two message sends. If this line is commented out, both operations are carried out; if not, then neither operation is carried out.

Open the client application in the previous example. Click on the Send button, and replace the code with the following:

C#

```
private void btnSend_Click(object sender, System.EventArgs e)
{
  int zero = 0;
  string queueName = ".\\private$\\test2";
  MessageQueueTransaction msgTx = new
  MessageQueueTransaction();
  MessageQueue mq;
  if (MessageQueue.Exists(queueName))
  {
    mq=new MessageQueue(queueName);
  }
  else
  {
    mq = MessageQueue.Create(queueName,true);
  }
  msgTx.Begin();
  try
  {
    mq.Send("Message 1",msgTx);
    zero = 5 / zero; // deliberate error
    mq.Send("Message 2",msgTx);
    msgTx.Commit();
  }
```

```
catch
{
  msgTx.Abort();
}
finally
{
  mq.Close();
}
}
```

VB.NET

```
Private  Sub btnSend_Click(ByVal sender As Object, _
    ByVal e As System.EventArgs)
Dim zero As Integer =  0
Dim queueName As String =  ".\private$\test2"
Dim msgTx As MessageQueueTransaction =  New _
    MessageQueueTransaction()
Dim mq As MessageQueue
If MessageQueue.Exists(queueName) Then
  mq=New MessageQueue(queueName)
Else
  mq = MessageQueue.Create(queueName,True)
End If
msgTx.Begin()
Try
  mq.Send("Message 1",msgTx)
  zero = 5 / zero ' deliberate error
  mq.Send("Message 2",msgTx)
  msgTx.Commit()
Catch
  msgTx.Abort()
Finally
  mq.Close()
End Try
End Sub
```

This code creates a queue as before. The Begin method initiates a transaction. This means that any changes to the queue will not physically take
place until the Commit method is called. If the Abort method is called, or
the computer crashes, then any statements issued directly after the Begin
method are ignored. In this case, an error occurs before the second message

is posted to the queue. This error throws an exception, which causes code to be executed that aborts the transaction.

To test this application, run it from Visual Studio .NET with the deliberate error left in the code. Press Send, and then open Computer Management and look at Message Queues. You will notice that a second queue has been created, but neither message has been posted. If you now remove the deliberate error from the code and rerun the application, then press the Send button, you will see both messages appearing in the Queue Messages list.

15.3.3   Acknowledgments

Most of the work done by MSMQ is behind the scenes and completely transparent to the application. If MSMQ fails for some reason, the application—and therefore the user—will not know that today's data was never transferred. Acknowledgments provide a mechanism for the sending application to verify that the receiving application has read the message and that the message queue is functioning correctly.

This example builds on the code for the first example in this chapter, so open that project in Visual Studio .NET and click on the Send button.

C#

```
private void btnSend_Click(object sender, System.EventArgs e)
{
  string queueName = ".\\private$\\test";
  MessageQueue mq;
  if (MessageQueue.Exists(queueName))
  {
    mq=new MessageQueue(queueName);
  }
  else
  {
    mq = MessageQueue.Create(queueName);
  }
  System.Messaging.Message myMessage = new
  System.Messaging.Message();
  myMessage.Body = tbMessage.Text;
  myMessage.AdministrationQueue =
  new MessageQueue(".\\private$\\test");
  myMessage.AcknowledgeType = AcknowledgeTypes.FullReachQueue
```

```
        AcknowledgeTypes.FullReceive;
        mq.Send(myMessage);
    }
```

VB.NET

```
Private  Sub btnSend_Click(ByVal sender As Object, _
ByVal e As System.EventArgs)
  Dim queueName As String =  ".\private$\test"
  Dim mq As MessageQueue
  If MessageQueue.Exists(queueName) Then
    mq=New MessageQueue(queueName)
  Else
    mq = MessageQueue.Create(queueName)
  End If
  Dim myMessage As System.Messaging.Message = New _
  System.Messaging.Message()
  myMessage.Body = tbMessage.Text
  myMessage.AdministrationQueue = New MessageQueue( _
  ".\private$\test")
  myMessage.AcknowledgeType = _
  AcknowledgeTypes.FullReachQueue or _
  AcknowledgeTypes.FullReceive
  mq.Send(myMessage)
End Sub
```

The preceding code checks for a private queue named \private$\test. If one is not found, a queue is then created. A message is then created, ready for posting to this queue. This message is set to acknowledge reaching the queue (AcknowledgeTypes.FullReachQueue) and reaching the end-recipient (AcknowledgeTypes.FullReceive). Acknowledgments are set to appear in the same test queue.

To test this piece of code, run it from Visual Studio .NET, type some text into the box provided, and press send. On opening Computer Management→Message Queuing→Private Queues→Test, you will notice acknowledgment messages interspersed throughout the list. Acknowledgment messages have a body size of 0 and carry a green circle on the envelope icon (Figure 15.8). The receiver program can recognize acknowledgment messages when a message has its MessageType set to MessageType.Acknowledgment.

Figure 15.8
MSMQ
acknowledgments.

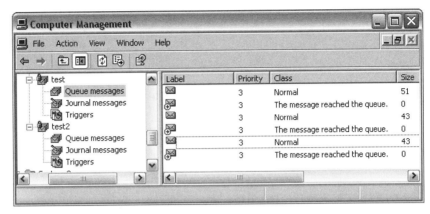

Note: When each message is received, a second acknowledgment message will appear in the queue, labeled "The message was received."

15.4   Timeouts

"Late data is bad data" is an expression that applies particularly to MSMQ. Imagine a scenario in which MSMQ were used to coordinate last-minute hotel bookings. When a client (a hotel) could not be contacted for more than 24 hours after a booking, it would be imperative that alternative action be taken, such as having an operator call the hotel to confirm the booking manually.

Timeouts provide a mechanism to age messages, such that if they do not reach their destination in time, the message can be deleted or moved to a dead-letter queue so that alternative actions can be taken.

In this example, messages are sent with a five-second timeout. This means they will only appear in the queue for five seconds after being sent, before they are either read by a receiving application or discarded to the dead-letter messages queue. This example builds on the preceding example.

Open the preceding example in Visual Studio .NET, and click on the Send button. Then enter the following code:

C#

```
private void btnSend_Click(object sender, System.EventArgs e)
{
    string queueName = ".\\private$\\test";
```

```
MessageQueue mq;
if (MessageQueue.Exists(queueName))
{
  mq=new MessageQueue(queueName);
}
else
{
  mq = MessageQueue.Create(queueName);
}
System.Messaging.Message myMessage = new
System.Messaging.Message();
myMessage.Body = tbMessage.Text;
myMessage.TimeToBeReceived = new TimeSpan(0,0,0,5);
myMessage.UseDeadLetterQueue = true;
mq.Send(myMessage);
}
```

VB.NET

```
Private  Sub btnSend_Click(ByVal sender As Object, ByVal e As
System.EventArgs)
  Dim queueName As String =  ".\private$\test"
  Dim mq As MessageQueue
  If MessageQueue.Exists(queueName) Then
    mq=New MessageQueue(queueName)
  Else
    mq = MessageQueue.Create(queueName)
  End If
  Dim myMessage As System.Messaging.Message = _
  New System.Messaging.Message()
  myMessage.Body = tbMessage.Text
  myMessage.TimeToBeReceived = New TimeSpan(0,0,0,5)
  myMessage.UseDeadLetterQueue = True
  mq.Send(myMessage)
End Sub
```

In this code, the TimeToBeReceived for the message is set to five seconds. A related property TimeToReachQueue can also be used to time-out messages that do not reach the queue in a timely fashion. By setting UseDeadLetterQueue to true, all messages that pass their expiration time are moved into the dead-letter queue for administrative purposes.

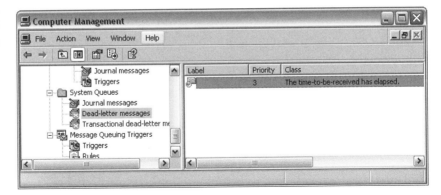

Figure 15.9
*MSMQ message
timeouts.*

To test this piece of code, run it from Visual Studio .NET. Type something into the box provided and press Send. Quickly open Computer Management, and click on the test queue (you may need to right-click and press Refresh). You should see a new message in the list. The messages will disappear again if you refresh the queue after five seconds. Click on System Queues→Dead-letter messages to view expired messages (Figure 15.9).

15.5 Journal

Journaling is where a record is kept of incoming and outgoing messages to and from remote machines. To specify that the message should be recorded in the journal, the UseJournalQueue method is used.

In the following example, you will need to have the message receiver program described earlier in this chapter close at hand. When sending a message that uses the Journal queue, it will only be transferred to that queue once it has been received. This differs from acknowledgment because the body of the message is stored rather than simply flagging an empty message.

Open the preceding example in Visual Studio .NET, and click on the Send button. Then enter the following code:

C#

```
private void btnSend_Click(object sender, System.EventArgs e)
{
  string queueName = ".\\private$\\test";
  MessageQueue mq;
  if (MessageQueue.Exists(queueName))
  {
    mq=new MessageQueue(queueName);
```

```
    }
    else
    {
      mq = MessageQueue.Create(queueName);
    }
    System.Messaging.Message myMessage = new
    System.Messaging.Message();
    myMessage.Body = tbMessage.Text;
    myMessage.UseJournalQueue = true;
    mq.Send(myMessage);
  }
```

VB.NET

```
Private Sub btnSend_Click(ByVal sender As Object, _
ByVal e As System.EventArgs)
  Dim queueName As String =  ".\private$\test"
  Dim mq As MessageQueue
  If MessageQueue.Exists(queueName) Then
    mq=New MessageQueue(queueName)
  Else
    mq = MessageQueue.Create(queueName)
  End If
  Dim myMessage As System.Messaging.Message = _
    New System.Messaging.Message()
  myMessage.Body = tbMessage.Text
  myMessage.UseJournalQueue = True
  mq.Send(myMessage)
End Sub
```

This piece of code creates a queue as before and posts a string as a message to the queue. Because UseJournalQueue is set, the message will be moved to this system queue after it has been received.

To test this piece of code, run it from Visual Studio .NET. Type something into the box provided and press Send. Open Computer Management and look at the test queue to confirm that the message is in the system. Start the message receiver program, and press Listen. The message should appear in the textbox of the receiver program and be removed from the queue. Clicking on System Queues→Journal messages should show the message once again (Figure 15.10).

Figure 15.10
MSMQ, Journal
messages.

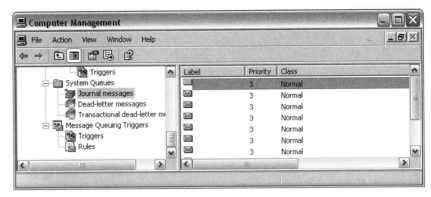

15.6 **Queued Components**

The bulk of the MSMQ code examples to date are very much concerned with the underlying plumbing of sending and receiving messages. You may wish to write code that abstracts away from the underlying MSMQ send & receive mechanisms and concentrate more on business logic.

MSMQ can work in tandem with COM+ component services to provide a means of asynchronous, queued invocation of object methods via Queued Components. In the below example, a component that can perform database updates is created, and a corresponding client is used to call methods on this component. If there were an impermanent connection to this database, then the component may fail during an update, MSMQ handles retries, and queues method calls whenever the component is unavailable.

An example application of the below code is where a database update is required, but is of lower priority than other code which must not be delayed whist waiting for the update to complete.

You may create a queued component by firstly generating a strong name key file by typing sn –k CompPlusServer.snk at the VS.NET command prompt. You can then start a new class library project in Visual Studio .NET, and enter the following code

C#

```
[assembly: ApplicationName("ComPlusServer")]
[assembly: ApplicationActivation(ActivationOption.Server)]
[assembly: AssemblyKeyFile("..\\..\\ComPlusServer.snk")]
[assembly: ApplicationQueuing(Enabled=true,
QueueListenerEnabled=true)]
namespace ComPlusService
```

```csharp
{
    public interface IComPlusServer
    {
        void ExecSQLAsync(string SQL,string strDSN);
    }
    [InterfaceQueuing(Interface="IComPlusServer")]
    public class ComPlusServer : ServicedComponent,
    IComPlusServer
    {
        public void ExecSQLAsync(string SQL,string strDSN)
        {
            OleDbConnection DSN =  new
            OleDbConnection(strDSN);
            DSN.Open();
            OleDbCommand oSQL = new OleDbCommand("",DSN);
            oSQL.CommandText = SQL;
            oSQL.ExecuteNonQuery();
            DSN.Close();
        }
    }
}
```

VB.NET

```vbnet
<assembly: ApplicationName("ComPlusServer")>
<assembly: ApplicationActivation(ActivationOption.Server)>
<assembly: AssemblyKeyFile("..\..\ComPlusServer.snk")>
<assembly: ApplicationQueuing(Enabled := True, _
    QueueListenerEnabled := True)>
Public Interface IComPlusServer
Sub ExecSQLAsync(ByVal SQL As String, ByVal _
    strDSN As String)
End Interface
<InterfaceQueuing([Interface] := "IComPlusServer")>  _
Public Class ComPlusServer
    Inherits ServicedComponent
    Implements ServicedComponent, IComPlusServer
    Public Sub ExecSQLAsync(ByVal SQL As String, _
        ByVal strDSN As String)
        Dim DSN As New OleDbConnection(strDSN)
        DSN.Open()
        Dim oSQL As New OleDbCommand("", DSN)
```

```
            oSQL.CommandText = SQL
            oSQL.ExecuteNonQuery()
            DSN.Close()
        End Sub
    End Class
```

The above code defines an interface, IComPlusServer, which contains a function prototype for the ExecSQLAsync method. The latter method opens a DSN connection to the specified database, executes an insert, update, or delete, and then closes the connection. A limitation of queued components is that they cannot have return values.

You will require the following namespaces at the head of your code.

C#

```
using System;
using System.Reflection;
using System.EnterpriseServices;
using System.Data;
using System.Data.OleDb;
```

VB.NET

```
Imports System
Imports System.Reflection
Imports System.EnterpriseServices
Imports System.Data
Imports System.Data.OleDb
```

In order to use this DLL as a queued component, there are some further steps that must be taken.

1. Import the DLL into the global assembly cache (GAC) by typing gacutil /I:ComPlusService.dll at the command prompt

2. Import the DLL into component services by typing regsvcs ComPlusService.DLL at the command prompt

3. Disable authentication on the component by opening Component Services from Administrative Tools, Expand Computers→My Computer→COM+ Applications. Right Click ComPlusServer, select properties→Security. Uncheck Enforce access checks for this application.

4. Right click ComPlusServer, and click start.

At this point you can now write a client to begin calling methods on this component. Here, we simply create a Windows Forms application in Visual Studio .NET. Add a reference to the ComPlusService DLL created in the previous example, and then draw two textboxes, tbSQL and tbDSN, and a button named btnExecSQL. Double click the button and enter the following code:

C#

```
private void btnExecSQL_Click(object sender, System.EventArgs
e)
{
   ComPlusService.IComPlusServer ComPlusServer = null;
   ComPlusServer = (IComPlusServer)
   Marshal.BindToMoniker
   ("queue:/new:ComPlusService.ComPlusServer");
   ComPlusServer.ExecSQLAsync
     (this.tbSQL.Text,this.tbDSN.Text);
   Marshal.ReleaseComObject(ComPlusServer);
}
```

VB.NET

```
Private Sub btnExecSQL_Click(ByVal sender As Object, _
ByVal e As System.EventArgs) Handles btnExecSQL.Click
  Dim ComPlusServer As ComPlusService.IComPlusServer = _
  Nothing
  ComPlusServer = _
  CType(Marshal.BindToMoniker( _
  "queue:/new:ComPlusService.ComPlusServer"), _
  IComPlusServer)
  ComPlusServer.ExecSQLAsync(Me.tbSQL.Text, Me.tbDSN.Text)
  Marshal.ReleaseComObject(ComPlusServer)
  End Sub
```

The above code does not directly execute the ExecSQLAsync method on the ComPlusService component. Instead it writes an instruction to the ComPlusService queue in MSMQ, which is then read back by component services, which executes the method on the component.

You will need the following namespaces at the head of the code in your application.

Figure 15.11
*Test COM+
Client.*

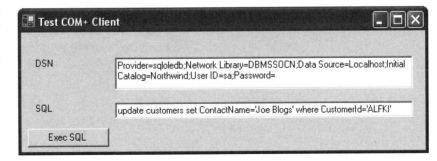

C#

```
using ComPlusService;
using System.Runtime.InteropServices;
```

VB.NET

```
Imports ComPlusService
Imports System.Runtime.InteropServices
```

To test the application, run the client from Visual Studio .NET, type in a valid DSN and SQL statement, then press the 'Execute SQL' button. You will see that the database is updated within a few moments (Figure 15.11). If you temporarily stop the component from component services, and continue to use the client, then the changes will be applied as soon as you restart the component.

15.7 Security

Using MSMQ gives an attacker another point of access to sensitive information. Without encryption and authentication, MSMQ could never be used to handle credit card details or other financial transactions.

To encrypt a message in MSMQ, you set the `UseEncryption` property to `true` before sending the message. This prevents the message from being snooped while in transit, but it is decrypted transparently at the receiving end.

The encryption algorithm can be selected using the `EncryptionAlgorithm` property. This can be set to either RC2 or RC4. The latter is a stream cipher and is thus faster than RC2.

To use authentication in a message in MSMQ, you set the `UseAuthentication` property to `true` before sending the message. This will guarantee to the receiver that the message sender is legitimate, but it does not secure against packet snooping.

The hashing algorithm can be selected using the `HashAlgorithm` property. This can be set to MAC, MD2, MD4, MD5, SHA, or none. The default algorithm is MD5, although MAC (keyed hash) is the most secure.

An authenticated message needs to be accompanied by an external certificate, as contained within the `SenderCertificate` property. An external certificate must be registered with the directory service of MSMQ. An external certificate contains information about the certification authority, the certificate user, the validity period of the certificate, and the public key of the certificate user, the certification authority's signature, and so forth.

In cases where message properties usually set by MSMQ are not suited for a particular application, it is possible to tweak low-level security aspects of MSMQ manually. This includes the `DestinationSymetricKey` property. The latter is simply a byte array used to encrypt and decrypt the message on sending and receipt. The `ConnectorType` property must be set to a genuinely unique identifier (GUID) to access this property.

Low-level authentication properties that can be altered once `ConnectorType` is set are `AuthenticationProviderName`, `AuthenticationProviderType`, and `DigitalSignature`. These methods specify the name, type, and credentials of authentication applied to the message, defaulting to `Microsoft Base Cryptographic Provider, Ver. 1.0`, `RSA_FULL` and a zero-length array, respectively.

Where MSMQ is used over HTTP, it is possible to employ standard Web security systems, such as HTTPS. In this case, the MSMQ server domain name would be prefixed with `https://`.

As shown in chapters 8 and 9, it is easy to use ultrastrong encryption algorithms on strings (and serialized objects). Coupled with the use of X.509 certificates, issued by an internationally trusted certificate authority, strong authentication could be easily applied to message queues.

To illustrate the example based on the previous hotel booking center analogy, imagine that the booking center also forwarded credit card details to the hotelier via MSMQ. The booking center would need to be absolutely sure that when someone dialed into the MSMQ server, it was in fact the hotelier and not a hacker. Furthermore, it would be a disaster if a technically savvy clerk at the hotel could snoop credit card details from the network installed at the hotel.

First, the hotel would need to acquire an X.509 certificate from a certificate authority such as Verisign or Thawte. The certificate containing the private key would remain at the hotel, but the public keyed certificate would be sent to the booking center.

When a phone order arrived at the booking center, a message would be placed in the queue, which would be encrypted with the public key from the certificate. At this point, a hacker could still receive the message, but could not read it; however, a problem still remains because the hotelier would not know whether there was ever a new message or if it had been stolen.

To avoid this situation, the booking center would require an acknowledgment from the hotel that the booking had been received. The acknowledgment would simply be an acknowledgment reference number encrypted with the private key from the certificate. An attacker would not be able to generate this message, so the message could be reposted awaiting pickup from the correct recipient.

15.8 Scalability

When computer systems scale upward, so does the volume of data being sent between them. MSMQ needs to be able to handle larger volumes of data and larger networks, when needed.

Note: When installing an MSMQ server behind a firewall, you will need to ensure that TCP 1801 is open.

MSMQ can consume a lot of disk space; therefore, it may be necessary to ensure that some queues do not grow to a size that they fill the hard disk and prevent other queues from operating. To do this, set the Queue Quota by opening Computer Management, clicking on Message Queuing, and then selecting the queue in question (i.e., Private Queues→test2). Right-click on the queue and select Properties (Figure 15.12). The queue quota is contained in the Limit message storage to (KB): box. The computer quota can be set in the same manner.

Another space-consuming item that is vital to the correct operation of MSMQ is the MQIS database, an internal database that contains queue information and network topology. This is a distributed database, so more than one MSMQ server can hold the data.

Figure 15.12
*MSMQ queue
settings dialog.*

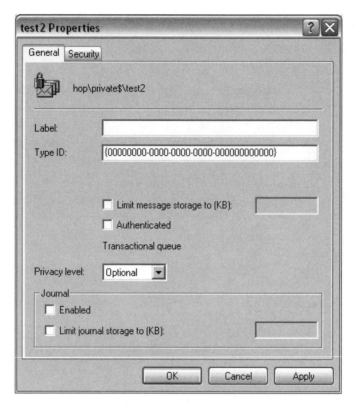

In situations where multiple segments in a network are all interconnected with impermanent connections, multiple MSMQ servers can be
deployed in each segment. A sample case would be an international chain of
shops that centralize their point-of-sale data at the regional office for end-
of-day processing and send it once a week to the head office for auditing.

In MSMQ terminology, the entire chain is called an *enterprise*, each
regional office is a *site*, and every shop is a *client*. The MSMQ server located
in the head office is called the primary enterprise controller (PEC), and the
servers at the regional offices are called Primary Site Controllers (PSCs).
Three other types of MSMQ servers are available: backup site controllers
(BSCs), routing servers, and connector servers.

A BSC requires both a PEC and PSC and stores as a read-only backup
of a PSC's database. This ensures that if the PSC goes offline, clients can
still read from the BSC.

A routing server provides a mechanism to forward messages through
alternate routes if a network connection goes down. To illustrate this feature, envisage two sites, New York and Toronto, and a head office in Dallas.

If the link between Toronto and Dallas is broken, but links between the other cities are still operational, then a routing server could relay messages from New York through Toronto.

A connector server is used as a proxy between MSMQ and third-party messaging systems, such as IBM MQSeries.

The shops can be either dependent clients or independent clients. The difference is that an independent client can store messages locally and forward them to the regional office whenever a connection becomes available. A dependent client requires an always-on connection to the regional office. This may seem disadvantageous, but a dependent client uses less disk space, will run on Windows 95, and becomes one less point of administration

Note: You cannot install an independent client when disconnected to the PSC because it requires access to MQIS data to initialize properly.

15.9 Performance issues

MSMQ can operate in a multitude of ways, from running locally as an interprocess communications (IPC) mechanism for applications or as a complex structure of hundreds of machines working in tandem. MSMQ is an effective IPC mechanism when the messages are sent in the Express format, where messages are held in RAM rather than on disk. This does mean that the data will be erased on power failure, but the applications will also be stopped abruptly, so it shouldn't matter. The only IPC that would outperform MSMQ would be Windows messaging (specifically `WM_COPY`), but this is not an easy undertaking.

When operating MSMQ over a network, it is common for all messages to be stored on disk to ensure that no data is lost in the event of a system failure. These messages are known as *recoverable messages*. They come in two flavors: transactional and nontransactional.

Transactions are carried out as a series of in-memory operations and then committed to disk when the operation is complete. They can be coordinated by MSMQ or by the Microsoft Distributed Transaction Coordinator (MSDTC); the former is the more efficient. Nontransactional messages cannot be rolled back, but they are faster than transactional messages.

When many messages need to be written to a queue in one operation, a higher performance can be achieved if a thread pool is used. This only applies to writing messages to a queue; reading from a queue using multiple threads actually decreases performance. When using threads, it is important to make sure the connection to the MSMQ server is not reopened in every thread, but rather, a connection is shared among all threads.

Where network bandwidth is a concern (e.g., over dial-up connections), actions can be taken to reduce the size of the message body by using binary formatters rather than the default XML formatter.

This can be implemented by setting the `Formatter` property to `New BinaryMessageFormatter()` before calling the Send method. A new feature in MSMQ 3.0 is the use of multicast from within MSMQ. Where a single message is destined for multiple recipients, multicasting can greatly reduce network traffic. This does require access to the MBONE network and, thus, may not be applicable to all situations.

The most common performance problem with MSMQ is handles to queues being repeatedly opened and closed. This process is extremely wasteful, and it is imperative that a handle to the queue should be maintained for as long as possible. A few bytes from each message can be cut by omitting the system identification (SID), but this is only an option if security features are not being used. Another pitfall could be that the client is requesting too many acknowledgments from the server, which may put an unnecessary strain on both the client and server.

15.10 Conclusion

There is little real voodoo behind message queuing, and it would be an easy task to implement a store-and-forward-type proxy server using socket-level programming; however, this chapter is meant to illustrate the advantage of moving to industry-standard techniques by demonstrating the wealth of additional functionality built into MSMQ. After an initial learning curve, MSMQ can easily be seen as a much more scalable solution than any in-house solution developed in the same timeframe.

The next chapter deals with a subject that may not directly impinge on developer's lives now, but by 2005, it is set to overhaul the entire Internet as we know it, and interoperability with it will become a major selling point with future-proof software products.

Make way for IPv6.

16

IPv6: Programming for the Next-generation Internet

16.1   Introduction

IPv6 will be the largest overhaul of the Internet since its commercialization. It is due to arrive in 2005 and will incrementally replace the Internet protocol (IP). Many existing network programs will become obsolete as they become incompatible with the emerging networks. This will inevitably create a great opportunity for network programmers who are familiar with the new protocol.

Such a large overhaul is extremely expensive, but the simple fact is that the IP cannot accommodate the explosion in market demand for Internet access. In the long run, the migration to IPv6 makes perfect sense and is inevitable. IPv6 will create a bigger, faster Internet that will continue to accommodate the world's bandwidth-hungry population into the twenty-second century. Making your application IPv6 compatible from the outset will ensure that you will not have to go through a costly overhaul once IPv6 becomes mainstream.

This chapter is divided into two sections, beginning with a discussion of IPv6 in general and the utilities you can use to manage IPv6 on your network. The chapter concludes with an example of how to communicate over IPv6 from within a .NET application.

16.2   What is IPv6?

IP addresses are 32 bits long, which provides four billion unique addresses. The number of assigned IP addresses is fast approaching this mark. Contributing to this consumption of IP addresses are professionals in the developed world who may have several computers dedicated for their use. The largest source of IP wastage is the way in which addresses are assigned in blocks of 256 or 65,355, which could be hundreds or thousands more addresses than are required by one organization.

IPv6 addresses this issue by extending the address to 128 bits, which provides 3 billion billion billion billion unique addresses. Even if the world's computer usage were to double every year, it would take 100 years for the same problem to occur again.

There is no provision in IPv4 for storing routing information. It is possible for a router to predict the fastest route for a packet many hops in advance, but the IPv4 packet can only hold the next-hop address, so the receiving router has to recalculate the fastest route. This consumes router processing power and delays packets unnecessarily.

IPv6 can hold routing information in its header and can, therefore, be forwarded through routers with minimal time wastage. Furthermore, the header is expandable with optional fields, such that it could hold the routing information the whole way from a computer in Europe to a server in the United States.

IPX was once a strong contender to IP, but it was unfortunately not adopted by router vendors and, thus, cannot be used for Internet communications; however, its unique identifier was based on the hardware (MAC) address and, thus, was easily configurable, with no need for assignation protocols such as DHCP, unlike IP. A MAC address is 48 bits long, and therefore can be contained within the IPv6 address. This then negates the need for ARP and DHCP, thus simplifying the job of the network administrator.

Systems that implement security features, such as HTTP-form authentication, are built on top of IP. This leaves security holes open for people who have the resources to perform IP spoofing (i.e., the impersonation of IP addresses). IPv6 contains built-in headers to protect against IP spoofing, with encryption, authentication, and privacy.

The final difference between IPv6 and IPv4 is the quality-of-service (QoS) provision. In this way, data with absolute priority, such as voice over IP (VOIP) will be forwarded through routers before emails, where it doesn't matter if they're a few seconds late.

16.3 The history of IPv6

In 1993, the IETF issued RFC 1550, "IP: Next Generation (IPng) White Paper Solicitation." This could almost be described as a request for tenders for a replacement of IP. This was followed by a requirements document in RFC 1726, "Technical Criteria for Choosing IP: The Next Generation

(IPng)." In January 1995, the initial specification for IPng, RFC 1752, was issued as "The Recommendations for the IP Next Generation Protocol." Despite the best efforts of the IETF, IPng became commonly known as IPv6 with the release of its final specification in RFC 1883.

The first layer 3 protocol to support large addresses was CLNP, more commonly known as TUBA (TCP and UDP over bigger addresses). This had huge 160-bit addresses and was well-established within certain fields; however, it was inefficient in comparison to IP and lacked the ability to multicast.

In 1993, two new protocols emerged: simple IP (SIP) and policy IP (PIP), both of which were extensions on IP. SIP addressed the scalability issue, proposing a 64-bit address, whereas PIP addressed policy routing for efficiency. The two protocols were merged to form SIPP and extended to 128-bit addressing. The findings were published in 1994. This led to the development of an experimental protocol, IPv5. This protocol was designed to coexist with IPv4, but used the same addressing scheme. When the limitations in IPv5 were addressed, a new protocol, IPv6, emerged.

IPv6 will have knock-on effects to routing and auxiliary protocols such as OSPF, BGP, IDRP, and SNMP. It is predicted that RIP will be replaced by RIP-2 with the rollout of IPv6.

16.4   So what changes?

IPv6 is backward compatible with IPv4, so there will be a gradual migration toward the technology. When the last block of IP addresses is assigned, organizations will be given the chance to use IPv6 instead. This may involve buying more expensive IPv6-compatible routers, hubs, and switches. The higher-level protocols, such as TCP and UDP, will not change, although some higher-level protocols may have some compatibility problems (e.g., the PASV command in FTP).

Many applications designed for IPv4 will not work on IPv6, producing a market void in IPv6-compatible software. Because some large firms, such as Microsoft, IBM, and Digital Equipment Corporation (DEC), have developed their own IPv6 implementation, it is unlikely that the changeover will affect their software.

The first and most obvious difference is the change in the format of the IP address. IPv6 addresses consist of a combination of six identifiers: (1) a 3-bit format prefix (FP), which is always 001 for aggregatable unicast addresses; (2) the 13-bit top-level aggregator (TLA), which would be a number assigned to a backbone service provider; (3) an 8-bit reserved field, set to 0; (4) the 24-bit next-level aggregator (NLA), which would represent an ISP; (5) the 16-bit site-level aggregator (SLA), which would represent the subnet; and (6) the 64-bit interface ID, which identifies a specific interface on a host. The definitive description of this format is described in RFC 2374.

A global IPv6 address, therefore, takes the following form:

`[FP][TLA]:[Reserved][NLA]:[SLA]:[Interface ID]`

16.5   IPv6 naming conventions

With Ipv4 addresses, it was practical to write each byte in decimal format, such as `195.233.254.33`; however, with a 128-bit address, it becomes awkward to write 16 three-digit numbers to represent a single IP address. Therefore, a new naming convention is used to quote IPv6 addresses. IPv6 addresses are quoted in hexadecimal, not decimal. They are broken into 16-bit segments, rather than 8 bits, as was the case with IPv4. Therefore, one would write `FFFF:FFFF` rather than `255.255.255.255`.

To abbreviate long sequences of zeros, the double colon (`::`) is used. Sequential blocks of 16 zero bits are replaced with the double colon for brevity. The IPv6 address `2001:0db8:1000:0000:0000:0000:0000:0027` is abbreviated to `2001:db8:1000::27`.

When an IPv6 address encapsulates an IPv4 address, the IPv4 address is represented in its standard form within the IPv6 address. An example of this would be `::192.44.75.70 ::ffff:192.44.75.70`.

In order to separate the IPv6 prefix from the IPv6 interface identifier, it is common practice to append a forward slash followed by the length of the prefix to the end of an IPv6 address. For example, in the case of

`2001:db8:2000:240:290:27ff:fe24:c19f/64,`

the prefix is

`2001:db8:2000:240.`

16.6 Installing IPv6

If you have Windows XP, you can install IPv6 by simply typing `IPv6 install` at the command prompt. To test IPv6 on Windows 2000 (Service Pack 1) or later, you need to download an add-on from *www.microsoft.com/ windowsserver2003/technologies/ipv6/default.mspx*. You will need an Ethernet Network adapter, and TCP/IP must be installed.

To install IPv6 on Windows 2000, follow these steps:

1. Download the add-on from Microsoft.com.

2. Click Start→Settings→Network and Dial-up Connections.

3. Right-click on your Ethernet card and click Properties.

4. Click Install.

5. In the Select Network Component Type box, click Protocol and then click Add.

6. In the Select Network Protocol box, click Microsoft IPv5 Protocol.

7. Click OK and then Close.

To install IPv6 on previous versions of Windows, links to third-party vendors are located at *www.ipv6.com*.

To uninstall IPv6 from a host, in Windows XP, you simply type `Ipv6 uninstall` at the command line and reboot the computer.

16.6.1 Auto configuration

Similar to the loopback address in IPv4 (`127.0.0.1`), you will always be given an IP address whether you are online or not. In IPv6, the equivalent of the loopback address is the link-local address. This is `FE80::1`.

Non-link-local addresses, such as site-local addresses or global addresses, are automatically assigned based on the receipt of IPv6 router advertisements (akin to DHCP in IPv4). An IPv6-compatible router is required to issue router advertisements.

16.7   Using IPv6 utilities

If you have Windows XP, you will be happy to know that several handy IPv6 utilities come preinstalled, which is helpful for implementing IPv6 applications.

16.7.1   IPv6

IPv6 is a command-line-based utility that is similar, in some ways, to `ipconfig`. To use this application in a meaningful way, you should install the IPv6 protocol thus:

```
IPv6 install
```

After a few seconds, it should report "succeeded." At this point, you can view your IPv6 address and other technical information about the IPv6 stack. You will be allocated several interfaces, through which you can access the Internet. This includes the physical network interface and hybrid interfaces. You can list the interfaces on your system by typing the following:

```
IPv6 if
```

To specify an interface, you can type `IPv6 if <number>`, such as in Figure 16.1, where interface 4 was a network card.

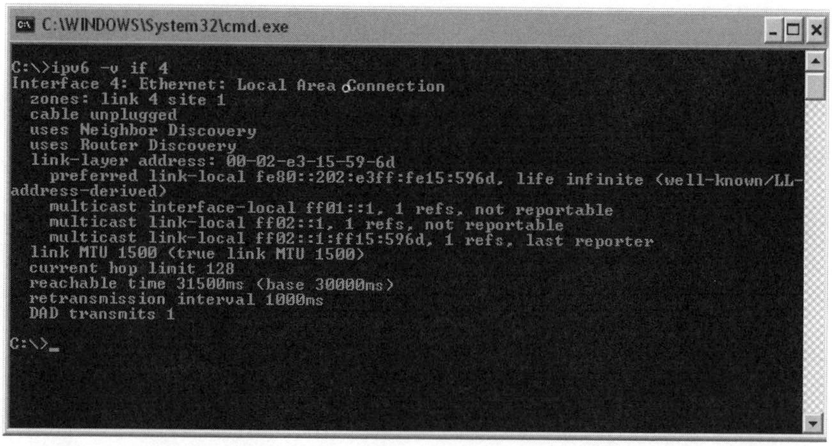

Figure 16.1
IPv6 MS-DOS utility.

```
C:\WINDOWS\System32\cmd.exe

C:\>ipv6 -v if 4
Interface 4: Ethernet: Local Area Connection
  zones: link 4 site 1
  cable unplugged
  uses Neighbor Discovery
  uses Router Discovery
  link-layer address: 00-02-e3-15-59-6d
    preferred link-local fe80::202:e3ff:fe15:596d, life infinite (well-known/LL-
address-derived)
    multicast interface-local ff01::1, 1 refs, not reportable
    multicast link-local ff02::1, 1 refs, not reportable
    multicast link-local ff02::1:ff15:596d, 1 refs, last reporter
  link MTU 1500 (true link MTU 1500)
  current hop limit 128
  reachable time 31500ms (base 30000ms)
  retransmission interval 1000ms
  DAD transmits 1

C:\>_
```

Global configuration parameters for the IPv6 stack can be viewed by typing `IPv6 gp`. A typical response would be:

```
DefaultCurHopLimit = 128
UseAnonymousAddresses = yes
MaxAnonDADAttempts = 5
MaxAnonLifetime = 7d/24h
AnonRegenerateTime = 5s
MaxAnonRandomTime = 10m
AnonRandomTime = 2m21s
NeighborCacheLimit = 8
RouteCacheLimit = 32
BindingCacheLimit = 32
ReassemblyLimit = 262144
MobilitySecurity = on
```

To view the prefix policy table for the IPv6 stack, you can use `IPv6 ppt`, typical response being the following:

```
::ffff:0:0/96 -> precedence 10 srclabel 4 dstlabel 4
::/96 -> precedence 20 srclabel 3 dstlabel 3
2002::/16 -> precedence 30 srclabel 2 dstlabel 2
::/0 -> precedence 40 srclabel 1 dstlabel 1
::1/128 -> precedence 50 srclabel 0 dstlabel 0
```

16.7.2 NETSH

This useful utility can be used to read information from the IPv6 stack, as well as to perform many of the tasks of the previous utility. It is more user-friendly than the `IPv6` utility and provides much the same level of information (Figure 16.2).

To view your IPv6 address using NETSH, type the following at the command line:

```
Netsh interface ipv6 show address
```

16.7.3 Ping6

There are no prizes for guessing what *ping6* does. It is simply an IPv6 implementation of the *ping* utility. It is a stripped-down version of ping, but it uses IPv6 addresses rather than IPv4 addresses (Figure 16.3). Parameters that are not supported by the *Ping6* utility (but not necessarily IPv6)

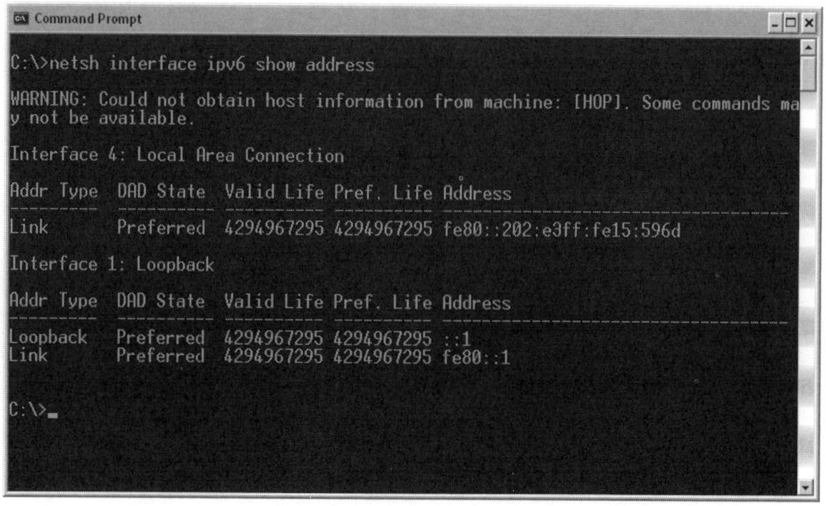

Figure 16.2
*NETSH MS-DOS
utility.*

are TTL, fragment flag, type of service (TOS), and loose and strict routing.
The parameters that are supported are listed in Table 16.1.

Table 16.1   *Command-line parameters for Ping6.*

Parameter	Purpose
`-t`	Pings the host until the user presses CTRL + C
`-a`	Resolves IP addresses to host names
`-n <count>`	Sends a specified number of pings
`-l`	Sends buffer size; default is 32 bytes
`-r`	Uses the routing header to test the reverse route as well as the forward route
`-s <address>`	Uses the specified source address in the ping requests
`-w <milliseconds>`	Discards any replies delayed longer than the specified time

16.7.4   Tracert6

This program is a migration of the *tracert* utility from IPv4 to IPv6 (Figure
16.4). Some command-line parameters have changed from the original version, including the j, s, and r command-line parameters. Like *ping6,*

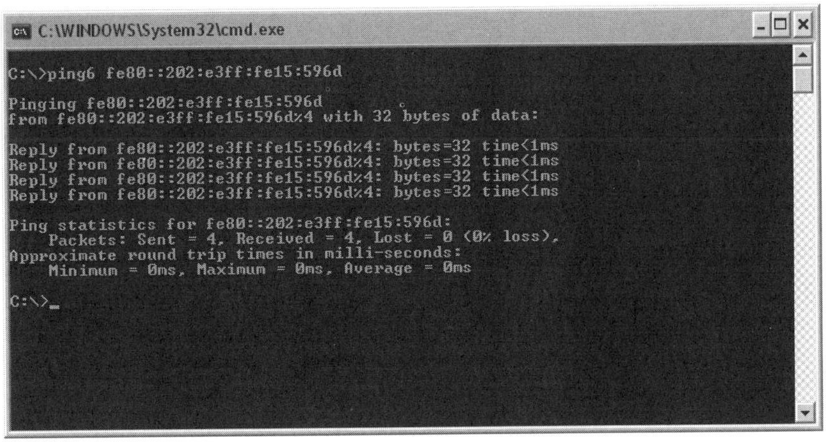

Figure 16.3
*Ping6 MS-DOS
utility.*

tracert6 no longer supports loose and strict routing (j parameter), although
it does support the parameters in Table 16.2.

Table 16.2   *Command-line parameters for Tracert6.*

Parameter	Purpose
-d	Suppresses the resolving of IP addresses to domain names
-h <hops>	Specifies the maximum number of hops between source and destination
-w <milliseconds>	Discards any replies delayed longer than the specified time
-s	Uses the specified source address in the ping requests
-r	Uses the routing header to test the reverse route as well as the forward route

16.7.5   IPSec6

IPSec6 is a utility that manages IP-level security. This is a long-awaited
security feature that effectively makes it impossible for hackers to forge IP
addresses. To view the security policies on your system, you can type
IPSec6 sp at the command prompt. This displays the contents of the
IPSec6 security policies database (illustrated in Figure 16.5; described in
Table 16.3). You can also view the security associations database (Table
16.4) by typing IPSec6 sa at the command prompt.

Figure 16.4
*Tracert6 MS-DOS
utility.*

Table 16.3   *Fields in the IPv6 security policies database.*

Field	Purpose
Policy	An identifier for the policy, similar to a primary key in a database
RemoteIPAddr	The IP address from which the packet has originated
LocalIPAddr	The IP address at which the packet is arriving
Protocol	The higher-level protocol in use
RemotePort	The port from which the packet came
LocalPort	The port at which the packet arrived
IPSecProtocol	The version of the IPSec protocol in use; default is NONE
IPSecMode	The mode of operation of IPSec
RemoteGWIPAddr	The remote gateway IP address
SABundleIndex	The security association bundle index; default is NONE
Direction	The direction of travel of the packet. The default is BIDIRECT
Action	The action to be taken on any particular packet; default is BYPASS
InterfaceIndex	The interface on which the packet arrives

Figure 16.5
*IPSec6 MS-DOS
utility.*

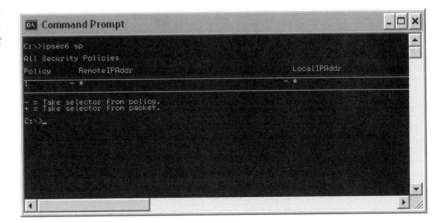

Note: The default for all fields is * (all) unless otherwise specified.

Table 16.4 *Fields in the IPv6 security associations database.*

Field	Purpose
SAEntry	An identifier for the policy, similar to a primary key in a database
DestIPAddr	The destination IP address of the packet
SrcIPAddr	The source IP address of the packet
Protocol	The higher-level protocol in use
DestPort	The destination port of the packet
SrcPort	The source port of the packet
AuthAlg	The authorization algorithm in use
KeyFile	The symmetric or public key in use
Direction	The direction of travel of the packet
SecPolicyIndex	The security policy index

16.7.6 Windows 2000 specific

The IPv6 implementation comes with some extra utilities, such as *6to4cfg*
and *checkv4*. The first of those two utilities is for use on hybrid IPv6/IPv4
networks. The latter is used to help migrate C++ Windows socket code to

IPv6 compliance. C++ network programming code was concerned mainly with interfacing directly into wsock32.dll, which luckily C# or VB.NET programmers are not obliged to do.

16.8   IPv6 routing

Every device that runs IPv6 will maintain a routing table, opposed to all routing information being stored in routers. It is logical that PCs should provide some of the processing power to route packets, rather than leaving it up to routers.

When a router encounters an IPv6 packet, it will match the destination IPv6 address with entries in the destination cache to determine the next-hop address and forwarding interface. If no matching entry is found in the cache, then the destination IPv6 address is compared against the prefixes in the routing table. The closest match with the lowest cost (as determined from the preference or metrics field) is used.

A routing table consists of eight different fields:

- The *address prefix*, similar to a subnet mask, will match specific IPv6 addresses to particular routes. The prefix can be any length between 0 to 128 bits long. This column is named Prefix in the Windows XP routing table.

- The *network interface* for each prefix contains an index of the interface over which the packet should be retransmitted. This column is named Idx in the Windows XP routing table.

- The *next-hop address* holds the IPv6 address of the host or router to which the packet is to be forwarded. This column is named Gateway/ Interface Name in the Windows XP routing table.

- A *preference or metric for any particular route* is used to provide routers with a means to select what route to send packets when two routes are available. The preference value could be set manually to reduce the cost of bandwidth billable connections.

- The *route lifetime* is an optional field that can be used to provide for automatic routing cache purges.

- The *availability of a routing advertisement* is, once again, an optional field, but it can be used to determine if the connecting network is IPv6 compliant.

- The *aging of the route* is an optional field that aids in keeping router caches up to date.

- The *type of route* is an optional field that can determine if a destination is directly attached, remote, an endpoint host, or the default route.

The routing table is constructed automatically and does not require manual input, in the same way as the ARP cache of IPv4 computers is not accessible to users. It is not mandatory for every IPv6 device to maintain a routing table; in fact, it is quite likely that many computers will store only the default route (::/0, i.e., an IPv6 address consisting only of zeros) to the nearest router.

To go into a little more detail on the route type field, four different types of routes can be stored in the routing table: directly attached, remote, endpoint host, or the default route. It can be estimated from the route type how far the destination is from the router.

A *directly attached route* is where a subnet is physically attached to the router. In this case, the prefix length would typically be 64 bits, and the distance between the router and the destination would typically only be two hops.

A *remote route* is where the packet is forwarded to a subnet or address space that is not physically connected. In this case, the prefix would be 64 bits or less, and the distance to the destination would typically be over two hops.

A *host route* is where the packet is being routed to an endpoint host, such as a computer. In this case, the prefix length is 128 bits long, and the distance would typically be one hop or less.

16.8.1 **Route determination process**

When the sending host does not specify the source address, then the entire routing table is checked for matches. If a source address is specified, then only entries for interfaces designated to handle that source address are checked.

The IPv6 destination address is compared against each entry in the table, looking for matches between the prefix and the high-order bits in the IPv6 destination address. Where a prefix is only 64 bits long, and therefore shorter than the IPv6 address, only the highest 64 bits of the IPv6 address are relevant for this comparison process.

If there is more than one match between the IPv6 destination addresses and the prefixes held in the routing table, the prefix with the longest length is selected. When two matching prefixes have the same length, the route with the lowest cost (as determined from the metrics or preference field) is selected. The default route is used only in the case where there are no successful matches.

The route selection provides a next-hop address and a forwarding interface. In the case where the next-hop address is not the endpoint host, but another router, then the next-hop address is stored in the next-hop address field in the packet.

In the case where the destination host or subnet is unreachable, then the router returns an ICMPv6 packet to the sender of the packet, stating that the host was unreachable. This is analogous to the action of ICMP in IPv4.

16.8.2 Administering the IPv6 routing table

The IPv6 routing table is mostly self-maintaining. It builds entries from routing advertisements from other routers and phases out out-of-date or out-of-service routes over time. In the case where the network infrastructure has changed significantly, however, or for experimentation purposes, it may be necessary to configure the routing table of an IPv6 router manually, or in this case, a Windows XP server running the Internet connection sharing (ICS) service.

To show the IPv6 routing table (Figure 16.6) on your PC, type the following at the command line:

```
netsh interface ipv6 show routes
```

If any routes are stored in the routing table, information will follow the form described in Table 16.5.

Assume that you wish to add a route to the routing table, where you want packets with a destination IPv6 address starting with 3ffe to be forwarded to the loopback address (fe80::1). For debugging purposes, we can name this route a. Therefore, you may use the following syntax:

```
netsh interface ipv6 add route 3ffe::/16 "a" fe80::1
```

Figure 16.6
IPv6 routing table.

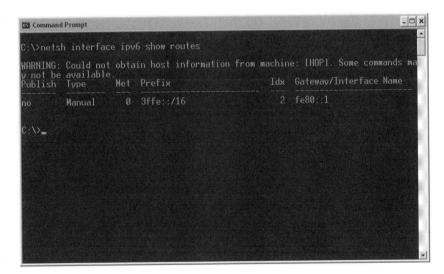

```
C:\>netsh interface ipv6 show routes

WARNING: Could not obtain host information from machine: [HOP]. Some commands ma
y not be available.
Publish  Type      Met  Prefix                      Idx  Gateway/Interface Name
-------  ----      ---  ------                      ---  ----------------------
no       Manual    0    3ffe::/16                   2    fe80::1


C:\>_
```

Table 16.5 *Fields in the IPv6 routing table.*

Field	Purpose
Publish	Specifies whether the route is advertised in a routing advertisement message.
Met	Specifies the metric or preference used to select between multiple routes with the same prefix. The lowest metric is the best matching route.
Prefix	Specifies the address prefix; it can have a length between 0 and 128 bits.
Idx	Specifies the interface index, over which packets that match the address prefix may be transferred. Interface indexes can be viewed by typing `netsh interface ipv6 show interface` at the command prompt.
Gateway/Interface Name	Specifies either an interface name or a next-hop IPv6 address. Remote network routes list a next-hop IPv6. Directly attached network routes list the name of the relevant interface.
Type	Specifies the type of the route. Routes configured by user applications are listed with a route type of `Manual`. Routes configured by the IPv6 protocol are listed with a route type of `Autoconf`.

To remove this link, you can use the following command:

```
netsh interface ipv6 delete route 3ffe::/16 "a" fe80::1
```

The IPv6 addresses assigned to interfaces can also be changed. Extra IPv6 addresses can be added to each interface if required. To give a quick example, if you ping6 the IPv6 address `fe80::10`, it will fail, but if the address is assigned to your local computer thus:

```
netsh interface ipv6 add address "loopback" fe80::10
```

if you ping6 `fe80::10`, the ping will succeed because your computer is now multihomed with a second IPv6 address. To remove this address, you can use the command:

```
netsh interface ipv6 delete address "loopback" fe80::10
```

16.8.3   IPv6 routing advertisements

As previously mentioned, the IPv6 routing table is generally populated from received advertisements from other routers. These advertisements contain information about the advertising router's subnet and optional information such as the prefix information option and the route information option.

The prefix information option is described definitively in RFC 2461. It provides the receiving router with the address prefix from which the auto-configured addresses derive.

The route information option is specified in an Internet draft entitled "Default Router Preferences and More-Specific Routes." This optional data contains prefix and routing information for subnets accessible from the advertising router. This provides a redundancy mechanism, such that if the router that sent the advertisement ever goes offline, it may still be possible to communicate with subnets behind that router if an alternative route exists.

A Windows XP machine will not send routing advertisements on the network by default, but it can be set to do so with the following command:

```
netsh interface ipv6 set interface <interface id>
forwarding=enabled advertise=enabled
```

where the interface ID can be determined from the following command, under the `Idx` field:

```
Netsh interface ipv6 show interface
```

16.9 IPv6 coexistence

IPv6 will not replace IPv4 overnight. Instead, there will be a considerable period when both IPv6 and IPv4 will coexist on the Internet. In time, IPv4 will be phased out entirely. This transitional period is important for developers of mass-market software where the network infrastructure of the end-user can be one of several different hybrid systems.

IPv6 deployment will take place in a much more organized way than the MBONE project did. The ad hoc deployment of MBONE created islands of multicast supporting infrastructure and left entire countries with no access to multicast networks. With IPv6, networks that have not yet migrated to IPv6 will still be capable of transporting IPv6 data, once it is encapsulated within IPv4 packets.

The encapsulation of IPv6 data within IPv4 packets can take place using one of two mechanisms: the intrasite automatic tunnel addressing protocol (ISATAP) or 6to4. The crucial difference between these two systems is the IPv4 address that each uses to represent the destination. An IPv6 address consists of an interface and subnet identifier. With 6to4, this subnet identifier is created from a public IPv4 address, whereas ISATAP uses a local IPv4 address to create the subnet identifier. Regardless of the mechanism used, the IPv4 packet will contain enough information to determine the source and destination of the packet. Having said that, there will be designated pockets of the Internet that natively support IPv6, known as the 6bone. This region of the Internet will support more efficient and faster transfer of IPv6 data, but IPv6 accessibility will not be limited only to this region.

16.9.1 The 6to4 protocol

The 6to4 mechanism is an elegant solution to ferry IPv6 data across IPv4 networks. It is described definitively in RFC 3056. Although hosts employing 6to4 address assignment would not require any manual configuration, it is likely that 6to4-compliant routers will require some level of configuration.

6to4 generates a global IPv6 address from an IPv4 address by suffixing the IPv4 address with a global address prefix (2002 hex), appending the

IPv4 address, and retaining the subnet and interface identifier. This creates an IPv6 address of the form:

```
2002 : HIGH IPv4 : LOW IPv4 : SUBNET : INTERFACE
```

where high IPv4 is the high-order 16 bits from the IPv4 address and low IPv4 is the low-order 16 bits from the IPv4 address. This type of address is not suited to multicast applications.

The high 64 bits of the 6to4 address (which includes the subnet) are used to provide routing information between 6to4-compliant routers. Routers advertise this route to other routers within the IPv6 intranet and also to 6to4 routers outside the network.

Any 6to4 network traffic that does not belong within the intranet is forwarded to a router on the border of the intranet. This data then has to be encapsulated into an IPv4 packet because non-IPv6-compliant routers would simply discard native IPv6 packets. The 6to4 router would extract the IPv4 address from the IPv6 address and use it in the header to direct the packet.

In Windows XP, the 6to4 service is included with the IPv6 protocol. This service can be administered from Administrative Tools→Services→ 6to4. This service automatically generates 6to4 addresses for all IPv4 addresses assigned to the local computer. It also provides a facility to encapsulate IPv6 packets with IPv4 headers when required and attempts to locate a 6to4 relay router on the Internet using a DNS query.

If ICS were enabled on that computer, as it would be with many home or small office networks, the computer will enable IPv6 forwarding on the private interface and broadcast router advertisements, such that any other IPv6 hosts on the network could communicate natively. This effectively configures that computer to become a 6to4 router.

Note: Technically, neither the ICS nor 6to4 service provides IPv4/IPv6 address translation, but for all practical purposes, it can be seen as such.

In situations where you cannot or do not want to run ICS on the server, it is possible to configure the machine as a 6to4 router without using ICS. In order to configure the computer as a 6to4 router, it must have a publicly accessible IPv4 address and must not have a 6to4 pseudointerface in its routing table. A 6to4 pseudointerface is created when a host computer receives a routing advertisement from an IPv6 or ISATAP router. This generates an entry in the routing table, prefixed `2002::/16` and pointing to a 6to4 relay router on the IPv4 Internet.

Enable forwarding and advertising on all interfaces connected to the Internet, and enable forwarding on the 6to4 pseudointerface using the following command (with the interface ID substituted accordingly):

```
netsh interface ipv6 set interface <interface id>
forwarding=enabled advertise=enabled
```

Add routes to the 6to4 pseudointerface using the following command (with interface ID, subnet ID, and the IPv4 address substituted accordingly):

```
Netsh interface ipv6 add route 2002:<High bytes IPv4>:<Low
bytes IPv4>:<Subnet ID>::/64 <interface ID> publish=yes
```

The subnet ID is, by convention, the index of the interface being used, but it can be any two-byte hex number.

16.9.2   The ISATAP protocol

ISATAP serves much the same purpose as 6to4 in providing a means to transport IPv6 data over the existing IPv4 architecture. It has not gained the same level of support as 6to4, but it still remains a valid and usable technology. An ISATAP address uses the following form:

```
::0:5EFE:[IPv4 Address]
```

The ISATAP address can be combined with an IPv6 prefix, including 6to4 prefixes if required. Again, ISATAP is not suited to multicast applications.

On Windows XP, the ISATAP address for each local interface is automatically configured. This address enables ISATAP hosts to communicate over IPv4 within the same intranet. To allow communication over the Internet, the host must have previously received a router advertisement from the border router from the foreign network. Once this advertisement has been received, the host can then determine other ISATAP addresses from within that network.

ISATAP uses an IPv4 address to derive the interface ID. Because it defeats the purpose to have the uniqueness of an IPv6 address depend on the availability of a unique IPv4 address, it is possible to have two identical ISATAP interface IDs for two hosts in separate sites because they would both have different IPv6 addresses, thanks to the unique subnet ID.

To configure a computer as an ISATAP router, it must have at least two LAN connections, one of which is connected to the IPv6 network and another connected to the IPv4 network. The first step in configuring a Windows XP machine as an ISATAP router is to enable forwarding on all interfaces connected to the Internet and enable both forwarding and advertising on the automatic tunneling pseudointerface, using the following command (with the interface ID substituted accordingly):

```
netsh interface ipv6 set interface <interface id>
forwarding=enabled advertise=enabled
```

Add routes to the automatic tunneling pseudointerface using the following command (with interface ID, subnet ID, and the IPv4 address substituted accordingly):

```
Netsh interface ipv6 add route 2002:<High bytes IPv4>:<Low
bytes IPv4>:<Subnet ID>::/64 <interface ID> publish=yes
```

Add a default route to the physical LAN interface using the following command (with interface ID and the IPv6 address substituted accordingly):

```
Netsh interface ipv6 add route ::/0 <interface id>
nexthop=<IPv6> publish=yes
```

ISATAP hosts use DNS to discover the ISATAP router by resolving the name ISATAP (Windows Server 2003) or _ISATAP (Windows XP). It is therefore necessary either to name the router computer ISATAP or to enter the record into the local DNS server(s). If this cannot be done, you must run the following command on all ISATAP hosts and the router computer itself:

```
Netsh interface ipv6 isatap set state router=<IPv4 Address>
```

16.9.3   The 6over4 protocol

6over4 and 6to4 are similar protocols, but they are different in some significant respects. They are both used to ferry IPv6 data over IPv4 networks; however, 6over4 is designed for use in multicast environments, unlike 6to4 or ISATAP. 6over4 is defined definitively in RFC 2529.

6over4 is disabled by default on Windows XP, but it can be enabled with the command line (substituting the IPv4 address with that of the local computer):

```
netsh interface ipv6 add 6over4tunnel "6over4" <ipv4 address>
```

From this point, 6over4 can be configured in an identical way to ISATAP; however, it should be noted that the underlying IPv4 network must already support multicasting for IPv6 multicasting to be functional.

16.10 IPv6 in .NET

IPv6 is supported in version 1.1 of .NET. Migrating code to support IPv6 isn't difficult. All that is required is a new parameter to be passed to the socket constructor `AddressFamily.InterNetworkV6`. Locally bound endpoints are created differently, too, using `IPAddress.IPv6Any` as the loopback address.

Support for IPv6 in .NET 1.1 is disabled by default, so before you can begin programming, you need to adjust the configuration for .NET. Using a text editor, open the `machine.config` file, located in the `C:\WINDOWS\Microsoft.NET\Framework\v1.1.4322` folder. Replace the XML `<!--<ipv6 enabled="false "/> -->` with `<ipv6 enabled="true"/>`.

The following example demonstrates how to transmit some text via TCP/IPv6. There are two parts to this example: a client and a server. We shall start by first implementing the server. Create a new project in Visual Studio .NET. Draw a textbox on the form, named `tbMessages`, with `multiline` set to `true`.

First, add a public variable named `port`. This variable will hold the port number on which the server will listen:

C#

```
public class Form1 : System.Windows.Forms.Form
{
```

```
public static int port;
```

VB.NET

```
Public Class Form1
    Inherits System.Windows.Forms.Form
    Public Shared port As Integer
```

This server is dual threaded, where the main thread is used to keep the UI responsive, and a secondary "worker" thread is used to accept and handle incoming connections. This server would be incapable of handling more than one connection at a time. In the form Load event, the port is set to 9999, and the worker thread is started.

C#

```
private void Form1_Load(object sender, System.EventArgs e)
{
  port = 9999;
  Thread thdListener = new Thread(new ThreadStart(listener));
  thdListener.Start();
}
```

VB.NET

```
Private Sub Form1_Load(ByVal sender As System.Object, _
ByVal e As System.EventArgs) Handles MyBase.Load
  port = 9999
  Dim thdListener As Thread = New Thread( _
        New ThreadStart(AddressOf listener))
  thdListener.Start()
End Sub
```

The Listener function works by binding a socket to the IPv6 loopback address on port 9999. It uses Socket.SupportsIPv6 to determine if the .NET run time is capable of handling IPv6. If so, the socket is bound to the address and begins listening. Once a connection is received, a new socket is created, which will read data from the network in 256-byte chunks. It outputs all data to the screen immediately. Once there is no more data, both sockets close, and the server will no longer accept connections.

C#

```
public void listener()
{
```

```csharp
Socket sckListener;
Socket clientSocket;
IPEndPoint ipepLocal =
new IPEndPoint(IPAddress.IPv6Any, port);
byte[] RecvBytes = new byte[Byte.MaxValue];
Int32 bytes;
if(!Socket.SupportsIPv6)
{
  MessageBox.Show("Cannot support IPv6");
  return;
}
sckListener = new Socket(
AddressFamily.InterNetworkV6, SocketType.Stream,
ProtocolType.Tcp
);
sckListener.Bind(ipepLocal);
sckListener.Listen(0);
clientSocket = sckListener.Accept();
while(true)
{
  bytes = clientSocket.Receive(RecvBytes);
  if (bytes<=0) break;
  tbMessages.Text += Encoding.ASCII.GetString(RecvBytes);
}
tbMessages.Text += "\n";
clientSocket.Close();
sckListener.Close();
}
```

VB.NET

```vbnet
Public Sub listener()
  Dim sckListener As Socket
  Dim clientSocket As Socket
  Dim ipepLocal As IPEndPoint = New _
    IPEndPoint(IPAddress.IPv6Any, port)
  Dim RecvBytes() As Byte = New Byte(Byte.MaxValue) {}
  Dim bytes As Int32
  If (Not Socket.SupportsIPv6) Then
    MessageBox.Show("Cannot support IPv6")
    Return
  End If
```

```
    sckListener = New Socket( _
     AddressFamily.InterNetworkV6, SocketType.Stream, _
        ProtocolType.Tcp)
    sckListener.Bind(ipepLocal)
    sckListener.Listen(0)
    clientSocket = sckListener.Accept()
    Do
       bytes = clientSocket.Receive(RecvBytes)
       If bytes <= 0 Then Exit Do
       tbMessages.Text += Encoding.ASCII.GetString(RecvBytes)
    Loop
    tbMessages.Text += vbCrLf
    clientSocket.Close()
    sckListener.Close()
End Sub
```

You will also need to add the following namespaces to your code:

C#

```
using System.Net;
using System.Net.Sockets;
using System.Threading;
using System.Text;
```

VB.NET

```
Imports System.Net
Imports System.Net.Sockets
Imports System.Threading
Imports System.Text
```

Once the server is written, let us turn our attention to implementing the client. Open a new project in Visual Studio .NET. Draw two textboxes on the form: tbIPv6Addr and tbMessage. Then add a button named btnSend.

First, add a public variable named port. This variable will hold the port number, on which the server will listen:

C#

```
public class Form1 : System.Windows.Forms.Form
{
   public static int port;
```

VB.NET

```
Public Class Form1
    Inherits System.Windows.Forms.Form
    Public Shared port As Integer
```

As in the server, the port needs to be set to 9999. This is set from within the form Load event.

C#

```
private void Form1_Load(object sender, System.EventArgs e)
{
  port = 9999;
}
```

VB.NET

```
Private Sub Form1_Load(ByVal sender As System.Object, _
  ByVal e As System.EventArgs) Handles MyBase.Load
  port = 9999
End Sub
```

Now, double-click on the Send button, and enter the code below. This works by creating a socket with an address type of IPv6. This socket establishes a connection with the remote server in the normal way and transfers the string by converting it to a byte array.

C#

```
private void btnSend_Click(object sender, System.EventArgs e)
{
  byte[] msg;
  if(!Socket.SupportsIPv6)
  {
    MessageBox.Show("Cannot support IPv6");
    return;
  }
  IPAddress ipAddrv6 = IPAddress.Parse(tbIPv6Addr.Text);
  IPEndPoint ipEPv6 = new IPEndPoint(ipAddrv6, port);
  Socket socket = new Socket(
   AddressFamily.InterNetworkV6, SocketType.Stream,
   ProtocolType.Tcp
  );
```

```
    socket.Connect(ipEPv6);
    msg = Encoding.ASCII.GetBytes(tbMessage.Text);
    socket.Send(msg);
    socket.Close();
}
```

VB.NET

```
Private Sub btnSend_Click(ByVal sender As System.Object, _
 ByVal e As System.EventArgs) Handles btnSend.Click
  Dim msg() As Byte
  If Not Socket.SupportsIPv6 Then
    MessageBox.Show("Cannot support IPv6")
    Return
  End If
  Dim ipAddrv6 As IPAddress = _
  IPAddress.Parse(tbIPv6Addr.Text)
  Dim ipEPv6 As IPEndPoint = New IPEndPoint(ipAddrv6, port)
  Dim ipv6Socket As Socket
  ipv6Socket = New Socket( _
   AddressFamily.InterNetworkV6, SocketType.Stream, _
     ProtocolType.Tcp)
  ipv6Socket.Connect(ipEPv6)
  msg = Encoding.ASCII.GetBytes(tbMessage.Text)
  ipv6Socket.Send(msg)
  ipv6Socket.Close()
End Sub
```

You will also need to add the following namespaces to your code:

C#

```
using System.Net;
using System.Net.Sockets;
using System.Text;
```

VB.NET

```
Imports System.Net
Imports System.Net.Sockets
Imports System.Text
```

To test this example, run the server from Visual Studio .NET. Find the IPv6 address of the server computer, using the `Ipv6 if` command. If you are

Figure 16.7
TCP/IPv6 client and server.

using only one computer, then this is FE80::1. Now run the client program, enter the server IPv6 address into the box provided, and type a message into the second box. Press Send, and the message should appear in the text window of the server, as depicted in Figure 16.7.

16.11 Conclusion

IPv6 compliance may not be a big issue today, but in the near future it will be key and may be an absolute requirement in certain software products. This chapter should provide enough information for you to set up an experimental IPv6 network and provide a test platform for IPv6 compliance in software. It should also give insight into how to upgrade legacy protocols without alienating existing clients.

IPv6 may be a headache for network administrators, but it is a gold mine of opportunity for developers. When IPv4 begins to make its exit from the Internet, it is almost certain that people will start looking at other protocols. FTP, for instance, is incompatible with IPv6 because of IPv4-dependent features of the protocol, such as the PASV command. Another example is X.25, which currently forms the backbone of financial institutions, but has no native mechanism to tunnel over IPv6, so it may also be replaced. The list is virtually endless.

The final chapter deals with two of the technologies introduced with .NET that have been heralded as a revolution in distributed computing: remoting and Web services.

17

Web Services and Remoting

17.1 Introduction

Web services are one of the most hyped features of .NET. They facilitate the sharing of information and services among companies and individuals on a programmatic level more elegantly than any other existing technology. The real benefit of using Web services in Visual Studio .NET is that you require nothing more than a simple URL to begin coding against a Web service residing on a remote server as if it were a local object. This cuts out the complexity of establishing network connections, formatting requests, and parsing replies.

From a business perspective, Web services can drastically reduce the development and integration time in rolling out affiliate programs. Online retailers can make their price listings available publicly via Web services to enable third parties to resell their products, knowing that items sold are currently in stock.

Although Web services may make information freely available, this does not imply that all of these services are free. Pay-per-use Web services such as SMS, credit card processing, and postal address lookup can be bought and used by third parties as part of larger applications with minimal effort.

17.2 Creating a Web service

In order to create a Web service, you will require access to an IIS server with the .NET framework installed. You will need administrative rights on this server to develop the Web service directly from Visual Studio .NET. When you install VS.NET, it will install and configure IIS for you.

This first Web service is used to report server variables from the server that hosts the service. This may not seem immediately useful, but one of the server variables (REMOTE_HOST) indicates the remote IP address of the client connecting to it. This information is useful to determine if a client is running behind a firewall or proxy, because in this case the local IP address on the client will not be the same as the IP address that would connect to a remote server. There is no easy way to determine this IP address using only code running on the client.

Another use of tracking the requester's IP address is to limit the number of queries made against a service in any one day. This effectively prohibits data mining, but it could be a hindrance when many users use the service behind the same outgoing proxy or firewall.

Start a new project in Visual Studio .NET, selecting a project of type ASP.NET Web Service. The default path for this new project is on the local IIS server (*http://localhost*).

Note: If you receive an error concerning the "debugging users group" on IIS, this generally means you have not enabled Integrated Windows Authentication under Directory Security on the server.

A server will have many variables associated with it, although the names of these variables do not change from server to server; for flexibility, we can provide a method that returns an array of all the server variables stored on this machine.

Enter the following code in the asmx file:

C#

```
[WebMethod]
public String[] getServerVariableNames()
{
  System.Collections.Specialized.NameValueCollection col;
  col=Context.Request.ServerVariables;
  String[] arr = col.AllKeys;
  return arr;
}
```

VB.NET

```
<WebMethod> _
Public Function getServerVariableNames() As String()
```

```
    Dim col As _
      System.Collections.Specialized.NameValueCollection _
      col=Context.Request.ServerVariables
      Dim arr() As String =  col.AllKeys
    Return arr
  End Function
```

Notice the [WebMethod] attribute placed before the function name. This exposes the function for use over the Internet. The array returned from this method would be instantly recognizable by any ASP or ASP.NET developer. It would include strings such as REMOTE_HOST, representing the IP address of the client, and HTTP_USER_AGENT, representing the software being used by the client.

To retrieve the value of each of these variables, we can implement a second function as follows:

C#

```
[WebMethod]
public string[] getServerVariable(string variableName)
{
  System.Collections.Specialized.NameValueCollection col;
  col=Context.Request.ServerVariables;
  String[] arr = col.GetValues(variableName);
  return arr;
}
```

VB.NET

```
<WebMethod> _
Public Function getServerVariable(ByVal variableName As _
  String) As String()
  Dim col As _
  System.Collections.Specialized.NameValueCollection _
  col=Context.Request.ServerVariables
  Dim arr() As String =  col.GetValues(variableName)
  Return arr
End Function
```

This function returns the value of a server variable when passed its name. It returns an array because some server variables return more than one result. To cite an example, HTTP_ACCEPT, the variable that enumerates the MIME types that the browser can render, will generally return an array of several different file types.

To test this service, run it from Visual Studio .NET, and you will see a browser open with an automatically generated Web page that details the public functions of your Web service. This Web page should be used for debugging purposes only because the default security setting is that the HTML interface is only available to browsers running on the local machine. End-consumers will use a programmatic interface to access this service. Click on `getServerVariableNames` and then Invoke.

You will see a new browser window opening with XML content, as shown in Figure 17.1. The XML is formatted as SOAP.

Take note of a server variable of interest, such as `REMOTE_ADDR`. Press Back on the first browser window, and select `getServerVariable`. Enter the name of the server variable in the box provided, and press Invoke. You will see a new window open and the Web service's XML response encoded as SOAP.

You will notice the URL in the address bar changing as you navigate within this interface to the Web service. An HTTP `GET` request in the following format can be used to invoke a Web service method:

Figure 17.1
*SOAP result
returned from a
Web service.*

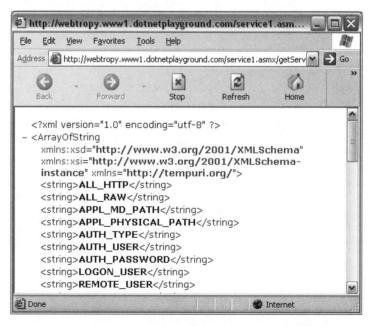

```
http://[ASMX file]/[function name]?[function parameters]
```

It is possible to use a GET request to invoke a Web service programmatically, but this is ill advised. Using the query string to pass objects is only possible with primitive types, and there are better ways to use a Web service programmatically.

Another HTTP GET request can be made against the Web service in the form

```
http://[ASMX file]?WSDL
```

This displays the formal definition of the Web service in Web Service Definition Language (WSDL) format. The WSDL definition allows Visual Studio .NET to determine the methods exposed by the Web service and to generate a suitable wrapper or proxy class for it. This step is generally done behind the scenes, but for the interested reader, it is possible to perform this step manually using the WSDL.EXE utility provided with .NET. The calling syntax is as follows:

```
WSDL http://[ASMX file]?WSDL
```

This will generate a C# proxy class in the same folder as WSDL.EXE. To generate a VB.NET class, precede the URL with /Language:VB.

17.2.1 Deploying a Web service

Having a Web service running on your local machine is fine for development purposes, but in order to make the service meaningful, it should be uploaded to a publicly accessible IIS server. Web services that are deployed publicly must have a unique namespace to distinguish them from other Web services on the Internet. Coding convention dictates that the namespace should be in the form of a domain name that you control. The namespace may look like a URL, but it does not need to point to anything on the Web in particular.

C#

```
[WebService(Namespace="http://www.myserver.com/")]
```

VB.NET

```
<WebService(Namespace:="http://www.myserver.com/")> _
```

If you want to make it easy for people to find your Web service, one of the first places you should advertise it is at *http://uddi.Microsoft.com* or *http://test.uddi.Microsoft.com*. These are public repositories for Web services and generally the first place developers go when looking for a particular online service.

Universal description discovery integration (UDDI) is an open standard that can be accessed programmatically by using the `Microsoft.Uddi.Sdk` namespace provided with the UDDI SDK.

17.3   Using a Web service

As mentioned earlier, the automatically generated Web interface for a Web service is not designed for public use. Instead, you generate a proxy class that accesses the service programmatically, and you can code against the Web service as if you are using a local object.

In Visual Studio .NET, you don't need to code a proxy class yourself; it will be created for you. All you need to do is enter the URL of the Web service, and all of the behind-the-scenes work is taken care of.

Start a new project in Visual Studio .NET and select Windows Forms Application. Click Project→Add Web Reference, and then enter the URL of the ASMX file created in the previous example. Press Add Reference once you have found the Web service. In the following example, the Web service is assumed to reside on the local machine and to be named `Service1`.

Draw a list view on the form, and name it `lvServerVariables`. A button named `btnPopulate` is also required.

Click on the form and add the following code:

C#

```
private void Form1_Load(object sender, System.EventArgs e)
{
  lvServerVariables.View=View.Details;
  lvServerVariables.Columns.Add("Name",
     lvServerVariables.Width/2,
     HorizontalAlignment.Left);
  lvServerVariables.Columns.Add("Value",
```

```
        lvServerVariables.Width/2,
        HorizontalAlignment.Left);
    }
```

VB.NET

```
    Private Sub Form1_Load(ByVal sender As Object, ByVal _
      e As System.EventArgs)
      lvServerVariables.View=View.Details
      lvServerVariables.Columns.Add("Name", _
          lvServerVariables.Width/2, _
          HorizontalAlignment.Left)
      lvServerVariables.Columns.Add("Value", _
          lvServerVariables.Width/2, _
          HorizontalAlignment.Left)
    End Sub
```

This code simply lays the list view out on the screen in a neat way, with the column headers equally spaced across the screen.

Click on the Populate button, and add the following code:

C#

```
    private void btnPopulate_Click(object sender,
    System.EventArgs e)
    {
      string[] serverVariableNames;
      localhost.Service1 webservice = new localhost.Service1();
      serverVariableNames = webservice.getServerVariableNames();
      lvServerVariables.Items.Clear();
     foreach (string serverVariableName in serverVariableNames)
      {
        ListViewItem lvItem = new ListViewItem();
        lvItem.Text = serverVariableName;
        string[] serverVariableValues;
        serverVariableValues =
        webservice.getServerVariable(serverVariableName);
        if (serverVariableValues!=null)
        {
          lvItem.SubItems.Add(serverVariableValues[0]);
        }
      lvServerVariables.Items.Add((ListViewItem)lvItem.Clone());
      }
    }
```

VB.NET

```
Private  Sub btnPopulate_Click(ByVal sender As Object, _
  ByVal e As System.EventArgs)
  Dim serverVariableNames() As String
  Dim webservice As localhost.Service1 = New _
    localhost.Service1
  serverVariableNames = webservice.getServerVariableNames()
  lvServerVariables.Items.Clear()
  Dim i As Integer
  For each serverVariableName as string in _
    serverVariableNames
    Dim lvItem As ListViewItem = New ListViewItem
    lvItem.Text = serverVariableName
    Dim serverVariableValues() As String
    serverVariableValues = _
      webservice.getServerVariable(serverVariableName)
    If Not serverVariableValues Is Nothing Then
      lvItem.SubItems.Add(serverVariableValues(0))
    End If
    lvServerVariables.Items.Add(CType(lvItem.Clone(), _
      ListViewItem))
  Next
End Sub
```

This code would seem to have nothing to do with networking code, but in fact, it communicates extensively with the remote server via the proxy class every time a method is called on the webservice object.

If you would like to view the proxy class, you can click on show all files in the Solution Explorer, and click Localhost→Reference.map→ Reference.cs. It is not advisable to edit the proxy class manually.

The rest of the code above is concerned with displaying the data returned from the Web service on-screen. Only the first element in the array returned from getServerVariable is actually rendered on-screen, for the sake of simplicity.

To test the Web service client, run it from Visual Studio .NET, ensure that IIS is running on the local machine, and then press Populate. You should see a list appearing on-screen, which should resemble Figure 17.2.

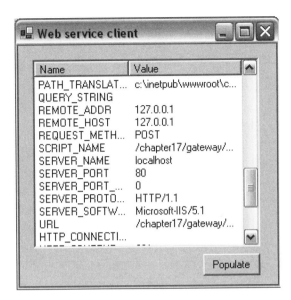

Figure 17.2
*Web service client
application.*

17.4   Asynchronous calls to Web services

If the same Web service were deployed on several geographically separated
Web servers, clients could connect to several Web services at once in order
to improve performance. This may only be applicable in situations where
several calls have to be made and each call takes a significant amount of
time to complete.

To understand the scenario, we could envisage a situation where an
application displays live stock values of a large share portfolio. A Web service is hosted on a server in the United States, which is linked into the
NASDAQ exchange, and another server is located in Japan, which is linked
into the Nikeii exchange. A customer in question has shares in Microsoft
and Toyota. If the client were to issue a request for the value of the
Microsoft shares, wait for the response, and then request the value of the
Toyota shares, the process would take twice as long as if both requests were
made simultaneously.

Several techniques can be used to manage simultaneous Web service
calls. The following code examples perform the same function: They make
two calls to a Web service and measure the response times to the calls. IIS is
multithreaded, so it handles both of these requests in parallel. In a real-
world example, the same Web service would be mirrored on more than one
server, so that the two requests would be handled at exactly the same time.

Each of the following samples requires a simple user interface consisting of only a button and a label. To create this interface, open a new project in Visual Studio .NET, and select a Windows form application. Draw a button on the form and name it `btnMakeCall` and then draw a label named `lblStatus`.

You will also require a Web reference to the Web service as described earlier in this chapter. This Web reference should be named `localhost`, for the purposes of these code examples. The Web service does not necessarily need to be hosted on the local machine.

17.4.1 Wait handles

A wait handle is equivalent to a `do-nothing while` loop using polling, but it is less processor intensive. This should only be used in a separate thread, or the client application will be nonresponsive to the user. This technique should only be used when useful client-side processing can be performed before data is returned from any of the Web services.

Click on the Make Call button and enter the following code:

C#

```
private void btnMakeCall_Click(object sender,
System.EventArgs e)
{
  long timeStart = DateTime.UtcNow.Ticks;
  localhost.Service1 svc = new localhost.Service1();
  IAsyncResult result1;
  IAsyncResult result2;
  result1 = svc.BegingetServerVariableNames(null,null);
  result2 =
  svc.BegingetServerVariable("REMOTE_ADDR",null,null);
  result1.AsyncWaitHandle.WaitOne();
  result2.AsyncWaitHandle.WaitOne();
  string[] varNames = svc.EndgetServerVariableNames(result1);
  string[] response = svc.EndgetServerVariable(result2);
  lblStatus.Text = "Time elapsed:" +
  (DateTime.UtcNow.Ticks - timeStart);
  lblStatus.Text += " ticks";
}
```

VB.NET

```
Private  Sub btnMakeCall_Click(ByVal sender As Object, _
```

```
ByVal e As System.EventArgs)
Dim timeStart As Long = DateTime.UtcNow.Ticks
Dim svc As localhost.Service1 = New localhost.Service1()
Dim result1 As IAsyncResult
Dim result2 As IAsyncResult
result1 = svc.BegingetServerVariableNames( _
    Nothing,Nothing)
result2 = _
    svc.BegingetServerVariable( _
    "REMOTE_ADDR",Nothing,Nothing)
result1.AsyncWaitHandle.WaitOne()
result2.AsyncWaitHandle.WaitOne()
Dim varNames() As String = _
    svc.EndgetServerVariableNames(result1)
Dim response() As String = _
    svc.EndgetServerVariable(result2)
lblStatus.Text = "Time elapsed:" & _
    (DateTime.UtcNow.Ticks - timeStart)
lblStatus.Text += " ticks"
End Sub
```

To test this code, run the application from Visual Studio .NET, and press the make Call Button. The user interface will become unresponsive until the call is received. In a production environment, the code detailed above should be contained within a separate thread.

17.4.2 Callbacks

Callbacks produce the least amount of processor overhead while waiting for Web service calls to return. They are ideal in situations where no useful client-side processing can be performed before all of the data is received; however, it could be difficult to determine when the last call has returned successfully or erroneously.

Click on the Make Call button and enter the following code:

C#

```
public localhost.Service1 svc;
public long timeStart;
private void btnMakeCall_Click(object sender,
System.EventArgs e)
{
```

```csharp
    timeStart = DateTime.UtcNow.Ticks;
    svc = new localhost.Service1();
    svc.BegingetServerVariableNames(new
    AsyncCallback(ServiceCallback1),null);
    svc.BegingetServerVariable("REMOTE_ADDR",new
    AsyncCallback(ServiceCallback2),null);
}

private void ServiceCallback1(IAsyncResult result)
{
  string[] response = svc.EndgetServerVariableNames(result);

  lblStatus.Text = "Time elapsed:" +
  (DateTime.UtcNow.Ticks - timeStart);
  lblStatus.Text += " ticks";
}

private void ServiceCallback2(IAsyncResult result)
{
  string[] response = svc.EndgetServerVariable(result);
  lblStatus.Text = "Time elapsed:" +
  (DateTime.UtcNow.Ticks - timeStart);
  lblStatus.Text += " ticks";
}
```

VB.NET

```vbnet
Public svc As localhost.Service1
Public timeStart As Long
Private Sub btnMakeCall_Click(ByVal sender As Object, _
  ByVal e As System.EventArgs)
  timeStart = DateTime.UtcNow.Ticks
  svc = New localhost.Service1()
  svc.BegingetServerVariableNames(New _
     AsyncCallback(AddressOf ServiceCallback1),Nothing)
  svc.BegingetServerVariable("REMOTE_ADDR",New _
     AsyncCallback(AddressOf ServiceCallback2),Nothing)
End Sub
Private  Sub ServiceCallback1(ByVal result As IAsyncResult)
  Dim response() As String = _
     svc.EndgetServerVariableNames(result)
  lblStatus.Text = "Time elapsed:" & _
```

```
   (DateTime.UtcNow.Ticks - timeStart)
   lblStatus.Text += " ticks"
End Sub

Private  Sub ServiceCallback2(ByVal result As IAsyncResult)
   Dim response() As String = _
     svc.EndgetServerVariable(result)
   lblStatus.Text = "Time elapsed:" & _
     (DateTime.UtcNow.Ticks - timeStart)
   lblStatus.Text += " ticks"
End Sub
```

To test this code, run the application from Visual Studio .NET, and press the Make Call button. The time displayed is the time that has elapsed between the issuing of the Web methods and the last response received. A more robust solution would be to use a global array that would track the progress of each call.

The `BeginGetServerVariableNames` function takes two parameters; the first parameter indicates the procedure to be called once the web-method returns, and the second, as shown in the code example above, is set to `null` or `Nothing`. This parameter can optionally contain objects that can be passed to the callback via the `result` object.

17.5 Interoperability

When developing a Web service, it should be straightforward for any developer working on any platform to implement a client. The previous example should demonstrate that it is easy to implement a Web service client in .NET, but if your service is to be made available to third-party Web site developers, you have to make sure that you do not needlessly complicate their job simply for the sake of using this new buzzword in Web technology.

Although it may not seem like your responsibility to support third-party developers that integrate into your software, it would be lunacy (and bad for business!) to provide a service that was so difficult to use from platforms other than .NET that developers would simply give up and find a different supplier.

Most languages now support XML. With this, it is easy to extract primitive types such as strings, numbers, and arrays from SOAP responses; however, if complex objects such as datasets and nested classes are rendered as SOAP, it is likely that the average PHP Web developer will throw his hands up in despair. Therefore, if it is envisaged that there may be a user base that may not use Microsoft scripting languages to run their Web sites, then the clarity of XML returned from Web service methods should be closely examined.

If the third party wishing to access your Web service is running a Microsoft platform and does not intend to use .NET (e.g., if he or she are using classic ASP or Visual Basic 6), then you cannot force these people to migrate to .NET in order to use your Web service; however, you could mention the SOAP toolkit from Microsoft (*msdn.microsoft.com/webservices/building/soaptk/*), which can greatly simplify the task of adding Web service support to a legacy Windows application.

17.6 Performance

The first thing that may strike you when running the code sample above is that it can take several seconds to populate a short list of information. Web services are slow on first access because of background .NET compilations. It may look as if Web services were designed more for interoperability than speed.

In chapter 4, remoting was discussed. This technology is similar to Web services. With remoting, there were many ways to improve performance by using more simplistic protocols. With Web services, there is no easy way to use anything other than SOAP. Having said this, the one-protocol-only way of doing things makes life easier for system integrators who are working on different platforms. The trade-off between interoperability and performance has to be decided on a case-by-case basis. It should be clear enough that SOAP is more interoperable than Microsoft's proprietary binary format.

In benchmarking tests, a Web service and remoting object both made queries to a database in response to client requests. Under high-load conditions (60 requests per second for a single database entry), a remoting object hosted on a Windows service using a binary formatter over TCP outperformed the Web service by 50%.

Although remoting objects can be configured for higher performance than Web services, when a remoting object communicates with SOAP over HTTP, it is actually slower than a Windows service by about 25% under the same load as stated above. Furthermore, it is more difficult to use a remoting object than a Web service because there is no automatic mechanism to discover the interface of a remoting object, whereas Web services use WSDL. Some other configurations of the remoting object also succeeded in outperforming the Web service. They were binary format over HTTP and SOAP format over TCP.

When a remoting object is hosted on IIS rather than in a Windows service, the performance level drops substantially. When a remoting object uses the binary format, it only barely surpasses Web services performance at 20 requests per second; however, using other configurations, such as SOAP over HTTP on IIS, dropped the performance to 35% under Web services.

To sum up, in order to achieve maximum performance, with a user base that is exclusively .NET clients, and where you have access to a dedicated Windows server, then use a Windows service hosting a remoting object using binary format over TCP. If the user base could include non-.NET clients, however, or if you have only shared access to a server, then you should use a Web service.

17.7 Security

Web services run on IIS servers, so an IIS server with SSL certificates installed provides secure Web services. This rather simplistic view of security in Web services is nonetheless probably the best approach to take when implementing a secure Web service at the moment.

Web site security is more concerned with ensuring that the server is authenticated to the client than vice versa, but this makes good sense because it means that customers will know they are giving their credit card details to a reputable supplier, but the supplier doesn't really care who enters the details, as long as money is involved in the transaction.

With Web services, the typical user would have paid for the privilege of using the service. The user would not care exactly who is providing the service, just that the information is correct; however, the Web service provider would need to know that the client was in fact a paying customer.

HTTPS provides for client authentication, so there is no need to reinvent the wheel here. In an intranet environment, a Windows authentication system will undoubtedly already be in place on the network. To provide credentials with a Web service call, it is a matter of setting the `Credentials` property of the Web service, such as in the following code snippet:

C#

```
localhost.Service1 webservice = new localhost.Service1();
CredentialCache cache = new CredentialCache();
```

```
NetworkCredential netCred =
      new NetworkCredential( "user", "pass", "myServerName"
);
cache.Add( new Uri(svc.Url), "Basic", netCred );
webservice.Credentials = cache;
```

VB.NET

```
Dim webservice As localhost.Service1 =  New _
   localhost.Service1()
Dim cache As CredentialCache =  New CredentialCache()
NetworkCredential netCred = _
   New NetworkCredential("user", "pass", "myServerName")
cache.Add(New Uri(webservice.Url), "Basic", netCred)
webservice.Credentials = cache
```

On the Web service side, it is possible to check credentials using the following statement:

```
Thread.CurrentPrincipal.Identity.Name
```

Which will return either an empty string or a user name in the following form:

```
[Domain]\[user]
```

Of course, this type of authentication is only useful for intranet situations. It is not applicable for globally accessible services when SSL is not used on the server. The best practice is to use client X.509 certificates, but this would be overkill for everything less than financial applications because it takes a lot of time and effort to get issued an X.509 client certificate with your name on it. An X.509 certificate can be included in the client request by adding it to the ClientCertificates collection thus:

C#

```
localhost.Service1 webservice = new localhost.Service1();
X509Certificate x509 = X509Certificate.CreateFromCertFile(
     "c:\\myCertificate.cer");
webservice.ClientCertificates.Add(x509);
```

VB.NET

```
Dim webservice As localhost.Service1 =  New _
   localhost.Service1()
X509Certificate x509 = X509Certificate.CreateFromCertFile( _
   "c:\myCertificate.cer")
webservice.ClientCertificates.Add(x509)
```

If your Web service needs to be secure enough to prevent nonpaying users from accessing it, but doesn't require the overhead of end-to-end strong encryption, an acceptable middle road is to use *hashing*, or as it is more correctly called, *digest authentication*. This is where each customer is allocated a username and password. The password is combined with the username and then hashed. The hash digest is then sent as a parameter to the Web method. If the digest matches the hash of the username and password pair held in the database, then the user can be authenticated. To increase security, a second digest could be created, composed from the current time (accurate to the minute) and the user's password. A hashed timestamp more than one minute old would be rejected. This means that a hacker listening on the wire could not record and replay Web service requests.

17.8   Web services enhancements

Web services can be made more flexible by installing Web Services Enhancements (WSE) from Microsoft. To save confusion over terminology, Global XML Web Services Architecture (GXA) was a joint proposal by IBM and Microsoft. WSE is Microsoft's adaptation of GXA, which is, for all intents and purposes, identical. The added features are attachments, security, routing, and referral.

WSE can be downloaded from *http://msdn.microsoft.com/webservices/ building/wse*. Once installed, it can be integrated into any .NET project by adding a reference to `Microsoft.Web.Services.dll` and by modifying the `Web.Config` file for the project by adding a type to `soapExtension-Types` thus:

```
<configuration>
 <system.web>
  ...
  <webServices>
   <soapExtensionTypes>
    <add type= "Microsoft.Web.Services.WebServicesExtension,
```

```
            Microsoft.Web.Services,
            Version=1.0.0.0,
            Culture=neutral,
            PublicKeyToken=31bf3856ad364e35"
            priority="1" group="0" />
        </soapExtensionTypes>
      </webServices>
    </system.web>
  </configuration>
```

17.8.1   Web service extensions: Attachments

If your Web service returns multimedia data, such as images or audio, you should consider using SOAP attachments. Including binary data as a SOAP attachment as distinct from plain text offers a performance advantage because the data will not be encoded and bloated in size. SOAP attachments use the direct Internet message encapsulation (DIME) format. This feature is included in WSE 1.0. Only the core features of the technology are described here.

To attach an image (such as c:\photo.jpg) to a SOAP response, you could use code similar to the following:

C#

```
string filePath = "C:\\myPhoto.jpg";
DimeAttachment dimeImage = new DimeAttachment(
    "image/jpeg", TypeFormatEnum.MediaType,
    filePath);
dimeImage.Id = "uri:" + Guid.NewGuid().ToString();
SoapContext cntxt = HttpSoapContext.ResponseContext;
cntxt.Attachments.Add(dimeImage);
```

VB.NET

```
Dim filePath As String =  "C:\myPhoto.jpg"
DimeAttachment dimeImage = New DimeAttachment( _
    "image/jpeg", TypeFormatEnum.MediaType, _
    filePath)
dimeImage.Id = "uri:" & Guid.NewGuid().ToString()
Dim cntxt As SoapContext =  HttpSoapContext.ResponseContext
cntxt.Attachments.Add(dimeImage)
```

You will require the following namespaces:

C#

```
using System.Web.Services;
using Microsoft.Web.Services;
using Microsoft.Web.Services.Dime;
```

VB.NET

```
Imports System.Web.Services
Imports Microsoft.Web.Services
Imports Microsoft.Web.Services.Dime
```

The Web service client could extract the image data from the SOAP response by using the following code:

C#

```
localhost.Service1 webservice = new localhost.Service1();
Stream attachment =
webservice.ResponseSoapContext.Attachments[0].Stream;
Bitmap myImage = new Bitmap(attachment);
```

VB.NET

```
Dim webservice As localhost.Service1 =  New _
   localhost.Service1()
Dim attachment As Stream
Attachment = _
   webservice.ResponseSoapContext.Attachments(0).Stream
Dim myImage As Bitmap =  New Bitmap(attachment)
```

There are several limitations to DIME in WSE 1.0. One significant limitation is that SOAP attachments are not reflected in the WDSL contract that is generated with the Web service. This means that clients will not be aware, until they make a request to your Web service, that there are any attachments in the response. Furthermore, DIME is not portable among different platforms and is proprietary to Microsoft. To make matters worse, COM clients using the SOAP toolkit will not be able to access attachments at all unless the WDSL is manually edited to contain the appropriate <dime:message> child elements and <wsdl:output> elements, as described in the WDSL specification.

Another limitation of DIME in WSE 1.0 is that security does not extend to the attachment. Therefore, whenever attachments need to be kept secure from prying eyes and made resistant to man-in-the-middle tampering, you will have to implement your own hashing and encryption mechanism. Alternately, as previously recommended, the Web service should run over SSL to provide end-to-end encryption and avoid security loopholes such as this one.

17.8.2   Web service extensions: Routing

When a Web service begins to scale upward, it may quickly outgrow a single-server environment and require hosting on several servers in parallel. Because Web services run over IIS, they can be scaled upward in much the same way as any Web site. This includes using load-balancing systems such as Cisco Local Director or Microsoft NLB.

Load-balancing systems do generally delegate workload equally among servers, and sometimes you may require more logic behind the load balancing. When talking specifically about Web services, you can use WSE to create an intermediary Web service. This Web service could be used to direct Web service calls to other servers, which may contain more up-to-date data or be otherwise more appropriate for that particular call.

17.8.3   A word on Project Hailstorm (MyServices)

Project Hailstorm, or MyServices, is a technology that was shelved by Microsoft in early 2002; therefore, it is best avoided. MyServices was a project put forward by Microsoft to permit people to store data they would use on a day-to-day basis on their servers via an array of custom-built Web services. Services such as .NET Contacts to store your personal address book, .NET Inbox to store your email, and .NET Wallet to store your credit card details would be available through MyServices. The idea is technically sound, but many people and companies balked at the idea of Microsoft being in control of so much personal information.

17.9   .NET remoting

Remoting is .NET's equivalent of Java remote method invocation (RMI) and Visual Basic's Distributed Common Object Model (DCOM). It facilitates the use of complex objects on remote computers, using the same syntax as if they were in the same application. The advantage that remoting affords is the abstraction of the network infrastructure. This greatly simplifies the implementation of client/server applications in which the server must perform a variety of tasks based on instructions from the client.

Imagine a scenario in which a distributed billing system is being developed, where the client's systems are high-street hire-purchase outlets, and a central server at the head office handles customer invoicing, debt collection, and so forth. Clients would require the server to perform tasks such as perform credit check, record start of lease, terminate lease, process credit card payment, and other such tasks. Of course, the same effect could be achieved by sending strings over TCP/IP, which the server would parse it on the remote side, but it is simpler to make a call to customer.terminateLease() and let .NET handle the network transmission.

17.9.1   How remoting works

When using remoting, you still need to create a client and server. You also need to create an object that performs whatever functions you require. Both ends of the connection need to know the type of the object. The client needs to know the IP address and port of the server. Other than that, .NET does the rest.

Although you don't see what is being passed over the network, you do have a choice whether to go for SOAP over HTTP (portable) or binary over TCP (performance). SOAP used for remoting differs from the industry format somewhat and would be less portable than an equivalent Web service.

Note: Channel sinks can be used to view or modify the data immediately before it is sent across the wire. This can be used to add security or queuing features.

To prevent clients from draining the server's resources by creating millions of objects and abandoning their instances, remoting has a built-in garbage-collection system. Objects can be created so that their lifetime lasts only as long as the execution time of the function (singlecall) or as long as the class (singleton) or a server-defined lifetime (published objects). Remote object lifetimes, with the exception of published objects, are specified in the call to RemotingConfiguration.RegisterWellKnownService-Type, as we shall see later.

Published objects are instantiated slightly differently, where, instead of the call to RegisterWellKnownServiceType, the object is created thus:

C#

```
RemoteObject obj = new RemoteObject(1234);
RemotingServices.Marshal (obj,"RemotingServer");
```

VB.NET

```
Dim obj as RemoteObject
obj = new RemoteObject(1234);
RemotingServices.Marshal(obj,"RemotingServer")
```

After which the object behaves as a singleton. The benefit of creating an object in this way is that it is possible to create objects with nondefault constructors. This could include constructors that require user intervention and, thus, are unsuitable for arbitrary client activation.

The key to remoting is to create a class that derives from `MarshalBy-RefObject`. This object is then capable of running within the context of a server and exposes its methods and properties through that server. While running in the context of the server, local resources such as files and databases located on the server are accessible through the class. Objects that are returned as a result of calling methods on this class, however, are run in the context of the client. These objects are called By Value objects.

By Value objects cannot access server resources, such as databases or files; however, they can be prepopulated with data taken from server resources such as these. For instance, the ubiquitous `DataSet` is perfectly acceptable as a By Value object. A remote object returns a By Value object by serializing it and transferring it over the network to the client. This mechanism will only work if two conditions are met: (1) the object must be marked `[Serializable]` or implement `ISerializable`, and (2) the client must hold at the metadata for the By Value object, such that it can correctly deserialize it.

17.9.2   Implementing remoting

This example demonstrates a simple remoting application, where the client application may request a number from a server, which is incremented on every call.

Start a new Class library project in Visual Studio .NET, and enter the following code:

C#

```
using System;
namespace RemoteObject
{
  public class IDGenerator : System.MarshalByRefObject
  {
```

```
      private int lastID =0;
      public int getID()
      {
        return(lastID++);
      }
    }
  }
```

VB.NET

```
Imports System
Namespace RemoteObject
  Public Class IDGenerator
   Inherits System.MarshalByRefObject
    Private lastID As Integer = 0
    Public Function getID() As Integer
      lastID = lastID + 1
                    return(lastID)
    End Function
  End Class
End Namespace
```

You will note that the class derives from System.MarshalByRefObject. This enables the object to be transferred over a remoting channel.

Compile the object, and note the location of the resultant DLL. The next step is to create the server application to host this object.

Create a new Windows form project in Visual Studio .NET. Click Project→Add References→Browse, and then click on the DLL created in the last compilation. You will also need to select the System.Runtime.Remoting namespace.

C#

```
private void Form1_Load(object sender, System.EventArgs e)
{
  HttpChannel channel = new HttpChannel(8085);
  ChannelServices.RegisterChannel(channel);
  RemotingConfiguration.RegisterWellKnownServiceType(
        typeof(RemoteObject.IDGenerator),
        "RemotingServer",
        WellKnownObjectMode.Singleton);
}
```

VB.NET

```
Private   Sub Form1_Load(ByVal sender As Object, _
ByVal e As System.EventArgs)
  Dim channel As HttpChannel =  New HttpChannel(8085)
  ChannelServices.RegisterChannel(channel)
  RemotingConfiguration.RegisterWellKnownServiceType( _
  (New RemoteObject.RemoteObject.IDGenerator).GetType(), _
        "RemotingServer", _
        WellKnownObjectMode.Singleton)


End Sub
```

Certain things can be immediately ascertained by looking at this code. The communications will take place on port 8085, using SOAP over HTTP. The object is to be created as a `Singleton`, which means that it is state-full, and the value of `LastID` will be maintained between calls.

You will also require the supporting namespaces:

C#

```
using System.Runtime.Remoting;
using System.Runtime.Remoting.Channels;
using System.Runtime.Remoting.Channels.Http;
using RemoteObject;
```

VB.NET

```
Imports System.Runtime.Remoting
Imports System.Runtime.Remoting.Channels
Imports System.Runtime.Remoting.Channels.Http
Imports RemoteObject
```

Create a new Windows forms project in Visual Studio .NET. Click Project→Add References, click Browse, and then click on the DLL created in the last compilation. Draw a button on the form and name it `btnGetID`. Now click on the `btnGetID` button and enter the following code:

C#

```
private void btnGetID_Click(object sender, System.EventArgs
e)
{
```

```
RemoteObject.IDGenerator remObject =
(RemoteObject.IDGenerator)Activator.GetObject(
        typeof(RemoteObject.IDGenerator),
        "http://localhost:8085/RemotingServer");
 if (remObject==null)
  MessageBox.Show("cannot locate server");
 else
  MessageBox.Show(Convert.ToString(remObject.getID()));
}
```

VB.NET

```
Private  Sub btnGetID_Click(ByVal sender As Object, _
  ByVal e As System.EventArgs)
  Dim remObject As RemoteObject.IDGenerator = _
    CType(Activator.GetObject( _
    (New RemoteObject.IDGenerator).GetType(), _
    "http://localhost:8085/RemotingServer"), _
        RemoteObject.IDGenerator)
  If remObject Is Nothing Then
    MessageBox.Show("cannot locate server")
  Else
    MessageBox.Show(Convert.ToString(remObject.getID()))
  End If
End Sub
```

In this code, the call to the remote object is discretely written as remObject.getID(). It is worthwhile to note that this is a synchronous call, and if the client could be doing other things while waiting for the method to return, then either an asynchronous or one-way call should be employed, as explained later.

Again, you will also require the supporting namespaces:

C#

```
using System.Runtime.Remoting;
using System.Runtime.Remoting.Channels;
using System.Runtime.Remoting.Channels.Http;
using RemoteObject;
```

VB.NET

```
Imports System.Runtime.Remoting
Imports System.Runtime.Remoting.Channels
```

Figure 17.3
*Remoting Client
and remoting
Server.*

```
Imports System.Runtime.Remoting.Channels.Http
Imports RemoteObject
```

To test the application, execute the client and server together (Figure 17.3), and then press the button on the client a few times. You will see the number in the message box increasing.

17.9.3 Asynchronous use of remote objects

Asynchronous use of remote objects can be achieved by using delegates, which are the .NET equivalent of function pointers. They are declared within the same class as the client, but outside any of its methods. It would have the same function prototype as the synchronous method you wish to call. For instance, a remote method named `getDetails()` returning `string` would have a corresponding delegate such as the following:

C#

```
delegate String GetDetailsDelegate();
```

VB.NET

```
Delegate Function GetDetailsDelegate() as string
```

Assuming the remote object is already instantiated and named `obj`, the `getDetails()` method can be called thus:

C#

```
GetDetailsDelegate gdDelegate = new
GetDetailsDelegate(obj.GetDetails);
IASyncResult gdAsyncres = gnDelegate.BeginInvoke(null,null);
```

VB.NET

```
Dim gdDelegate as GetDetailsDelegate
Dim gdAsyncres as IASyncResult
gdDelegate = new GetDetailsDelegate(AddressOf obj.GetDetails)
gdAsyncres = gnDelegate.BeginInvoke(nothing,nothing)
```

This code returns immediately, and the server will begin executing the `GetDetails` method on the remote object. In order to retrieve the return value from the call, the client must execute `EndInvoke` on the delegate. This method is blocking and will only return once the server has responded. It is called as follows:

C#

```
String details = gdDelegate.EndInvoke(gnAsyncres);
```

VB.NET

```
Dim details as string
Details = gdDelegate.EndInvoke(gnAsyncres)
```

Although this method should be sufficient for most purposes, there is another way to invoke a remote object asynchronously, by using the `OneWay` attribute. One-way calls are made in the same way as standard asynchronous calls from the client; however, the `EndInvoke` method will be nonblocking and is guaranteed to return immediately, whether the server has responded or not. This is useful for noncritical "call-and-forget" methods, where overall application speed is more important than guaranteeing execution of selected peripheral functions.

To implement a one-way function, simply mark a method within the interface definition with the attribute `[OneWay()]`.

17.9.4   **Deployment of a remoting service**

When using remoting in a commercial application, a few tricks of the trade
help your software become more robust and manageable. The client must
be able to tell the type of the object it is to receive at compile time. This
means that if you have already deployed your client to a million users
worldwide, you can't make changes to the object or all of the clients will
stop working. The way around this dilemma is to have the client refer to the
interface of the object rather than the object itself, which means you can
change the implementation of the object's methods without breaking compatibility. Perhaps a more important aspect is that if you are sharing the
implementation of your software with third parties, they could possibly
decompile or otherwise reverse-engineer your DLL, using ILDASM or
MSIL-to-C# (*www.saurik.com*).

An interface to the `RemoteObject.IDGenerator` class above is as follows:

C#

```
using System;
public Interface IIDGenerator
{
  public int getID();
}
```

VB.NET

```
Imports System
Public Interface IIDGenerator
  Public Function NextOrder() As int
End Interface
```

Using shared interfaces is not the only way to provide clients with access
to remote objects. The two main drawbacks are that third parties working
with your remote object must be sent the new interface whenever any of the
public methods or properties in the object change; furthermore, you cannot
pass these objects as parameters to functions running in a different context.

An alternate method is to use shared base classes. This is where the client
is provided with an abstract base class. The server would inherit from this
base class and implement the required functionality. This would make these
classes capable of being passed to functions running in different contexts;
however, it is impossible to create new objects using the `new` operator, only
the `Activator.GetObject()` can be used in this instance.

In order to address the deployment issue, Microsoft has created a utility named *soapsuds*. This command-line utility can be used to extract metadata from remote objects. It is invoked from DOS thus:

```
soapsuds —url:<URL>?wsdl -oa:<OUTPUT>.DLL —nowp
```

This generates a DLL file, which client programs can use to communicate with the remote object. This DLL does not contain any implementation details, only interfaces. The —nowp, or no-wrap, parameter is used to indicate whether the URL of the remote object should be hard-coded into the DLL. An unwrapped proxy DLL does not contain URL information, but a wrapped proxy DLL does. The benefit of hard-coding the URL into the DLL is that the remote object can be created using the new operator. Otherwise, the client has to use `Activator.GetObject()` to instantiate the object.

17.9.5 Configuration

One major issue regarding deployment of remoting services is the ability to configure clients quickly and easily. For instance, if you are forced to change the IP address of the server hosting the remote object, it could be tricky to change the code to point to the new IP address, recompile the application, and request that all customers upgrade their software. A more acceptable solution is to hold the location of the remote object in a separate XML file, which could be replaced with a hot-fix patch when required. Therefore, .NET provides a means of providing configuration files for remoting clients. A configuration file takes the following form:

XML

```xml
<configuration>
 <system.runtime.remoting>
  <application>
   <channels>
    <channel ref="http" port="1234" />
   </channels>
   <service>
    <wellknown mode="Singleton" type="myNamespace.myClass,
     myAssembly" objectUri="myClass.soap">
   </service>
  </application>
 </system.runtime.remoting>
</configuration>
```

Assuming this file is saved as `MyApp.exe.config`, you can instantiate the remote object from the client using the following code:

C#

```
String filename = "MyApp.exe.config";
RemotingConfiguration.Configure(filename);
MyClass obj = new MyClass();
```

VB.NET

```
Dim filename as string
Filename = "MyApp.exe.config"
RemotingConfiguration.Configure(filename)
Dim obj as MyClass
Obj=new MyClass()
```

Of course, the client still requires the definition of the class `MyClass` in order to create an instance of the class. You could provide the implementation of `MyClass` to the client, but this poses code security risks and deployment problems. Neither the shared interface nor the shared base class method is suitable for the above example for providing class definitions, so in this case you should use `soapsuds` to generate a DLL for the client to reference in order to create these remote objects. The `-nowp` switch should be used with `soapsuds` to ensure that the DLL does not have hard-coded parameters.

In most cases, this should be all that is required to deploy a remoting service with configuration files; however, some developers may run into a problem where a remote object returns a By Value object, containing its own methods. In this case, the client must have a local reference to the By Value object, so it can deserialize the object and execute its methods. But a problem occurs because the namespace generated by `soapsuds` will be the same as the By Value object's namespace. To avoid this namespace name clash, you should manually edit the `soapsuds`-generated proxy DLL from its source code, which can be obtained by calling `soapsuds` with the `-gc` switch. Once the C# code can be edited, the namespace can be changed to something else, thereby avoiding the namespace clash.

17.9.6   Hosting remote objects within IIS

Remote objects, as described thus far, have been hosted in simple Windows applications. In reality, remote object servers generally do not require a user interface, but they often require the ability to execute on a computer regardless of whether a user is actively logged in. For this reason, you will probably want to run your remote object server as a service. Chapter 10 covers this topic in more detail.

Another alternative, which may be more applicable for shared hosting environments, is to host the remote object within IIS. This can be achieved by adding a little XML to the `web.config` file thus:

XML

```
<configuration>
  <system.runtime.remoting>
    <application>
      <service>
        <wellknown
          mode = "Singleton"
          type = "RemoteObject.IDGenerator,RemotingServer"
          objectUri = "RemoteObject.soap"
        />
      </service>
    </application>
  </system.runtime.remoting>
</configuration>
```

17.9.7 Hosting remote objects within a Windows service

When an application is designed to run unattended on a computer, and has no need for a user interface, it should run as a Windows service. Windows services run in the background even when no user is currently logged on. They are controlled via Control Panel→Administrative Tools→Services, where you can start, stop, and restart the service, as well as view information about it.

It is possible to use IIS as a host for remoting objects, but if you are developing a mass-market software product, not all users have IIS on their computers, nor will they want to go to the hassle of installing it.

This example requires the client and object from the previous example, so if you have not done so, now is a good time to type it in. Start a new Windows service (not application) project in Visual Studio .NET, scroll down the code to the `OnStart` and `OnStop` methods, and add the following code:

C#

```
Thread thdServer;
protected override void OnStart(string[] args)
{
  thdServer = new Thread(new ThreadStart(serverThread));
  thdServer.Start();
}
```

VB.NET

```
Dim thdServer As Thread
Protected Overrides  Sub OnStart(ByVal args() As String)
      thdServer = New Thread(New ThreadStart( _
                    AddressOf serverThread))
      thdServer.Start()
End Sub
```

The two events OnStart and OnStop are triggered whenever the service is started or stopped from Administrative Tools→Services. The above code will simply start a new thread at the serverThread function. Note that the thread variable is outside of the method call, which provides a means for OnStop to disable the service by stopping the thread.

C#

```
protected override void OnStop()
{
  thdServer.Abort();
}
```

VB.NET

```
Protected Overrides  Sub OnStop()
  thdServer.Abort()
End Sub
```

ServerThread is taken verbatim from the chapter 4 example. It opens an HTTP channel on port 8085 for the RemoteObject assembly.

C#

```
public void serverThread()
{
  HttpChannel channel = new HttpChannel(8085);
```

```
ChannelServices.RegisterChannel(channel);
RemotingConfiguration.RegisterWellKnownServiceType(
    typeof(RemoteObject.IDGenerator),
    "RemotingServer",
    WellKnownObjectMode.Singleton);
}
```

VB.NET

```
Public  Sub serverThread()
  Dim channel As HttpChannel = New HttpChannel(8085)
  ChannelServices.RegisterChannel(channel)
  RemotingConfiguration.RegisterWellKnownServiceType( _
    (New RemoteObject.RemoteObject.IDGenerator).GetType(), _
      "RemotingServer", _
      WellKnownObjectMode.Singleton)
End Sub
```

As before, the code establishes a connection channel using HTTP over port 8085. The object is hosted in `singleton` mode, meaning that only one instance of the object is ever created. This mode is required for this application because the object needs to maintain a private variable, which is shared between all clients that call the remote object.

Services cannot be run directly from the command line; they must be installed. To prepare a service for deployment, right-click on the service in design view and select Add Installer. Click on `ServiceInstaller1`, and set the `ServiceName` property to `MyService`. Set the `Account` property of `ServiceProcessInstaller1` to `LocalSystem`.

Finally, you need to add three references: one to `System.Configuration.Install.dll`, one to `System.Runtime.Remoting`, and another that points at the compiled DLL for the `IDGenerator` assembly. Then add the required namespaces as shown:

C#

```
using System.Configuration.Install;
using System.Runtime.Remoting;
using System.Runtime.Remoting.Channels;
using System.Runtime.Remoting.Channels.Http;
using System.Threading;
```

VB.NET

```
Imports System.Configuration.Install
Imports System.Runtime.Remoting
Imports System.Runtime.Remoting.Channels
Imports System.Runtime.Remoting.Channels.Http
Imports System.Threading
```

Compile the application in Visual Studio .NET. You will not be able to run it directly. You need to install the service first. To do so, you now must go to the DOS command prompt. Navigate to the path where the compiled .exe file resides, and then type the following at the command prompt:

DOS

```
path %path%;C:\WINDOWS\Microsoft.NET\Framework\v1.0.3705
installutil service.exe
net start MyService
```

Note: The path C:\windows\Microsoft.NET\Framework\v1.0.3705 may differ among computers. If you have two versions of the .NET framework on your machine, use the latest version.

Figure 17.4
*Remoting Server
running as a
Windows service.*

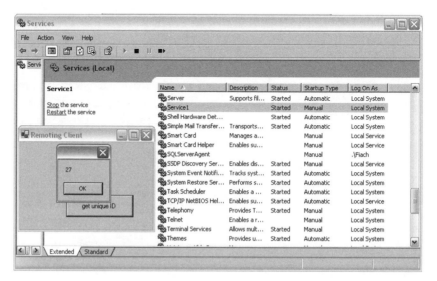

You may be prompted to enter a valid Windows username and password during the installation process. To test the application, open the Services snap-in at Control Panel→Administrative Tools→Services. If you scroll down the list, you should see an entry named "Service1" (Figure 17.4), which should be already started. Now open the client program that was created for the example in chapter 4. Press Get unique ID, and you should see a message box appear with a number on it.

17.9.8 Distributed garbage collection

Garbage collection occurs when an object is loaded into memory and no program holds a reference to it. In a distributed environment, it is much more difficult to monitor which programs hold references to a remote object, especially if the programs in question are hundreds of miles away over unreliable dial-up connections.

There are two ways to solve this problem: client activation and server activation. *Server activation* is where the client has no control over the lifetime of the object, and *client activation* is where the client has full control over the lifetime of the object.

Table 17.1 *Significant members of the* `ILease` *interface.*

Method or Property	Purpose
`InitialLeaseTime`	Specifies the amount of time a remote object will stay in memory before it is garbage-collected, assuming no action was taken on the object. The default is five minutes.
`CurrentLeaseTime`	Represents the amount of time left before the remote object is garbage-collected.
`RenewOnCallTime`	Specifies the amount of extended lease time that should be added if the object is called. The default is two minutes.
`SponsorshipTimeout`	Indicates the amount of time the lease manager will wait for a sponsor to respond before moving to another sponsor or garbage-collecting the object. The default is two minutes.
`LeaseManagerPollTime`	Specifies the interval of time between scans for expired leases by the underlying lease manager process. The default is ten seconds.

When the object is created using the `Activator.GetObject()` command, then the object is server activated. Server activation comes in two forms: singleton and single call. *Singleton activation* is where one, and only one, instance of the object is created on the server. This implies that state information for the object is shared between all clients. *Single-call activation* is a second form of server activation in which the object is created whenever any method is called on it. The object will be destroyed again once the method call is complete. This implies that there is no state information held in the object.

Client-side activation manages objects by lifetime leases, which means that a client can instruct the server to create an object and to keep it in memory for a specified time before destroying it. Client-side activation occurs when the object is created using `Activator.CreateInstance()`.

In order to modify the lease parameters of a remote object, you simply override the `InitializeLifetimeService` method and change the properties of the `ILease` interface (Table 17.1).

C#

```csharp
using System;
using System.Runtime.Remoting.Lifetime;
namespace RemoteObject
{
  public class IDGenerator : System.MarshalByRefObject
  {
    private int lastID =0;
    public override Object InitializeLifetimeService()
      {
        ILease lease =
        (ILease)base.InitializeLifetimeService();
        if (lease.CurrentState == LeaseState.Initial)
        {
          lease.InitialLeaseTime = TimeSpan.FromMinutes(5);
          lease.SponsorshipTimeout = TimeSpan.FromMinutes(6);
          lease.RenewOnCallTime =
          TimeSpan.FromSeconds(7);
        }
        return lease;
      }
    public int getID()
      {
```

```
      return(lastID++);
    }
  }
}
```

VB.NET

```
Imports System
Imports System.Runtime.Remoting.Lifetime
Namespace RemoteObject
  Public Class IDGenerator
   Inherits System.MarshalByRefObject
    Private lastID As Integer = 0

    Public Overrides Function _
    InitializeLifetimeService() As [Object]
      Dim lease As Ilease
      Lease = _
      CType(MyBase.InitializeLifetimeService(), ILease)
          If lease.CurrentState = LeaseState.Initial Then
            lease.InitialLeaseTime = TimeSpan.FromMinutes(5)
            lease.SponsorshipTimeout = _
                  TimeSpan.FromMinutes(6)
            lease.RenewOnCallTime = TimeSpan.FromSeconds(7)
          End If
      Return lease
      End Function

    Public Function getID() As Integer
    lastID = lastID + 1
    return(lastID)
    End Function
  End Class
End Namespace
```

Looking closely at the code above, you can see that this is the same object as described earlier in the chapter. The difference is the overridden function, which provides access to the lease parameters of the object. To obtain an interface to the lease parameters, a call is made to base.Initial-izeLifetimeService(), which returns the lease interface.

Some lease parameters cannot be changed once the object has been instantiated, thus the lease's current state is checked with the lease.Cur-

`rentState` property to ensure that the object is just in the process of being created.

The `InitialLeaseTime`, `SponsorshipTimeout`, and `RenewOnCallTime` properties are set to five, six, and seven minutes, respectively. This will keep the object in memory longer than the default object lifetime.

To test this code, compile the object, and run the client program as described earlier. Calls to the object will work fine for the first five minutes, but any call made more than seven minutes after the previous call will cause incorrect operation because the object will have been garbage collected.

17.10 Conclusion

Web services have been very much hyped as the next big thing in information technology. They are arguably one of the simplest remote procedure call systems ever developed and possibly the most interoperable technology ever developed by Microsoft. Having said that, remoting can outperform Web services under most conditions, and the technology is still in its infancy. Many features, especially within WSE 1.0, are underimplemented and could easily cause headaches for some developers.

As this concludes this book on .NET networking, I hope it proves beneficial to you and helps you to further your career as a professional developer. Good luck, and may your programs be bug free and efficient!

Index